DECISION SUPPORT SYSTEMS ENGINEERING

WILEY SERIES IN SYSTEMS ENGINEERING

Andrew P. Sage

ANDREW P. SAGE AND JAMES D. PALMER
Software Systems Engineering

WILLIAM B. ROUSE
Design for Success: A Human-Centered Approach to Designing Successful Products and Systems

ANDREW P. SAGE
Decision Support Systems Engineering

DECISION SUPPORT SYSTEMS ENGINEERING

ANDREW P. SAGE
School of Information Technology and Engineering
George Mason University

A Wiley-Interscience Publication
JOHN WILEY & SONS, INC.
New York / Chichester / Brisbane / Toronto / Singapore

In recognition of the importance of preserving what has been
written, it is a policy of John Wiley & Sons, Inc., to have books
of enduring value published in the United States printed on
acid-free paper, and we exert our best efforts to that end.

Copyright © 1991 by John Wiley & Sons, Inc.

All rights reserved. Published simultaneously in Canada.

Reproduction or translation of any part of this work
beyond that permitted by Section 107 or 108 of the
1976 United States Copyright Act without the permission
of the copyright owner is unlawful. Requests for
permission or further information should be addressed to
the Permissions Department, John Wiley & Sons, Inc.

Library of Congress Cataloging in Publication Data:
Sage, Andrew P.
    Decision support systems engineering / Andrew P. Sage.
      p. cm. — (Wiley series in systems engineering)
    "A Wiley-Interscience publication."
    Includes bibliographical references.
    1. Decision support systems.   I. Title. II. Series.
T58.62.S25   1991
658.4′03—dc20   91-15539
ISBN 0-471-53000-X   CIP

Printed in the United States of America

10 9 8 7 6 5 4 3 2 1

Contents

Preface		**ix**
1	**An Introduction to Decision Support Systems Engineering**	**1**
	1.1 Introduction to, and Taxonomies of, Decision Problems	2
	1.2 Frameworks for Designing Decision Support Systems	7
	1.3 Data-Base Management Systems (DBMS)	13
	1.4 Model-Base Management Systems (MBMS)	14
	1.5 Dialog Generation and Management Systems (DGMS)	15
	1.6 Design and Evaluation of Decision Support Systems Designs	15
	1.7 Individual Information-Processing Realities	16
	1.8 A Framework for Group DSS Design	21
	1.9 Group Decision Support System (GDSS) Design	26
	1.10 Information Technology Support Environments for DSS	30
	1.11 Summary	35
	Problems	35
	References	36
2	**Data-Base Management Systems**	**39**
	2.1 DBMS Design, Selection, and Systems Integration	42
	2.2 Data Models and Data-Base Architectures	44
	2.2.1 Record-Based Models	50
	2.2.2 Structural Models	54
	2.2.3 Expert Data-Base Models	61

	2.3	Distributed and Cooperative Data-Base Issues	69
	2.4	DBMS Software Evaluation	72
	2.5	Summary	78
		Problems	78
		References	79

3 Model-Base Management Systems — 81

- 3.1 Models and Modeling — 82
  - 3.1.1 Issue, or Problem, Formulation Models — 83
  - 3.1.2 Models for Analysis — 88
  - 3.1.3 Interpretation Models — 91
- 3.2 Decision Models — 93
  - 3.2.1 Models for Decision Making Under Risk — 94
  - 3.2.2 Decision Making with Multiattributed Outcomes — 103
  - 3.2.3 Screening-Based Approaches, and Imprecise Information — 104
- 3.3 Model-Base Management — 120
- 3.4 Summary — 125
  - Problems — 125
  - References — 126

4 Dialog Generation and Management Systems — 131

- 4.1 Preliminary Comments and Terminology for DGMS — 133
- 4.2 Interaction Styles — 134
- 4.3 Dialog Generation Objectives — 139
- 4.4 Dialog Independence — 148
- 4.5 Representations of the Human–Computer Interface (HCI) — 148
- 4.6 Evaluation of Interfaces, Interface Development Tools, and Human–Computer Dialogs — 150
- 4.7 Errors in Interface Design — 153
- 4.8 Summary — 157
  - Problems — 158
  - References — 159

5 Design and Evaluation of Decision Support Systems — 161

- 5.1 The Emergence of Systems Design Engineering — 163
- 5.2 The Nature of Systems Design Engineering — 166
- 5.3 Systems Design Methodology — 167
- 5.4 Information Requirements for Design — 171
- 5.5 The Environment for DSS Design and Characteristics of Successful Designs — 177
  - 5.5.1 Requirements Specifications — 180
  - 5.5.2 Preliminary Conceptual Design — 182

	5.5.3	Detailed Design and Testing Phase, and Implementation Phase	184
	5.5.4	The Operational Test and Evaluation Phase	184
	5.5.5	Operational Deployment	186
	5.5.6	The Value of System Design and the System Design Life Cycle	187
5.6	Operational Evaluation of Decision Support Systems	188
	5.6.1	Empirical Evaluation of Decision Support Systems	188
	5.6.2	Measurement Frameworks for DSS Evaluation	196
5.7	Summary	201
	Problems	201
	References	202

6 Information Processing in Individuals and Organizations — 205

6.1	Motivations for the Study of Information-Processing Models	206
6.2	Human Information-Processing Models	211
	6.2.1	Piaget's Model	211
	6.2.2	The Rasmussen Model of Judgment and Choice	214
	6.2.3	The Klein Model	217
	6.2.4	The Dreyfus Model	218
	6.2.5	The Janis and Mann Model	222
	6.2.6	Interpretation of the Human Information-Processing Models	226
6.3	Organizational Information Processing and Decision Making	228
6.4	Rationality Perspectives and Models of Individual and Organizational Information Processing	235
	6.4.1	Economic Rationality	236
	6.4.2	Technical Rationality	236
	6.4.3	Satisficing or Bounded Rationality	237
	6.4.4	Social Rationality	238
	6.4.5	Political Rationality	239
	6.4.6	Legal Rationality	239
	6.4.7	Substantive Rationality	239
	6.4.8	Procedural Rationality	239
	6.4.9	Bureaucratic Politics, Incrementalism, or "Muddling-Through" Rationality	240
	6.4.10	Organizational Processes Rationality	241
	6.4.11	Garbage Can Rationality	242
	6.4.12	Comparison of Approaches	244
6.5	Human Information-Processing Biases	247
	6.5.1	A Summary of Identified Biases	249
	6.5.2	Debiasing	253
	6.5.3	Contrasting Views	254

	6.6	Information-Processing Concerns in Decision Support Systems Design	255
	6.7	Summary	256
		Problems	257
		References	257

7 Group and Organizational Decision Support Systems — 263

	7.1	Characteristics of Organizations	266
	7.2	Information Needs for Group and Organizational Decision Making	267
	7.3	GDSS Design Constructs	275
	7.4	Distributed GDSS Design Issues	294
		7.4.1 Individual Information-Processing Realities	296
		7.4.2 Distributed Multiagent and Organizational Information-Processing Realities	300
	7.5	GDSS Evaluation Needs	302
	7.6	Summary	305
		Problems	305
		References	306

8 Operational Implementation, System Integration, and Environments for Decision Support Systems — 309

	8.1	Implementation and Integration	310
	8.2	Management of DSS Implementation and Integration	315
	8.3	System Integration Needs in DSS Engineering	317
	8.4	DSS Engineering Design Environments	322
	8.5	DSS Effects on the Environment	330
	8.6	Summary	332
		Problems	332
		References	334

Index — 335

Preface

This book is addressed to two groups of people. The first are information systems engineering professionals who *design* decision support systems that aid knowledge workers in a variety of judgment and choice activities. It is also addressed, through the provision of appropriate overviews, to those who *utilize* decision support systems in any of a number of important contemporary activities. These activities include the design of complex technological systems, such as aircraft flight control systems. They include management systems to enable better financial decisions. They also include decision support systems that enhance judgment and choice in areas in which there is a need for integration of technological, economic, and sociopolitical concerns, such as group decision support systems that enable identification and choice among alternatives to improve urban and regional transportation mobility. Specific examples of "real-world" decision support are generally not discussed, although all of the presentation is relevant to DSS design and use. It is my hope, by addressing both the design and user communities, to present a reasonably complete and comprehensive treatment of this important subject area that will have a wide scope of utility for each group.

The first part of the book focuses on a description of the generic technological components of a decision support system: data-base management systems, model-base management systems, and dialog generation and management systems. The emphasis on these information systems engineering design concerns is relatively technological. The focus is also on the basic and applied technology that makes the application of decision support systems feasible and practical. Emphasis is placed on decision support system requirements analysis and specification, the use of alternative analytical methods, and iterative design approaches for realization of decision support systems. A portion of the first part is also concerned with how decision support systems can be evaluated.

In the second part of the text, approaches are described for developing appropriate integrated information systems architectures that result in effective decision support. These approaches are discussed in the framework of a total life-cycle systems management process. Emphasis is placed on the formulation of user needs, the translation of user needs into system requirements, the hardware and software allocation of these requirements, and the development of suitable hardware and software architectures for decision support systems.

There has been much research in cognitive and behavioral psychology concerning human information processing in judgment and choice situations. Major results of these studies indicate that human information processing is often very flawed. A number of these human information-processing biases have been identified. This second major portion of this text first discusses the general subject of cognitive systems engineering and concludes with a presentation of the way in which decision support systems can be utilized to avoid cognitive information-processing biases and errors.

The second major part of the book provides a discussion of computing, communication, and decision support technologies and associated design efforts that result in useful systems for the formulation, analysis, and interpretation of unstructured issues by groups and organizations. Available systems are described as well as the impact of group decision support systems on decision making in design and management situations. Command and control system design and corporate planning systems will be briefly examined from the perspective of group decision support systems. We discuss design and user environments for decision support systems. This will serve both as the concluding portion of the text and as a vehicle for integrating the material presented earlier. References are presented on a chapter-by-chapter basis. Problems and case-study suggestions are presented at the end of each chapter.

This text is written for beginning graduate students in systems engineering, information systems, computer science, and management. Prerequisites for the text are moderate. The discussion of data-base management systems assumes a moderate background in data structures and some familiarity with applications systems programming. The discussion of model-base management assumes a moderate background in calculus and, to a lesser extent, linear programming. This is specifically needed only for that part of the material that deals with decision analysis and related material. The treatment of human and organizational information-processing concerns is nearly self-contained. For the most part, this is the case also with respect to the group decision support systems design discussions. Some elementary knowledge of computer communications and architecture will be helpful but not required for the group decision support systems and the design and environments chapters (Chapter 7 and Chapter 8, respectively).

Each of the chapters in this text is interrelated. For this reason, Chapter 1 provides a relatively detailed overview of much of the material in this book. This perspective should support the design and evaluation efforts discussed in Chapters 2–5. While this effect could be obtained by placing this technological material after the behavioral and organizational material, the discussion of the organizational and behavioral material would suffer because of the need for knowledge of the support systems design features.

The book is designed for a one-semester graduate course for students in the areas mentioned earlier. It has been used for this purpose by the author in courses taken by students with the same general core background of virtually all students in engineering, computing, and management-related areas.

This text should also be attractive to and suitable for use by the many professionals in industry concerned with decision support systems, information systems, and software development for these purposes. The book has a good many applied discussions from the area of information-processing psychology and it may be of interest to those concerned with human–computer interface design as well.

Many people contribute to an effort as large as a textbook. I must first acknowledge the many who have written research papers and monographs. Generally, these are acknowledged by the references at the end of each chapter. Doubtlessly, I have forgotten, or unintentionally neglected, to mention some authors and for this I apologize in advance. Contributions were also made by students in an information technology graduate course at George Mason University who were thoughtful enough to spend time marking class notes with corrections and suggestions. Particularly helpful in this regard were Pershing Anderson, Philip Barry, Raymond Curts, Lynne Fellman, Jianhong Liang, Richard Librizzi, Michael McFerren, and Kwang-Su Yang.

ANDREW P. SAGE

Fairfax Station, Virginia
June 1991

DECISION SUPPORT SYSTEMS ENGINEERING

Chapter 1

An Introduction to Decision Support Systems Engineering

In very general terms, a decision support system (DDS) is a system that supports technological and managerial decision making by assisting in the organization of knowledge about ill-structured, semistructured or unstructured* issues. The primary components of a decision support system are a *data-base management system* (DBMS), a *model-base management system* (MBMS), and a *dialog generation and management system* (DGMS). Emphasis in the use of a DSS is on provision of support to decision makers in terms of increasing the effectiveness of the decision-making effort. As we will see, this involves the *formulation* of alternatives, the *analysis* of their impacts, and *interpretation* and selection of appropriate options for implementation. Efficiency in terms of time required to evolve the decision, while important, is usually secondary to effectiveness.† Generally, DSS are intended for use in strategic and tactical situations, and less in operational situations. (In operational situations, which are often well structured, an expert system may often be gainfully employed to assist novices. Those very proficient in operational tasks generally do not require support, except perhaps for automation of some routine and repetitive chores.) In this chapter, we will provide an introduction to decision support systems engineering.

There are many application areas in which the use of a decision support system is potentially promising. These include management and planning [1], command and control [2], system design [3], health care, operations management, and essentially any area in which management has to cope with decision situations having an initially unfamiliar structure.

---

*For our purposes, a structured issue is one that has a framework with elements and relations between them that are understood.
†In those instances in which decision-making speed is essential to effectiveness, an appropriate DSS *will* provide primary support in enabling quick decision response.

1.1 INTRODUCTION TO, AND TAXONOMIES OF, DECISION PROBLEMS

Numerous disciplinary areas have contributed to the development of decision support systems. These include computer science, which provides the hardware and software tools necessary to implement decision support systems design constructs. In particular, computer science provides us with the *data-base design* and programming support tools that are needed in a decision support system. The field of management science and operations research has provided the theoretical framework in decision analysis that is necessary to design useful and relevant normative approaches to choice making, especially those that are concerned with systems analysis and *model-base management*. The areas of organizational behavior, and behavioral and cognitive science, provide rich sources of information concerning how humans and organizations process information and make judgments in a descriptive fashion. Background information from these areas are needed for the design of effective systems for *dialog generation and management*. The area of systems design engineering is concerned with building large systems of hardware and software, including systems for decision support.

There have been many attempts to classify different types of decisions. Among the classifications of particular interest here is the decision type taxonomy of Anthony [4]. He describes four types of decisions:

1. *Strategic Planning Decisions:* decisions related to choosing highest-level policies and objectives, and associated resource allocations.
2. *Management Control Decisions:* decisions made for the purpose of assuring effectiveness in the acquisition and use of resources.
3. *Operational Control Decisions:* decisions made for the purpose of assuring effectiveness in the performance of operations.
4. *Operational Performance Decisions:* day-to-day decisions made while performing operations.

Figure 1.1 illustrates the way in which these decisions are related and the way in which they normatively influence organizational learning.* A key point in this figure is that low-consequence decisions are made less frequently that high-consequence decisions. Also, strategic decisions are associated with higher consequences and are likely to involve more significant risk, and must be made on the basis of considerably less perfect information than operational control and operational performance decisions. These latter two decisions relate to specific tasks and may be called task control decisions [4].

Simon [5] describes decisions as structured or unstructured depending on whether the decision-making process can be explicitly described prior to the time when it is necessary to make a decision. This taxonomy would seem to lead directly to that in which expert skills (wholistic reasoning), rules (heuristics), or formal reasoning (holistic evaluation) are normatively used for judgment. Generally, operational performance decisions are more likely than strategic planning decisions to be pre-

---

*Learning is needed or there will generally be no way to do things better next time.

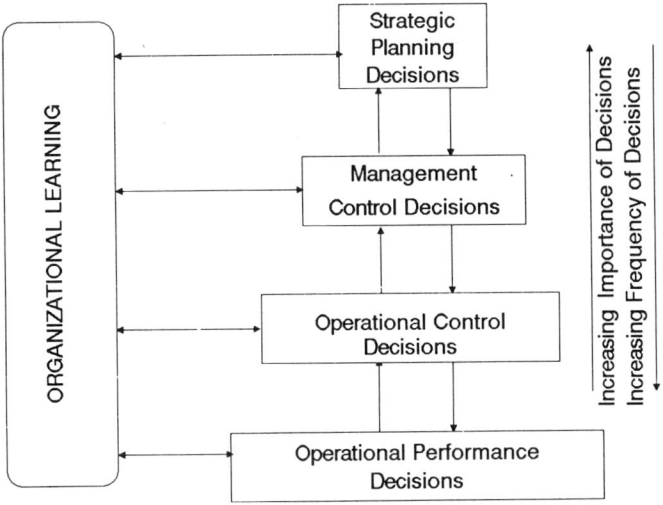

Figure 1.1 Organizational information and decision flow.

structured. Thus, expert systems can usually be expected to be more appropriate for operational performance and operational control decisions than for strategic planning and management planning decisions. (Most expert systems are based on extensive use of what are generally called *production rules*. This *rule-based reasoning* may not be suitable for situations that require either formal knowledge based reasoning or skill-based expert reasoning. From this perspective, *expert systems* might well be more appropriately called *proficient systems;* but, this is getting ahead of our story as we will have more to say later about this. Much research is currently being undertaken to overcome limits to expert systems.) In a similar way decision support systems will often be more appropriate for strategic planning and management control than they are for operational control and operational performance.† We will provide some discussions relative to the use of expert system (AI) tools for decision support, such as expert data-base systems, and expert model-base management systems. This will be a relatively small part of the coverage, and these discussions will always be put into the perspective of decision support system design and use. Basically, there is no need for the decision *support* of well-structured decisions. It may be desirable to automate well-structured decisions, such that the decision maker is relieved of the need to accomplish relatively routine tasks and thereby increase the time available for significant decision-making activities. Alternatively, a person inexperienced at the task at hand may be asked to perform it. An *expert system* may be of support to such a person, for whom the required decision tasks may not be well structured. We will have much more to say about these issues later.

It is very important to note that expertise is a relative term that depends on familiarity with task and the operational environment into which it is embedded.

†Decision making systems generally make use of *formal reasoning based* knowledge.

Since decision environments do change, and since novices become experts through learning and feedback, it is clear that there should exist many areas in which the proper form of knowledge-based support is a hybrid of an "expert system" and a "decision support system." This suggests that there will be a variety of decision-making processes in practice and that an effective support system should support multiple decision processes. In a similar way, the information requirements for decision making can be expected to be highly varied, and an effective support system should support a variety of data-base and model-base management needs.

There are a number of abilities that a decision support system should support. It should support the decision maker in the *formulation* or framing or assessment of the decision situation in the sense of recognizing needs, identifying appropriate objectives by which to measure successful resolution of an issue, and generating alternative courses of action that will resolve the needs and satisfy objectives. It should also provide support in enhancing the abilities of the decision maker to obtain the possible impacts on needs of the alternative courses of action. This *analysis* capability must be associated with provision of capability to improve the ability of the decision maker to provide an *interpretation* of these impacts in terms of objectives. This interpretation capability will lead to evaluation of the alternatives and selection of a preferred alternative option. These three steps of formulation, analysis, and interpretation are very fundamental ones for formal analysis of difficult issues. They are the fundamental steps of systems engineering and are discussed at some length in the chapter on DSS design (Chapter 5). It is essential to note that the purpose of a decision support system is *to support humans in the performance of primarily cognitive tasks that involve decisions, judgments, and choice.* Ultimately, there may be some human supervisory control of a physical system through use of these decisions. Nevertheless, the primary purpose of a DSS is support for cognitive activities that involve human information processing and associated judgment and choice.

Associated with these three steps—formulation, analysis, and interpretation—must be the ability to acquire, represent, and utilize information or knowledge, and the ability to implement the chosen alternative course of action. All of this must be accomplished with due consideration to the particular rationality perspective that is used for decision making. As will be discussed in Chapter 6, these include economic and technical rationality, satisficing rationality, organizational process rationality, incremental or bureaucratic politics rationality, and other forms.

There are many variables that will influence the information that is, or which should be, obtained relative to any given decision situation. These variables are very clearly task dependent. Keen and Scott-Morton [6], who wrote an early seminal text in this area, identify eight information relevant variables:

1. *Inherent Accuracy of Available Information.* Operational control situations will often deal with information that is relatively certain and precise. The information in strategic planning situations is often uncertain, imprecise, and incomplete.
2. *Needed Level of Detail.* Often very detailed information is needed for operational-type decisions. Highly aggregated information is often desired for strategic decisions.

3. *Time Horizon for Information Needed.* Operational decisions are typically based on information over a short time horizon, and the nature of the control may be changed frequently. In contrast, strategic decisions are founded on information and predictions based on a long time horizon.
4. *Frequency of Use.* Strategic decisions are made infrequently, although they are perhaps refined fairly often. Operational decisions are made quite frequently, and are relatively easily changed.
5. *Internal or External Information Source.* Operational decisions are often based on information that is available internal to the organization, whereas strategic decisions are much more likely to be dependent on information content that can only be obtained external to the organization.
6. *Information Scope.* Generally, operational decisions are made on the basis of narrow-scope information related to well-defined events internal to the organization. Strategic decisions are based on broad-scope information and a wide range of factors that often cannot be fully anticipated prior to the need for the decision.
7. *Information Quantifiability.* In strategic planning, information is very likely to be highly qualitative, at least initially. For operational decisions, the available information is often highly quantified.
8. *Information Currency.* In strategic planning, information is often rather old, and it is often difficult to obtain current information. For operational control decisions, very current information is often needed.

The extent to which a support system possesses the capacity to assist a person or a group to formulate, analyze, and interpret issues will depend on whether the resulting system should be called a management information system (MIS), a predictive management information system (PMIS), or a decision support system (DSS). We can provide support to the decision maker at any of these several levels, as suggested by Figure 1.2. Whether we have a MIS, a PMIS or a DSS depends on the type of automated computer-based support that is provided to the decision maker to assist in reaching the decision. Fundamental to the notion of a decision support system is assistance provided in assessing the situation, identifying alternative courses of action, formulating the decision situation, structuring and analyzing the decision situation, and then interpreting the results of analysis of the alternatives in terms of the value system of the decision maker.

In a classical management information system, the user inputs a request for a report concerning some question, and the MIS supplies that report. When the user is able to pose a *"what if?"* type question and the system is able to respond with an *"if then..."* type of response, then we have a predictive management information system. In each case, there is some sort of *formulation* of the issue and this is accompanied by some capacity for *analysis*. The classic MIS need only be able to respond to queries with reports.* The typical MIS is comprised of the following

---

*Thus, it would respond to a request for inputs concerning airline flights from Washington to Chicago on July 4 with a report of available flights on that date. Search of an electronic file cabinet, or perhaps a relational data base, would provide information from which a report generator could construct the desired report.

6 AN INTRODUCTION TO DECISION SUPPORT SYSTEMS ENGINEERING

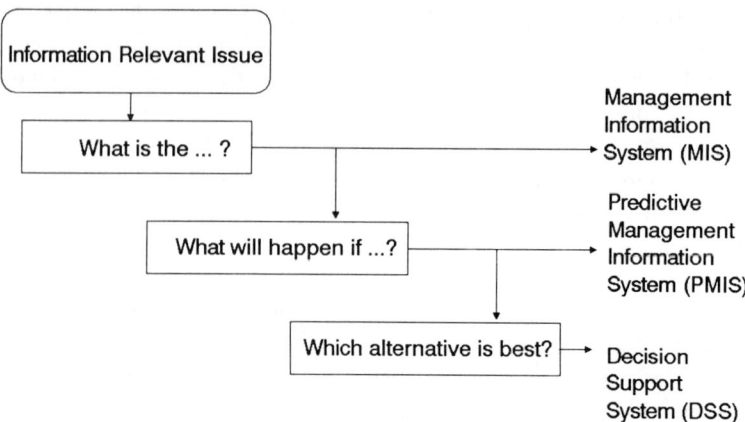

Figure 1.2 Conceptual differences between MIS, PMIS, and DSS.

capabilities: a focus on data processing and structured data flows at an operational level, and summary reports for the user. The predictive management system would also include an additional amount of analysis capability.[†] This might require an intelligent data-base query system, or perhaps just the simple use of some sort of spreadsheet or macroeconomic model.

To obtain a decision support system, we would need to add the capability of model-base management to a MIS. But much more is needed, for example, than just the simple addition of a set of decision trees and procedures to elicit examination of decision analysis based paradigms. We also need a system that is flexible and adaptable to changing user requirements such as to provide support for the decision styles of the decision maker as these change with task, environment, and experiential familiarity of the support system users with task and environment. We need to provide analytical support in a variety of complex situations. Most decision situations are fragmented in that there are multiple decision makers, and their staffs, rather than just a single decision maker. Also there are temporal and spatial separation elements involved. Further, as Mintzberg [7] has indicated, managers have many more activities than decision making to occupy themselves with, and it will be necessary for appropriate DSS to support many of these other information-related functions as well. Thus, the principal goal of a DSS is *improvement in the effectiveness of organizational knowledge users through use of information technology*. This is not a simple objective to achieve, as has been learned in the process of past DSS design efforts.

[†]For example we might desire a response to a "what if" type question such as "What will likely happen if we drill for oil at location x?" The computer might then respond with "Based on the physical characteristics of source x it is predicted that if you drill at this source then you should likely expect..."

1.2 FRAMEWORKS FOR DESIGNING DECISION SUPPORT SYSTEMS

As we have discussed there are three principal components of a decision support system:

- Data-base management system (DBMS)
- Model-base management system (MBMS)
- Dialog generation and management systems (DGMS)

and an appropriate decision support system design framework will consider each of these three component systems and their interrelations and interactions. Figure 1.3 illustrates the interconnection of these three generic components and shows the interaction of the decision maker with the system through the DGMS.

Sprague and Carlson [8], authors of another early seminal book on decision support systems, have indicated that there are three technology levels at which a DSS may be considered. The first of these is the level of *DSS tools* themselves. This level contains the hardware and software elements and those system science and operations research methods that are needed to design a specific decision support system. The purpose of these DSS tools is to design a *specific* DSS that is responsive to a particular task or issue. The second level is that of a decision support system generator. The third level is the specific DSS itself. The specific DSS may be designed through the use of the DSS tools only, through use of the DSS generator only, or through combined use of these.

Often the best designers of a decision support system are not the specialists familiar with the DSS tools. The principal reason for this is that it is difficult for one person or small group to be very familiar with a great variety of tools, the requirements needed for a specific DSS, and the systems management skills needed to design

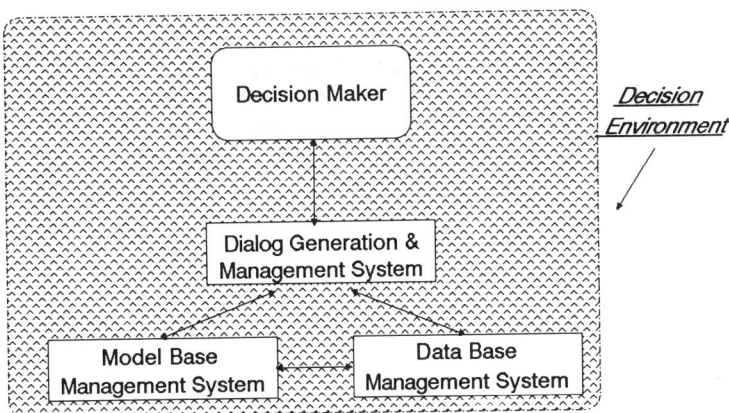

Figure 1.3 Generic components in decision support system.

a support process. This suggests an intermediate level, that of the *decision support generator,* as being a useful level for DSS system design. The DSS generator is a set of software, similar to a very high level programming language, that enables construction of a specific DSS without the need to formally use DSS, or other, micro-level tools in the initial construction of the specific DSS. A DSS generator contains an integrated set of features, such as inquiry capabilities, modeling language capabilities, financial and statistical (and perhaps other) analysis capabilities, and graphic display and report preparation capabilities. The major support provided by a DSS generator is that it allows the rapid construction of a prototype of the decision situation and permits the decision maker to experiment with the prototype and to refine it such that it is more representative of the decision situation and more useful to the decision maker. This generally reduces, often to a considerable degree, the time required to design and build a DSS. This notion is not unlike that of software prototyping, one of the principal macro-enhancement software productivity tools [9]. It will sometimes turn out that the process of constructing the prototype DSS through use of the DSS generator leads to a set of requirements specifications for a DSS that are then realized in efficient form using DSS tools directly.

There are many people that can become involved in the design and use of a decision support system. At a minimum, these include the DSS users and their staffs, the DSS designer, the technical support people who work with the DSS designer, the specialists in computer science and engineering who develop the hardware and source code in an appropriate programming language, and those who develop the operations research methods that ultimately become the algorithms for a specific DSS. The advantage of the DSS generator is that it is something that the DSS designer can use to directly interact with the DSS user group. This eliminates, or at least minimizes, the need for DSS user interaction with the content specialists more familiar with micro-level tools. Generally, a DSS user will seldom be able to specify the requirements for a DSS initially. In such a situation, it is very advantageous to have a DSS generator that may be used by the DSS designer in order to obtain prototypes of the DSS. The user may then be encouraged to interact with the prototype to assist in identifying appropriate requirements specifications for the evolving DSS design.

The third level in this DSS design and development effort results from adding a decision support systems management capability. Often, this will take the form of the dialog generation and management subsystem referred to earlier, except perhaps at a more general level, since this is a DGMS for DSS design rather than a DGMS for a specific DSS. Figure 1.4 illustrates these three levels for DSS design.

This DSS design approach is not unlike that advocated for large-scale systems engineering design [10]. A plethora of potential difficulties can affect the design of large-scale systems in general and DSS in particular. Among them are inconsistent, incomplete, and otherwise imperfect system requirements specifications; system requirements that do not provide for change as user needs evolve over time; and poorly defined management structures. The major problems associated with the production of trustworthy decision support systems have more to do with the *organization and management of complexity* than with direct technological concerns.

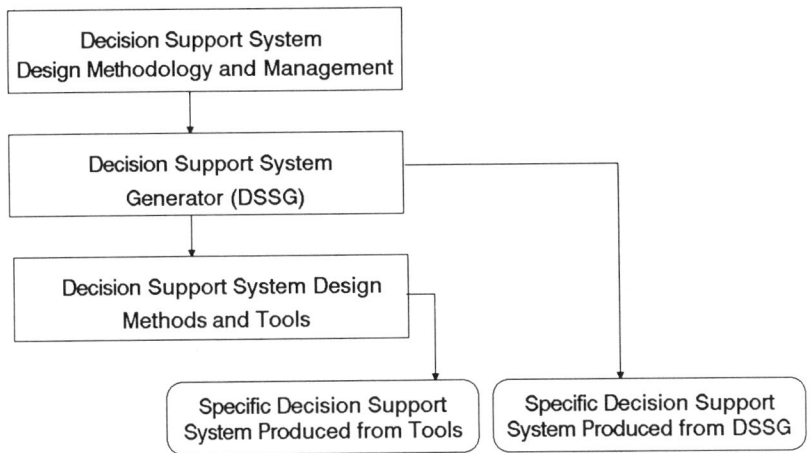

Figure 1.4 Three fundamental levels for systems design and two generic approaches for DSS design.

We envision an embedded hierarchy of performance levels for systems engineering efforts, such as shown in Figure 1.5. The resemblance between Figures 1.4 and 1.5 is striking in that it indicates the similarity of the DSS design approach of Sprague and Carlson [8], as presented here, and the systems engineering design approach.

For our purposes, we may define *systems engineering* as the need identification, architectural specification, design, production, and maintenance of functional, reliable, and trustworthy systems within cost and time constraints.* Our continued discussion of decision support systems, and of a systems engineering design and development process for DSS, will be assisted by the provision of a *structural, function,* and *purposeful* definition of systems engineering.† These three definitions are

1. *Structure.* Systems engineering is management technology to assist clients through the formulation, analysis, and interpretation of the impacts of proposed policies, controls, or complete systems on the need perspectives, institutional perspectives, and value perspectives of stakeholders‡ to issues under consideration.
2. *Function.* Systems engineering is an appropriate combination of theories and tools, made possible through use of a suitable methodology and systems management procedures, in a useful setting appropriate for the resolution of real-world problems, often of large scale and scope.

---

*We use the term *decision support systems engineering* to mean the systems engineering of decision support systems.
†A structural, functional, and purposeful definition of a DSS is also of interest, as are structural, functional, and purposeful definitions of decision support systems engineering.
‡A *stakeholder* is simply a person who has a stake in the outcome of some effort. Often, but not always, *stakeholder* and *client* are equivalent terms.

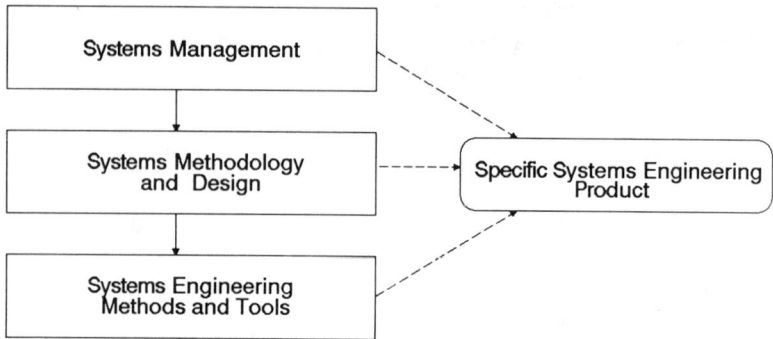

Figure 1.5 Three fundamental levels of systems engineering.

3. *Purpose.* The purpose of systems engineering is information and knowledge organization that assists clients who desire to develop policies for management, direction, control, and regulation activities relative to forecasting planning, development, production, and operation of total systems to maintain overall integrity and integration as related to performance and reliability.

Each of these definitions is important for our discussions in this book on *decision support systems engineering*. The functional definition of systems engineering, as applied to decision support systems engineering, says that we will be concerned with the various tools and techniques that enable us to design decision support systems. Often, these will be *systems science and operations research* tools, or perhaps they will be *computer science* tools. Also, it says that we will be concerned with a combination of these tools. We will use the term *systems design methodology* to denote the effort to obtain an ideal combination of design tools. Finally, the definition says that we will accomplish this in a useful and appropriate setting. We will use the term *systems management* to refer to the cognitive tasks necessary to produce a useful process from a systems methodology and design study. The product of this is an appropriate combination of systems science and operations research methods that is used, with suitable technical direction and leadership associated with systems management, to resolve issues. Each of the three functional levels shown in Figure 1.5 is important. None can be safely neglected.

We can provide a structural, functional, and purposeful definition of a decision support system as well.* The structural definition tells us that we will be concerned with a framework for decision problem resolution that, from a formal perspective at least, consists of three fundamental steps:

- Decision support issue *formulation*
- Decision support issue *analysis*
- Decision support issue *interpretation*

---

*This is left as an exercise for student input.

In Chapter 5, we will provide a detailed discussion of the framework that leads to these three steps, and a number of larger steps into which they may be further decomposed.

Regardless of the way in which the decision support system design process is characterized, and regardless of the type of process or system that is being designed, all characterizations will necessarily involve [11–13]:

1. *Formulation of the design problem*, in which the needs and objectives of a client group are identified, and potentially acceptable design alternatives, or options, are identified or generated.
2. *Analysis of the alternative designs*, in which the impacts of the identified design options are evaluated.
3. *Interpretation and selection*, in which the design options are compared by means of an evaluation of the impacts of the design alternatives. The needs and objectives of the client group are used as a basis for evaluation. The most acceptable alternative is selected for implementation or further study in a subsequent phase of design.

The model for formal DSS problem solution, by which we mean provision of systemic support for decision making, is also a model of the steps of the fine structure of the systems engineering process. Figure 1.6, a model of the systems engineering process, is based on this conceptualization.

The design and development of a DSS can, as we have noted, be patterned after the stages of the systems engineering process. This may be described briefly as follows. More often than not, the initial design of a system is first conducted in a preliminary way to obtain several concepts that might work. Several options are identified and subjected to at least a preliminary evaluation in order to eliminate clearly unacceptable alternatives. The surviving alternatives are then subjected to more detailed design efforts, and more complete architectures or specifications are obtained. The result of this is a decision,* and an associated action plan, that can be subject to detailed design testing, and at least preliminary operational implementation. Once this has occurred, operational evaluation and test of the implemented system can occur. This system design may be modified as a result of this evaluation and this will, hopefully, lead to an ultimately improved system and operational implementation.

This leads us to a systems engineering design methodology, which is also applicable for DSS design, that consists of seven phases:

1. Identification of requirements specifications
2. Preliminary conceptual design
3. Logical design and architectural specifications

---

*When we use the term *a decision*, we also mean such terms as alternative, option, policy, process, technology, or the like. The term *decision* is, therefore, used in a very broad sense. Fundamentally, a decision is an unalterable allocation of resources.

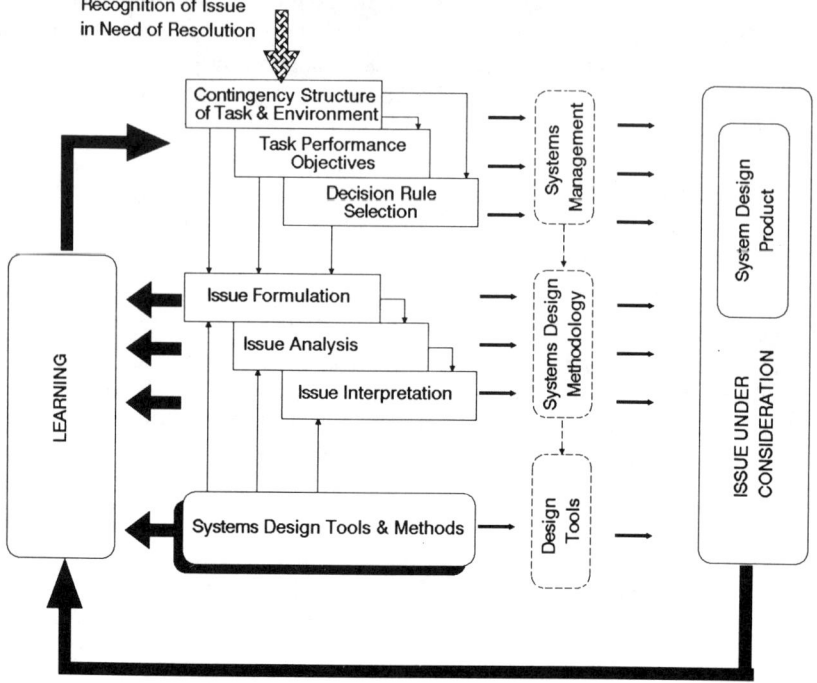

Figure 1.6 The process of systems engineering.

4. Detailed design and testing
5. Operational implementation
6. Operational test and evaluation, and modification
7. Operational deployment and maintenance

which are sequenced in an iterative manner. There are many descriptions of systems design methodology and associated frameworks [11] and we use only one here. In Chapter 5, we will expand considerably upon this systems design framework.

Since a decision support system is intended to be used by decision makers with varying experiential familiarity and expertise with respect to a particular task, it is especially important that a DSS design consider the variety of issue *representations* or frames that decision makers may use to describe issues; the *operations* that may be performed on these representations to enable formulation analysis and interpretation of the decision situation; the automated *memory aids* that support retention of the various results of operations on the representations; and the *control mechanisms* that assist decision makers in using these representations, operations, and memory aids. A very useful control mechanism results in the construction of heuristic procedures, perhaps in the form of a set of production rules, to enable development of efficient standard operating policies to be issued as staff directives. Other control mechanisms are intended to help the decision maker direct and control the use of the DSS. This process-independent approach toward development of the necessary capabilities of a specific DSS is due to Sprague and Carlson [8] and is known as the ROMC approach (ROMC is an acronym for representations, operations, memory aids, and control mechanisms). It also serves to specify the capabilities that a useful DSS generator, or the specific DSS tools, must have in order to be capable of building an effective decision support system. In Chapter 5, we will discuss this approach.

1.3 DATA-BASE MANAGEMENT SYSTEMS (DBMS)

A data-base management system is one of the three fundamental components of a decision support system. An appropriate DBMS must be able to work with data that is internal to the organization and data that is external to it. In almost every instance in which there are multiple decision makers, there will exist the need for personal, local, and systemwide data bases. Some of the desirable characteristics of a DBMS include the ability to cope with a variety of data structures that allow for probabilistic, incomplete, and imprecise data, and data that is unofficial, and personal, as contrasted with official and organizational. The DBMS should also be capable of informing the support system user of the types of data that are available and how to gain access to them.

In order to construct a data base, we must first identify a data model. A data model is a collection of data structures, operations that may be applied on the data structures, and integrity rules that are used to constrain or otherwise define permissible values of the data. There are at least five models that may be used to represent data. The most elementary of these is the individual record model. The relational model is a powerful generalization of the record model. A relation is the fundamental data structure in the relational model, and there may be a number of fields in any given relation. The relational model enables mathematical set operations on records in terms of insertion of new records; updating fields within existing records; deleting existing records; creating relations that may be contained in records; deleting relations that may be contained in records; joining or combining two or more relations based on their containing common fields; selecting records by virtue of their containing certain specified relations; and projection so as to enable selection of a subset of the fields that exist in a relation.

The hierarchical or tree data model is a relatively efficient representation of data. In a hierarchical model, the structure represents the information that is contained in the fields of a relational record. In a hierarchical model, there will be certain records that must exist before other records can exist, since every data structure must have a root record. Because of this structured aspect of the model, it will be necessary to repeat some of the data that need be stored only once for a relational model. The network model is a generalization of the hierarchical model in that there are links between records which enable a given record to participate in several relationships. There are often major problems associated with insertions, deletions, and updating in both the hierarchical and network data models owing to the need to maintain a consistent data base. These do not exist in the relational model, since the same data is never entered more than once. Also, there is additional search complexity, because a search can start anywhere in the network structure. Searches are, however, generally more efficient than they are in a relational model.

Owing to the potential need to accommodate expert system type capabilities in a decision support system, it is desirable to consider a production rule model as a fifth data model. This will enable inferences to be made. Thus, this is an especially desirable form of data model when we desire to use many predictive management information system capabilities. The "if then" type response to "what if" queries is especially natural in this representation. Much additional discussion of DBMS design approaches [14–16] will be found in Chapter 2, where we will also present a relatively brief overview of expert data-base systems and a closely related data-base type, object-oriented data bases.

1.4 MODEL-BASE MANAGEMENT SYSTEMS (MBMS)

The desire to provide recommendation capability in a decision support system leads us to a discussion of model-base management systems. It is through the use of MBMS that we are able to provide for sophisticated analysis and interpretation capability in a decision support system. The single most important characteristic of a MBMS is that it enables the decision maker to explore the decision situation through use of the data base by a model base of algorithmic procedures and associated model management protocols. This can occur through use of modeling statements, in some procedural or nonprocedural language; through use of model subroutines, such as mathematical programming packages, that are called by a management function; and through use of data abstraction models. This latter approach is close to the expert system approach in that there will exist element, equation, and solution procedures that will together comprise an inference engine. Advantages to this approach include ease of updating and use of the model for explanatory and explication purposes.

Typically, it will be desirable to allow for the use of multiple models to accommodate decision makers' desires for flexibility. For example, a mixed scanning approach might be incorporated to allow for an initial scan to eliminate grossly unacceptable alternatives. After this is accomplished, further evaluation of alternatives might be accomplished by a compensatory trade-off evaluation, or one based on a dominance search procedure [17].

The subject of model-base management, and its use in managing decision models, is a new and very important one for decision support systems development. A number of concepts will be discussed in Chapter 3. Among the new developments in this area are the use of expert systems for rapidly constructing models, the use of heuristic search techniques for selection and integration of models into the DSS, and the development of approaches for interpretation of the analysis results of model use.

The MBMS should provide flexibility upon system user request through a variety of prewritten models that have been found useful in the past, such as linear programming and multiattribute decision analysis models, and procedures to use these models. It should also permit the development of user-built models and heuristics that are developed from established models. It should also be possible to perform sensitivity tests of model outputs, and to run models with a range of data in order to obtain the response to a variety of "what if" type questions.

1.5 DIALOG GENERATION AND MANAGEMENT SYSTEMS (DGMS)

The dialog generation and management system portion of a decision support system is designed to satisfy knowledge representation, and control and interface requirements of the DSS. It is the DGMS that is responsible for presentation of the information outputs of the DBMS and MBMS to the decision makers and for acquiring and transmitting their inputs to the DBMS and the MBMS. The DGMS is responsible for producing DSS output representations, for obtaining the decision maker inputs that result in the operations on the representations, for interfacing to the memory aids, and for explicit provision of the control mechanisms that enable the dialog between user input and output and the DBMS and MBMS. The dialog generation and management system should be regarded as a critical aspect of DSS design, as it is through the DGMS that the user interacts with the system.

There are a number of possible dialogs. These are inherently linked to the representational forms that are used for the DBMS and the MBMS. Menus, command languages, and direct manipulation interfaces are some of the formats that may be used as a basis for dialog system design. Generally, several of these should be used, as the support system user may wish to shift among these formats as the nature of issues and experiential familiarity when the issue under consideration changes. The DGMS should be sufficiently flexible to allow review and sensitivity analysis of past judgments, and to be able to provide partial judgments based on incomplete information. Of course, the DGMS should be "user friendly" through provision of various HELP facilities that prompt the DSS user in an acceptable and appropriate manner. At all costs, it is necessary to avoid a system that destroys naturalistic perspectives and to encourage a system that enhances them. Chapter 4 will discuss dialog generation and management systems. A successful DGMS is essential if the DSS is to be sought after for use by humans, that is to say, *acceptable*. Providing an acceptable system is, naturally, a primary objective of systems design.

1.6 DESIGN AND EVALUATION OF DECISION SUPPORT SYSTEMS DESIGNS

A number of behavioral implications to decision support systems introduction are very important. User involvement in the design process, management support for the DSS design effort, and the availability of user training activities are but a few of the many requisites for a successful DSS implementation. It is especially important that potential system users not regard it as too difficult to learn to use, too hard or too time-consuming to actually use, or as producing inaccurate, incomplete, or out-of-date results or recommendations. Perhaps the most damning charge of all that affect potential user willingness to use the system is the feeling that it significantly interferes with the "normal" way of thinking about problems, or that it cannot adapt to changes in problem specifications, that it does not produce intermediate results of value, or that it does not really address the actual problems that exist. The design requirements for a DSS and the implementation concerns will depend considerably on these variables. All of this will influence operational test and evaluation of the effects of DSS introduction as well. These issues are examined in Chapter 5.

1.7 INDIVIDUAL INFORMATION-PROCESSING REALITIES

Having discussed technological design details relative to DSS design, we turn our attention to human and organizational information-processing concerns. There are a number of human information-processing capabilities and limitations that interact with organizational arrangements and task requirements. These strongly influence resource allocations in DSS environments. Among individual information-processing characteristics are the following:

1. Humans have extensive wholistic (intuitive affect, reasoning by analogy, etc.) information-processing abilities.

The judgments that follow from wholistic skill-based reasoning may well be very sound, but will often be quite difficult to explain. Consequently, there exists the need for decision and knowledge support efforts that will enable construction of knowledge bases and judgment guidelines that follow from skill-based experiential reasoning. This is particularly essential in group situations in which all participants will not have the same level of expertise, but need to understand the rationale behind expert wholistic judgment. Information sharing is one of the many features of individual and group decision activities. An inherent advantage to knowledge support approaches that allow for the "blending" of formal reasoning, rule based knowledge, and skill-based expert knowledge is that explanations for judgments are potentially available from each knowledge perspective. This capability considerably enhances the potential contribution of all participants using a DSS by enabling them to use the type of information, and associated information presentation format, most appropriate to the perspectives from which they approach the task at hand. To bring these potential advantages to fruition requires considerable attention to dialog management and associated information presentation principles in relevant and prototypical DSS situation.

A second reality is that

2. Humans use potentially definable and identifiable judgmental guidelines, perspectives, and rules that are more or less appropriate, depending on their applicability to the task at hand.

The judgmental perspectives that are actually used in a given situation will depend strongly on the format that is used to present various situation-assessment and decision-relevant information, and the experiential familiarity of an individual with respect to the task and the environment into which the task is embedded. That it is possible to identify judgmental perspectives is more a desiderata than a present-day reality. It is crucial that we be able to accomplish this identification for a variety of knowledge acquisition, representation, and use tasks. It is well known that a diagram is worth many words [18], but we are only beginning to develop a theory of information presentation such that we are able to design information presentation aids for purposes such as situation assessment. Although there is much more to learn, we do know that

2.1. When deemed appropriate, especially for unfamiliar and unstructured or semistructured situations, when *vigilant information processing* is needed, humans will attempt to use approaches that may be characterized by the formal reasoning based constructs of Janis and Mann [19].

2.2. The particular blend of knowledge (skill-based, rule-based, or formal reasoning based in the typology of Rasmussen [20]) used to reach judgments is a function of the contingency task structure. This structure consists of three elements: the internal and external environment in which the task need is embedded; the decision task requirements, including the stress associated with the decision and the "cost" to the decision maker of exercising various judgment strategies; and decision maker experiential familiarity with the environment and the decision task requirements.

Both formal reasoning and rule-based reasoning approaches contribute to the accumulation of skill-based experiential knowledge through a learning process. In practice, as well as prescriptively, diagnosis of the contingency task structure leads to determination of the appropriate knowledge perspective and the decision concerning how to decide. We learn through experience.* Thus, the contingency task structure, for a given individual, changes with experience. Therefore, we envision a structure for knowledge acquisition, representation, and use such as that shown in Figure 1.7.

In this figure, we see a symbiotic relationship among three fundamental knowledge perspectives. A *meta-level reasoning*† process results in a decision concerning *how to decide how to decide* [21]. On the basis of this meta-level decision, a balance of skill-based, rule-based, and formal knowledge based reasoning is used to identify a decision option or problem solution. This will often result in some sort of physical controlling action. Learning occurs, as both a direct and as a feedback process, through observation of what results.

---

*And in other ways, as well. Experientially based learning is often, but not always an excellent base for decision making. It is not guaranteed to be good. An important objective for a DSS is to improve learning through experience.

†*Meta* is Greek for "higher level." Hence a *meta-rule* is a rule on how to make a rule. *Meta-reasoning* is reasoning about how to reason.

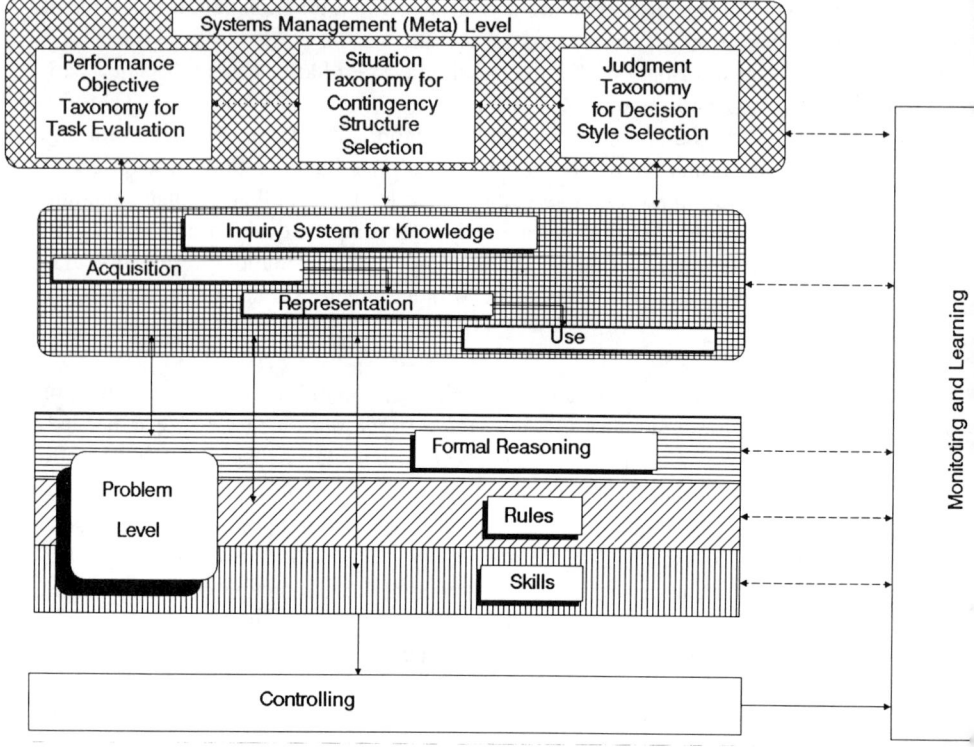

Figure 1.7 Reasoning perspectives and learning in decision making.

In an especially discerning analysis, Klein and Calderwood [22] have identified no less than 38 problem-solving and decision-making strategies. These 38 strategies have been aggregated to form eight upper-level perspectives. In turn these could, with some trepidation, be cautiously aggregated into the trilogy that we have identified here. A possible problem in doing this is that at no level are the identified knowledge perspectives mutually exclusive or collectively exhaustive. In practice also, humans use a blend of factors in their development of realistic approaches to problem solving and decision making. A number of other taxonomies of problem-solving strategies can and have been developed, and will be discussed in Chapter 6.

It is certainly now recognized that the mere insertion of a computerized aid for problem solving or decision making will in no way guarantee an increase in either the effectiveness or explicability of the resulting problem-solving or decision-making task. Just the opposite may well occur. The complexity of tasks may increase, owing to technology infusion, such that there is a reduction in the quality of the resulting information processing and judgments. Clearly then, the amount and extent of technology infusion impact each dimension of the contingency task structure.

The complexity of a situation and the task requirements, together with the experiential familiarity of an individual with these, will influence how an issue under consideration is decomposed into aspects, elements, or components believed to be tractable by that individual. High complexity will also encourage that this be done in such a way as to minimize the interaction among the elements so that the human decision maker is able to cope with the resulting disaggregated issue. At least in a formal sense, this complexity will encourage modularization, the hierarchical structuring of issues, and distributed processing of the subcomponents of these issues. On the basis of this hypothesis, it follows that

3. As the amount of information imperfection increases, there will exist a much greater need for cooperative interaction among the various human, technological, and organizational elements that comprise the task.

This appears needed owing to the difficulty, especially when the available information about system behavior is of poor quality, of appropriately disaggregating task requirements into more elemental ones. This need is particularly acute when expressed for the multiple-agent case, since there will then exist a large shared distributed data, information, or knowledge base with sophisticated devices to obtain the sensory inputs that enable contributions from a number of individuals who each participate in various aspects of a problem-solving task.

Klein and Calderwood [22] have made the observation that decision-making issues, in which the fundamental objective is to select a best course of action, are often sublimated into problem-solving issues. In these, the primary goals are situation understanding and immediate selection of a prescribed course of action once a situation is understood. Information imperfections are a primary cause of this lack of understanding and resulting sublimation. They describe three types of ambiguities that determine whether a given issue is regarded as a decision-making issue or a problem-solving issue: problem situation ambiguities, appropriate goal ambiguities, and ambiguities in relations to alternative options that will achieve goals. Thus, there exists a need for techniques to enable individuals and groups to deal with potentially competing and conflicting hypotheses such that they can resolve discordances due to uncertain, imprecise, or other forms of imperfect information and knowledge. This suggests a relationship between the quality of information available in a given situation and the degree of expertise that a specific person will have about that situation. This does not *in any way* suggest that more information will lead to reduced information equivocality and, hence, better judgment. Just the opposite may well happen! It does suggest the major role of information, and value of information constructs, as major determinants of situation understanding as well as of decision-making and problem-solving behavior.

This last observation is related to another one that pertains to human allocation of human resources to judgment and decision tasks:

4. The majority of studies of human decision making, especially in organizational settings, shows that people rarely concentrate on one problem at one time but generally consider, in a simultaneous, often nonsystematic, and parallel manner, a diversity of problem-solving situations [7].

This also leads to the observation that

5. Human performance may suffer when the task requirements suggest performance of several subtasks, often in diverse stages of completion, in parallel.

As has often been noted, humans are limited in their cognitive ability to cope with many bits of stimulus information. The effect of this is often selective perception, in which only a portion, often that portion confirming a decision that the decision maker would like to make, of available information is used in the process of judgment and choice. These studies, many of which are reprinted in Kahneman, Slovic, and Tversky [23], show that

6. Humans are limited in their unaided ability to process aleatory, or statistical, information.

For example, base rates or prior statistics will not be accorded the weight that they should be allocated, as compared to individuating information. A large number of cognitive information-processing biases that degrade the quality of the resulting judgments have been identified and many of these are discussed in Chapter 6. It is also true, as noted by Cohen [24], Baron [25], and Kyburg [26], that

7. Humans often reason quite well based on epistemic and evidential information. Confirmation and denial rules, while potentially very flawed from the strict viewpoint of mathematical logic, often yield very acceptable judgments and often represent the only types of information available for judgment.

At least two considerations suggest very real limits to the behavioral decision theory, or judgment and choice, viewpoint of humans as intellectual cripples who are prone to the use of seriously flawed information-processing heuristics and the resulting cognitive biases. The first of these is that, on an individual basis, the continuous adaptive nature of operational judgmental processes acts in such a way as to overcome the discrete biases discovered in the laboratory [27]. The second is that there is the *potential* for group-based judgments to be of higher quality than individual judgments.

Concerns arise when these notions are considered in a distributed multiagent environment. The concepts of *information sharing* and *shared-concept models* then become important. There are many ingredients in this. Some of them are the communication nodes and links that exist, the perceptions that the different agents have regarding the internal and external environment, and the situation-assessment and decision-making needs of the different agents or actors. A central need in distributed multi-agent situations is translation of thoughts and ideas into some, more or less common language such that these can be shared. Thus, questions of dialog generation and management, including information presentation, become particularly influential. Needs in this area have led to the development of *group decision support systems* (GDSS). The purposes of these computerized aids to planning, problem solving, and decision making have been discussed in a noteworthy article by DeSanctis and Gallupe which we will soon discuss. They include

- Removing a number of common communication barriers.
- Providing techniques for structuring decisions.
- Systematically directing group discussion, and associated problem solving and decision making, in terms of the patterns, timing, and content of the information that influences these actions.

1.8 A FRAMEWORK FOR GROUP DSS DESIGN

Much recent research in human judgment and choice suggests the need for incorporation of behavioral perspectives in all aspects of system design, including DSS design. A DSS design framework to support information processing and associated judgment and choice should be comprised of three principal interrelated components:

Knowledge acquisition and representation, so as to enable effective understanding of the decision situation and to model how people might use information when making a decision.

Information presentation of these representations in a distributed multiagent situation such as to enable evaluation of alternatives from perspectives that are commensurate with experiential familiarity with the task at hand.

DSS organizational structures and architectures, which results in a network of communication channels, in which distributed multiagent decision making takes place.

A purpose for this framework is to guide the design of distributed information systems [28,29], including GDSS. It is important, in a distributed group situation, to effectively allocate resource distribution across nodes in the communication network and associated information presentation so that it becomes possible to

- Indicate the kinds of interactions between people in distributed decision tasks that result in enhancing support for, or interference with or lack of support to, these distributed decision tasks.
- Understand how one mode of information presentation, for both situation understanding and decision-making purposes, may be better than another mode in encouraging request for other information that aids in better understanding of the decision situation.

- Predict the characteristics of a DSS that provides support for distributed multiagent decision making, such as to make information easy to understand, to relate to other relevant information presentations, and to encourage effective decision making.
- Evaluate decision support systems with respect to the extent to which they encourage "effective" decision making (and thereby)
- Develop a methodology for the design of decision support systems, especially organizational and group decision support systems, that aids information processing in systems and organizations [30].

Among the many concerns relevant for a design theory for DSS, four are particularly important:

1. Time sequencing of elements, such as activities and events.
2. Spatial separation between elements in the decision situation, such as cooperating decision makers.
3. Containment of elements within other elements of the decision situation, such as the incremental decisions of a person who must integrate, contain, and coordinate the incremental decisions according to some strategic plan.
4. The inherent uncertainty and imprecision, and other forms of imperfection, that are associated with information inputs and knowledge of the consequences of actions that might be undertaken.

These four concerns, especially that associated with information imperfection [31] in knowledge representation, must be given particular attention in developing a design methodology for decision support systems engineering. Several conclusions are suggested by, and which follow from, these observations:

1. The design of decision support systems, that assist humans in cognitive tasks, requires substantial comprehension of the human intellectual activities supporting judgment and choice on both an individual and organizational basis.

This comprises studies of skill-based, rule-based, and formal reasoning based judgment, or the seemingly equivalent larger-dimensioned frameworks concerning judgmental perspectives. Importantly also, it involves the way in which use of these types of knowledge depends on the contingency task structure. It also encompasses a study of ways in which humans process information, especially in distributed environments that are subject to considerable message delays, node failures, and associated uncertainties and imprecision in the resulting data base or knowledge base.

2. Identification of appropriate ways to represent and use knowledge in a multiple-agent support system is a critical issue.

This requires attention to studies that deal not only with the formal reasoning methods common to normative decision analysis, but also to studies of how humans can be aided in reasoning wholistically and affectively, such as reasoning by analogy. Perhaps more significantly, it requires studies of how holistic and wholistic knowledge can each normatively support one another to aid the decision-making processes of individuals and groups in distributed multiagent situations. It also requires knowledge of

> 2.1. How information queries are made, in terms of the number of requests and their distribution across communication nodes.
> 2.2. The amount of information potentially available across network communication nodes.
> 2.3. How much of this is used and unused.
> 2.4. The amount of information ambiguity and imperfection that is present in a given situation.

Progress in this area must typically be very concerned with information-processing behaviors in organizational settings. Studies in this category are especially important, since it has been shown that people in an organization will often ignore relevant information in their possession, simultaneously ask for more, and then ignore that new information [32]. Of value also are ways in which information is combined. Thus,

> 3. Information fusion studies and studies of the diverse interpretations that can result from the same knowledge presentation are important current issues.

There is the need to blend descriptive and normative approaches in doing this so that the resulting prescriptive knowledge support process is behaviorally acceptable.

> 4. Acquisition and representation of knowledge from multiple perspectives are needed, as well as studies of how to accommodate this within the framework of specific model-base management system constructs.

This is needed in order to provide the input to the model base management system and associated inference mechanisms that access the knowledge base of a support system. These must be designed in such a way as to consider the special needs that should be associated with a query language structure that may be used to elicit knowledge from the knowledge base, and the physical locations for various portions of the knowledge base, such as data bases and model bases.

> 5. There exist many needs relative to integration of the various knowledge bases, model bases, including data bases and so as to enable communication within a distributed multiagent knowledge environment by users of the system.

In a representative situation, it will typically not be possible, due to time constraints and other complexities, to evolve a *"complete"* set of action alternatives or plans, and possible ways to implement them. These realities must be considered in system conceptualization, and the resulting system architecture, such that the resulting design is one that people may and will use in an efficient way to develop appropriate and explicable judgments.

If there is a single purpose for an overall decision support systems engineering design effort, it must be *to enhance the value of information* in the resulting judgment and decision-making tasks. There have been many approaches suggested for the study of information value, including empirical, information theoretic, information economics, and multiattribute utility theoretic approaches. Value of information is a very multifaceted concept. It implies much more than the information theoretic notions concerning this might. One of the fundamental reasons for this is that much of the information that people ask for is requested for surveillance purposes in an effort to uncover potentially embarrassing "surprises" and not strictly for the purposes of decision making [32]. There are also a number of factors, such as interpersonal conflicts and power struggles, that encourage intentional and unintentional misrepresentation of information. This again indicates that information is not "innocent" and must be suspected of (many potential forms of) bias. Also, information is a symbol that suggests rationality and there are many incentives to displaying what looks like, but which may not be, this symbol. *It looks very bad to not display what can be regarded as this symbol!* As a consequence, there will often be an expressed need for great quantities of the symbol that is information, but there may not be an equivalent desire to use the information that is requested appropriately. The information presentation system should encourage parsimonious requests for that information that is truly used for and that will be appropriately used in resolving the decision situation.

Thus, we see that for an information systems engineering design effort to lead to a functional and trustworthy DSS design product, the design effort must necessarily be concerned with behavioral realities, as well as with the strictly technological issues. Knowledge representation perspectives are particularly critical here. Unfortunately, there does not seem to be a unique way to proceed from one knowledge representation perspective to another, and a number of interesting approaches may need to be examined further to determine suitable architecture that encourages and enables effective knowledge acquisition, representation, and use—and efficient transitions from one form of knowledge representation to another. Some very general observations that need to be addressed relative to this are

1. What happens when an individual decision maker discovers an incongruity between the knowledge representation that the information presentation system (somehow) constructs and the schema that the individual believes to be correct?

These discrepancies may be of a structural, functional, or purposeful nature. The implications of various discordances may be significantly different for different individuals.

2. How do we deal with the *three* possible knowledge bases that may exist for a given decision situation? These are
    2.1 A personal and private knowledge base that the individual may not wish to transmit over the system to others. This is not sinister in any way, necessarily. We all have hypotheses that we believe to be "half-baked" and that we desire to personally explore before telling others about them.
    2.2 A personal knowledge base that an individual wishes to transmit openly to everyone on the system.
    2.3 A personal knowledge base that the individual wishes to selectively transmit to others, for any of a variety of reasons.

There are, at least in principle, various sorts of "centralized" knowledge bases that might represent, in some way, group wisdom. Depending on the manner used to aggregate individual beliefs, or alternatively to use maps in a collective inquiry situation for judgment and choice, incongruities may or may not appear. Although the basic decision support system design effort may well be concerned with the short-term effects of various problem-solving, decision-making, and information presentation formats, the actual knowledge that a person brings to bear on a given problem is a function of the accumulated experience that the person possesses, and hence long-term effects need to be considered, at least as a matter of secondary importance.

We remarked earlier that a major purpose of a DSS is to enhance the value of information. Three attributes of information appear dominant in our discussions so far relative to value for problem-solving purposes, and in the literature in general. These are

1. *Equivocality Reduction* It is generally accepted that high-quality information may reduce imperfection or equivocality. This equivocality usually takes the form of uncertainty, imprecision, inconsistency, or incompleteness. It is vital to note that it is neither necessary nor desirable to obtain decision information that is unequivocal or totally "perfect." Information need only be sufficiently unequivocal or unambiguous for the task at hand. For instance, if we know that alternative A dominates alternative B, then the fact that there is imprecision among the weights of the attributes or among the utilities of the alternatives across the attributes is not bothersome. We should not be willing to pay anything to reduce this equivocality *if* we know that the information precision is sufficient to ensure that A dominates B.
2. *Task Relevance.* Information must be relevant to the task at hand. It must allow the decision maker to know what needs to be known in order to make an effective decision. Relevance varies considerably across individuals, as a function of the contingency task structure, and in time as well.
3. *Representational Appropriateness.* In addition to the need that information be relevant to the task at hand, it must be represented in a form that is appropriate for use by the person who needs the information.

Each of these top-level attributes may be decomposed into attributes at a lower level. Each are needed as fundamental metrics for valuation of information quality. It has just been indicated that the components of equivocality or imperfection are uncertainty, imprecision, inconsistency, and incompleteness. Two of the attributes of representational appropriateness are naturalness or transformability to naturalness, and conciseness. These attributes of information presentation systems effectiveness relate strongly to overall value of information concerns and should be measured as a part of the information systems evaluation effort even though any one of them may appear to be a secondary theme in a specific dialog generation and management situation.

Accordingly, we see that there are many relations between human information-processing concerns and the resulting DSS design. An effort to interpret this concept in terms of contemporary literature has been made here. Answers to the many concerns raised here enable more precise specification of decision support systems architecture. Among these are questions concerning the robustness of knowledge representation frameworks relative to accommodating skill-, rule-, and formal reasoning based knowledge, and questions concerning how the transformation from various representations and perspectives should be accomplished. A purpose of an information system for decision support is information selection and retention, and decision enactment based on this information in an interactive and adaptive fashion. An ancillary purpose is to enhance the value of information in terms of equivocality reduction, task relevance, and appropriateness of form. An evaluation effort that encourages use and evaluation of the entire information presentation system concept, as contrasted with controlled experiments involving a portion of the system, are an essential part of the information system design effort. Thus, this portion of the text is essential to an effort to describe the *engineering design* of decision support systems. This is true for decision support systems to aid individual judgment and choice. It is especially true for group and organizational decision support systems [33], in a centralized or group setting. A presentation of these topics will conclude the portion of the text devoted to information processing in organizations and systems.

1.9 GROUP DECISION SUPPORT SYSTEM (GDSS) DESIGN

There have been a number of related definitions of decision support and group decision support systems. As has been stated, at least implicitly, *a DSS is an interactive computer-based system of hardware, software and interfaces that supports the decision-making process that involves resolution of unstructured problems*. A GDSS, then, *is simply a DSS that supports a group of people or, more to the point, a group of decision makers*.

It is important to note that the group of people may be centralized at one sport, or decentralized in space and/or time. Also, the decision considered by each individual in a decision-making group may or may not be the *ultimate* decision. The decision being considered may be sequential over time and may involve many component decisions. Alternatively, or in addition, many members in a decision-making group may be formulating and/or analyzing options, and preparing a short list of these for review by a person with greater authority. Figure 1.8 illustrates a generic GDSS. Basically, what we have shown is a collection of DSS with some means of communications among the individuals that comprise the group.

A GDSS may influence the *process* of group-decision making. A GDSS has the potential for changing the *information-processing characteristics* of individuals in the group. A GDSS provides *a mechanism for group interaction*. A GDSS may impose any of various *structured processes* on individuals in the group—for example, a particular voting scheme. A GDSS may impose any of several *management control processes* on the individuals on the group—such as that of imposing or removing the effects of a dominant personality. The design of the GDSS and the way in which it is used are the primary determinants of these.

It is possible to develop a taxonomy of GDSS based on the levels of support just discussed. From this perspective, a level-I GDSS would simply be a medium for enhanced information interchange that might lead ultimately to a decision. Electronic mail, large video screen displays that can be viewed by a group, or a *decision room* that contains these features could represent a level-I GDSS. A level-I GDSS provides only a mechanism for group interaction. What we show in Figure 1.8 could actually be regarded as a level-I GDSS.

A level-II GDSS would provide various decision structuring and other analytic tools that could act to reduce information imperfection. A decision room that contained software that could be used for problem solution would represent a level-II GDSS. Therefore, spreadsheets would primarily represent a level-II DSS. To become a level-II GDSS, there would also have to be some means of enabling group communication. Figure 1.9 represents a level-II GDSS. It is simply a communications medium that has been augmented with some tools for problem structuring and solution with no prescribed management control of the use of these tools.

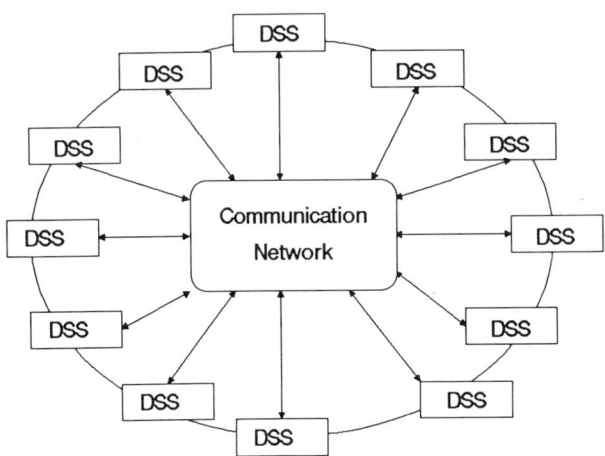

Figure 1.8 Generic GDSS as electronic communication among people.

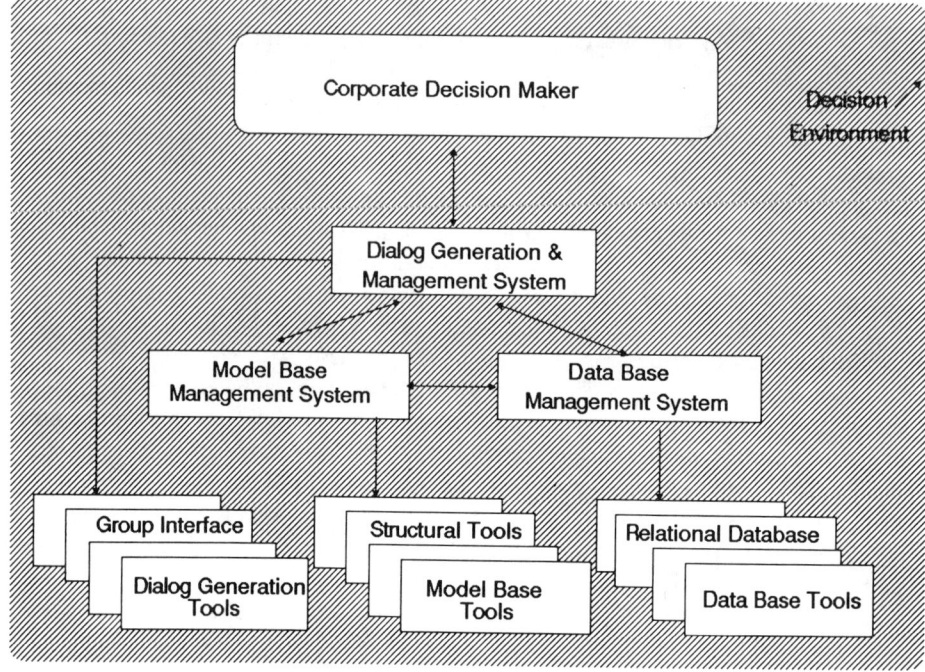

Figure 1.9 Generic level-II GDSS.

A level-III GDSS also includes the notion of management control of the decision process. Hence, there is a notion of *facilitation* of the process, either through the direct intervention of a human in the process, or through some rule-based specifications of the management control process that is inherent in level-III GDSS. Clearly, there is no sharp transition line between one level and the next and it may not always be easy to identify at what level a GDSS is operating. The DSS generator, such as discussed in our preceding section, would generally appear to produce a form of level-III DSS.

As noted by George Huber [34–36] and others, much of the concern in the design of GDSS should relate to the need for trade-offs among

1. Human decision-making needs for greater information sharing, and
2. The lack of time for, and other resistance to, attending a large number of group meetings.

There is considerable contemporary interest in the subject of GDSS design. Gerardine DeSanctis and Brent Gallupe [37], who initiated the notion of three levels of DSS support just discussed, have provided a recent definitive overview of foundations for the study of GDSS. The taxonomy of GDSS settings that DeSanctis and Gallupe identify include group proximity* and group size.† Within this, they identify four recommended approaches: decision rooms for small group face-to-face meetings, legislative sessions for large group face-to-face meetings, local area decision networks for small dispersed groups, and computer-mediated conferencing for large groups that are dispersed. They discuss the design of facilities to enable this, as well as techniques whereby the quality of efforts such as generation of ideas and actions, choosing from among alternative courses of action, and negotiating conflicts may be enhanced. On the basis of this, these authors recommend six areas as promising for additional study: GDSS design methodologies; patterns of information exchange; mediation of the effects of participation; effects of (the presence or absence of) physical proximity, interpersonal attraction, and group cohesion; effects on power and influence; and performance–satisfaction trade-offs. Each of these issues is examined in Chapter 8.

Other relevant efforts and interest areas involving GDSS include group processes in computer-mediated communications, the computer support for collaboration and problem solving in meetings study of Stefik et al. [33], the organizational planning study of Applegate et al. [38], and the knowledge management and intelligent information-sharing systems study of Malone et al. [39]. Particularly interesting current issues surround the extent to which cognitive science and engineering studies that involve potential human information-processing flaws can be effectively dealt with, in the sense of design of debiasing aids, in GDSS design.

Interesting complications arise in group decision situations where the objectives, perhaps owing to different interpretations of information, are in partial conflict. Even this limited discussion makes it quite clear that the role of the individual in a decentralized, distributed, group effort may be much different from that traditionally assumed for an individual in a single-person, centralized decision situation. In particular, it is essential that individuals in roles such as these be able to combine the tasks of information acquisition, representation, analysis, and interpretation; and associated action planning and implementation. This is not at all an uncomplicated effort, since each individual will have a partially different knowledge base that represents beliefs about others as well as beliefs about the environment and the intentions of others. Further, activities selected for implementation will not necessarily be accomplished to full fruition. Activities may be brought to full fruition. Alternatively, they may be eliminated, or modified, owing to the identification of new activities that have higher priority. These affect, to a considerable extent, the roles of the individual in a decentralized, distributed environment with respect to such activities as

- Situation assessment
- Gathering information or sensing information distribution to others
- Potential plan identification or generation
- Evaluation of potential plans

*From face-to face communication to dispersed communication.
†Small groups to large groups.

- Resolution of conflicts with respect to information and activities
- Execution of selected plans or action alternatives

Knowledge representation efforts are, again, seen to be very important, since the form and structure of knowledge exert a strong influence over the way in which knowledge is used. Knowledge use includes retrieval of information from the knowledge base, and aggregation of this knowledge with values to enable judgment formation. If a decision support system for a single individual is to be ultimately useful, it must allow for expansion and adaptation in such a way that the knowledge base is consistent and nonredundant. In a group decision support-agent situation, additional concerns emerge. Data inputs from distributed sources and sharing of data now become requirements. These should be accomplished, from an efficiency viewpoint, such that only needed redundancy is obtained, only needed consistency is maintained, and integrated management of the composite knowledge base is possible. Data independence concepts then become an additional desirable requirement that will ensure efficiency, in that modifications to a data base can easily be accomplished. We should like to make the analogous statement concerning information and knowledge. That we cannot easily do this is indicative of additional needs for efforts that better enable us to consider information and knowledge as data. To accomplish this well is a central purpose of a model-base management subsystem in a GDSS.

Security of data, information, and knowledge in terms of authentication, authorization, and various protection mechanisms also becomes significant. The need for local and personal data and knowledge bases is easily established. A top-level manager may, for example, wish to test various hypotheses concerning especially sensitive resource deployment strategies. The impacts of various strategies will, after implementation, influence other items in the knowledge base. For a variety of reasons, a particular decision maker may not wish these impacts to become part of the shared data or knowledge base immediately. This illustrates the desirability of personal data and knowledge bases in a group decision support situation. In a similar way, loss of a portion of the shared data base may require the replacement of the now-missing data with very subjective data, such as that contained in a personal data base. Figure 1.10 illustrates the role of these various data bases in a GDSS.

In our detailed discussions of these topics, we will provide a broad perspective on group decision support group and organizational decision-making functions. Rather than concentrate on one or two specific systems, we will paint a picture of the many requirements that must be satisfied to produce an acceptable design for GDSS. This will be built on our earlier discussions of individual and group information-processing characteristics and the file of information technology in these. Hardware and Software concerns related to the design of group and organizational DSS will be examined. A brief overview of existing systems will also be presented.

1.10 INFORMATION TECHNOLOGY SUPPORT ENVIRONMENTS FOR DSS

Expressions such as *information technology environments* or *environment for systems design* are open to a wide range of interpretations. At one end of the spectrum is an

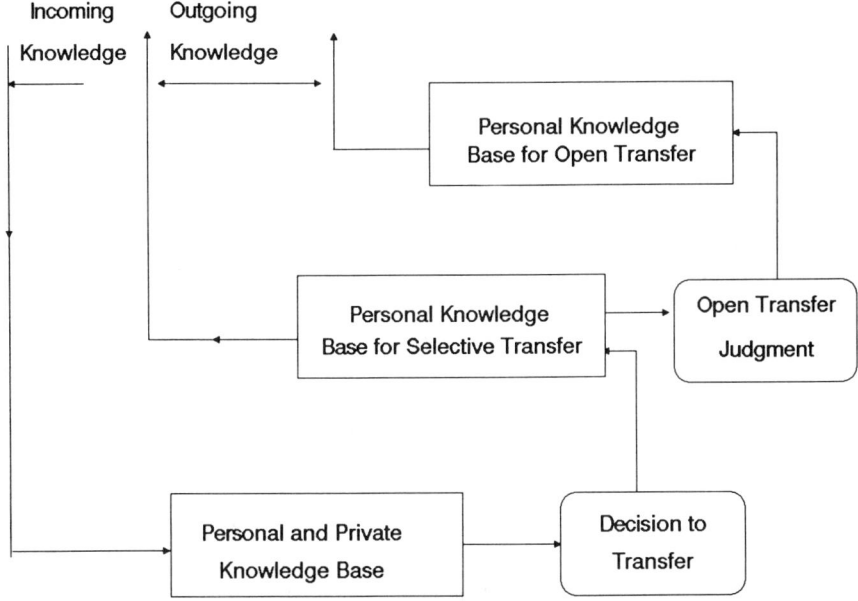

Figure 1.10 Conceptual model of three types of personal knowledge bases.

interpretation that suggests a set of *computer-aided system design tools,* or perhaps just a classic collection of design approaches that have not been subject to computerization at all. At another end of the spectrum are uses of the term that imply an aid that provides *machine intelligence* or *expert system* type support to aid systems design and development, potentially through the entire life-cycle phases of information system evolution. These two notions are related. The first refers to the environment of the designer and the second to the environment of the client or system user. Still another common use of the term *environment* relates to the *surroundings* in which the designed information system will be used for decision support purposes.

The term *environment* includes not only the present time and contests surrounding information systems designers and users, but the anticipated future contexts for users and designers as well. A *proper* design environment is one that is integrated with the user environment and that allows for system evolution over time, system integration with other systems in the operational environment as necessary to satisfy the evolving needs of the system user.

Thus, *information technology support environments* represent a fundamental ingredient throughout the life cycle of an information system, and in particular the life cycle of a decision support system.

Environment may be defined as follows: *A system design and development environment is the set of methods, design methodologies, and systems management processes that, associated with the operational situation extant of the user, is used to produce a trustworthy system.* The methods portion of this definition represents those analytical tools that support the design process. For information systems design for example, this would include the design tools that produce the data-base and model-base management systems. Design methodologies represent the sets of open procedures that enable problem solving. In other words, a methodology relates to the ways in which the methods and tools are used. The term *systems management* refers not only to the way in which problems are formulated, but also to the way in which a problem-solving effort is formulated.

It is potentially significant to note that this definition indicates that an appropriate information systems design environment is *much more* than an integrated set of methods and tools, regardless of their sophistication, that are useful throughout the technical life cycle of a system. It is important, of course, to surround the system designer with an appropriate set of tools. But this alone will generally not be sufficient for the design of trustworthy systems that satisfy user needs and that are usable by the user.

Hence, contemporary efforts in *decision support systems engineering* contain a focus on tools and methods, on the system design methodology that enables appropriate use of these tools, and on the systems management approaches that enable the embedding of design approaches within organizations and environments. The use of appropriate tools, as well as systems methodology and management constructs, enables *system design for more efficient and effective human interaction* [40]. Clearly, this is a product of an effective information systems engineering design environment.

To achieve truly useful system design environments for the design of a trustworthy and functional DSS, there will have to be specific tools that are primarily useful in only some system life cycle phases. This suggests the need for a systems engineering environment to support *transitioning* from one phase to the other, and to support integration and interoperability across phases and the products of different vendors.

The early phases of the system life cycle are conceptual formulation or *framing*-type efforts in which the primary tasks are associated with problem or issue characterization and representation. Then follows a detailed design and analysis, or *production* sequence of phases in which a system is actually produced. The final phases in the system life cycle are devoted to interpretation and *evaluation* of the produced system and associated maintenance and modification of the system to make it more effective as time evolves. We can associate an environment with each of these, and we can also speak of a *generic* environment, and of tools associated with this environment. These tools would consist of very general purpose instruments that would be useful across the other more specialized environments.

This notion of four environmental phases (i.e., framing, production, evaluation, and generic) is not unrelated to several of the other environmental constructs that have been identified. We choose this particular set of four since they so closely correspond to the general efforts of formulation, analysis, and interpretation that are the fundamental systems engineering steps. The fourth environment, a generic environment, corresponds to tools and support that are ubiquitous across the other three. Figure 1.11 illustrates this concept.

The primary objectives of the development and use of a DSS design and use environment are to evolve an integrated suite of analysis and design tools, method-

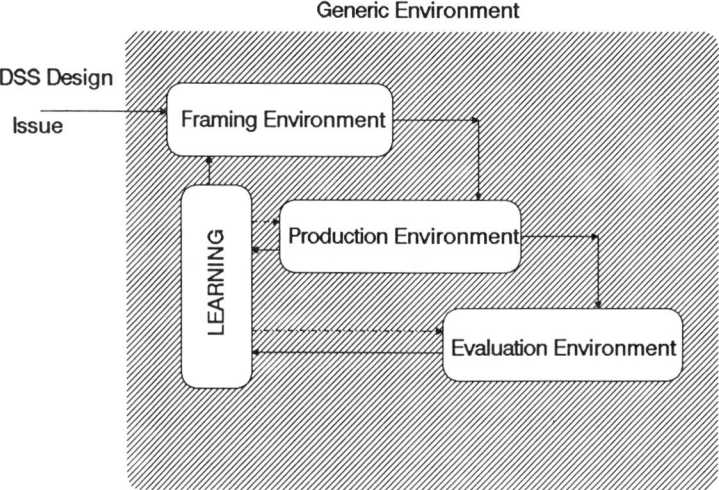

Figure 1.11 Four environmental phases for DSS design: framing, production, evaluation, generic.

ologies, and systems management processes that support the effective design of a complex information systems of large scale and scope to support information processing and judgment and choice (that is to say, decision support). The system design environment should have six major functional elements:

1. A system builder or system generator that selects appropriate algorithms and software packages.
2. Data retrieval, entry, and editing capability to allow relevant design data and information to be used by the selected system design algorithms.
3. Exercise of the specific design algorithm that is selected to be used for a particular application.
4. Generation of output displays and reports, and presentation of these to the user.
5. A user–system–designer interface to support human machine communication from both conceptual and linguistic points of view and to assist the system user in efficient and effective use of the resulting *prototype* system such as to enable iterative adjustments toward a *better* system.
6. A knowledge base life-cycle assistant to determine the implications of design changes throughout the development life cycle.

Generally, neither application systems designers, software systems engineers, or users are very knowledgeable about all characteristics of the end system under consideration. This is because they will not have sufficient experiential familiarity with the knowledge domains of the other group to enable full appreciation of the implications of the system design and development decisions. This is one of the primary purposes of the *DSS design support environment* and why one is quite needed.

An ideal DSS development environment is not unlike a software development and use environment [9,41,42]. This desirable environment is one in which the end user is able to identify system requirements through an interactive human–machine interface that enables visualization of the impact of alternative requirements specifications. Through this, the user should be able to refine these requirements iteratively and throughout the process, so as to produce the software system closest to that required to fulfill identified needs. The ultimate operational goal of a information systems development environment is to facilitate automated production of requirements specifications and to be able to ultimately enable these to be translated into operational code that meets all of the operational functionality requirements of reliability, maintainability, availability, portability, interoperability, verifiability, validability, and trustability. This process implies the need to look beyond the conventional "waterfall life cycle" and potentially other production life-cycle models, to take advantage of the opportunities afforded by emerging information technology advances: expert systems, artificially intelligent interfaces, open systems architectures, distributed data bases, graphic interfaces, and cognitive interfaces.

As noted in our foregoing discussions on environment characteristics, information needs abound in each of the activities of DSS development. We have presented the requirements for an ideal information systems development environment as one in which the DSS developer is

1. Able to identify system requirements through an interactive human–machine interface that enables visualization of the impact of alternative requirements specifications.
2. Provided with an extensive software toolkit that automates the development of specifications to include all data elements, data dictionary information, data flows, structured design flows.
3. Able to extend the concept of reusability through libraries of code, specifications, testing procedures, and so on.
4. Provided with prototyping for early review and for code generation.
5. Able to incorporated concepts of verification, validation, and maintenance in all phases of design and development.
6. Able to take advantage of all automated processes such as fourth-generation language (4GL) generators and documentation generators.

The operational goal of such a DSS development environment is to enable

1. Automated production of system requirements specifications.
2. Translation of these into operational code that meets all the operational functionality requirements of performance, reliability, maintainability, availability, and portability.

3. Full DSS performance verification and validation.
4. DSS modification, as needed, over the entire useful life of the system.

There are at least five issues that must be addressed in a DSS development environment in order to improve DSS productivity significantly.

1. Shorten the DSS development time.
2. Reduce the DSS development cost.
3. Achieve higher quality and reliability with products.
4. Achieve predictability for DSS development in terms of cost, schedule, and performance.
5. Achieve better communication between the DSS developers and the end users.

Obviously, efforts in DSS development environments have not yet produced these results. But progress is being made. And this is why the subject of DSS design environments is such an important one at this time.

1.11 SUMMARY

This chapter has provided an overview of decision support systems engineering. The goal was to produce a commentary that would have initial value on first reading and that would be of later value as well for its intermediate-level summary of DSS and GDSS design and development issues.

PROBLEMS

1.1. Provide a definition of ill-structured, poorly structured, semistructured, and unstructured decision situations.

1.2. Why do you believe that we have been careful to distinguish between formal Wnowledge, rule-based knowledge and skill-based knowledge?

1.3. Define a decision support system from a structural perspective, a functional perspective, and a purposeful perspective.

1.4. Describe the purpose of a DBMS, MBMS, and DGMS.

1.5. Why do you believe that the study of human information processing is important for understanding of design principles for DSS and GDSS?

1.6. What is rationality? What does it mean in the context used here?

1.7. Identify 10 words or phrases used in this chapter with which you were initially unfamiliar. Define each of them in the context that they were used.

1.8. Identify a DSS support need with which you are familiar. Describe the needed DSS.

1.9. A DSS has the potential to support the formulation, analysis, or interpretation of issues. What would be some ways in which this might be done? Would any different DSS requirements be present for these three problems?

1.10. What is the primary difference between a DSS and an expert system? Under what circumstances would either be appropriate? Under what circumstances would both be appropriate? Under what circumstances would neither be appropriate?

1.11. Comment on the assertion that a DSS user is primarily concerned with purpose, a DSS designer with structure, and a DSS toolsmith with function.

1.12. Are the adjectives structural, functional, and purposeful mutually exclusive and collectively exhaustive? In particular is it possible to have a strucural representation of system purpose?

References

[1] Alter, S. L., *Decision Support Systems: Current Practice and Continuing Challenges,* Addison-Wesley, Reading, MA, 1982.

[2] Andriole, S. J., and Halpin, S. M. (Eds.), *Special Issue on Information Technology for Command and Control, IEEE Transactions on Systems, Man and Cybernetics,* Vol. 16, No. 6, November/December 1986 (also IEEE Press, 1991).

[3] Rouse, W. B., *Design for Success: Human-Centered Design of Complex Systems,* Wiley, New York, 1990.

[4] Anthony, R. N., *Planning and Control Systems: A Framework for Analysis,* Harvard University Press, Cambridge, 1965. [Major extensions are provided in Anthony, R. N., *The Management Control Function,* Harvard University Press, 1988.]

[5] Simon, H. A., *The New Science of Management Decision,* Harper & Row, New York, 1960.

[6] Keen, P. G. W., and Scott Morton, M. S., *Decision Support Systems: An Organizational Perspective,* Addison-Wesley, Reading, MA, 1978.

[7] Mintzberg, H., *The Nature of Managerial Work,* Harper & Row, New York, 1973.

[8] Sprague, R. H., Jr., and Carlson, E. D., *Building Effective Decision Support Systems,* Prentice-Hall, Englewood Cliffs, NJ, 1982.

[9] Sage, A. P., and Palmer, J. D., *Software Systems Engineering,* Wiley, New York, 1990.

[10] Sage, A. P., "Methodological Considerations in the Design of Large Scale Systems Engineering Processes," in Haimes, Y.Y. (Ed.), *Large Scale Systems,* North-Holland, Amsterdam, 1982, pp. 99–141.

[11] Sage, A. P., *Methodology for Large Scale Systems,* McGraw-Hill, 1977.

[12] Sage, A. P. (Ed), *Systems Engineering: Methodology and Applications,* IEEE Press, New York, 1977.

[13] Sage, A. P., "A Methodological Framework for Systemic Design and Evaluation of Computer Aids for Planning and Decision Support," *Computers and Electrical Engineering,* Vol. 8, No. 2, 1981, pp. 87–102.

[14] Date, C. J., *An Introduction to Data Base Systems,* 2nd ed., Addison-Wesley, Reading, MA, 1977.

[15] Date, C. J., *Database: A Primer,* Addison-Wesley, Reading, MA, 1983.

[16] Martin, J., *Managing the Data Base Environment,* Prentice-Hall, Englewood Cliffs, NJ, 1983.

[17] Sage, A. P., and White, C. C., "ARIADNE: A Knowledge Based Interactive System for Decision Support," *IEEE Transactions on Systems, Man and Cybernetics,* Vol. 14, No. 1, January 1984, pp. 35–47.

[18] Larkin, J. H., and Simon, H. A., "Why a Diagram is (Sometimes) Worth Ten Thousand Words," *Cognitive Science,* Vol. 11, No. 1, 1987, pp. 65–99.

[19] Janis, I. L., and Mann, L., *Decision Making: A Psychological Analysis of Conflict, Choice, and Commitment,* Free Press, New York, 1977.

[20] Rasmussen, J., *Information Processing and Human-Machine Interaction: An Approach to Cognitive Engineering,* North-Holland, New York, 1986.

[21] Simon, H. A., "On How to Decide What to Do," *Bell Journal of Economics,* Vol. 10, 1978, pp. 494–507.

[22] Klein, G. A., and Calderwood, R., *A Preliminary Assessment of Factors Affecting Decision Complexity,* Report No. 96-86.1-F, Klein Associates, Yellow Springs, OH, 1986.

[23] Kahneman, D., Slovic, P., and Tversky, A. (Eds.), *Judgments under Uncertainty: Heuristics and Biases,* Cambridge University Press, New York, 1982.

[24] Cohen, L. J., "Can Human Irrationality Be Experimentally Demonstrated," *Behavioral and Brain Sciences,* Vol. 4, 1981, pp. 317–331.

[25] Baron, J., *Rationality and Intelligence,* Cambridge University Press, Cambridge, 1985.

[26] Kyburg, H. E., "Rational Belief," *Behavioral and Brain Sciences,* Vol. 6, No. 2, June 1983, pp. 231–274.

[27] Hogarth, R. M., "Beyond Discrete Biases: Functional and Disfunctional Aspects of Judgmental Heuristics," *Psychological Bulletin,* Vol. 90, No. 2, 1981, pp. 197–217.

[28] Sage, A. P., "Information Systems Engineering for Distributed Decision Making," *IEEE Transactions on Systems, Man and Cybernetics,* Vol. 17, No. 6, November 1987, pp. 920–936.

[29] Decker, K. S., "Distributed Problem Solving Techniques: A Survey," *IEEE Transactions on Systems, Man, and Cybernetics,* Vol. 17, No. 5, September 1987, pp. 729–740.

[30] Sage, A. P. (Ed.), *Information Processing in Systems and Organizations,* Pergamon Press, Oxford, UK, 1990.

[31] Stephanou, H., and Sage, A. P., "Perspectives on Imperfect Information Processing," *IEEE Transactions on Systems, Man and Cybernetics,* Vol. SMC 17, No. 5, September 1987, pp. 780–798. [Also in Garcia, O. N. and Chien, Y. T. (Eds.) *Knowledge-Based Systems: Fundamentals and Tools,* IEEE Computer Society Press, forthcoming.]

[32] Feldman, M. S., and March, J. G., "Information in Organizations as Signal and Symbol," *Administrative Science Quarterly,* Vol. 26, 1981, pp. 171–186.

[33] Stefik, M., Foster, G., Bobrow, D. G., Kahn, K., Lanning, S., and Suchman, L., "Beyond the Chalkboard: Computer Support for Collaboration and Problem Solving in Meetings," *Communications of the ACM,* Vol. 30, No. 1, January 1987, pp. 32–47.

[34] Huber, G. P., "Issues in the Design of Group Decision Support Systems," *MIS Quarterly,* Vol. 8, No. 3, 1984, pp. 195–204.

[35] Huber, G. P., and McDaniel, R. R., "The Decision Making Paradigm of Organizational Design," *Management Science,* Vol. 32, No. 5, May 1986, pp. 572–589.

[36] Cats-Baril, W. L., and Huber, G. P., "Decision Support Systems for Ill-Structured Problems: An Empirical Study," *Decision Sciences,* Vol. 18, 1987, pp. 350–372.

[37] DeSanctis, G., and Gallupe, R. B., "A Foundation for the Study of Group Decision Support Systems," *Management Science,* Vol. 33, No. 5, May 1987, pp. 547–588.

[38] Applegate, L. M., Chen T. T., Konsynski, B. R., and Nunamaker, J. F., "Knowledge Management in Organizational Planning," *Journal of Management Information Systems,* Vol. 3, No. 4, Spring 1987, pp. 20–38.

[39] Malone, T. W., Grant, K. R., Turbak, F. A., Brobst, S. A., and Cohen, M. D., "Intelligent Information Sharing Systems," *Communications of the ACM,* Vol. 30, No. 5, May 1987, pp. 390–402.

[40] Sage, A. P. (Ed.), *Systems Design for Human Interaction,* IEEE Press, New York, 1987.

[41] Charette, R. N., *Software Engineering Environments: Concepts and Terminology,* McGraw-Hill, New York, 1986.

[42] Evans, M. W., *The Software Factory: A Fourth Generation Software Engineering Environment,* Wiley, New York, 1989.

Chapter **2**

Data-Base Management Systems

As we have noted, a data-base management system (DBMS) is one of the three fundamental technological components in a decision support system. Figure 1.3 indicates the generic relationship among these components, or subsystems.* We can consider a data-base management system as comprised of a *data base*† *(DB)* and a *management system*. This sort of expansion holds for the model-base management system also. Figure 2.1 indicates the resulting expanded view of a DSS. The DBMS block itself can be expanded considerably. Figure 2.2 indicates one possible expansion to indicate many of the very useful components of a data-base management system that we will define and examine later in this chapter.

Three major objectives for a DBMS are *data independence, data redundancy reduction,* and *data resource control.* (There are other major objectives that are particularly useful for distributed data bases, and data 1bases that are based on object-oriented and expert system approaches. We will discuss these later in the chapter.) Data independence relates to design of the data base such that software to enable applications to use the DBMS and the data processed are independent.‡ The major advantage to data independence is that application systems developers do not need to be explicitly concerned with the details of data organization in the computer, or how to access it explicitly for information-processing purposes (one typical use is query processing). Elimination or reduction of data redundancy will assist in lessening the effort required to make changes in the data in a data base. It may also assist,

---

*A DSS is comprised of a data-base management system (DBMS), a model-base management system (MBMS) and a dialog generation and management system (DGMS).
†Often spelled as one word.
‡If this is no accomplished, then such simple changes to the data structure as adding four digits to the zip code number in an address might require rewriting many applications programs.

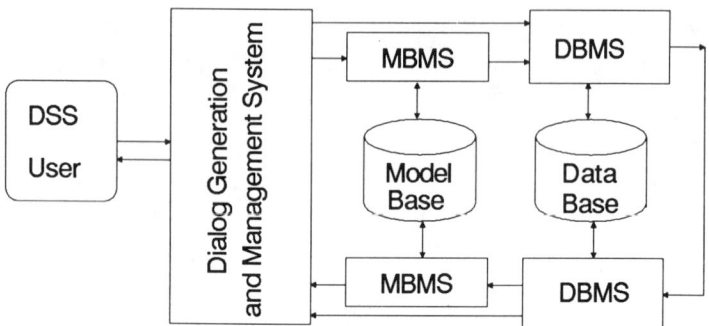

Figure 2.1 Expanded view of DSS indicating data base and management system for DBMS.

generally greatly, in eliminating the inconsistent data problem that often results from updating data items in one part of a data base but (unintentionally) not updating this same data that exist elsewhere in the data base because of data redundancy. With many people potentially using the same data base, resource control is essential. The presence of these three features in a DBMS is the major factor that differentiates it from a file management system.

The management system for a data base is comprised of the software* that is beneficial to the creation, access,† maintenance, and updating of a data base. A data base contains data that is of value to an individual or to an organization and that an individual or an organization desires to *maintain*; Maintenance should be such that the data survives even when the DBMS system hardware and/or software fails. Thus, maintenance of data is one of the very important functions provided for in DBMS design.

There are many tasks that we desire to perform using a data base:

1. *Capturing* relevant data for use in the data base.
2. *Selection* of relevant data from the data base.
3. *Aggregation* of data to form totals, averages, moments, and other items that support decision making.
4. *Estimation, forecasting, and prediction* in order to obtain extrapolations of events into the future, and such other activities as
5. *Optimization* in order to enable selection of a "best" alternative.

We note that these data-base use notions raise issues that are associated with the model-base management system. In a similar way, the dialog generation and manage-

---

*This is generally so, although there could be some hardware that might be specifically designated as belonging *exclusively* to the DBMS.
†Access is used, also, to denote restricting access, such as would be needed when data-base security is required.

ment system determines how (and what) data is viewed and is, therefore, also important for use of a DBMS.

The discussions in this chapter will begin with an overview of the importance of a DBMS in a DSS. We will then discuss three fundamental data models and associated data-base system architectures. This will lead to an examination of the various data-base requirements for a DSS. We will do this by developing an evaluation strategy, and attributes, for a DBMS. Our discussions in Chapter 1 have also indicated the several types of data bases (i.e., personal, local, and systemwide) we can expect to encounter in a DBMS. Some consideration will also be given to data-base access languages (this also includes data-base query languages) here, as well as distributed data-base systems. This will enable us to develop a systems design perspective for the design of the DBMS component of a DSS. Finally, we will discuss some of the

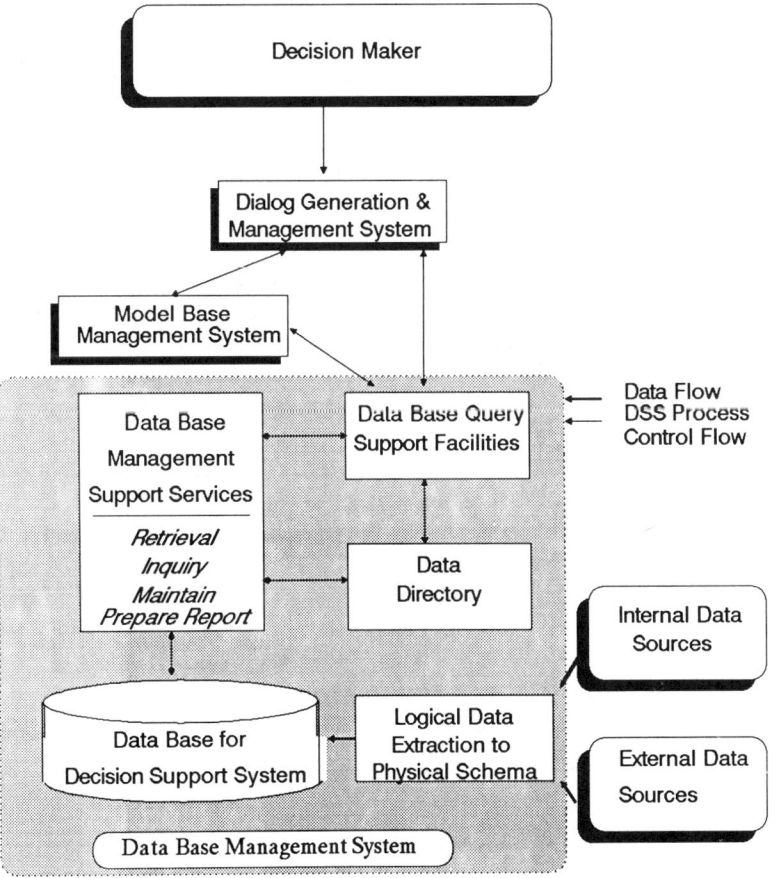

Figure 2.2 Generic components in decision support system with expansion of data base management system (DBMS).

emerging research concerning expert data-base systems,* and indicate the role of expert data bases in decision support systems. A brief commentary will also be provided regarding recent advances in interactive graphical and statistical systems for enhanced communications with humans that use DBMS in problem-solving situations. Much more about this important topic will be said in Chapter 4 which discusses the dialog generation and management.

2.1 DBMS DESIGN, SELECTION, AND SYSTEMS INTEGRATION

As with any information systems engineering based activity, DBMS design should start with an identification of the DBMS design situation and the user requirements. From this, identification of the *logical or conceptual data requirements* follows specification of a logical data-base structure in accordance with what is known as a *data definition language* (DDL). After this, the *physical data base structure*[†] is identified. This structure must be very concerned with specific computer hardware characteristics and efficiency considerations. Given these design specifications, an operational DBMS is constructed, and DBMS operation and maintenance efforts begin. The logical data-base design and physical data-base design efforts can each be disaggregated into a number of related activities. The typical data-base management system life cycle will follow the systems engineering development life cycle as discussed in Chapter 1, or some similar life cycle.

The three important DBMS requirements—data independence, redundancy reduction, and increased data resource control—are generally applicable both to logical data and to physical data.[‡] It is highly desirable, for example, to be able to change the structure of the physical data base without affecting other portions of the DBMS. This is denoted *physical data independence.* In a similar way, *logical data independence* denotes the ability of software to function using a given applications-oriented perspective on the data base even though changes in other parts of the logical structure (and perhaps physical and/or conceptual data structure, as well) have been made. The requirements specification, conceptual design, logical design, and physical design phases of the DBMS development life cycle are specifically concerned with satisfaction of these requirements.

A number of questions need to be asked and answered successfully in order to design an effective DBMS. Among them are [1]:

1. Are there data models that are appropriate across a variety of applications?
2. What are DBMS designs that enable data models to support logical data independence?

---

*This includes natural language processing systems for DBMS design.

[†]This is *physical data*, in the sense that data is to be physically stored in computer memory in accordance with the design specifications identified here.

[‡]This is also desirable as well, although to a lesser extent, for conceptual data.

3. What DBMS designs enable data models to support logical data independence, and what are the associated physical data transformations and manipulations?
4. What features of a data description language will enable a DBMS designer to control both the logical and physical properties of data independently?
5. What features need to be incorporated into a data description language in order to enable errors to be detected at the earliest possible time so that users will not be affected by errors that occur at a time prior to their personal use of the DBMS?
6. What are the relationships between data models and data-base security?
7. What are the relationships between data models and errors that may possibly be caused by concurrent use of the data base by many users?
8. What are design principles that will enable a DBMS to support a number of users having diverse and changing perspectives?
9. What are the appropriate design questions such that *applications programmers*,[*] *technical users*,[†] and *DBMS operational users*[‡] are each able to function effectively?

The bottom-line question that summarizes all of these is, *How does one design a data model and data description language to enable efficient and effective data acquisition, storage, and use?* There are many related questions; one of them concerns the design of *standard query languages* (SQLs) such that it is possible to design a specific DBMS for a given application.

It is very important that, whenever possible, a specific DBMS be selected before design of the rest of the DSS. There are a variety of reasons why this is desirable. The collection and maintenance of the data through the DSS are simplified if there is a specified single DBMS structure and architecture. (The simplest situation of all occurs when all data collection and maintenance is accomplished prior to use of the DSS. The DBMS is not then used in an interactive manner as part of DSS operation.) The set of data-base functions that the DSS needs to support is controlled when we have the freedom to select a single DBMS structure and architecture before design of the rest of the DSS. The resulting design of the DSS is, therefore, simplified. Further, the opportunities for data sharing among potentially distributed data bases are increased when the interoperability of data bases is guaranteed.

Many difficulties result when this is not possible.[§] If it is required to use existing DBMS that are different in structure and architecture, data sharing across data bases

---
[*]The computer science content specialists who actually construct and build the DBMS.
[†]This person, who is knowledgeable concerning highly technical aspects of DBMS use in specific applications, is often called a *data-base administrator* (DBA).
[‡]Generally, these are nontechnically trained "operators."
[§]Data in a DBMS may be classified as *internal data*, stored in an internal data base, and *external data*, stored in an external data base. Every individual and organization will necessarily have an internal data base. While there may be no problem in ensuring DBMs structure and architecture compatibility for internal data, this may be difficult to do for external data. *If* both of these data can be *(continued)*

is generally difficult, and it is often then necessary to maintain redundant data. This can lead to a number of difficulties in the systems integration that is undertaken to ensure compatibility across different data bases. (When there are multiple sources of the same or related data, problems with data consistency will often arise. This can lead to a number of issues involving such interesting concepts as *data fusion*, or *data integration*. These are important areas of concern but, sadly, outside the scope of our present efforts.)

In this chapter, will will generally assume that the DBMS is preselected prior to design of the rest of the DSS, and that the same DBMS structure and architecture are used for multiple data bases that may potentially be used in the DSS. This is often appropriate for purposes of DSS design, since DBMS design technology [2, 3] is now relatively mature in contrast to MBMS and DGMS design. It is usually possible, and generally desirable, to select a DBMS, based on criteria we will soon discuss, and then design the MBMS and DGMS based on the existing DBMS. This will usually, but surely not always, allow selection of *off-the shelf* DBMS software. The alternative approach of designing a MBMS and DGMS first and then specifying the requirements for a DBMS based on these is possible and may, in some cases, be needed. Given the comparatively developed state of DBMS software development, as contrasted with MBMS and DDGMS software, this approach will usually be less desirable from the point of view of design economy.

2.2 DATA MODELS AND DATA-BASE ARCHITECTURES

We will now expand on our introductory comments concerning data model representations, and associated architectures for data-base management systems. Some definitions are appropriate. A *data model* defines the types of data objects that may be manipulated or referenced within a DBMS. The concept of a *logical record* is a central one in all DBMS. Some DBMS designs are based on mathematical relations, and the physical data base is a collection of consistent tables in which every row is a *record* of a given type. This is an informal description of a *relational* data-base management system, a DBMS type that is a clear outgrowth of the file management system philosophy. Other DBMS may be based on *hierarchical* or *network structures* that resemble the appearance of the data in the user's world.* More sophisticated DBMS may be based on artificial intelligence constructs or may contain extensive graphical and interactive support characteristics.

There are several approaches that can be taken to describe data models. Date [2], for instance, discusses the three-level representation described in Figure 2.3. The three *levels* of data models are

---

(footnote continued) collected and maintained before use of a DSS, there will generally be no data integration needs. Often, however, this will not be possible. As we will often be unable to control the data structure and architecture of data obtained externally, the difficulties we cite will often be real, especially in what we will call *real-time, interactive environments*.

*Actually, the first DBMS were based on hierarchical data models. Developments in network data models followed, as did development of relational data-base models by Codd in 1970. About a decade later, relational data bases became available for mini- and microcomputers.

2.2 DATA MODELS AND DATA-BASE ARCHITECTURES   45

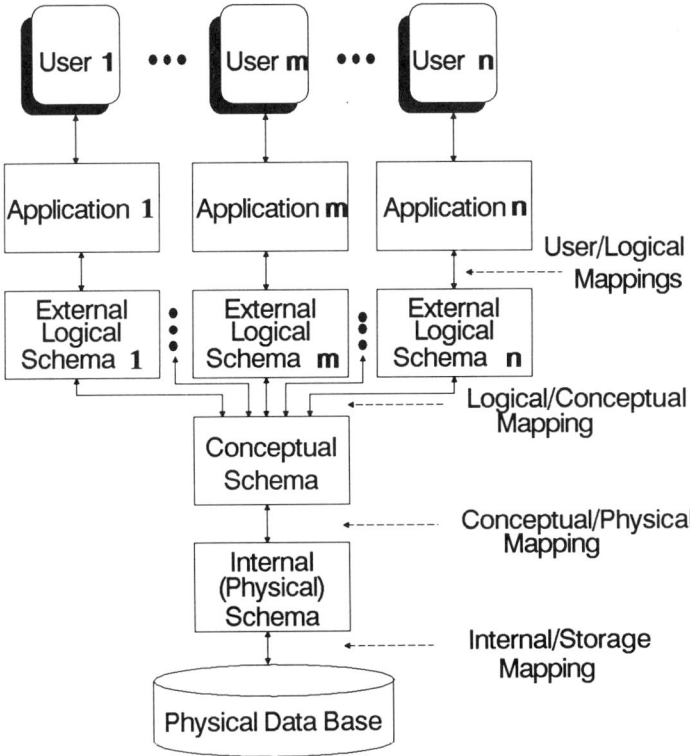

Figure 2.3 Three levels of data schemas.

1. An *external model* which represents a data model at the level of the user's application, and is the data model closest and most familiar to users of a DBMS or DSS.
2. A *conceptual model* which is an aggregation model that envelopes several external models.
3. An *internal model* which is a technical-level model that describes how the conceptual model is actually represented in computer storage.

In Figure 2.4, which is a generic diagram indicating the mapping and data translations needed to accommodate the different levels of data models and architectures, the relations between the various levels are called *mappings*. The mappings specify and describe the *transformations* that are needed to obtain one model from another. The user supplies specifications for the source and target data structures in a *data description language* (DDL) and also describes the mapping that is desired between source and target data. Figure 2.5 represents this general notion of data transformation. This could, for example, represent target data in the form of a table that is obtained from a source model comprised of a set of lists. There are other language types that are useful in DBMS applications and we will soon discuss them. It is helpful to first

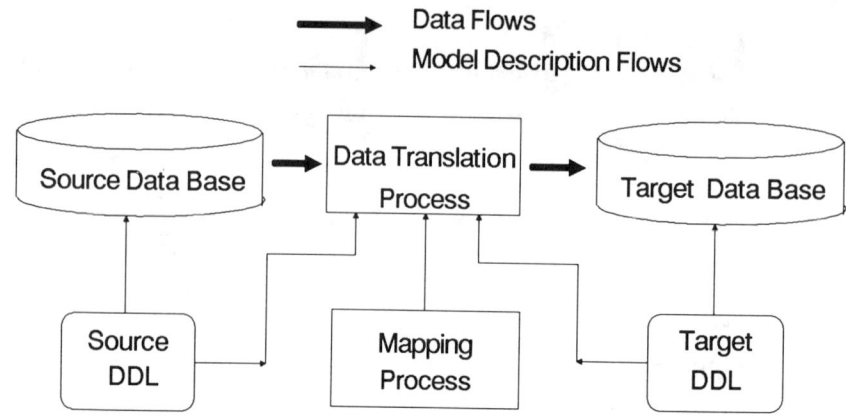

Figure 2.4 Data transforms and model mappings.

define some other terms that are common in data-base management system design and development.

Figure 2.5 depicts just a simple illustration of the more general problem of mapping between various *schemas*. Simply stated, a schema is an image used for comparison purposes. A schema can also be described as a data structure for representing generic concepts. Thus, schemas represent knowledge about concepts and are structurally organized about some theme. In terms appropriate here, the user of a data base must interpret the real world that is outside of the data base in terms of real-world objects (objects are entities and relationships between entities) and activities that exist and that involve these objects. The data-base user will interact with the data base to obtain needed data for use or, alternatively, to store outlined data for possible later use. But a DBMS cannot function in terms of real objects and operations. Instead, a DBMS must use data objects (which are comprised of data elements and relations between them) and operations on data objects. Therefore, a DBMS user must perform some sort of mapping or transformation from perceived real objects and actions to those objects and actions representations that will be used in the physical data base.

The single-level data model, conceptually illustrated in Figure 2.5, represents the nature of the data objects and operations that the user understands when receiving data from the data base. It is in this fashion that the DBMS user models the perceived real world. To model some action sequence, or impact of an action sequence on the world, the user maps these actions to a sequence of operations that are allowed by the specific data model. It is the *data manipulation language* (DML) that provides the basis for the operations submitted to the DBMS as a sequence of queries or programs. The development of these schemas, which represent logical data, results in a *DBMS architecture* or *DBMS framework*. This architecture or framework describes the types of schemas that are allowable and the way in which these schemas are related through various mappings. We could, for example, have the two-schema framework shown in Figure 2.6.

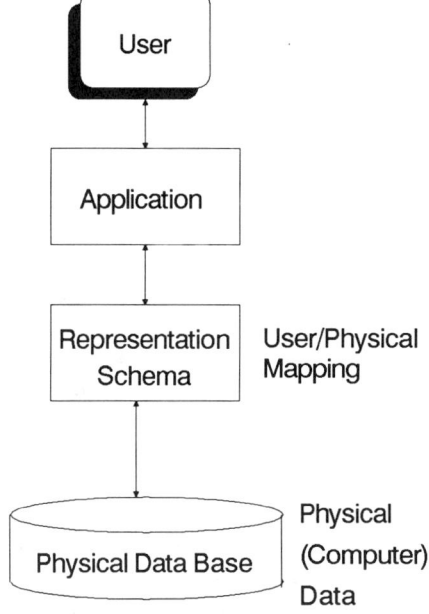

Figure 2.5 Single-level model of data schema.

The three-schema framework, illustrated in Figure 2.3 [2, 3], appears to be the most popular representation at this time. Here, the external schemas* define the logical subset of the data base that may be presented to a specific DBMS user. The conceptual schemas define conceptual models as represented in the data base. The internal schema describes physical data structures in the data base. These data structures provide support to the conceptual models. The mappings used establish correspondence between various objects and operations at the three levels shown in Figure 2.3. If consistency of the conceptual models is to be assured, we must be able to map the internal, or physical, and external, or logical, schemas to the conceptual schemas.

Useful documentation about the data-base structure and architecture is provided through the various schemas, which represent explicit data declarations. These declarations represent *data about data*. The central repository in which these declarations are kept, called a *data dictionary* or *data directory* (often abbreviated to DD), stores the definitions of the schemas and the mappings between schemas. Generally, a data dictionary can be queried in the same manner as the data base, thereby enhancing the ability of the DBMS user to pose questions about the availability and structure of data. It is often possible to query a data directory with a high-level, or fourth-generation, query language.

---

*The plural of schema is schemata, although schemas is often used, especially in the computer science and information systems areas.

A data dictionary is able to tell us what the records in the data dictionary consist of. It also contains information about the logical relationships that pertain to each of the particular elements in the data base. The development of a data dictionary generally begins with formation of lists of desired data items or fields that have been grouped in accordance with the entities that they are to represent. A name is assigned for each of these lists, and a brief statement of the meaning of each is provided for later use. Next, the relationships between data elements should be described and any index keys or pointers determined. Finally, the data dictionary is implemented within the DBMS. In many ways, a data dictionary is the central portion of a DBMS. It performs the critical role of retaining high-level information relative to the various applications of the DBMS and hence enables specification, control, review, and management of the data of value for decision making relative to specific applications.

For very large system designs, the data dictionary development process must be automated. A typical data dictionary for a large system may include several thousand entries. It is physically impossible to maintain a dictionary of this size manually or to retain consistent and unambiguous terms for each data element or composite of data elements. Therefore, automated tools are needed for efficient development and maintenance of a data dictionary. These are provided in contemporary DBMS.

This ability to specify data-base structures, through use of schemas, enables effective management of data resources. This is necessary for access control. The use

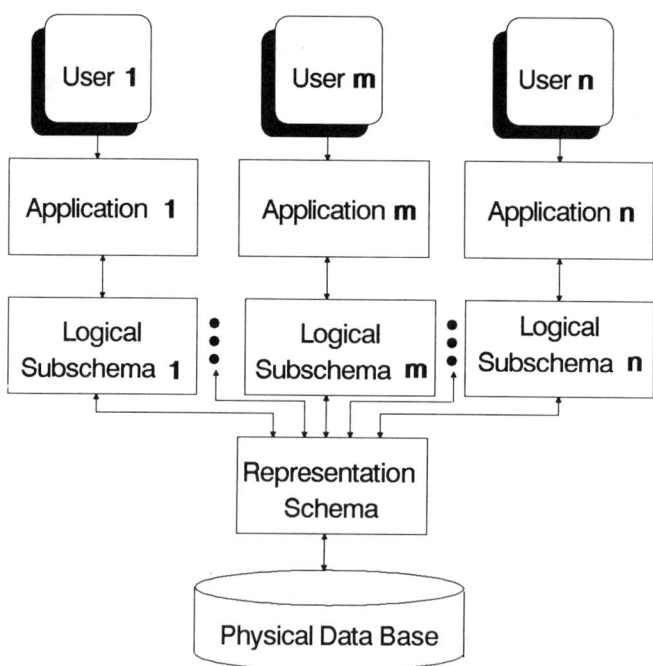

Figure 2.6 Two-level model of data schemas.

of one or more *subschemas* generally simplifies access to data bases. It may also provide for data-base security and integrity for authorized users of the DBMS. Since complex physical (computer) structures for data may be specified, independent of the logical structure of the situation that is perceived by DBMS users, it is thereby possible to improve the performance of an existing and operational data base without altering the user interface to the data base. This provides for simplicity in use of the DBMS.

The data model gives us the constructs that provide a foundation for the development and use of a data-base management system. It also provides the framework for such tools and techniques as user interface languages. The three types of user interface languages are

1. *Data definition languages* (DDLs) provide the basis for definition of schemas and subschemas.
2. *Data manipulation languages* (DMLs) are used to develop data-base applications.
3. *Data query languages* (DQLs), or simply *query languages* (QLs), are used to write queries and reports. (There has been much effort to develop *standard query languages* (SQLs), often pronounced "see-quell," that are interoperable across a variety of hardware and on a number of operating systems. Although these are potentially suitable for a number of applications, the SQLs available to date are DBMS SQLs.)

Of course, it is possible to combine a DDL, DML, and DQL into a single data-base language. As mentioned earlier, the user of these languages is often called a *data-base Administrator* (DBA).

The discussion in the remainder of this section will be specifically applicable to the three-level data model discussed at the beginning of this section and illustrated in Figure 2.3. In general, a data model is a paradigm for representation, storing, organizing, and otherwise managing data in a data base. There are three component sets in most data models. These, and their functions [4] are

1. A set of *data structures* which define the fields and records which are allowed in the data base. Examples of data structures include lists, tables, hierarchies, and networks.
2. A set of *operations* which define the admissible manipulations that are applied to the fields and records that comprise the data structures. Examples of operations include retrieval, combine, subtraction, addition, and update.
3. A set of *integrity** *rules* which define or constrain allowable or legal states or changes of state for the data structures that must be protected by the operations.

---

*Formally, the *integrity* of a data base is the consistency between the data values that are in the data base and the attributes of the real objects that are represented by these values. Integrity of a data base also refers to the consistency between the records in the data base and the real object that these records represent.

(An example of an integrity rule is that only dates between 06/01/89 and 07/30/90 can be utilized. Another example is that a royalty payment must be rounded off to a whole dollar amount and cannot be negative.)

We will soon identify three generically different types of data model representations, and several variants within these three representations. Each of these is applicable as an internal, external, or conceptual model. For our principal purpose here, the design of decision support systems, we will be primarily concerned with these three modeling representations as they affect the external, or logical, data model. (See Figure 2.3 for an illustration of the three-level model and the role of the external model in DBMS architectures.) This model is the one with which the user of a specific DSS interfaces. For use in a DSS generator, the conceptual model is of importance, since it is the model that influences the specific external model that various users of a DSS will interface with after an operational DSS is realized. This does not mean that the internal data model is unimportant. It is very important for the design of a DBMS. Through its data structures, operations, and integrity constraints, the data model controls the operation of the DBMS portion of the DSS.

The three fundamental data models for use in the external model portion of a DSS [5] are record-based models, structurally based models, and expert systems based models. Each of these will now be described.

2.2.1 Record-Based Models

We are very accustomed to using forms and reports, often prepared in a standard fashion for a particular application. *Record-based models* are computer implementations of these spreadsheetlike forms. Two types can be identified. The first of these, common in the early days of *file processing systems* (FPS) (sometimes also referred to as *file management systems* [FMS]), is the individual record model. This is little more than an electronic file drawer in which records are stored. It is useful for a great many applications. More sophisticated, however, is the relational data-base data model in which mathematical relations are used to electronically "cut and paste" reports from a variety of files. Relational data-base systems have been developed to a considerable degree of sophistication, and many commercial products are available.*

2.2.1.1 Individual Record Model This is surely the oldest data model representation, and is illustrated in Figure 2.7 for our student records example. While the simple single-record tables shown in this figure may appear quite appealing, the logic operations and integrity constraints that must be associated with the data structure are often undefined, and are perhaps not easily defined. Here, the data structure is simply

---

*dBase and *Oracle* are two leading examples for personal computers. *MicroSTEP*, from Syscorp International in Austin, Texas, is a CASE (computer-aided software engineering) tool based relational DBMS generator for microcomputers. There are many others. Chapter 1 of Stonebraker [4] provides an interesting overview of early DBMS developments and commercial products.

Student Record				
Name	SSN	Major	Address	Advisor
Jones, A.	123-45-6789	Business	House 1	Advisor 1

Student Record				
Name	SSN	Major	Address	Advisor
Smith, P.	234-56-7891	Computer Sci.	House 2	Advisor 2

Grade Record				
Course	SSN	Date	Section No.	Grade
CS-101	234-56-7891	12/15/89	20234	A

Grade Record				
Course	SSN	Date	Section No.	Grade
CS-101	123-45-6789	12/15/89	20294	C

Grade Record				
Course	SSN	Date	Section No.	Grade
CS-101	345-67-8912	12/15/89	20294	C

Registration Record		
Course	SSN	Section No.
BU-202	123-45-6789	3023

Registration Record		
Course	SSN	Section No.
BU-202	345-67-8912	3023

Registration Record		
Course	SSN	Section No.
BU-202	456-78-9123	3023

Figure 2.7 Individual record model of data.

a set of records, with each record consisting of a set of fields. When there is more than a single type of record, one field contains a value that indicates what the other fields in the record are named.

In Figure 2.7, we illustrate three types of records. The *student record* contains such information as name, social security number, college major, address, and advisor name. The *grades (received) record* indicates the courses the student has taken, the date taken, and the section number in which the student was enrolled as well as the final grade received. The *(current) registration record* contains the courses the student is currently taking and the assigned section number.* The overall data structures for the *individual record model* are comprised of fields that have been aggregated into *records*. The complete data base is a collection of these records.

There are a number of operations on records in the data base that are admissible. These include creating new records, selecting and printing a record, updating fields in a record, and deleting a record. Formally, this is usually accomplished by transferring the record to be deleted from the set of active records to those that have been archived. This might be done after a student has not taken courses in a long time, such as 20 years, and the probability of receiving a request for information is low. Integrity constraints can also be placed on the records. (It might be quite desirable, for example, to prevent students from, intentionally or unintentionally, being assigned a nonexisting grade of "Q.") It is generally most important that one of these constraints be the requirement for a field whose value is unique among all records of a given type. Such a field is usually called a *key field*, and is generally also an *index field*. "Social security number" is an appropriate key field in the specific record model considered here. Multiple field keys are possible also. Here, it is not possible to use student name only as a key field, as two or more students may have the same name. "Social security number" is a somewhat cumbersome key field in that few people want to be called by their social security number. The solution to the nonuniqueness of name problem is to use both social security number and name as a multifield key.

2.1.2.2 Relational Model The relational model is a modification of the individual record model that limits its data structures and that thereby provides a mathematical basis for operation on records. Data structures in a relational data base may consist only of *relations*, or field sets that are related. Every relation may be considered as a table. Each row in the table is a *record* or *tuple*. Every column in each table or row is a *field* or *attribute*. Each field, or attribute, has a *domain* that defines the admissible values for that field.

Figure 2.8 presents a relational version of the just-considered student data base. We note that there is only a modest difference in structure between this relational model and the individual record model. The major difference is that relationships are represented by fields in the various records of the individual record model, whereas relationships (among fields or attributes in a relation) are denoted by the name of the relation.

While the structural differences between the relational model and the individual record model are minimal, there are major differences in the way in which the integrity constraints and operations may affect the data base. The operations in a relational data base form a set of operations (generally spoken of and known, collectively, as an *algebra*, or *relational algebra*) that are defined mathematically. The operations in a relational model must operate on entire relations, or tuples, rather

---

*It is interesting to note that it may be desirable for this record to also indicate instructor name. This information is redundant, as it must surely be included in teaching assignment records. To include it in the student record would add complexity in record maintenance through the associated redundancy, although this does reduce the time required to list the instructors currently teaching a particular student.

Student Record

Name	SSN	Major	Address	Advisor
Jones, A.	123-45-6789	Business	House 1	Advisor 1
Smith, P.	234-56-7891	Computer Sci.	House 2	Advisor 2

Grade Record

Course	SSN	Date	Section Number	Grade
CS-101	234-56-7891	12/15/89	20234	A
CS-101	123-45-6789	12/15/89	20294	C
CS-101	345-67-8912	12/15/89	20294	C

Registration Record

Course	SSN	Section Number
BU-202	123-45-6789	3023
BU-202	345-67-8912	3023
BU-202	456-78-9123	3023

Figure 2.8 Relational model of data.

than only on individual records. The operations in a relational data base are independent of the data structures and, therefore, do not depend on the specific order of the records or the fields. There is often controversy about whether or not a DBMS is *truly* relational. Although there are very formal definitions of a relational data base [6], a rather informal one is sufficient here. A relational data base is one in which

- Data are presented in tabular fashion without the need for navigation links, or pointer structures, between various tables.
- A relational algebra exists and can be used to automatically prepare *joins* of logical record files.
- New fields (and such related items as *field indices*) can be added to the data base, without the necessity to rewrite any programs that used previous versions of the data base.*

If a DBMS does not satisfy these three criteria, it is almost surely *not* a relational data base.† There are a great many other interesting observations and extensions that could be made about relational data bases [2, 7–9]. The overview presented here is generally sufficient for our interests in decision support systems and we will not develop the many possible extensions here.

---

*Also, presently existing fields can be deleted from the data base with the need to change only those components of presently existing programs that refer to the deleted field(s).

†In Ref. 6, structural, manipulative, and integrity attributes of a data base are identified. Relational data bases are disaggregated into minimally relational, relationally complete, and fully relational. Nonrelational data bases are called tabular data bases. Categorization is suggested on the basis of relational satisfaction of these attributes.

2.2.2 Structural Models

In many instances, data is intended to be associated with a natural structural representation. Figure 2.9 represents a hierarchical structure of an organization. A more general representation than a hierarchy, or tree, is known as a network. Figure 2.10 illustrates a network structure for a matrix organization.

2.2.2.1 The Hierarchical Model It is often possible to represent a logical data model with a hierarchical data structure. As shown in Figure 2.9, we have a number

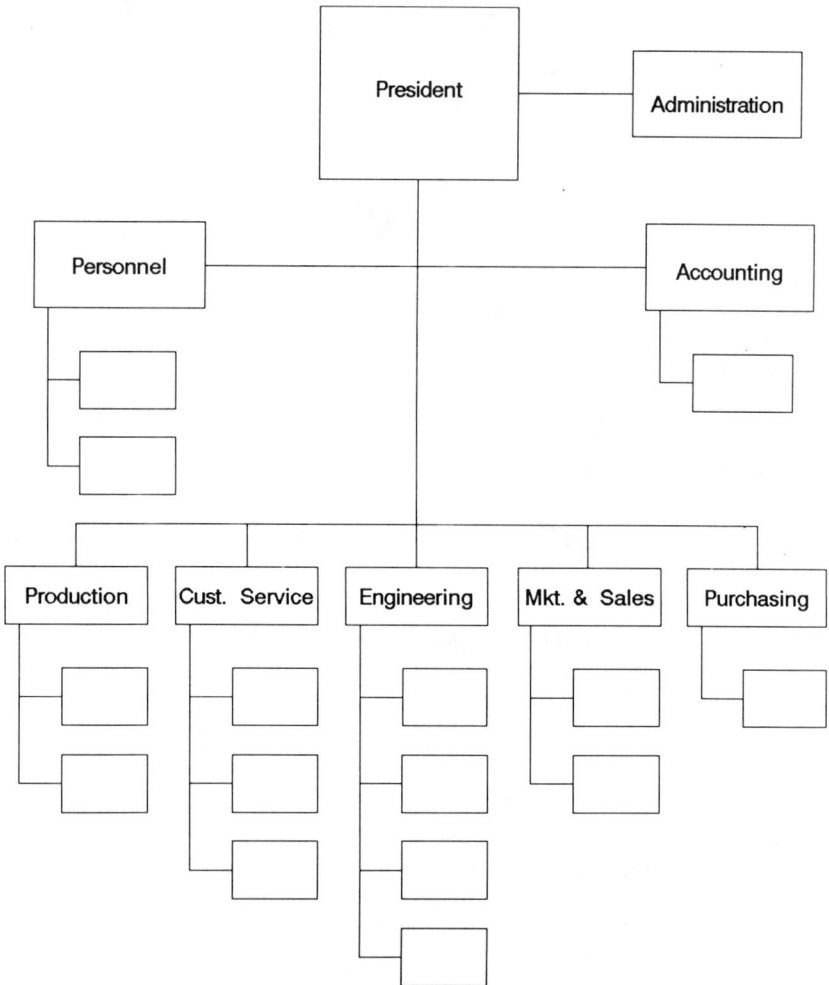

Figure 2.9 Hierarchical, or tree, structure of an organization.

2.2 DATA MODELS AND DATA-BASE ARCHITECTURES

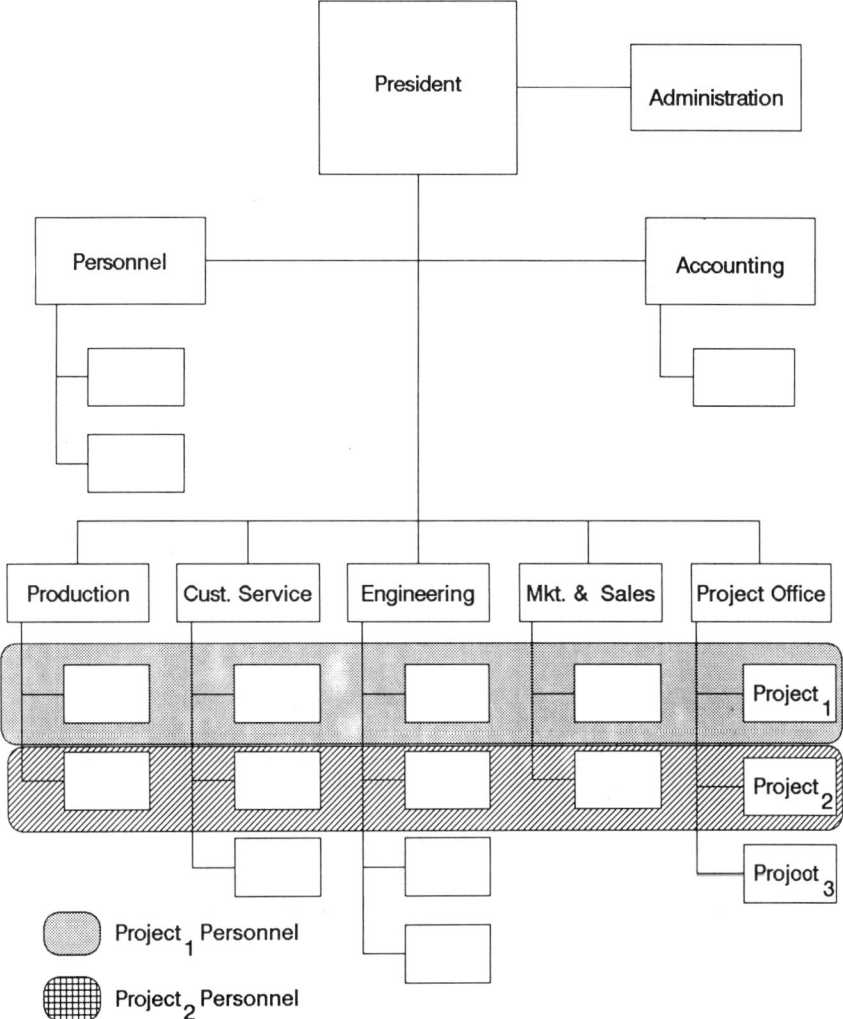

Figure 2.10 Network structure of a matrix management organization.

of nodes that are connected by links, and all links are directed.* The basic operation in a hierarchy is that of searching a tree to find items of value. When a query is posed with a hierarchical data base, all branches of the hierarchy are searched and those nodes that meet the conditions posed in the query are noted and then returned to the DBMS system user in the form of a report.

Some comparisons of a hierarchical data model with a relational data model are of interest here. The structures in the hierarchical model represent the information that

---
*They point in the direction from "child" to "parent."

is contained in the fields of the relational model. In a hierarchical model, certain records must exist before other records can exist. The hierarchical model is generally required to have only one key field. In a hierarchical data model, it is necessary to repeat some data in a *descendant record* that need be stored only once in a relational data base regardless of the number of relations. This is so since it is not possible for one record to be a descendant of more than one parent record.*

There are some unfortunate consequences of the mathematics involved in creating a hierarchical tree, as contrasted with relations among records. Descendants cannot be added without a root leading to them, for example. This leads to a number of undesirable characteristic properties of hierarchical models that may affect our ability to add, delete, and update or edit records easily.

Figure 2.11 presents a hierarchical tree model, or schema, for the student data base that we have been considering. There are three record types: student, courses taken, and courses in progress. In the particular representation chosen here, a new student cannot be added unless the student is currently registered for at least one course. In general, hierarchical models are not as well suited as relational models for use in a DSS because they are not as easily analyzed as a relational model. The multiple entry of the same data reality can make data modifications difficult, as has been noted,

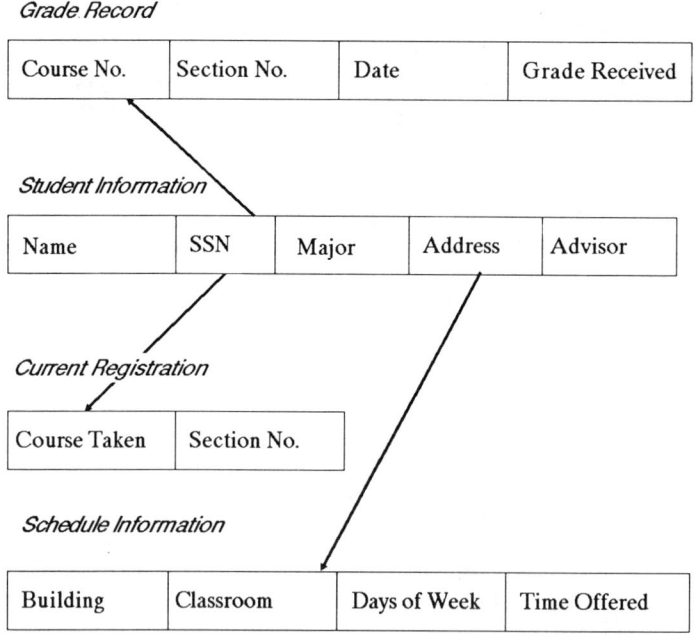

Figure 2.11 Hierarchical model, or schema, for student data base.

*Or we would not have a hierarchical model. We would, however, have a network model.

owing to the associated data redundancy. One primary advantage of the hierarchical model is that access is generally quite rapid.

2.2.2.2 The Network Model A network model is quite similar to but more general than the hierarchical model. In a hierarchy, data has to be arranged such that one child has only one parent (that is to say, the data is *strictly nested*). There are many instances when this is unrealistic. If we force the use of a hierarchical representation in such cases, data will have to be repeated at more than one location in the hierarchical model. This redundancy can create a number of problems. A record in a network model can participate in several relationships. This leads to two primary structural differences between hierarchical and network models. Some fields in the hierarchical model will become relationships in a network model. Further, the relationships in a network model are explicit and may be bidirectional. The navigation problem in a network data model can become severe. Since search of the data base can start at several places in the network, there is added complexity in searching, as well.

Figure 2.12 presents a network model for the student data-base example that we have been considering.

2.2.2.3 The Entity–Relationship (ER) Model While spreadsheet-type relational records are useful for many purposes, it has been observed [10] that not all views of a situation, or human cognitive maps, can be represented by relational data models. This has led to interest in entity- and object-oriented data models, and to data models based on artificial intelligence techniques (which we will discuss next).

The basic notion in use of an ER model is to accomplish data-base design at the conceptual level in the three-level model of Figure 2.3, rather than at the logical

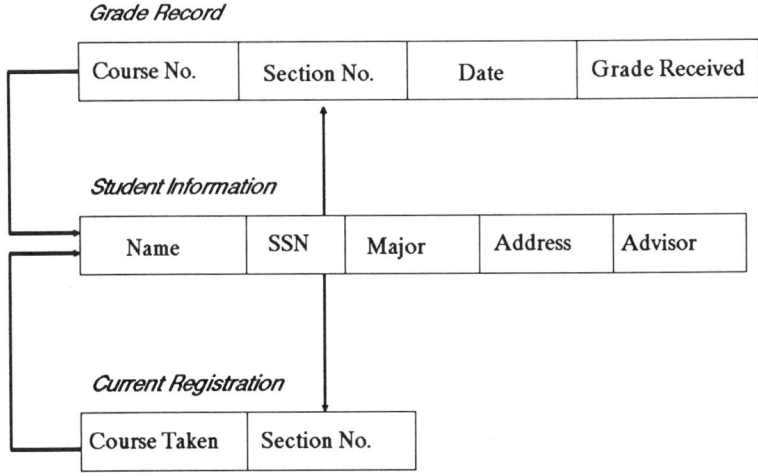

Figure 2.12 Network model, or schema, for student data base.

and/or physical levels. Entity–relationship* models [11] are relatively simple and easy to understand and use, in large part because of the easy graphical visualization of the data-base model structure. Also, ER modeling capability is provided by many *computer-aided software engineering* (CASE) tools. While there are such limitations as lack of a very useful query language [12], much interest in ER data models, especially at the conceptual level, exists at this time. Figure 2.13 illustrates this conceptual orientation of the ER modeling approach.

Entity–Relationship Models are based on two premises [11]:

- Information concerning entities and relationships exist as a cognitive reality.
- This information may be structured using entities and the relationships among them as data.

An entity–relationship data model is a generalization of the hierarchical and network data models. It is based on well-established graph theoretic developments [13], and is a form of *structured modeling* [14, 15]. Structured modeling concepts are associated in [14, 15] with the *Framework* software package, which is especially appropriate for dealing with relational tables and organizational trees, to produce a modeling environment that is, essentially, ER-like.

We will use four items to illustrate entity–relationship models:

1. *Rectangles* will be used to represent entities.
2. *Diamonds* will be used to represent relationships.
3. *Circles* will be used to represent attributes of entities.
4. *Relational tables* will be used to represent a collection of entities.

Items 3 and 4 are not necessary for entity–relationship modeling. They are not formally contained in the graph theoretic notation, but are useful for more compact and more descriptive models. Use of the latter item (relational table) enables us to show the equivalence of the ER data model to the relational data model. Also, one of the possible uses of the ER data modeling construct is as a preliminary step to the design of a relational data base.

A six-step approach to entity–relationship data base design and description has been suggested [11]:

1. Identify the entities that are of interest and appropriate relationships with which to link the entities.

---

*An *entity* is some distinct thing, or object, or element, that can be explicitly identified. Appropriate elements could represent objectives for a corporation or people in the corporation. A *relationship*, in contextual relation, is a directed association among entities. Quite clearly, the same item could be an entity *or* a relationship. In the expression "John is the father of Mary," "John" and "Mary" are entities, and "is the father of" is a (contextual) relationship. On the other hand, "father" is an element in the statement, "a father must be older than his child." The environment and context in which ER statements are made is a strong influencer of whether an item of data is an entity or a relationship. The data-base administrator will generally need to define elements or entities, and (contextual) relationships for a data base.

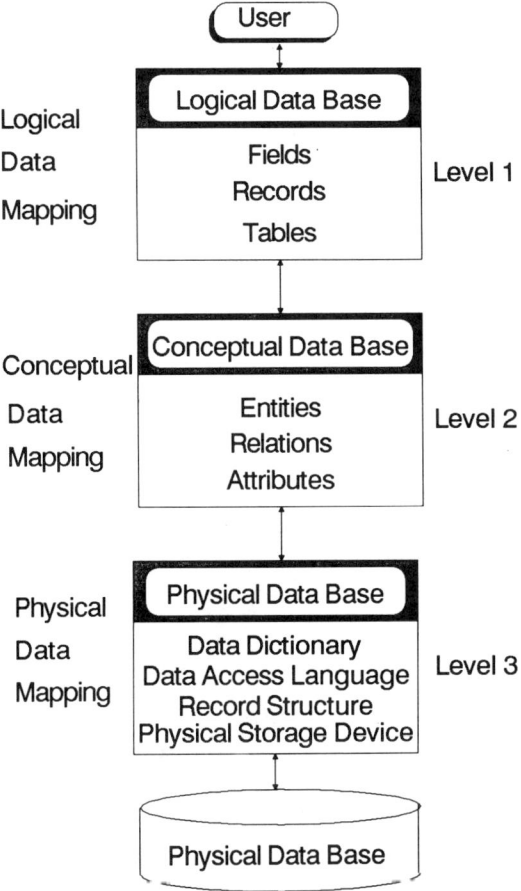

Figure 2.13 The potential role of entity–relationship data models at the conceptual data level.

2. Identify potentially important semantic information in the relationships (e.g., degree of fulfillment, or how necessary is necessary, etc.).
3. Identify attributes desirable in providing an appropriate description of entities and numerical value sets (e.g., inventory part number, or student number, and including allowable values for valid entities, etc.) for these attributes.
4. Organize the data into entity–relationship relations, and decide on index keys for the data base.
5. Validate the ER diagrams and determine that the lowest needed level of decomposition has been achieved.
6. Repeat the process until the primitive-level diagram has been found and that all needed entity–relationships have been found and are retained.

One relatively simple way to go about constructing an ER data model is to first consider only entities and relations, and then construct a model that is initially based only on entities and relations. After this, attributes may be added to describe the model more fully. It will often be desirable to subdivide the initial entity portrayals into more finely grained entity portrayals. In a university, for instance, courses might be associated with a prefix to describe the department or educational program to which they belong. Figures 2.14 and 2.15 illustrate ER data models for the student/course data base discussed here.

The major advantage of the ER approach is that it provides a realistic view of the structure and form for the DBMS design and development effort. This should naturally support the subsequent development of appropriate software. In addition, the approach readily leads to the development of the data dictionary. The primary difficulties that may impede easy use of the ER method are in the need for selection

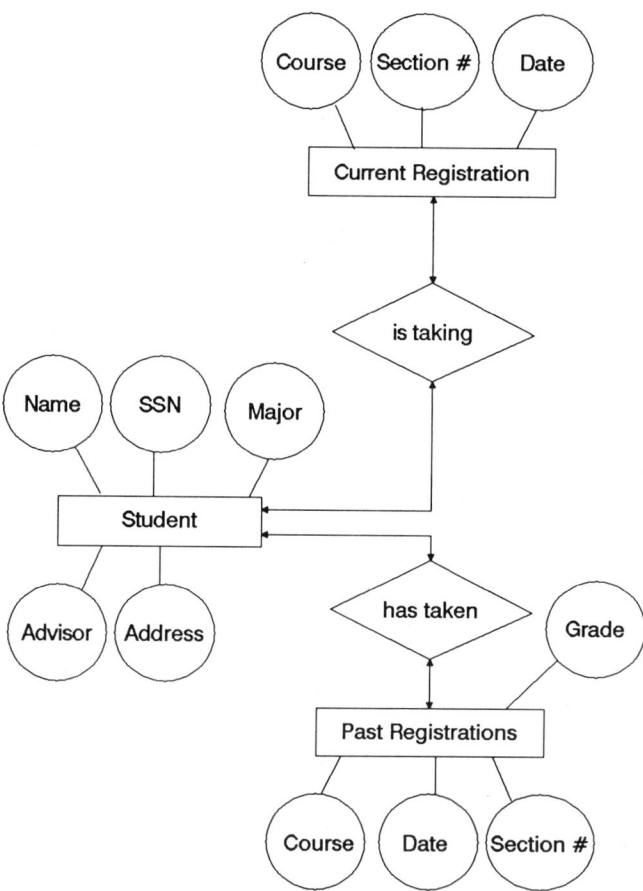

Figure 2.14 Entity–relationship model of student data base.

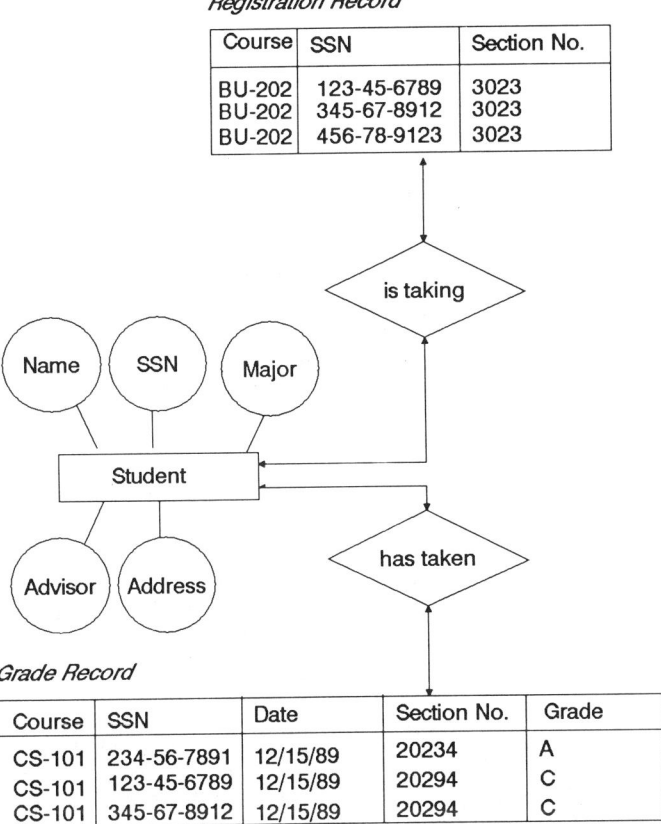

Figure 2.15 Entity-relationship data base showing relational tables for current registration and courses taken.

of appropriate verbs for use as contextual relationships, elimination of redundancy of entities and assurances that all of the needed entity–relationships have been determined and properly used. Often, it may take a considerable amount of time to identify a suitable set of entities and relations and to obtain an appropriate structural model in the form of an ER diagram.

2.2.3 Expert Data-Base Models

An expert data-base model, as a specialized expert data-base system, involves the use of artificial intelligence technology. The goal in this is to provide for data-base functionality in more complex environments that require at least some limited form of intelligent capability. To allow this may require adaptive identification of system characteristics, or learning over time as experience with an issue and the environment into which it is embedded increases. The principal approach that has been developed to date comprises an *object-oriented data base* (OODB) design with any of the several knowledge representation approaches useful in expert system development. The field is very new and we can anticipate new and potentially exciting developments in the future.* We will discuss some of the central features of this approach as described much more fully in Refs. 16–20.

2.2.3.1 Object-Oriented Data-Base Management Systems (OODBMS) The efforts to date in this area almost exclusively concern what might be more appropriately named as object-oriented data-base management systems design. The objective in OODBMS design is to cope with data-base complexity, potentially for large distributed data bases, through a combination of object-oriented programming and expert systems technology. Object-oriented design approaches generally involve notions of separating internal computer representations of elements from the external realities that lead to the elements.† A primary reason for using an object-oriented language is that it naturally enables *semantic* representations of knowledge through use of [19]:

1. *Information hiding*, to increase the reliability and maintenance of the system by reducing interdependencies among system elements. *Information Hiding*, or *encapsulation*, is the principle of system design that enables each portion of a system to encapsulate only a single purpose or function. In addition, the design of the interface to each module is such that little, if any, of the inner workings or microstructure of the module is revealed.
2. *Data abstraction*, so as to provide a set of operators similar to abstract data types and a way of utilizing information hiding. *Abstraction* is the principle of suppressing those perspectives of an issue that are not fully relevant to the purpose at hand such as to be able to visualize and deal with a characterization of the issue that is simpler and more fully relevant to the task at hand.
3. *Dynamic binding and object identity*, such as to provide for a unique identifier for each object that is independent of the particular attribute values that the object may have in order to allow the addition of new classes of objects without the need to modify existing code. *Dynamic Binding* is the principle of deferred, or delayed, integration, or linking, of elements and relations into a specific functional description.
4. *Inheritance*, so as to provide economies of specification by allowing generic properties to be defined for the higher-level objects, and more specialized

---

*The first object-oriented DBMS, *GemStone* became available in late 1986. It runs on microcomputers and is similar in use to Smalltalk-80, an object-oriented language.
†In the more conventional approach, information and manipulation of information are each a separate type of entity. In object-oriented representations, an *object* may represent both information and information manipulation. In object-oriented systems, information is manipulated by sending *messages* to objects that represent manipulations. Thus an *object* is a set of information and the descriptions of manipulations. A *message* is the specification of one of the manipulations of an object. Usually, object-oriented representations make a distinction between an object and the description of an object.

properties to be associated with lower-level objects through property inheritance. *Inheritance* is the principle of specifying attributes of issues such that *siblings* are represented as explicitly inheriting the properties of their ancestors. The need to represent attributes more than once is minimized.

5. *Message handling*, to enable objects to communicate with one another through sending messages that have sending and receiving object identifiers, as well as the message name and message contents.
6. *Object-oriented graphical interfaces*, to enable complex objects to be better understood and manipulated.
7. *Transaction management*, to enable effective input to and output from the object oriented system.
8. *Reusability* through the proficient modularity of the resulting system.
9. *Partitioning* is the principle of dividing or disaggregating an issue into parts such that it can be more effectively represented or more easily understood through a description of the parts.
10. *Projection* is the principle of describing a system from *multiple perspectives*, or viewpoints. These could include, for example, social, political, legal, and technoeconomic.

Three very desirable object oriented *primitives* that assist mightily in the representation of complex systems are: *abstraction, partitioning*, and *projection*. These were first identified as principles for use in the structuring of software requirements [20], they are actually useful functional and purposeful primitives as well, and are useful throughout the systems engineering life cycle. *Information hiding, inheritance*, and *dynamic binding* are two related primitives. There are many others. Among these are *polymorphisms, modularity, instantiation*, and other terms that are relatively esoteric and absent from common usage.

There are at least two approaches that we might use in modeling a complex large scale system: *functional decomposition and structuring*, and *purposeful or object decomposition and structuring*. Both approaches are appropriate and may potentially result in useful models. Most models of real world phenomena tend to be purposeful. Most conventional high level programming languages are *functionally*, or procedurally, oriented. To use them, we must write statements that correspond to the functions that we wish to provide in order to solve the problem that has been posed.

Our discussions here relate to object decomposition and structuring. An advantage to this approach is that it enables us to more easily relate the structure of a data base model to the structure of the real system. This is the case if we accomplish our decomposition and structuring such that *each module in the system or issue model represents an object or a class of objects in the real issue or problem space*. This is a statement of the *fundamental criterion for decomposing a system using object oriented design approach of Booch* [21].

Objects in object oriented methodology are not unlike elements or nodes in graph theory and structural modeling. It is possible to use one or more *contextual relations* to relate elements together in a structural model. An object may be defined as a collection of information and those operations that can be performed upon it. We request an object to perform one of its allowable operations by instructing it with a message.

From this perspective, *objects are abstractions of elements in the real world,* * *and encapsulations of information in the form of attributes of these elements.* A description of one or more similar objects is generally called a *class.* Thus, a class may describe one, or a whole set, of related or similar objects. Each of the objects described by a specific class is called an *instance* of that class. Thus, objects in object oriented models bear close resemblance to the way in which real world events are visualized.

Coad and Yourdon [22] suggest seven steps t use in order to identify objects for use in object oriented methodology:

1. Examine structure of the real world system or issue;
2. Identify possible other real world systems that may have mutual interactions with the system being represented;
3. Identify the information in the real world that will need to be stored for later retrieval and use;
4. Identify the roles that will need to be played by the various actors associated with the issue;
5. Identify physical locations that need to be known;
6. Identify organizations that the various actors belong; and
7. Identify inventories of repetitive, generally static, information about elements.

There are two basic object oriented structural types.

1. *Assembly structures* utilize the contextual relation *is a part of.*
2. *Classification structures* enable us to define a contextual relation such that all objects with common attributes inherit these attributes and we can distinguish between different classes of objects.

Both are important and they may be used separately, or in conjunction with one another.

Object-oriented data-base design is based on approaches to DBMS design in which we model knowledge about objects as well as traditional data modeling. Accordingly, we capture not only data, in the form of objects, properties and associations; we also capture the knowledge semantics in the form of rules, scripts, schemas, and other representational forms. A crucial feature of object-oriented design approaches is that of information hiding. This refers to the ability of an object to contain information that is hidden from view. An object can be created and modified only through *external*

---

*The terms *real world* and *problem space* are used interchangably in object-oriented design.

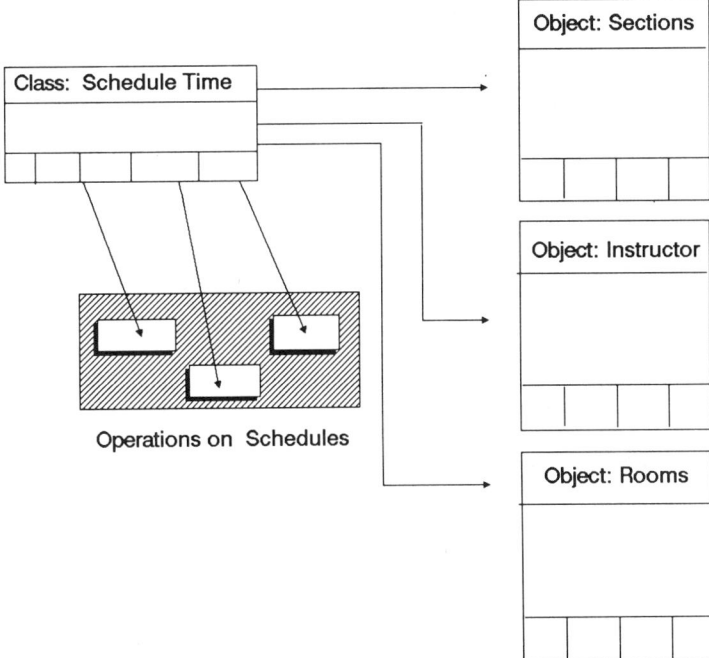

Figure 2.16 Object, operation, and message relationships applied to student registration data model.

operations. *Internal* implementation details used to implement objects and operations on them are not visible by those externally accessing and modifying the objects. Figures 2.16 and 2.17 illustrate some salient features of OODB design as applied to our student information system. Specifically, they provide an example of possible relationships between objects, attributes, operations, and messages [21].

Object-oriented design approaches differ from the functional approaches used for conventional DBMS designs.* Object-oriented DBMS design relies on the precise definition of objects and the relationships between objects and operations. Object-

---

*These earlier approaches use such higher-order languages as FORTRAN, Cobol, Ada, or C. The database design issue is approached through design of data models of the problem domain that use predefined data and control structures. In such DBMS design efforts, software design typically is based on a functional decomposition approach and is accomplished using procedural processes that involve the specific language to be used to develop the final software product. The evolution of higher-order languages brought about the introduction of concepts that included abstraction and information-hiding, together with data flow and data structure design approaches. The development of Pascal and other high-order languages brought on a greater variety of data structures and strong data typing. During the 1970s, the development of discrete-event digital simulation languages, such as GPSS and SIMULA and later Smalltalk, introduced the notion of data representation as objects and classes of objects that were acted on by procedures called operations. GPSS and SIMULA are discrete-event simulation languages. Smalltalk, which evolved from these discrete-event simulation languages, is a true object-oriented language often used for object-oriented DBMS.

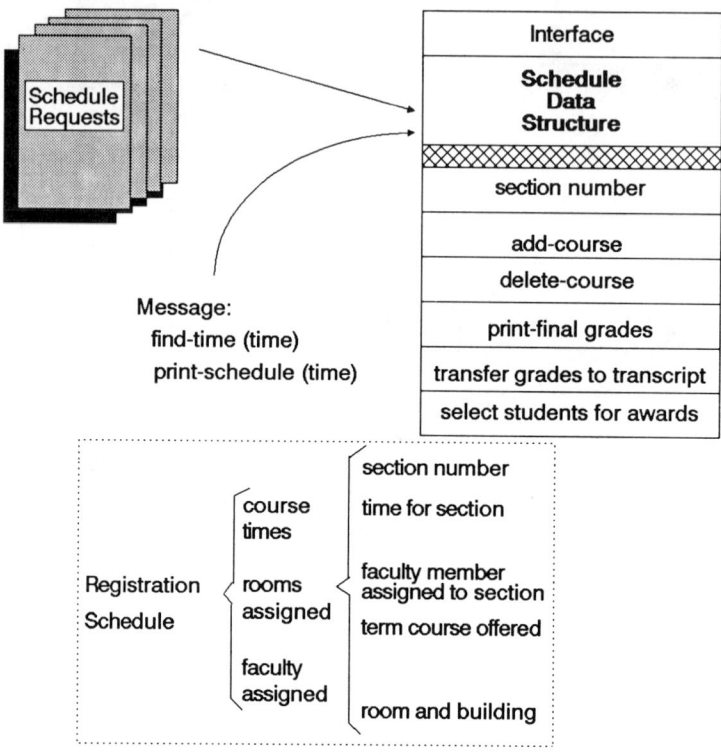

Schedule data structure

Figure 2.17 Object-oriented design perspective for student registration portion of student records data model.

oriented languages permit us to achieve functional decomposition in a simpler, more natural way than second- and third-generation languages, which necessarily involve many programming details not needed for object-oriented languages. There are three developmental approaches to obtaining object-oriented designs [18]:

1. *Novel Language Usage.* The most widely used object-oriented language is Smalltalk-80 [22, 24].
2. *Language Extensions.* There have been a number of recent augmentations to existing (third-generation) languages to provide them with object-oriented capabilities.*
3. *Object-Oriented Style* using an existing third-generation language. This involves using the discipline of object-oriented programming, to the extent that it can be used, and a high-level, nonobject-oriented language.

*C^{++} is one such example; Objective C, Turbo Pascal Plus, and Flavors are others.

2.2 DATA MODELS AND DATA-BASE ARCHITECTURES   **67**

Figure 2.18 illustrates the major conceptual difference between using a conventional programming approach and using an object-oriented approach. In the conventional approach, procedures are at the nexus and procedures update and otherwise manipulate data and return values. In the object-oriented approach, the collection of independent objects (or data) are at the nexus and communicate with each other through messages (or procedures). Objects investigate requests and behave according to these messages.

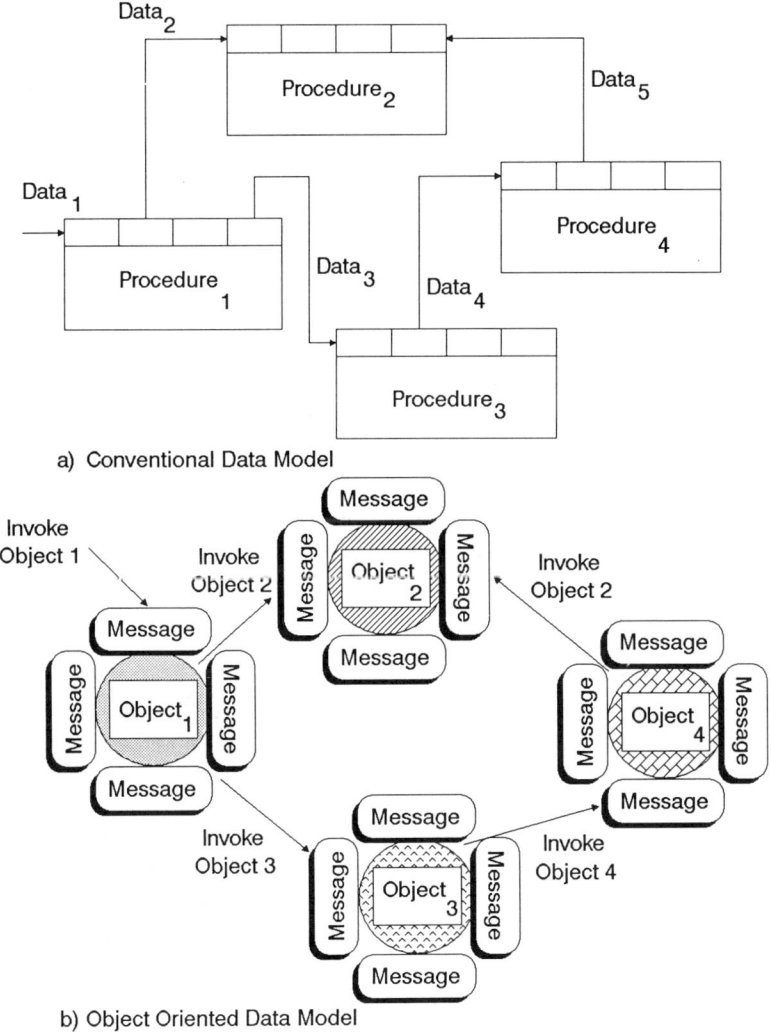

Figure 2.18 Conventional and object oriented data models.

Object-oriented design often provides a clear and concise interface to the problem domain in that the only way to interact with an object is through the operations or messages to the object. These messages call for operations that may result in a change of state in the object in question. This message will affect the particular object called and only that one, as no other object is affected. This provides a high degree of modularity, increased ability to verify and validate outcomes, and thus provides an increased sense of reliability in the resulting DBMS design. Object-oriented languages are, for the most part, very high level languages used to accomplish precisely the same results as high-level languages. By focusing on the entities of objects and the relationships between objects, they often provide a simpler way to describe precisely those elements needed in detailed design procedures.

Object-oriented DBMS design is based on appropriate linking of objects, or data items or entities, and the operations on these, such that the information and processing are concentrated on the object classes, attributes, and messages that transfer between them. The feature that sets object-oriented approaches apart from other approaches is the capability of object-oriented languages to support abstraction, information hiding, and modularity. The items used in object-oriented DBMS design are

1. *Objects*, abstracts, or physical entities that pertain to the domain of the system.
2. *Attributes*, or characteristics of objects.
3. *Operations*, or dynamic entities that may change with time.
4. *Messages*, or requests to an object to perform an operation.

Objects represent such real-world entities as machines, files, products, signals, persons, things, or places. They may be either physical entities or abstract representations. The attributes are characteristics that describe the properties ascribed to objects. Each attribute may be dynamically associated with a numerical value and the combination of these values together with the description of the object in the problem domain presents the state of the object. Therefore, the attributes are related to the object as subobjects. Attributes include such things as the name of the object, the number of specific objects in a file, or the name for the place, and the like. The basic attribute, one that may not be further decomposed, is the primitive type of object or subobject. Attributes may also be nonnumeric. Operations consist of processes and data structures that apply to the object to which it is directed. These are generally dynamic entities whose value may change over time. Each object may be subjected to a number of operations that provide information relative to control and procedural constructs that are applied to the object. Information hiding is achieved by defining an object to have a private part and then assigning a message to address the appropriate processing operation. Messages are passed between objects in order to change the state of the object, address the potentially hidden data parts of an object, or otherwise modify an object.

Steps we might use to implement an object-oriented design approach include the following [24]:

1. Define the problem and identify the objects.
2. Define messages passed between the objects.
3. Identify the attributes of the objects.
4. Analyze the class of objects and identify higher-level classes.
5. Identify the operations.
6. Associate operations and attributes with the class.
7. Define the implementation of objects and operations.
8. Determine lower-level objects in the class.

Others identify a similar set of steps. For example, Coad and Yourdon [22] distinguish five steps:

1. *Identify objects*, typically by examining the objects in the real world.
2. *Identify structures*, generally through various *abstracting* and *partitioning* approaches that result in a classification structure, an assembly structure, or a combination of these.
3. *Identify subjects*, through examining objects and their structures to obtain this more complex abstract view of the issue. Each classification structure and each assembly structure will comprise one subject.
4. *Identify attributes*, that impart important aspects of the objects that need to be retained for all instances of an object.
5. *Identify services*, such that we are aware of *occurrence* services, or creation or modification of instances of an object, *calculation* services, or the *monitoring* of other processes for critical events or conditions.

Steps such as these should generally be accomplished in an iterative manner, since there is no unique way to accomplish specification of a set of objects, or structural relations between objects.

A major result from using object-oriented approaches is that we obtain the sort of knowledge representation structures that are commonly found in many expert systems. Hence, object-oriented design techniques provide a natural interface to expert systems based techniques for DBMS design. This is the case since objects, in object-oriented design, are provided with the ability to *store information* such that learning over time can occur; *process information* by initiating actions in response to messages; *compute and communicate* by sending messages between objects; and *generate new information* as a result of communications and computations. Object-oriented design also lends itself to parallel processing and distributed environments.

2.3 DISTRIBUTED AND COOPERATIVE DATA-BASE ISSUES

We have identified three major objectives for a DBMS as *data independence, data redundancy reduction*, and *data resource control*. These objectives are important for a single data base. When there are multiple data bases potentially located in a distributed geographic fashion, and potentially many users of one or more data bases, additional objectives arise. These include

1. *Location independence or transparency*, to enable DBMS users to access applications across distributed information bases without the need to be explicitly concerned with where specific data is located.
2. *Advanced data models*, to enable DBMS users to access potentially nonconventional (nonconventional for a computer, that is!) forms of data such as multidimensional data, graphic data, spatial data, and imprecise data.
3. *Extensible data models*, that will allow new data types to be added to the DBMS, perhaps in an interactive real-time manner, as required by specific applications.

A significant feature of a distributed data-base management systems (DDBMS) is that provisions for data-base management are distributed. Only then can we obtain the needed "fail-safe" reliability and "availability" even when a portion of the system breaks down. There are a number of reasons why distributed data bases may be desirable. These include and are primarily related to distributed users and cost savings.* Of course, there are additional costs involved and these must be justified.

A distributed data-base management system will generally look much like replicated versions of a more conventional single-location data-base management system. We can thus imagine replicated versions of Figure 2.5. (This would be associated with a single or, more likely, multiple version of a data dictionary.) For simplicity, we will show only the physical data base, the data-base access interface mechanism, and the data dictionary for each data base. Figure 2.19 indicates one possible conceptual architecture of a distributed data base. There are two requests for data being simultaneously submitted in this figure. We will examine one of them in some detail, as the processing steps in obtaining data for each request are identical. They are (the numbers below also refer to the numbers shown in Fig. 2.19):

1. One user initiates a request for data. That request goes to the data dictionary belonging to that user. (This assumes that each data structure is the same, or that the data dictionary for each local user contains information concerning the data structure for all of the local data bases, or that the data structure for each local user is able to access a correct data structure and cause a translation of the data obtained into the proper format.)
2. This local data dictionary identifies those data elements and their location in the local host data base that are needed to satisfy the user's request.

---

*These are the primary advantages seen by DBMS users. They occur because of a number of highly technical provisions that include *transaction atomicity*, an abstraction that allows applications to ignore the effects that might otherwise be imposed by other applications that are concurrently addressing shared information, and *self-monitoring* and *staging independence* abstractions [18].

2.3 DISTRIBUTED AND COOPERATIVE DATA-BASE ISSUES

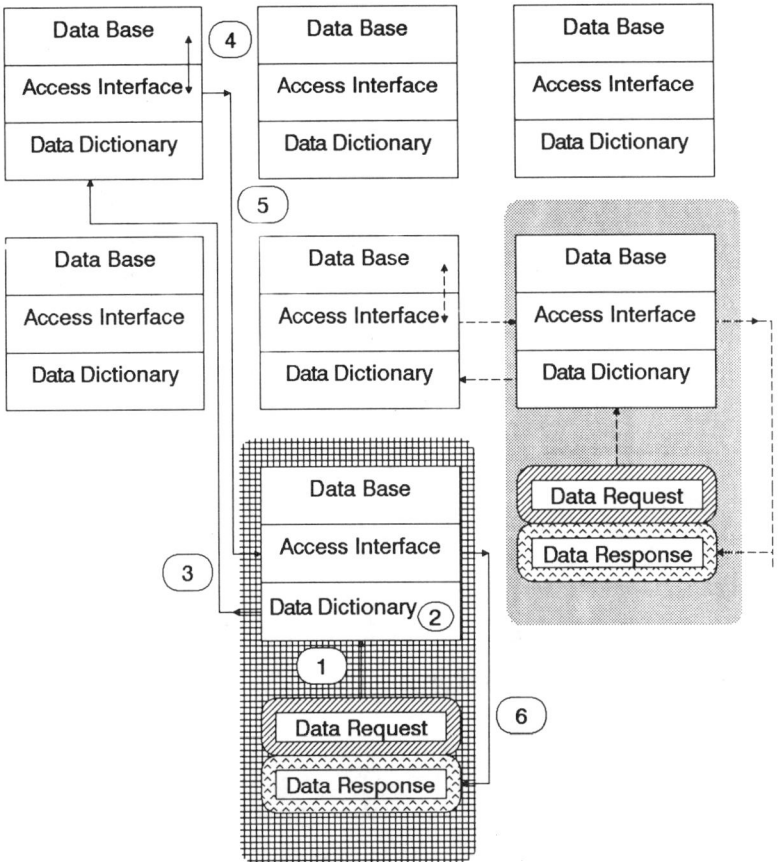

Figure 2.19 Distributed data-base management system.

3. The local data dictionary then causes the request to be routed to the request node of the distributed host that has the requested data through the two data dictionaries.
4. The interface access of that local host procures the requested data elements from the local data base.
5. The requested data elements are then routed from this interface access mechanism of the host to the interface access mechanism of the requesting user.
6. This data is provided, after being temporarily stored and potentially translated, as a response to the request.

Through use of protocols such as this, all requests for data are entered as if that data was stored in the data base of the requesting user. The data dictionaries of the distributed system are responsible for finding the requested data elements and delivering them to the requesting user. All of these auxiliary requests are accomplished in a manner that is transparent to the requesting data-base user. Data transmission rate concerns must be resolved for this to be done satisfactorily. Potentially, however, real-time access to all of the data in the entire distributed system can be provided to any local user.

It is important to note that completion of the above steps does not result in transfer of the requested data into the data base of the requesting user, except perhaps in some temporary storage fashion. The very good reason why this is not done is that doing so would result in data-base redundancy. Doing this would also increase data-base security difficulties.

An alternative approach to this distributing of data is to use what is often called *cooperative processing* or *cooperative data-base management.* This involves central data-base and distributed data-base concepts, blended to produce better results that can be had with either approach. Central to this are various approaches for the distribution and coordination of data. We could use function, geography, or organizational level as the basis for distributing and cooperating. Various perspectives concerning these issues have been taken [25–27]. Possible systems configurations may be based on background communications, microcomputer-based front-end processing for host applications, and peer-to-peer cooperative processing [28, 29].

2.4 DBMS SOFTWARE EVALUATION

In this section, we will suggest and examine some criteria for DBMS software selection. Our perspective will be that of a DSS developer. Later, in Chapter 5, some detailed discussions concerning DSS evaluation will be presented. Nevertheless, it is meaningful to examine, at least in a preliminary way, the attributes that contribute to DBMS success. This provides us with an appropriate summary of the critical and important factors in a DBMS. Moreover, it provides much motivation for the more detailed study that we will undertake, from a slightly different perspective, in Chapter 5.

It is important to present the perspective from which we approach DBMS software evaluation here. The following sequence of steps is suggested (we will concentrate on attribute identification here; justification of the multiple-attribute scoring approach suggested in our discussions will be provided in Chapters 5 and 6):

1. Identify DSS and user requirements for DBMS software.
2. Define critical attributes for the DBMS software. Identify the range of performance expected for each attribute (i.e., from best performance expected on a specific attribute to worst performance on that attribute). Also identify the importance worth of this performance range across each attribute.
3. Obtain literature describing potential software packages and arrange for an evaluation/demonstration of the software. If needed, iterate back to step 2 and refine attributes and attribute scoring measures.

4. Evaluate each software package according to its score on the various identified performance attributes.
5. Select the highest-scoring software package and conduct a sensitivity analysis of the results of the evaluation, if needed.

Each of these steps is necessary and should be followed.

In the first step, we identify critical user needs for the DBMS as a part of the DSS. When we speak of user requirements, we refer to the purposes and associated logical functions that the user wishes to, or needs to, perform using the to-be-obtained DBMS. These user requirements can be converted into *requirements specifications*, which are the more technical and structural characteristics of the DBMS. The high-level user requirements are, doubtlessly, related to such functions and purposes as [30, 31]:

1. Software company trustworthiness
2. Maintenance support available
3. Installation and delivery support
4. Training provisions
5. Ease of enhancements and modifications
6. Vendor contractual requirements
7. Software documentation
8. Ease of use and user friendliness
9. Data-base security and integrity
10. Flexibility
11. Development language (query languages, and other development languages)
12. End-user languages
13. Operating efficiency
14. Operating effectiveness
15. Data dictionary
16. Distributing and coordinating capabilities
17. Standards and portability concerns
18. System integration capabilities
19. Cost of the software

These performance requirements become attributes for the DBMS software evaluation. We will accomplish a cost-effectiveness evaluation. The first 18 attributes listed relate to effectiveness; the last relates to cost. We will describe two approaches to performance evaluation. The first of these is based on relative weights and relative performance scores across attributes of performance and performance alternatives.

In this *swing-weight* based approach, we identify the maximum performance expected on each of the identified performance attributes and associate these performance levels with a score of 1.0. The actual score used to indicate the maximum is arbitrary and the overall evaluation will not depend on this value. We could just as well use 100 as the maximum score possible. We identify the minimum performance expected on each attribute and associate these performance levels with a score of 0.

Now that we have established the performance ranges across each attribute that we expect to obtain from the candidate software packages, we must identify the importance weight to associate with each attribute. Clearly, some attributes will be important and some unimportant. These importance weights can be expected to vary, perhaps considerably, across specific DSS design situations. A possible way to identify weights for the attributes is to identify the most important performance attribute, in terms of the worst-to-best performance scores expected.* This attribute is assigned a value of 1.0. The next most important performance attribute, in terms of the range in performance expected, is identified. If the most important attribute has a weight of 1.0, then we should associate a lower weight, which is called a swing weight for this second most important attribute. This is continued until we have identified swing weights for all attributes of importance. These swing weights are then normalized such that they sum to 1.0. The normalized swing weight w_j becomes

$$w_j = \frac{W_j}{\left(\sum_{j=1}^{N} W_j\right)}$$

where N is the number of attributes considered and W_j is the (unnormalized) swing weight of the jth attribute.

Following this, we identify performance scores for each alternative on each attribute. We have already identified the 0 and 1.0 performance scores and their meaning and so the performance evaluation task is just that of placing the performance of each DBMS alternative within this range for each of the performance attributes. The final performance score is then determined from the weighted sum

$$PS_i = \sum_{j=1}^{N} (w_j S_{ji})$$

where w_j is the swing weight associated with the jth attribute and S_{ji} is the performance score of the ith software package on the jth attribute of performance.

The second approach is an *absolute-weight* based approach. It is founded on identifying an ideal performance alternative, one whose performance is *ideal* across all performance attributes, and then associating a performance score of 1.0 with this, for all attributes. The following associations of numerical scores with performance characteristics are somewhat mercurial, but may be of value in identifying an ideally performing DBMS package and in setting the standards for judgment of actual DBMS packages:

---

*It is necessary to identify this importance in terms of the performance ranges expected. If all software packages have virtually the same performance on some attribute, then the *relative* importance of this attribute is 0. Recall that there will be a performance score of 1.0 for the best-performing software package and a performance score of 0.0 for the worst-performing package on each performance attribute.

1.00 Package completely meets performance requirements on this attribute
0.75 Package is very acceptable on this performance attribute in all but very minor ways
0.50 Package generally satisfies maximum performance requirements on this attribute, but is deficient in some important aspects
0.25 Package fails to meet performance specifications associated with this attribute
0.00 Package is almost totally deficient in performance on this performance attribute

Now that we have defined the performance of an ideal standard DBMS package, and established performance scores across each attribute for less-than-ideal performance, we need to identify the importance weight to associate with each attribute. Clearly, some attributes will be very important and some very unimportant. These importance weights can be expected to vary, perhaps considerably, across specific DSS design situations. A possible way to identify the (absolute) attribute weights is to identify the most important performance attribute. This attribute is assigned a value of 1.0. The next most important performance attribute, in terms of the range in performance expected, is identified. We might associate weights in accordance with the following associations:

1.00 The feature described by the attribute in question is mandatory and very important
0.75 The feature described by the attribute in question is quite important
0.50 The attribute in question is moderately important, as is performance at the ideal level specified by a 1.00 performance score
0.25 Performance at the level specified by the ideal standard for this attribute is desirable, but not at all needed
0.00 Performance of this attribute is insignificant and this attribute can be disregarded in terms of performance evaluation

The process of listing the attributes in terms of ordinal importance continues. After they are identified, the absolute weight values are identified. These must be veridical to the ordinal listing.* These absolute weights are then normalized such that they sum to 1. The normalized absolute weight w_j becomes

$$w_j = \frac{W_j}{\left(\sum_{j=1}^{N} W_j\right)}$$

*One of the major potential problems associated with this particular approach is that of identigying a very large number of performance attributes and then assigning too high a worth to too many of them. A worth of 0.35 may not seem very high. However, if ther are 10 attributes with this weight, then it is possible to obtain a performance score of as much as 3.5 on these attributes alone. This is 3.5 times the maximum score of 1.0 that can be abtained due to performance on the most important attribute. For this reason, primarily, the author prefers the relative or swing-weight approach.

where N is the number of attributes considered and W_j is the (unnormalized) weight of the jth attribute. The final performance score is then determined from the weighted sum

$$PS_i = \sum_{j=1}^{N} (w_j S_{ji})$$

where w_j is the absolute weight associated with the jth attribute and S_{ji} is the performance score of the ith software package on the jth attribute of performance.

Even though our wording and the formulae to be used to compute the final software package worth appears to be the same for the two approaches, the interpretation placed on the attribute weights and alternative scores is quite different. Nevertheless, each method is subjective and potentially appropriate. The swing-weight approach has the greatest theoretical basis for use. It would be appropriate to evaluate the performance of candidate software packages using each approach and if there is a discrepancy in the final result, then explore the causes for this, perhaps by means of a sensitivity analysis and more refined definition of terms. We will explore a little more of the theoretical basis and implications associated with these multi-attribute approaches in Chapters 3 and 5. It turns out that the algorithms suggested here form a part of the *model base* for decision evaluation. Some available DSS software uses one of these algorithms as the, or a part of the, model-base management system for the DSS.

Example. As an example of DBMS software package evaluation, let us consider that four attributes are initially thought to be of importance:

1. Software company trustworthiness (W_1)
9. Data-base security and integrity (W_2)
14. Operating effectiveness (W_3)
15. Data dictionary (W_4)

and that three software packages are being considered for purchase. To use the swing-weight approach, we first determine the best- and worst-performing software packages across each alternative. This might result in the following partially filled in performance scoring matrix:

$$S_{ji} = \begin{bmatrix} 0.00 & 1.00 & & \\ 0.00 & 1.00 & & \\ 1.00 & & 0.00 & \\ & 1.00 & 0.00 & \end{bmatrix}$$

This says that we have determined that package 1, represented by the matrix column S_{j1} is the worst performer on the first two attributes we are using in the evaluation and the best performer on the third attribute. On the other hand, package 2 is the best performer on attributes 1, 2, and 4. It is not a worst performer on anything. Package

4 is neither a best- nor a worst-performing package on any attribute. It is important to note that there is a single 0.00 and a single 1.00 in each row.

Based on these assessments, we can evaluate the performance of the other alternative attribute pairs. Suppose that we obtain

$$S_{ji} = \begin{bmatrix} 0.00 & 1.00 & 0.60 & 0.80 \\ 0.00 & 1.00 & 0.90 & 0.80 \\ 1.00 & 0.00 & 0.00 & 0.90 \\ 0.40 & 1.00 & 0.00 & 0.90 \end{bmatrix}$$

Based on this definition of best and worst, we now need to determine the attribute swing weights. Suppose that we indicate that the difference between worst and best performance is such that attribute 4 is the most important. We then assign it an unnormalized weight of 1.00. Given this, we might say that attribute 3 is only 0.80 as important as attribute 1, and that attribute 1 is 0.40 and attribute 2 is 0.30 as important as attribute 4. We then calculate the normalized swing weights and obtain

$$W_1 = 0.40 \quad W_2 = 0.30 \quad W_3 = 0.80 \quad W_4 = 1.00$$
$$w_1 = 0.16 \quad w_2 = 0.12 \quad w_3 = 0.32 \quad w_4 = 0.40$$

The final evaluation scores are obtained using the equation

$$PS_i = \sum_{j=1}^{N} (w_j S_{ji})$$

as $PS_1 = 0.48$, $PS_2 = 0.58$, $PS_3 = 0.20$, and $PS_4 = 0.87$. Thus, we see that alternative 4 is the best alternative, actually by quite a fair amount.

To do this same evaluation using the absolute-weight approach, we might proceed as follows. First, we assign weights (actually the order of assigning weights and performance scores is immaterial here), perhaps as follows:

$$W_1 = 0.60 \quad W_2 = 0.50 \quad W_3 = 1.00 \quad W_4 = 1.00$$

and then calculate relative weights as

$$w_1 = 0.19 \quad w_2 = 0.16 \quad w_3 = 0.32 \quad w_4 = 0.32$$

Next, we assign performance scores. Ideally, it would be best to do this across all alternatives at a single attribute, and then proceed to a new attribute. To make this assignment across attributes for a single alternative is generally more cognitively demanding and invites cognitive bias. These might be

$$S_{ji} = \begin{bmatrix} 0.50 & 1.00 & 0.70 & 0.90 \\ 0.50 & 1.00 & 0.90 & 0.80 \\ 1.00 & 0.60 & 0.50 & 0.90 \\ 0.60 & 1.00 & 0.30 & 0.95 \end{bmatrix}$$

such that we obtain for the evaluation scores $PS_1 = 0.69$, $PS_2 = 0.86$, $PS_3 = 0.53$, and $PS_4 = 0.89$. Therefore, we see again that alternative 4 is the best, according to the criteria and approach used. Alternative 2 is a close competitor, however. In part, this is caused by the fact that we are working over a smaller range of performance scores in that no score is now less than 0.30 and many are close to 1.00.

2.5 SUMMARY

We have described some features of data-base management systems most useful for our continuing studies in decision support systems engineering. The data-base component of a DSS provides the memory prerequisite that is necessary for decision support. There must be some sort of management system associated with this data base, to provide the data acquisition and extraction capability needed for effective decision support. We have described a number of existing constructs for data-base management systems.

PROBLEMS

2.1. Obtain a set of data with which you are familiar. Structure it using the several data models we have discussed in this chapter. Which of these data models appears most appropriate, and why? Are the results you obtain dependent on the specific application area chosen?

2.2. Reconsider the student data-base examples we examined in this chapter. How should these be modified so that the DBMS can select students for special actions such as graduation, dean's list, suspension, and so forth?

2.3. How does a DBMS differ from a file management system?

2.4. From references, prepare a discussion of a typical fourth generation (query) language associated with a data base of your choice. Describe this programming language and indicate how it is used in the DBMS you choose.

2.5. Obtain documentation for three or four commercial microcomputer DBMS. Identify an apropriate set of attributes for evaluation of the suitability of the DBMS example for use in an application of your choosing. Evaluate the DBMS packages using the two evaluation approaches described here.

2.6. Write a brief paper discussing the subject of buying an existing DBMS or designing one, and coding it yourself, for an application of your own choosing. What are the trade-offs involved?

2.7. Perform a sensitivity analysis of the DBMS software package evaluation considered in Section 2.4. How much of a change needs to be made before alternative 2 is the best alternative?

2.8. Provide a structural, functional, and purposeful definition of the major DBMS types discussed in this chapter.

References

[1] Arden, B. W. (Ed.), *What Can Be Automated? The Computer Science and Engineering Research Study*, MIT Press, Cambridge, 1980, Chapter 10.

[2] Date, C. J., *An Introduction to Data Base Systems*, Addison-Wesley, Reading, MA, Vol. I, 4th Edition 1985, Vol. II, 1983.

[3] Date, C. J., *Database*, Addison-Wesley, Reading, MA, 1983.

[4] Stonebraker, M. (Ed.), *Readings in Database Systems*, Morgan Kaufman, San Mateo, CA, 1988.

[5] Sprague, R. H., Jr., and Carlson, E. D., *Building Effective Decision Support Systems*, Prentice-Hall, Englewood Cliffs, NJ, 1982.

[6] Codd, E. F., "Relational Database: A Practical Foundation for Productivity," *Communications of the ACM*, Vol. 25, No. 2, February 1982, pp. 109–117.

[7] Codd, E. F., "A Relational Model of Data for Large Shared Data Banks," *Communications of the ACM*, Vol. 13, No. 6, June 1970, pp. 377–387.

[8] Codd, E. F., "Extending the Database Relational Model to Capture More Meaning," *ACM Transactions on Database Systems*, Vol. 4, 1979, pp. 397–434.

[9] Sandberg, G.,"A Primer on Relational Data Base Concepts," *IBM Systems Journal*, Vol. 20, No. 1, 1981, pp. 23–40.

[10] Kent, W.,"Limitation of Record Based Information Models," *ACM Transactions on Database Systems*, Vol. 4, No. 1, 1979, pp. 107–131.

[11] Chen, P. P. S.,"The Entity-Relationship Model: Towards a Unified View of Data," *ACM Transactions on Database Systems*, Vol. 1, No. 9, 1976, pp. 9–36.

[12] Atzeni, P., and Chen, P. P.,"Completeness of Query Languages for the Entity-Relationship Model," in Chen, P. P. (Ed.) *Entity-Relationship Approach to Information Modeling and Analysis*, North-Holland, Amsterdam, 1983, pp. 109–121.

[13] Harary, F., Norman, R. Z., and Cartwright, D., *Structural Models: An Introduction to the Theory of Directed Graphs*, Wiley, New York, 1965.

[14] Geoffrion, A. M.,"An Introduction to Structured Modeling," *Management Science*, Vol. 33, No. 5, May 1987, pp. 547–588.

[15] Geoffrion, A. M.,"Computer Based Modeling Environments," *European Journal of Operations Research*, Vol. 41, No. 1, 1989, pp. 33–43.

[16] Kerschberg, L. (Ed.), *Proceedings of the International Conferences on Expert Database Systems*, Benjamin-Cummings, Menlo Park, CA, Vol. 1, 1987; Vol. 2, 1989.

[17] Mylopoulos, J., and Brodie, M. L. (Eds.), *Artificial Intelligence and Databases*, Morgan Kaufman, San Mateo, CA, 1989.

[18] Parsaye, K., Chignell, M., Khoshafian, S., and Wong, H., *Intelligent Databases: Object Oriented, Deductive, Hypermedia Technologies*, Wiley, New York, 1989.

[19] Zdonik, S. B., and Maiser, D., *Readings in Object Oriented Databases*, Morgan Kaufman, Los Altos, CA, 1989.

[20] Yeh, R., and Zave, P.,"Specifying Software Requirements," *Proceedings of the IEEE*, Vol. 68, No. 9, September 1980, pp. 1077–1085.

[21] Booch, G., *Object Oriented Design: With Applications*, Benjamin/Cummings, Redwood City, CA, 1991.

[22] Coad, P., and Yourdon, E., *Object Oriented Analysis*, Prentice Hall Inc., Englewood Cliffs NJ 1990.

[23] Goldberg, A., and Robson, D., *Smalltalk 80: The Language and Its Implementation*, Addison-Wesley, Reading, MA 1983.

[24] Goldberg, A., *Smalltalk 80: The Interactive Programing Environment*, Addison-Wesley, Reading, MA, 1984.

[25] Lorin, H., *Aspects of Distributed Computer Systems*, 2nd ed., Wiley, New York, 1988.

[26] Mullender, S. (Ed.), *Distributed Systems*, Addison-Wesley, Reading, MA, 1989.

[27] Ceri, S., and Pelagatti, G., *Distributed Databases: Principles and Systems*, McGraw-Hill, New York, 1984.

[28] Altman, R.,"An Assessment of Current Cooperative Processing Architectures," in Tinnirello, P. C. (Ed.), *Systems Management: Development and Support*, Auerbach, Boston, 1989, pp. 287–311.

[29] Ziegler, K. Z. Jr., *Distributed Computing and the Mainframe*, Wiley, New York, 1991.

[30] Clark, C. M.,"Software Package Selection Guidelines," in Tinnirello, P. C. (Ed.), *Systems Management: Development and Support*, Auerbach, Boston, 1989, pp. 317–331.

[31] Martin, J., *Managing the Data-Base Environment*, Prentice-Hall, Englewood Cliffs, NJ, 1983.

Chapter 3

Model-Base Management Systems

There is virtually no one in computer, information systems, or systems engineering related professional areas who has not heard the term *data-base management system* (DBMS). This is not the case at all with respect to the term *model-base management system* (MBMS). When asked, most professionals would say that the objectives of a DBMS include

1. Managing a large quantity of data in physical storage.
2. Providing logical data structures, with which humans interact, that are independent of the structure used for physical data storage.
3. Reducing data redundancy and maintenance needs, and increasing flexibility of use of the data, by provision of independence between the data and the applications programs that use it.
4. Providing effective access to data users who are not necessarily sophisticated in the micro-level details of computer science.

Many support facilities will typically be provided with a DBMS to enable achievement of these purposes. These include data dictionaries to aid in internal housekeeping, and information query, retrieval, and report generation facilities to support external use needs.

The function of a model-base management system* is quite analogous to that of a DBMS. The primary function of a DBMS is separation of system users, in terms of independence of the application, from the physical aspects of data-base structure

---

*Sometimes the term *model management system* (MMS) is used. We will use the MBMS terminology, even though the MMS usage appears to have predated it.

81

and processing. In a similar way, a MBMS is intended to provide independence between the specific models that are used in a DSS and the applications that use them. *The purpose of a MBMS is to transform data from the DBMS into information that is useful for decision making.* An auxiliary purpose might also include representation of information as data such that it can later be recalled and used.

The term *model management system* was apparently first used over 15 years ago [1]. Soon thereafter, the MBMS usage was adopted in Sprague and Carlson [2]. The functions of a MBMS [2] include creation, storage, access, and manipulation of models. Objectives for a MBMS include

1. Providing for efficient creation of new models for use in specific applications.
2. Supporting maintenance of a wide range of models that support the formulation, analysis, and interpretation stages of issue resolution.
3. Providing for model access and integration, within models themselves as well as with the DBMS.
4. Centralizing model-base management in a manner analogous and compatible with data-base management.
5. Ensuring integrity, currency, consistency, and security of models.

Just as we have physical data and logical data in a DBMS, so also do we find it appropriate to discuss two types of model processing efforts. We will call these *model processing MBMS* and *decision processing MBMS* [3]. The user would interact most directly with the decision processing MBMS,* whereas the model processing MBMS would be more concerned with provision of consistency, security, currency, and other technical modeling issues. Each of these support the notion of appropriate formal use of models that support all aspects of human judgment and choice.

There are several necessary ingredients for a study of MBMS. The first is a study of formal analytical *methods* of operations research and systems engineering that support the construction of models that are useful in issue formulation, analysis, and interpretation. To present even a small fraction of the analytical methods and associated models that are in current use would be a mammoth undertaking. Rather than do this, we will discuss models in a somewhat general context and then present a more detailed discussion of decision analysis based models for issue interpretation. Next, we will look at several approaches for management of analytical models. First, we will present a relational view, and then an entity–relational view of modeling. Then, we will discuss some new and evolving concepts in expert model-base systems.

3.1 MODELS AND MODELING

In this section we will briefly describe a number of models and methods that can be used as part of a systems engineering based approach to problem solution, or issue

---

*This is quite analogous to interacting with the logical data model in a DBMS.

resolution. Systems engineering* involves the application of a general set of guidelines and methods useful to assist clients in the resolution of issues and problems. Three fundamental steps may be distinguished in a formal systems based approach [4–8]:

1. Problem or issue *formulation*.
2. Problem or issue *analysis*.
3. *Interpretation* of analysis results, including evaluation and selection of alternatives, and implementation of the chosen alternatives.

These steps are conducted at a number of phases throughout a systems *life cycle*. As was indicated in Chapter 1, this life cycle begins with determination of requirements for a system through phases that include such efforts as system design, development, installation, and ultimate system maintenance, retrofit, or replacement.

We have chosen a systems engineering framework involving the three steps of formulation, analysis, and interpretation as the underlying structure ordering the methods we discuss here. We shall now briefly elaborate on each of the three systems engineering steps, giving particular attention to the methods and models suitable for assistance in each step. Figure 3.1 illustrates the three major steps in this systems engineering problem-solving framework.

3.1.1 Issue, or Problem, Formulation Models

The first part of a systems effort for problem or issue resolution is typically concerned with problem or *issue formulation*, including identification of problem elements and characteristics. The first step in issue formulation is normally that of definition of the problem or issue to be resolved. Problem definition is generally an outscoping activity (it also involves refinement of the problem and other efforts), as it enlarges the scope of what was originally thought to be the problem. Problem or issue definition will ordinarily be a group activity involving those familiar with or impacted by the issue or problem. It seeks to determine the needs, constraints, alterables, and social or organizational sectors affecting a particular problem and relationships among these elements.

Of special importance are the identification and structuring of objectives for the policy or alternative that will ultimately be chosen. This is often referred to as *value system design* [9]. Option generation [10], or alternative identification, is an important, and often neglected portion of a problem-solving effort. This option generation, or system or alternative synthesis, step of issue formulation is concerned primarily with the answers to three questions:

1. What are the alternative approaches for attaining objectives?
2. How is each alternative approach described?
3. How do we measure attainment of each alternative approach?

*Operations research and systems analysis methods are a part of systems engineering, from the perspective adopted here.

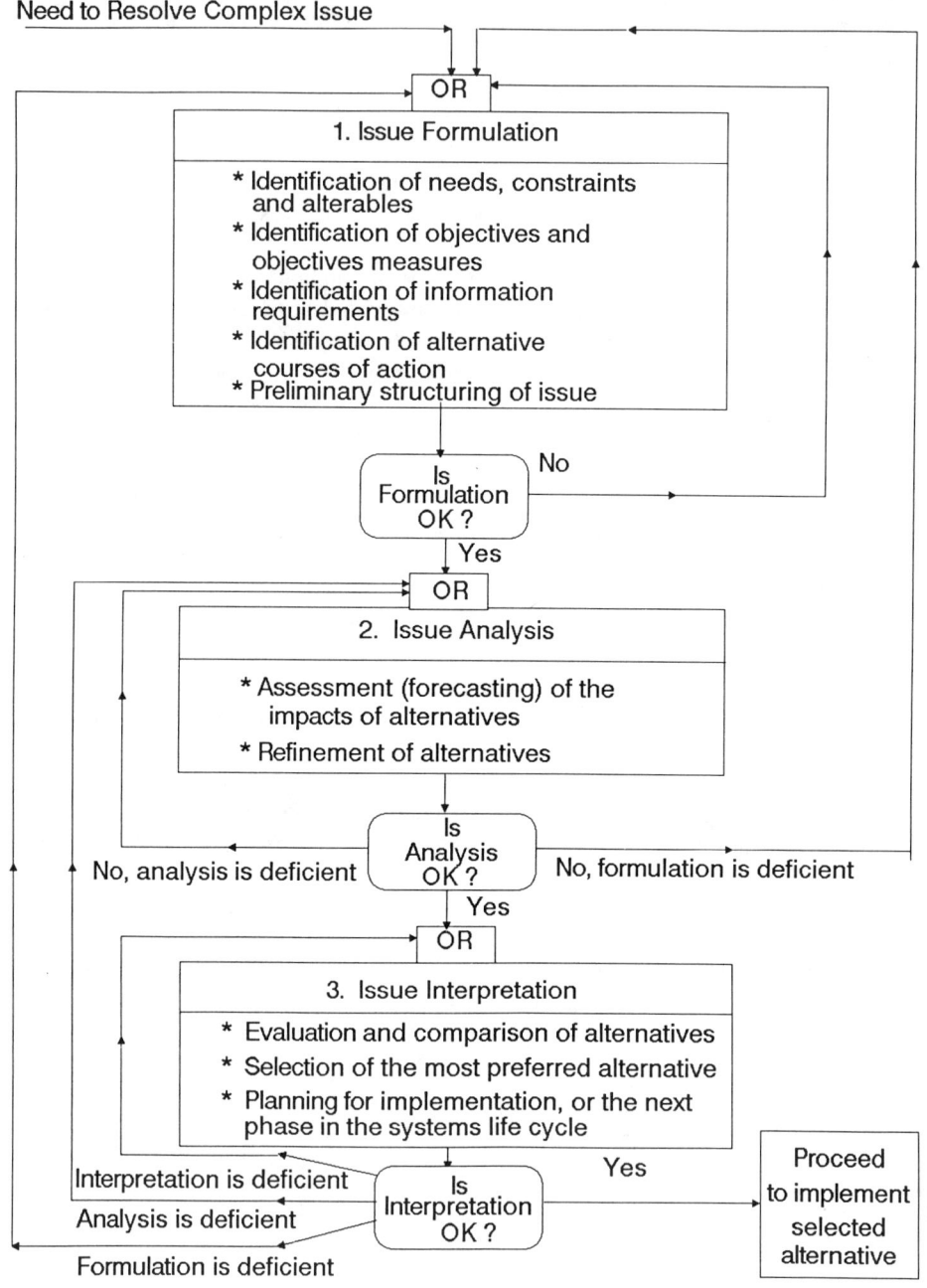

Figure 3.1 Flow chart of formal systems engineering approach to issue resolution.

The answers to these three questions lead to a series of alternative activities or policies and a set of activities measures.

Several of the methods that are especially helpful in the identification of issue formulation elements are based on principles of collective inquiry [11–13]. The term *collective inquiry** refers to the fact that a group of interested and motivated people is brought together in the hope that they will stimulate each other's creativity in generating elements. We may distinguish two groups of collective inquiry methods here, depending on whether or not the group is physically present at the same physical location.

Brainstorming, Synectics, and Nominal Group Technique. These approaches typically require a few hours of time, a group of knowledgeable people gathered in one place, and a group leader or facilitator. The nominal group technique is typically better than brainstorming in reducing the influence of dominant individuals. We will provide an expanded discussion of the nominal group technique in Chapter 7. Both methods can be very productive: 50–150 ideas or elements might be generated in less than one hour. Synectics, based on problem analogies, might be very appropriate if there is a need for truly unconventional, innovative ideas. Considerable experience with the method is a requirement, however, particularly for the group leader. The nominal group technique is based on a sequence of idea generation, discussion, and prioritization. It can be quite useful when an initial screening of a large number of ideas or elements is needed. Synectics and brainstorming are directly interactive group methods, whereas nominal group efforts are "nominally" interactive in that the members of the group do not directly communicate.

Questionnaires, Survey, and Delphi. These three methods of collective inquiry do not require the group of participants to gather at one place and time, but they typically take more time to achieve results than the methods above. In questionnaires and surveys, a usually large number of participants is asked, on an individual basis, for ideas or opinions, which are then processed to achieve an overall result. There is no interaction among participants. Delphi usually provides for written anonymous interaction among participants in several rounds. Results of previous rounds are fed back to participants, and they are asked to comment, revise their views as desired, and so on. A Delphi can be very instructive, but usually takes several weeks or months to complete.

Use of some of the many structuring methods, in addition to leading to greater clarity of the problem formulation elements, will typically lead also to identification of new elements and revision of element definitions. Most structuring methods contain an analytical component; and they may, therefore, be more properly labeled as analysis methods.† The following element structuring aids are among the many modeling aids available that are particularly suitable for the issue formulation step.

---
*See the article of this title in Ref. 7 for additional commentary and references.
†Since there are cycles within cycles, an issue formulation effort can be disaggregated into a formulation, analysis, and interpretation portion.

Interaction Matrices. These may be useful to identify clusters of closely related elements in a large set, in which case we have a *self-interaction matrix*; or to structure and identify the couplings between elements of different sets, for example, objectives and alternatives. In this case, we produce *cross-interaction matrices.* Interaction matrices are useful for initial, comprehensive exploration of sets of elements. Learning about problem interrelationships during the process of constructing an interaction matrix is a major result of use of these matrices. Figure 3.2 presents some prototypical self- and cross-interaction matrices as undirected graphs.

Trees. Trees are graphical aids particularly useful to portray hierarchical or branching-type structures. They are excellent for communication, illustration, and clarification of systemlike efforts. Trees may be useful in all steps and phases of a systems effort, especially in representing decision structures. A tree is a directed graph or structural model. Figure 3.3 represents a decision tree structure.

Structured Modeling. Structured or structural modeling methods are computer-assisted methods designed for individual and group use in structuring a large set of elements. The computer is programmed to perform the more straightforward bookkeeping tasks, thus allowing he user group to concentrate on the elements and their relations. These approaches are particularly useful in assisting an individual or group of people in their effort to create clarity concerning perceptions of a set of elements,

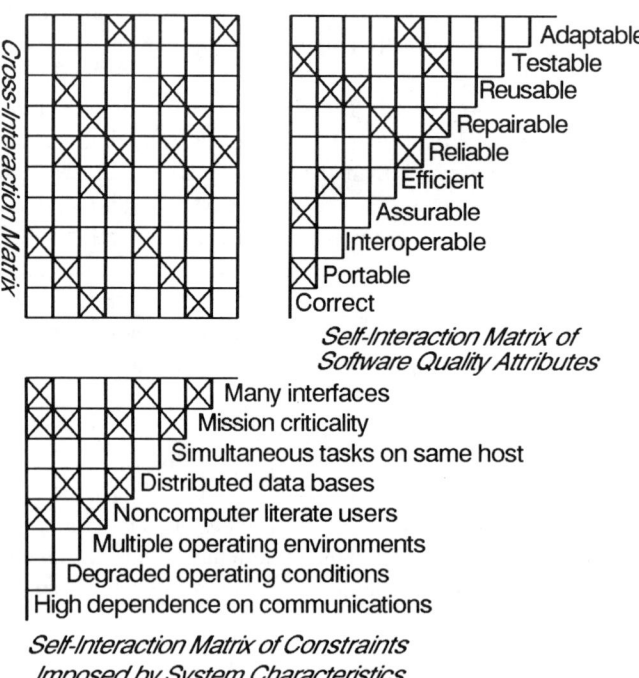

Figure 3.2 Self- and cross-interaction matrices for software development.

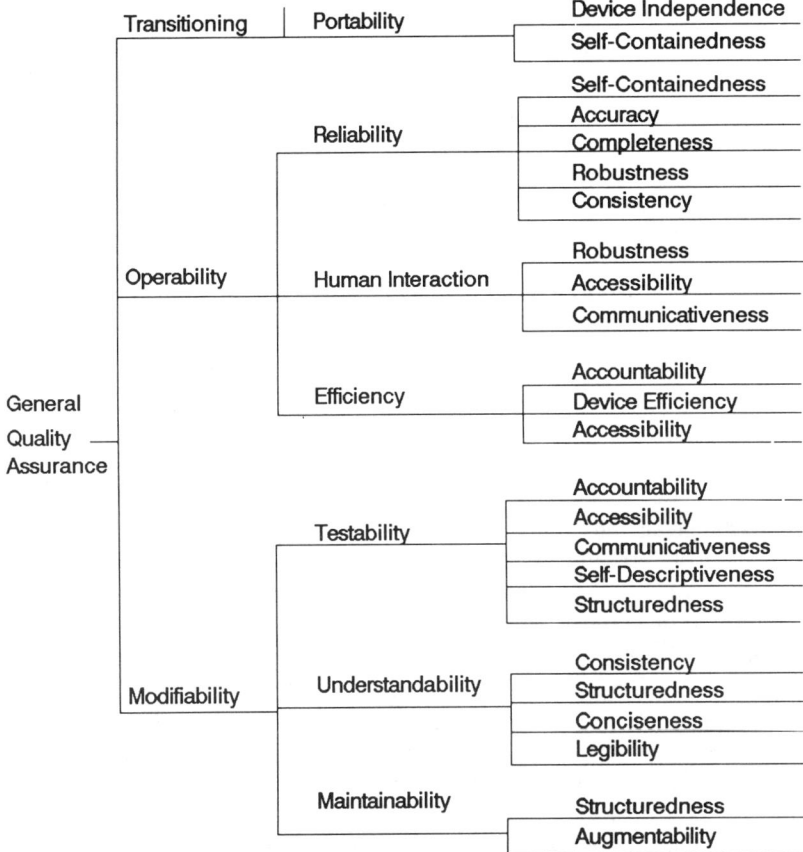

Figure 3.3 Tree structure of attributes for software quality assurance.

and to structure their discussion concerning the relationships in the set. Among the many structural modeling approaches are cognitive mapping, interpretive structural modeling [14], semantic networks, and frames. Our discussions to follow concerning the use of structured modeling concepts in model management will provide some additional commentary. In Chapter 2, we described DBMS based on structured modeling concepts.

Causal Loop Diagrams. A causal loop diagram [15] is a particular form of structural modeling that results in the representation of graphical pictures of causal interactions between sets of variables. They are especially helpful to make explicit one's perception of the causes of change in a system, and can serve very well as communication aids.

There are many approaches to problem formulation [16]. In general, these approaches assume that "asking" will be the predominant approach used to obtain issue formulation elements. Asking is often the simplest approach; but often valuable information can be obtained from observation of an existing and evolving system, or from study of plans and other prescriptive documents. When these three approaches fail, it may be necessary to construct a "trial" system and determine issue formulation elements through experimentation and iteration with the trial system. These four methods (asking, study of an existing system, study of a normative systems, experimentation with a prototype system) are each very useful for information requirements determination, a subject considered in Chapter 5.

3.1.2 Models for Analysis

The analysis portion of a DSS effort typically consists of two steps. First, the options or alternatives defined in issue formulation are analyzed to assess their expected impacts on needs and objectives. This is often called *impact assessment*. Second, a *refinement* or *optimization* effort is often desirable. This is directed toward refinement or fine-tuning a viable alternative through adjustment of the parameters within an alternative, such as to obtain maximum performance in terms of needs satisfaction, subject to the given constraints.

Simulation and *modeling* methods are based on the conceptualization and use of an abstraction, or model, which hopefully behaves in a way similar to that of the real system. Impacts of alternative courses of action are studied through use of the model, something that often cannot easily be done through experimentation with the real system. Models are, of necessity, dependent on the value system and the purpose behind utilization of a model. We want to be able to determine the correctness of predictions based on usage of a model and therefore be able to validate the model. There are three essential steps in constructing a model:

1. Determining those issue formulation elements that are most relevant to a particular problem.
2. Determining the structural relationships among these elements.
3. Determining parametric coefficients within the structure.

We should interpret the word *model* here as an abstract generalization of an object or system. Any set of rules or other relationships that describes something is a model of that thing. The MBMS of a DSS will typically contain formal models that have been stored in the model base of the support system.

When we model systems, we enhance our abilities to comprehend their nuances to understand their interrelationships and our relationship to them. A typical result of a model is the opportunity to see an issue from several viewpoints and perspectives, such as economic, technical, political, or environmental. A system model may be viewed as a physical arrangement, as a causal flow diagram, and/or as a set of actions and consequences that can be shown graphically through time, perhaps in a decision tree structure, as a simplified picture of reality. Developments and improvements in our ability to build models have become more important as systems have become more complex. This is, of course, facilitated by contemporary developments in information technology. Generally, large systems evolve as an aggregate of subsystems interacting with one another to create an interdependent whole. Hence, models of systems often contain submodels.

Gaming. This is a modeling method in which the real system is simulated by people taking on the roles of real-world actors. The approach is quite appropriate for studying situations in which people's reactions to each others' actions are of great importance, such as competition between individuals or groups for limited resources. It is also a very appropriate learning method. *Conflict analysis* [17,18] is an interesting and appropriate game theoretic based approach that may result in models that are particularly suitable for inclusion into the model base of a MBMS.

Trend Extrapolation or Time Series Forecasting Models. These modeling methods are especially useful when sufficient data about past and present developments are available but there is little theory about underlying mechanisms causing change. The method is based on the identification of a mathematical description or structure that will be capable of reproducing the data. Then, this description is used to extend the data series into the future, typically over the short-to-medium term. The primary concern is with input–output matching of observed input data and results of model use. Often, little attention is devoted to assuring process realism and this may create difficulties affecting model validity. While such models may be functionally valid, they may not be purposefully or structurally valid.

Continuous-Time Dynamic Simulation Models. These modeling methods are generally based on postulation and qualification of a causal structure underlying change over time. A computer is used to explore long-range behavior as it follows from the postulated causal structure. The method can be useful as a learning and qualitative forecasting device. Often, it is expensive and time-consuming to create realistic dynamic simulation models. These are quite common in the physical sciences and much of engineering, such as automatic control.

Input–Output Analysis. Models are especially designed for study of equilibrium situations and requirements in economic systems in which many industries are interdependent. Many economic data formats are directly suited for the method. It is relatively simple, conceptually, and can great handle many details. Commonly, input–output models are very large.

Econometrics or Macroeconomic Models are primarily applied to economic description and forecasting problems. They are based on both theory and data. Emphasis is placed on specification of structural relations, based on economic theory, and the identification of unknown parameters, using available data, in the behavioral equations. The method requires expertise in economics, statistics, and computer use. It can be quite costly and time-consuming. It has been widely used for short-to-medium-term economic analysis and forecasting.

Microeconomic Models represent an application of economic theories of firms and consumers. Behavior of economic agents in a free-market economy is described as that set of actions that will maximize total benefits or utility for the agent. Microeconomic models are used to study and forecast economic quantities. Closely related to microeconomic models are welfare economic models, which incorporate equity concepts into microeconomic models. There are a number of extensions [19], such as cost–benefit models.

Queuing Theory and Discrete Event Simulation Models are often used to study, analyze, and forecast the behavior of systems in which probabilistic phenomena, such as waiting lines, are of importance. Queuing theory is a mathematical approach, while discrete-event simulation generally refers to computer simulation of queuing-theory-type models. The two methods ar widely used in the analysis and design of systems such as toll booths, communications networks, service facilities, shipping terminals, scheduling, and so forth.

Hypothesis Testing Models provide a widely accepted set of rules for deriving conclusions on the basis of samples of information rather than full information. The approach is used widely in the social sciences, engineering, quality control, and in conjunction with regression analysis.

Regression Analysis Models and Estimation Theory Models are useful for the identification of mathematical relations and parameter values in these relations from sets of data or measurements. Regression and estimation methods are used frequently in conjunction with mathematical modeling, in particular with trend extrapolation and time series forecasting, and with econometrics. These methods are commonly also used to validate models. Often, these techniques are called system identification approaches when the goal is to identify the parameters of a system, within an assumed structure, so as to minimize a function of the error between observed data and the model response.

Mathematical Programming Models are used extensively in operations research systems analysis, and management science practice, for resource allocation under constraints, planning, or scheduling, and similar applications. They are particularly useful when the best equilibrium or one-time setting has to be determined for a given policy or system. Many analysis issues can be cast as mathematical programming problems. There have been a significant number of mathematical programming models developed, including linear, nonlinear, integer, and dynamic programming. There are many appropriate reference texts, including Ref. 20, that discuss this valuable class of modeling and analysis tools. A detailed implementation of a model management system for large-scale mathematical linear programs is discussed in Ref. 21.

Optimum Systems Control Models [22] address the problem of determining the best controls or actions when the system, the controls or actions, the constraints, or the performance index may change over time. A mathematical description of system change is necessary. Optimum systems control is especially suitable for determining controls or parameters in dynamic systems that are linear, or that can be linearized about a nominal trajectory. One particularly useful application, from the perspective of DSS utility, is that of developing a support system for control system design efforts.

Markov Decision Models have been designed to assist in determining the best overall strategy in a system in which future change over time can be described as a succession of random events occurring at discrete intervals of time. Applications have been reported in fields such as health care, maintenance strategy development, and inventory management.

3.1.3 Interpretation Models

The third step in a decision support systems effort starts with evaluation and comparison of alternatives, using the information gained by analysis. Subsequently, one of more alternatives are selected, and a plan for their implementation is designed. Thus, a MBMS must provide models for interpretation, including evaluation, of alternatives.

It is important to note that there is a clear and distinct difference between the refinement of individual alternatives, or optimization step of analysis, and the evaluation of sets of refined alternatives. In some cases, refinement or optimization of individual alternative policies is not needed in the analysis step. But evaluation of alternatives is always needed, for if there is but a single policy alternative, then there really is no alternative at all. It is especially important to avoid a large number of cognitive biases in evaluation and decision making. Clearly, the efforts involved in the interpretation step of evaluation and decision making interact most strongly with the efforts in the other steps of the systems process.

There are a number of methods for *evaluation* and *choice making* that are of value. A few will be described briefly here. Our next section will examine some decision analysis based approaches in greater detail.

Decision Analysis [23] is a very general approach to option evaluation and selection. It involves identification of action alternatives and possible consequences; identification of the probabilities of these consequences; identification of the valuation placed by the decision maker on these consequences; computation of the expected value of the consequences; and aggregating or summarizing these values for all consequences of each action. In doing this, we obtain an evaluation of each alternative act; and the one with the highest value is the most preferred action or option.

Multiple-Attribute Utility Theory [24] has been designed to facilitate comparison and ranking of alternatives with many attributes or characteristics. The relevant attributes are identified, structured, and a weight or relative utility is assigned by the decision maker to each basic attribute. The attribute measurements for each alternative are used to compute an overall worth or utility for each alternative. Multiple-attribute utility theory allows for various types of worth structures and for the explicit recognition and incorporation of the decision makers attitude toward risk in the utility computation.

Policy Capture (or Social Judgment Theory) [25,26] has also been designed to assist decision makers in making values explicit and known. It is basically a descriptive approach toward identification of values and attribute weights. By knowing these, one can generally make decisions that are consistent with values. In policy capture, the decision maker is asked to rank order a set of alternatives. Then, alternative attributes and their attribute measures or scores are determined by elicitation from the decision maker for each alternative. A mathematical procedure involving regression analysis is used to determine that relative importance, or weight, of each attribute that will lead to a ranking as specified by the decision maker. The result is fed back to the decision maker, who, typically, will express the view that some of his or her values, in terms of the weights associated with the attributes, are different. In an iterative learning process, preference weights and/or overall rankings are modified until the decision maker is satisfied with both the weights and the overall alternative ranking.

Elimination by Aspects [27] is a simple selection aid in which those alternatives not fulfilling certain minimum requirements on every aspect or attribute ar eliminated from further consideration. Alternatively, only alternatives exceeding a minimum aspiration level on each attribute may be retained. This is an extensively used heuristic. It is used in many areas as a screening method to select only those options for further consideration that meet a number of minimum requirements. It is appropriate for this purpose and we shall describe an approach that uses it in our next section. When used, as it often is in practice, to select a single "best" alternative, it can be very flawed.

Voting is a well-known and widely used method of group decision making. Different methods of voting may, and often will, lead to different results. Voting* is subject to a number of theoretical difficulties, the principal one being intransitivity.

Gantt Charts consist of a graphical representation of different activities in a project or plan, and the time during which they are (planned to be) carried out. Gantt charts are useful for communication, and for monitoring progress during implementation of a plan.

Project and Network Planning Methods include a wide variety of more specialized tools for planning complicated projects consisting of many activities, some of which must precede others in order to be meaningful. They are used extensively in the management of engineering projects, and have also received widespread acclaim in other areas. They are of great help in scheduling different activities, determining the expected duration of a project, estimating costs of reducing the project duration, identifying latest possible or necessary completion times of certain project tasks, scheduling activities to reduce overload, and so forth. After the selection of an alternative action or policy has been made, *implemention* of action plans is generally anticipated. There are many methods and tools that assist in planning for implementation of action. Many of them are based on various project charting and planning. A discussion of these approaches may be found in Ref. 28.

---

*See the article by this title in Ref. 7 for a summary of many voting strategies.

3.2 DECISION MODELS

Although a MBMS can and should contain models that assist in the formulation, analysis, and interpretation of issues, many operational decision support systems focus on approaches that specifically support the interpretation step. In this step, we are primarily concerned with evaluation of decisions. This is often called *decision analysis*.

The decision analysis problem may be described as follows. The decision maker is presented with a problem that requires a decision. Certain objectives are provided by those to whom the decision maker is responsible. Also available are certain alternative options or courses of action, each of which satisfies those objectives in some way. The problem is to choose the alternative course of action that best meets or satisfies these objectives. If there is more than one factor contributing to the satisfaction of those objectives, the decision maker must find some way to combine the contributions toward satisfaction of these objectives in some "best" or most appropriate way. Commonly, there are many alternatives that may be implemented, many objectives to be satisfied, and diverse group opinions concerning the worth of various alternatives.

Decision analysis can be subdivided into four categories:

1. Decision under certainty, in which each action results in one and only one outcome.
2. Decision under risk, in which one of several outcomes can result from given action depending on the state of nature, and these states occur with known probabilities.
3. The imperfect information problem, in which the problem formulation is incomplete, or otherwise imperfect. This is a generalization of what has been often called the *decision under uncertainty* problem. The decision under uncertainty situation is one in which one of several outcomes can result from a given action depending on the state of nature, and these states occur with unknown probabilities.
4. Decision under conflict, in which nature is replaced by a not necessarily hostile opponent.

Problems in category 1 are problems for which deterministic decision theory may be applied. They are of interest primarily in the multiattributed outcome situation. (We have already used this approach for a multiattribute evaluation issue in Chapter 2.) Problems in category 4 are game theoretic problems and the approaches of conflict analysis are applicable [17,18]. The domain for decision analysis models is generally restricted to categories 2 and 3. The majority of decision analysis efforts have been applied to issues in category 2, although current approaches to imperfect knowledge permit solution of some problems in category 3. We will initially concentrate on a description of problems in category 2, from which category 1 problems may be solved as a special case. Then, we will provide an overview of some solution methods for problems in category 3. We will not specifically discuss category 4 problems.

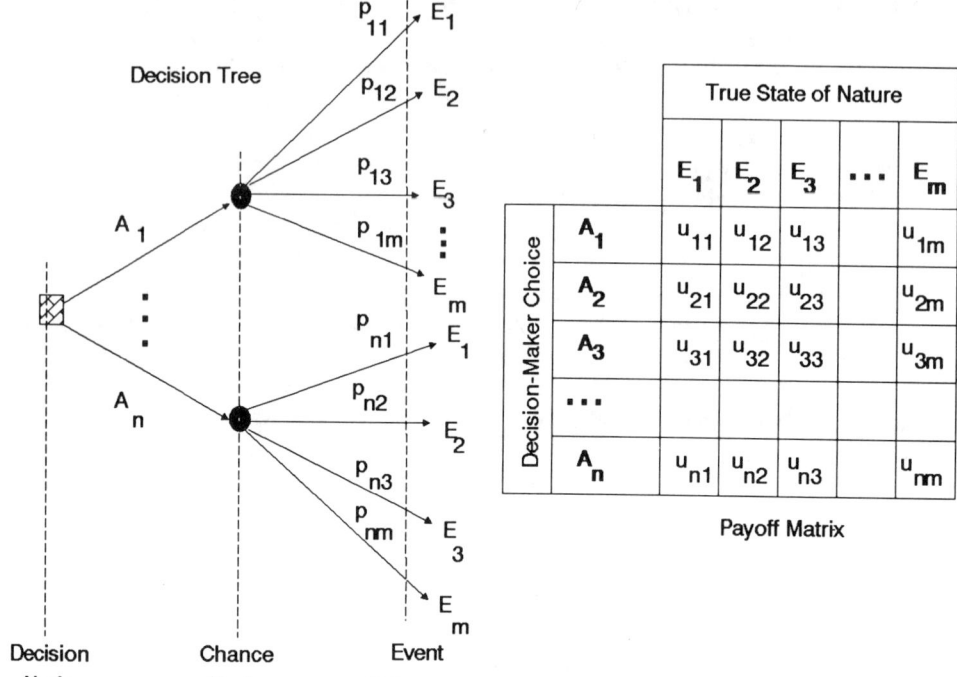

Figure 3.4 Decision analysis tree structure for simple, single decision lottery.

3.2.1 Models for Decision Making Under Risk

The theoretical foundations of decision analysis are probability theory and utility theory. Probability theory allows the decision maker to make maximum use of the information available,* while utility theory guarantees that the choice will reflect the decision maker's true preferences.† In decision analysis terminology, we speak of event outcome values and the utility of these values. Thus, utility is a more general concept than value. Figure 3.4 presents an illustration of the way we assume that alternatives, the event outcomes that follow from selecting alternatives, and utilities, can be represented. This forms the basis for the model that we will use for our brief study of decision analysis.

A decision analysis model contains five elements:

1. The set of n alternative actions $A = \{a(1), a(2), \ldots, a(n)\}$.
2. The set of m states of nature $E = \{e(1), e(2), \ldots, e(m)\}$.

---

*This is based on the tacit assumption that the structure of the situation is correct and that the parameters within this structure, including the probabilities of random parameters, are also known precisely.
†This is based on the tacit assumption that the utilities are accessed correctly *and* that the axioms on which formal decision analysis is based are accepted as reasonable.

3. The set of *nm* outcomes $Q = \{q(11), \ldots, q(ij), q(nm)\}$, where $q(ij)$ corresponds to the pair of action–event possibilities $(a(i)\ e(j))$.
4. A utility function $U = \{u(11), u(ij), \ldots, u(nm)\} = u_{ij}$, where $u(ij) = U(q(ij))$, that expresses the decision maker's utility at having selected alternative i and receiving state of nature j as a result.
5. The objective, a criterion or statement of what is desired.

It is desirable to reflect briefly on what is meant by the concept of utility. Formally, a utility function is a transformation that maps the set of outcomes of a decision problem into some interval of the real line. In other words, *a utility function assigns a numerical value to each outcome of a decision problem*. If the utility of outcome A is designated by $u(A)$, then the basic assumptions of utility theory may be described as follows:

1. Any two outcomes resulting from a decision may be compared. If A and B are two such outcomes, then one must either prefer A to B ($A \succ B$), prefer B to A ($B \succ A$), or be indifferent between A and B ($A \approx B$). An extension of this assumption results from the transitivity concept, which requires that if a rational decision maker prefers A to B and B to C, then the decision maker must also prefer A to C. If a decision maker is not transitive, all sorts of maladies can result, as can easily be demonstrated.* In the simple way posed here, every individual should normatively seek to be transitive relative to preferential expressions. Sadly, what applies to individuals does not apply to groups, as group preferences may well be intransitive, even though all individuals in the group have transitive preferences.†
2. Utilities may be assigned to lotteries involving outcomes as well as to the outcomes themselves. The term *lottery* is defined as a chance mechanism that yields outcomes $E_1, E_2, \ldots E_n$ with probabilities $p_1, p_2, \ldots p_n$, respectively, and where each $p_i \geq 0$, and where the sum over all p_i must be equal to 1. (This ensures that we have a valid probability function, but not necessarily that the probabilities we use are appropriate for the problem at hand.) A lottery such as the one we describe is denoted by $L = (p_1, E_1; p_2, E_2; \ldots p_n, E_n)$ and is illustrated in Figure 3.4. Obviously, a lottery is just a particular outcome alternative pair. It describes the alternatives that may be selected and the possible outcomes.

---

*For example, one can become a money pump. If for example, I have the preference structure $A \succ B$, then there should be some amount of money, say \$1, such that $A \approx B + \$1$. Now suppose that $B \succ C$ and $B \approx C + \$1$. If I have alternative C to start with, then I should be willing to trade in that alternative and \$1 for alternative B. If I have alternative B, then I should be willing to trade it and \$1 for alternative A. This new relation, $A = C + \$2$ is quite consistent with a transitive preference structure $A \succ C$, but very much a problem if I am intransitive and have $C \succ A$. If this were my preference structure, then I should be willing to pay someone to take away A and give me back C. Then the cycle can start all over again and continue *ad infinitum*!

†Many decision analysis texts demonstrate this, a generalization of which won a Nobel prize for Kenneth Arrow. For a discussion of voting intransitivities, see the article on voting in Ref. 7.

From this it follows that if one prefers alternative A to alternative B, then one should also prefer A to the lottery $(p, A; (1 - p), B)$, and one should prefer this lottery to alternative B. Further, if we prefer A to B, then we should prefer the lottery $L = (p, A; (1 - p), B)$ to the lottery $L' = (p', A; (1 - p'), B)$ if and only if $p > p'$.

3. There is no intrinsic reward in the lotteries themselves, or as it is more commonly expressed, there is "no fun in gambling." In other words, the decision maker's preferences should not be affected by the particular means chosen to resolve the uncertainty. If there is indeed "fun" in gambling, then this should be considered as one of the attributes of the alternative outcomes and multiattribute evaluation methods used. This is easily accomplished and the result is a situation in which there is no reward associated with the lotteries themselves.

4. If A is preferred to C and C preferred to B, then for sufficiently large p, the lottery $(P, A; (1 - p), B)$ is preferred to C. Similarly, for sufficiently small p, C is preferred to the lottery $(p, A; (1 - p), B)$. Therefore, there exists some p $(0 < p < 1)$ such that one has no preference concerning the choice of C or the lottery $(p, A; (1 - p), B)$. This fourth and final assumption deals with and ensures the continuity of the utility function.

Condition 4 contains the key to resolving a decision under risk problem through use of decision analysis techniques. In actual practice, a situation like the one described in condition 4 is used to measure the utility that a decision maker has for various outcomes. These four assumptions form a basic set for the establishment of a *utility theory*. While this theory is not at all complicated, putting the theory into practice successfully is exceedingly complicated. There are a number of important theoretical issues that can easily be overlooked.* There are many potential behavioral pitfalls, most of them more insidious than the theoretical and quantitative pitfalls, and some of these will be discussed in Chapter 6.

As was mentioned earlier, decision analysis or decision theory, as the subject is sometimes called, attempts to combine probability theory with the concept of a utility function. Only a summary of how this is accomplished is presented here. The perspective that we take is the construction of a decision analytic model based manager. Our approach will roughly parallel the treatment of the *ball-urn*-type problems so often used in the literature to illustrate decision analysis concepts [29].

---

*It is important, for instance, to keep in mind that the concept of preference precedes the concept of utility. In other words, A may be preferred to B ($A \succ B$), but not because the utility of A is greater than that of B, or $U(A) \succ U(B)$; on the contrary, we have the relation $U(A) \succ U(B)$ simply and directly because of the fact that A is preferred to B. Also, it is valuable to note that the numerical values assigned by the utility function are not unique. Given a utility function $U_1(x)$, it is possible to generate a new utility function $U_2(x)$ $= aU_1(x) + b$, where a is a positive constant, and b is any constant, such that the preferences are not altered. Thus, in a sense, a utility function may be viewed as a kind of *preference thermometer*. The utility function must also be monotonically nondecreasing in the sense that the highest utility is assigned to the most-preferred outcome and the lowest utility is assigned to the least-preferred outcome. Intermediate utility values and preferences are assigned in an analogous ordering.

We assume a situation model that is comprised of a collection of urns. Each of these contain a number of red balls and black balls. The decision maker knows in advance that there are n_1 urns, called type R_1, containing r_1 red balls and b_1 black balls, and there are n_2 urns, called type R_2, containing r_2 red balls and b_2 black balls. The decision maker is given an urn and must decide on the basis of this information whether it is of type R_1 or of type R_2. The reward will be a certain gain or loss, depending on both the choice of urn (R_1 or R_2) and the type of urn that the decision maker does in fact obtain. The reward matrix is given by Figure 3.5. Here, W stands for win and L stands for lose. The decision maker is faced with three possible choices if the option of refusing to play is allowed. The decision maker may choose R_1, R_2, or not to play. Which choice should be made? According to the basic rules of decision theory, a rational decision maker will choose the urn that maximizes the expected reward. If the R_1 urn is chosen, the expected reward will be $E(R_1) = W_1 p(R_1) + L_1 p(R_2)$. If the R_2 urn is chosen, the expected reward will be an $E(R_2) = L_2 p(R_1) + W_2 p(R_2)$, where $p(R_i)$ is the probability of being given an urn of type R_i. In this case, $p(R_1) = n_1/(n_1 + n_2)$ and $p(R_2) = n_2/(n_1+n_2)$. Figure 3.6 illustrates some salient details concerning this urn model.

Often, it is possible to obtain some useful information concerning the content of the urns. Generally, we will only be able to obtain this information at a price. This leads to some important notions regarding the *value of information*.

To illustrate some value of information concepts, let us now suppose that the decision maker has the option of picking one ball out of the unknown urn and observing the color of the ball. This will provide some information concerning the type of urn that is present. Of course, a price must usually be paid for this information.

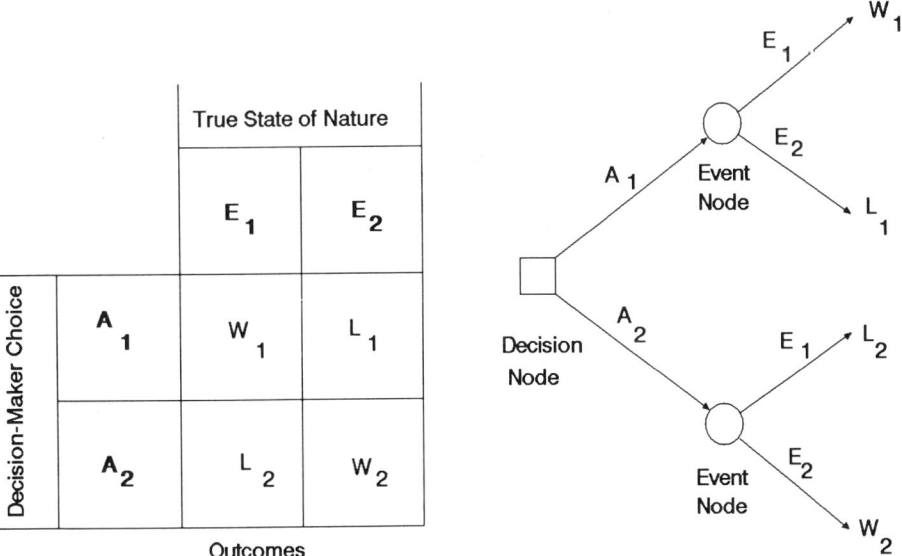

Figure 3.5 Payoff matrix and decision tree for simple decision options and outcomes.

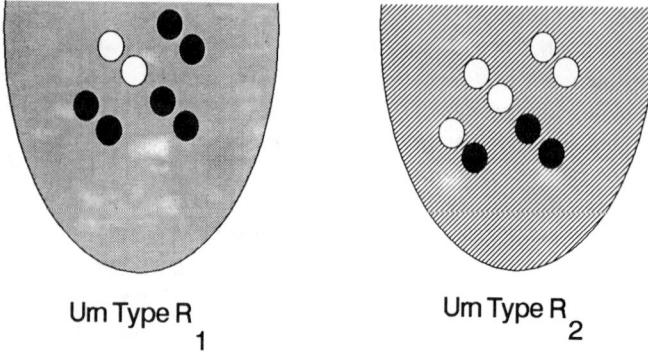

Figure 3.6 Generic urn model for decision analysis.

There is generally always a cost associated with information acquisition. Note that before this information is perhaps obtained, all of the decision maker's knowledge of $p(R_1)$ and $p(R_2)$ came from the relative proportion of type R_1 and type R_2 urns. These are called *a priori* probabilities, since they are known prior to sampling. Now the decision maker has picked a ball at random from the urn in question, has observed its color, and can use this knowledge, together with Bayes' rule, to update the assessment of $p(R_1)$ and $p(R_2)$. These are called *a posteriori* probabilities, since they are determined after sampling. With these updated probabilities, the decision maker again chooses the urn R_1 or R_2 that maximizes the expected reward. Of course, the decision maker must subtract the cost of the sample from the reward that might be obtained in order to get the net return. We note that the decision maker initially has four choices:

1. Don't play
2. Pick R_1
3. Pick R_2
4. Take a sample

If the decision maker chooses one of the first three of these alternatives, the outcome will be determined with no further actions required. If the fourth alternative is chosen, then after sampling one ball from the urn and observing the color of the ball chosen, the decision maker will be faced with another decision:

4.1. Pick R_1, or
4.2. Pick R_2

Obviously, we could extend this purchasing of information by now permitting the decision maker to, if desired, pay a price for looking at the color of another ball. (Alternatively, the decision maker could have had the option, at the start of information acquisition, to purchase n samples. This is different decision situation from the one described.) These urn-ball models are quite general and can be used to represent a number of information purchase situations.

Hence, the problem now becomes a sequential decision problem. More complex examples may be constructed and displayed in the form of a decision tree with alternating decision nodes and chance nodes. The optimal policy is developed by starting at the terminal nodes and working back through the tree in such a manner that at each decision node the decision maker chooses the path that maximizes his expected reward from that point. This approach is generally known as one of *averaging out and folding back* and is analogous to the solution of a dynamic programming problem. This is yet another analytical method that is very useful for issue analysis. Dynamic programming models could be incorporated into a MBMS.

Decision analysis may be applied to a wide variety of problems. The one common bond among formal decision analysis approaches to these problems is that they involve some kind of optimization. For example, in the model just described, the decision maker seeks to choose the alternative $a(i)$, which makes the resulting $u(ij)$ the best possible, in some sense. Often, "best" will mean "maximum." The utility $u(ij)$ will also depend on the particular value of the random variable $e(j)$, so the best the decision maker can do here is to maximize some function such as the expected value of the random variable $u(ij) = u_{ij}$:

$$\max_i EU\{a_i\} = \max_i \sum_{j=1}^{N} u_{ij} p(e_j)$$

where $p(e_j)$ is the probability that the state of nature is $e(j)$, and we have used the abbreviated notation $EU\{a(i)\}$ to mean the expected utility of taking action $a(i)$. Often, this is called the *subjective expected utility* and written SEU. The expression subjective is used to denote the fact that the probabilities may be *personal*, that is to say, belief probabilities.

When choosing among alternatives, a decision maker should be able to indicate values,* possible outcomes and resultant consequences, and associated preferences among alternatives. We are considering choice when there is some probabilistic risk or uncertainty associated with the outcome that will be obtained from a decision. To discuss utility in situations that involve risk, it is convenient to define and discuss a lottery in greater detail.

A lottery is a chance mechanism that results in an outcome with a prize or consequences $A(1)$ with probability $p(1)$, an outcome with prize or consequence $A(2)$ with probability $p(2), \ldots$, and an outcome with prize or consequence $A(r)$ with probability $p(r)$. The probabilities $p(i)$ must be such that they sum to 1:

$$\sum_{j=1}^{r} p(j) = p(1) + p(2) + \cdots + p(r) = 1$$

The lottery is denoted as

$$L = [p_1 A_1, p_2 A_2, \ldots, p_n A_n]$$

*A person who cannot express value preferences is *inchoate*.

We can now formally define a utility function as a transformation that maps the set of consequences into an interval on the real line. We will denote the utility of a consequence $A(i)$ as $U(A(i))$. We now make several assumptions. The number of assumptions varies from four to six, depending on which approach is taken. The basic approach taken by Luce and Raiffa [30] for example, in a classic and seminal work, utilized six assumptions. We have just described four assumptions or axioms, which enables establishment of subjective expected utility as the criterion of choice for rational decision making. (This *strong* statement is necessarily true *if* we accept the four axioms or assumptions stated earlier.) The result of these assumptions is that the utility function $U(ij)$ satisfies several properties. These utilities turn out to be indicators of preference and not absolute measurements. They are unique only up to a general linear transformation or, more properly stated, affine transformation.

A utility curve for money can be generated in the following manner. We arrange all the outcomes of a decision in order of preference. We denote the most preferred outcome W and the least preferred outcome L. We arbitrarily assign utility $U(W) = 1$ and $U(L) = 0$. Next, the decision maker is encouraged to, in effect, ask and then answer the question: "Suppose I owned the rights to a lottery that pays W with probability 1/2 and L with probability 1/2. For what amount, say $X_{0.5}$, would I be willint to see to rights to this lottery?" Since the decision maker is indifferent between receiving $X_{0.5}$ for certain and participating in the lottery $\{0.5, W; 0.5, L\}$, then $U(X_{0.5}) = 0.5u(W) + 0.5u(L) = 0.5$. Figure 3.7 illustrates this lottery in decision tree format.

It is potentially noteworthy that we could have picked any other lottery with outcomes W and L, such as, for example, $[0.01, W; 0.99, L]$. There are several

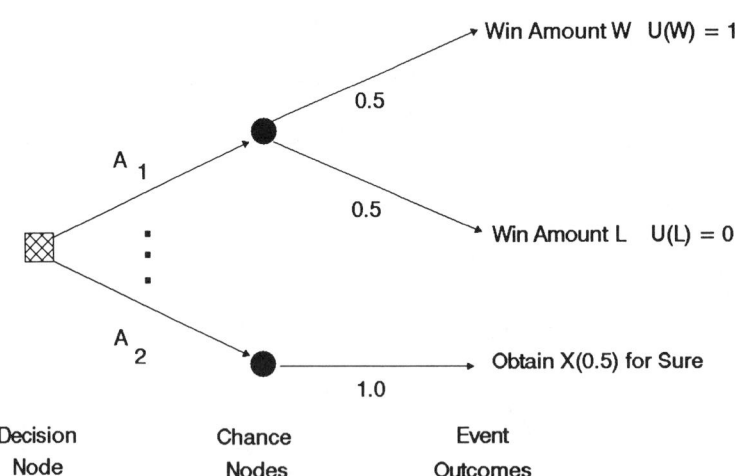

Figure 3.7 Decision analysis tree structure to determine decision maker utility for X(0.5).

analytical reasons, however, for choosing a lottery that gives W or L with equal probability, or $L = [0.5, W; 0.5, L]$.

1. It may be conceptually quite simple for the decision maker to imagine a lottery that gives W or L with equal probability. When W and L occur with equal probability, the decision maker need only be concerned with the relative preferences of W and L, since both are weighted equally. This may, however, be unrealistic. For instance, W might mean some enormous increase in profit to the firm and L might mean "go bankrupt." It might well be that a businessperson would so abhor a situation in which there is a 50 percent chance of going bankrupt that it would become impossible to think of utilities in these terms realistically.
2. Finally, the value of the lottery $[0.5, W; 0.5, L]$ occurs midway on the U axis between W and L and thus facilitates plotting the utility curve.

Next the decision maker is encouraged* to ask and answer the question: "Suppose I owned the rights to a lottery that paid W with probability 1/2 and $X_{0.5}$, which has a utility of 0.5, with probability 1/2. For what amount, call it $X_{0.75}$, would I just be willing to sell the rights to this lottery?" Here, the decision maker is indifferent when it comes to receiving $X_{0.75}$ for certain or participating in the lottery $[0.5, W; 0.5, X_{0.5}]$. Therefore, $U(X_{0.75}) = 0.5U(X_{0.5}) + 0.5U(L) = 0.75$. Next, we consider the lottery $[0.5, X_{0.5}; 0.5, L]$, and the amount to be determined is $X_{0.25}$. In this case, we obtain $U(X_{0.25}) = 0.5U(X_{0.5}) + 0.5U(L) = 0.25$. This process could be continued indefinitely. However, the three points generated here and the two end points are often sufficient to give an idea of the shape of the utility curve, which will usually take on the general shapes shown in Figure 3.8.†

The process of eliciting probabilities and associated utilities so that they veridically represent individual judgments concerning uncertain quantities is one of the major tasks in decision analysis. The seminal text by von Winterfeldt and Edwards [31] describes many of the approaches that have been taken to elicit these values.

Decision analysis provides a formal, rational, systematic framework of search, deliberation, evaluation, and selection. Its purpose is to facilitate the choice of a most preferred course of action for a decision maker in a complex decision situation. Typical activity steps in a decision analysis are as follows:

1. Structure the relationship between decision alternatives and outcomes, typically in the form of a decision tree.
2. Acquire information known by the decision maker or by others to describe the likelihood of occurrence of outcomes in uncertain situations.

---

*The encouragement might come from a human analyst, or a decision support system whose use may be under the guidance of a facilitator.
†It is rare that a decision maker is risk-prone. Hence, the typical utility curve is concave downward.

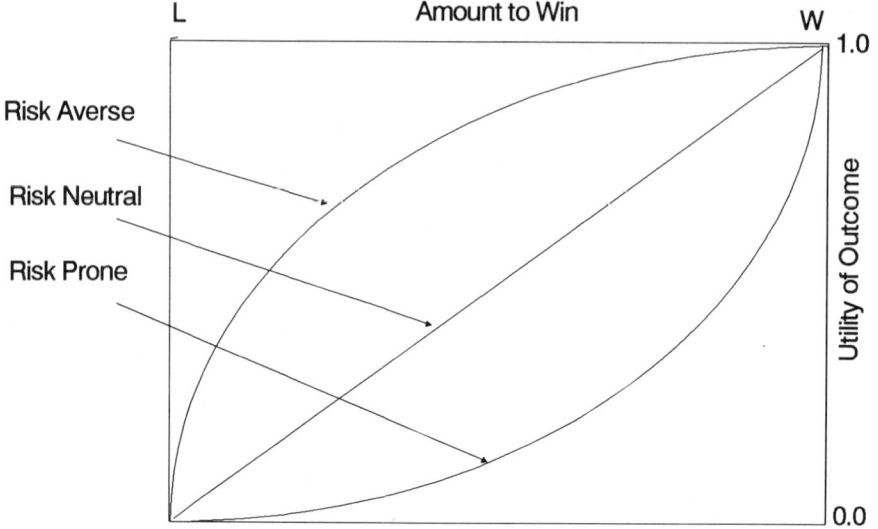

Figure 3.8 Hypothetical utility curve.

3. Assess decision-maker preferences for the various attributes characterizing the possible outcomes and then logically including decision-maker attitudes toward risk in uncertain situations. This will generally result in a utility function for each outcome.
4. Use this utility function, the attribute measures of the outcomes, and the probabilistic information to evaluate an overall utility score for the set of outcomes associated with each alternative.
5. Rank the outcomes, discuss these results with the decision maker, and iterate as necessary to enable final selection of a most preferred course of action.

The products of a formal decision analysis are

1. A decision tree that represents the real decision situation and that indicates probabilities assigned to outcomes, thereby expressing their occurrence probabilities.
2. A mathematical utility function describing the decision makers' preferences for the attributes that characterize the decision situation. This function might be useful to guide future decisions of a similar nature.
3. An evaluation and ranking of alternative courses of action according to their utility or value to the decision maker.
4. A description of the decision situation and the utility function, how it was elicited, and how the overall evaluation of each alternative was derived.
5. A sensitivity analysis of how the results might change for changes in uncertain inputs such as subjective probabilities, personal preferences, and attribute measures.

It is, of course, the DGMS that will provide displays of these products. Again, we see the care that must be taken to ensure that the various subsystems of the DSS are well integrated.

3.2.2 Decision Making with Multiattributed Outcomes

In this subsection, in which we describe an extension of the basic decision analysis paradigm to include situations where the outcomes have multiple attributes, we assume that a set of feasible alternatives $A = (a_1, \ldots, a_m)$ and a set $(X_1, \ldots, X_n)$ of attributes or evaluators of the alternatives can be identified. Associated with each alternative course of action a in A, there is a corresponding consequence $X_1(a), X_2(a), \ldots, X_n(a)$ in the n-dimensional attribute (consequence) space $X = X_1 X_2 \ldots X_n$.

The problem faced by the decision maker is to choose an alternative a in A so that the maximum pleasure with the payoff or consequence, $(X_1(a), \ldots, X_n(a))$, results. It is always possible to compare the values of each $X_i(a)$ for different alternatives, but in most situations, the values $X_i(a)$ and $X_j(a)$ for i not equal to j cannot be meaningfully compared, since they may be measured in totally different units. It would be convenient if we had a scaler utility value, as in our earlier efforts in this section. Therefore, a scaler-valued function defined on the attributes $(X_1, \ldots, X_n)$ is sought that will allow comparison of the alternatives across the attributes. The interested reader is referred to extended discussions in Keeney and Raiffa [24] and in Ref. 4. A summary of some of these is presented here, since major model management components of many DSS are based on decision analysis theory and practice.

A primary interest in multiattribute utility theory (MAUT) is to structure and assess a utility function of the form

$$U[X_1(a), \ldots, X_n(a)] = f\{U_1[X_1(a)], \ldots, U_n[X_n(a)]\} = \sum_{j=1}^{n} w_j U_j(a)$$

where U_i is a utility function over the single attribute X_i and f aggregates the values of the single-attribute utility functions so as to enable one to compute the scaler utility of the alternatives. We assume that the utility functions U and U_i are continuous, monotonic, and bounded. Usually, they are scaled by $U(x^+) = 1$, $U(x^-) = 0$, $U_i(x_i^+) = 1$, and $U_i(x_i^-) = 0$ for all i. Here, $x^+ = (x_1^+, x_2^+, \ldots, x_n^+)$ designates the most desirable consequence and the expression $x^- = (x_1^-, x_2^-, \ldots, x_n^-)$ denotes the least desirable consequence. The symbols x_i^+ and x_i^- refer to the best and worst consequence, respectively, for each attribute X_i. Thus, we have $x_i^+ = X_i(a^+)$, where a^+ is the best alternative for attribute i, and $x_i^- = X_i(a^-)$, where a^- is the worst alternative for attribute i. In the simplest situations, additive independence of attributes [24,4] exists such that the MAUT function may be written as

$$U(a_i) = w_1 U_1(a_i) + w_2 U_2(a_i) + \cdots + w_n U_n(a_i)$$

Here, the w_j are the weights of the various attributes of the decision alternative a_i and the U_j are the attribute scores for the alternative. It turns out that precisely this same form of expression is valid in the case where risk is involved. In cases where there is probabilistic risk, we use the utility of the multiattributed outcomes rather than the utility of the alternatives.

We have just described very briefly the case of certainty in a multiattribute decision-making framework. Associated with each alternative is a known consequence that follows with certainty from implementation of the alternative. The foundations for decision making under risk are provided by the classical work of von Neumann and Morgenstern [32] and we have discussed this subject earlier in this section. The implications of this work are that probabilities and utilities can be used to calculate the expected utility of each alternative and that alternatives with higher expected utilities should be preferred over those with lower ones. We simply calculate the scaler utility function of an outcome and use this scaler utility as we have done previously. It is important to note that these are *normative* concepts.

Even though the theory and procedures of multiattribute decision analysis are conceptually straightforward, there are circumstances that make its implementation complex. Putting the methodology into practice is much more involved than one might initially believe. Each of the foregoing decision analysis steps requires substantial interaction between the analyst and the decision maker if useful results are to be obtained. There are a number of subtleties associated with scaling and, of course, a number of simplified approaches that can be utilized [33].

A decision observation based approach is also of value in decision support. This consists of observing decision behavior in real-world or simulated real-world situations, and then inferring the parameters of a prestructured model from these observations. The research of Hammond and his colleagues on social judgment theory [25,26] makes extensive use of this concept. Techniques based on this approach have been shown to be particularly useful in policy formulation and analysis and are often called "policy capture" or "bootstrapping" techniques. Use of regression analysis is central to this *social judgment theory* approach. A number of other studies also make use of regression analysis based models to determine the parameters of a decision model. In one early study, for example, Dawes [34] used a regression analysis model to screen applications for admission to a graduate program.

3.2.3 Screening-Based Approaches, and Imprecise Information

One way to reduce the effort required in a decision selection is to accomplish a preliminary screening to eliminate alternatives that are quite inferior. Especially in prescriptive situations, screening procedures will often be needed to reduce the time, stress, and effort demanded from decision makers. Screening methods are generally intended to identify and reduce the size of the nondominated set of alternatives, that is, those that are not bettered by at least one other alternative on each and every one of the attributes of importance, through use of behaviorally relevant and easily available information.

One of the first to develop a screening method for decision making with incomplete knowledge of probabilities was Fishburn [35]. He was concerned with the use of incomplete information on probabilities in comparing alternative strategies in a typical formulation of decision making under risk. The criterion of choice or strategy that should normatively be used is the principle of maximum expected utility, so that the decision maker seeks a strategy a^+ which is the maximum over i of the expected utility of alternatives a_i. The utility function $U_j(a_i)$ is a precisely assessed multiattribute utility function defined on the set of possible strategies $\{a_i\}$, and p_j is a measure of the likelihood of the possible state of nature j given that particular strategy a_i was selected. The imprecise forms of the measure of probability that Fishburn considered were

1. No information about p_j
2. Ordinal measures (e.g., $p_1 \geq p_2 \geq p_3$) in terms of an ordering of p_j
3. Linear inequalities (e.g., $p_1 + p_2 \geq p_3$) in terms of ordering of the sums of the p_j
4. Bounded interval measures (e.g., $\alpha_i \leq p_i \leq \alpha_i + \beta_i$)

The search for the best alternative is, in this approach, performed by pairwise comparisons of expected utility among candidate strategies. Because of the restricted form of the available information on the p_j, it turns out that the search for the best alternative can be put, in general, into a straightforward linear programming problem.

Sarin [36] proposed a screening procedure similar to that of Fishburn with the additional assumption of additive independence on the set of attributes. This assumption simplifies the search for dominance structures and results in a procedure that can be formulated as a mathematical programming problem. The parameters of the mathematical programming formulation include probabilities, importance weights, and single-attribute utility functions. A simple procedure is then developed for the case when the probabilities and the importance weights are precisely known and utilities are stated in the form of linear inequalities, thereby resulting in simple linear programming formulations.

The *process* of choosing among multiattributed alternatives often involves an initial search for a dominance structure and ultimate identification of a set of *nondominated alternatives*. A nondominated alternative is one that is better than each other alternative on at least one attribute, as we have noted. In practice, in many decision situations, the decision maker typically "adjusts" the structure of the decision situation and parameter values within this structure so as to identify a dominance structure that contains a single nondominant alternative. In a situation in which there is a single nondominant alternative, that alternative must dominate all the others. This search may involve rational activities, such as aggregation of attributes and compensatory trade-offs through determination of judgmental weights. Alternatively, it may involve various rules that may be quite flawed. Examples of such rules are

1. *Lexicographic ordering*, in which the best alternative on the most important attribute is selected.
2. *Sequential pairwise comparison* of alternatives using a preference relation that is a function of the two alternatives being compared.

In this latter case, nontransitive preferences may easily result due to the fact that the contextual relation used to determine preferences will often change from one pairwise comparison to another and, often, this change will be subtle and unrecognized. A simple example of this is the statement, "I prefer house A to house B because it has a much nicer living room. I prefer house B to house C because it is closer to work." It may well be that house C is closer to work than house A is! We must be careful to resist the temptation to say that $A \succ B$ and $B \succ C$ and that, because of *transitivity*, we have $A \succ C$.)

The decision evaluation model discussed here [37] is based on the hypothesis that people are able to evaluate alternative plans and decisions effectively and with low stress when a clear dominance pattern exists among alternatives that allows the establishment of a sufficiently discriminatory priority structure. We will present some concepts for the design and evaluation of an interactive decision support system that combines, or permits the combination of, several evaluation rules and contingency structures frequently used as a basis for evaluation, prioritization, judgment, and choice. The support framework and model encourage search for a dominance structure that is behaviorally realistic and rational, from both a substantive and procedural viewpoint. The support system is called *alternative ranking interactive aid based on dominance structural information elicitation* (ARIADNE).* The discussion that follows is based on Ref. 37.

The efforts describe here concern decision-making situations under certainty and under risk, primarily for the single-decision node case. The decision situation structural model therefore may represent decisions under certainty or under risk. This formulation allows the consideration of a variety of imprecisely known parameters such as attribute trade-off weights, outcome state values on lowest-level attributes, event outcome probabilities, and various combinations of these. It does not formally represent decisions under uncertainty, since no probabilities of these imprecisely known parameters are assumed or needed. Parameter needs are determined from the structure of the decision situation, as elicited from the decision maker during the formulation and analysis steps of the decision support process.

The attribute tree representing the features of decision outcome states may be structured and/or parameterized in a top-down or bottom-up fashion through ARIADNE. A single-level structure or a multiple-level hierarchical structure of attributes may be used, the choice being at the discretion of the decision maker. Multiple-decision node situations may be approached through a goal-directed decision structuring method in which the growth of the structure of alternative decisions and event outcomes is guided by sensitivitylike computations [38–40] obtained by use of the ARIADNE algorithms.

In use of this approach, parameters are elicited from the decision maker in the form of equalities and inequality bounds for probabilities, attribute weights, and attribute scores or utilities. A variety of mathematical programming approaches and graph theory could be used to generate interactive displays of preference diagrams. These mathematical programming approaches are used to determine dominance structures for alternative prioritization that are based on parameter information elicited from the decision maker. We have been able to show that a linear programming approach will

---

*Ariadne, a character in Greek mythology, was the daughter of Minos. She gave Theseus a thread, thereby aiding him in escaping from the labyrinth.

yield necessary and sufficient conditions for determination of a priority structure. This requires that we elicit structural parameter information in a restricted form which we denote the *behaviorally consistent information set* (BCIS). Commonly, this BCIS will be in such a form that solution of the generally nonlinear programming problems associated with determination of dominance structures can be replaced by the solution of simple computationally amenable linear programs with bounded variables. The major simplification associated with eliciting parameter imprecision in a prespecified structural format, however, is in the natural language dialog needed to establish a model of the decision situation.

The set of activities needed to use the single-stage, or single-decision node, version of ARIADNE follows:

1. Formulation of the decision situation
    1.1 Define the problem or issue that requires decision making by identification of its elements in terms of needs, and constraints or bounds on the issue.
    1.2 Identify a value system with which to evaluate alternative courses of action, and identify objectives or attributes of the outcomes of possible decisions or alternative courses of actions.
    1.3 Identify possible alternative courses of action or operation generation.
2. Analysis of the decision situation
    2.1 Determine the outcome scenarios.
    2.2 Identify the decision situation structural model elements. These should include those elements or factors from the issue formulation framework that appear pertinent for incorporation into a decision situation structural model.
    2.3 Structure the decision situation model elements.
        2.3.1 Structure a decision tree.
        2.3.2 Structure an information acquisition and processing tree—which may be part of the basic decision tree.
        2.3.3 Structure an attribute tree or objectives hierarchy.
    2.4 Determine independence conditions among elements of the attribute tree and decision alternatives.
    2.5 Identify potential for the use of deficient information-processing heuristics, and provide appropriate debiasing procedures.
    2.6 Determine impacts of, or outcomes that may result from, alternative courses of action.
    2.7 Encode uncertainty elements in the form of event outcome probabilities, or bounds on these, to the extent possible.
    2.8 Identify risk-aversion coefficients, if needed, to the extent possible.
    2.9 Identify preference or value functions, or bounds on these functions, to the extent possible.

2.10 Identify attribute weights, or bounds on these functions, as much as possible.

2.11 Identify wholistic preferences among alternatives to the extent possible.

2.12 Identify possible disjunctive and conjunctive aspects, or thresholds for attributes, of identified alternative courses of action.

3. Evaluation and interpretation of the outcome of alternative courses of action

   3.1 Identify a decision-aiding protocol or plan for evaluation and interpretation of the decision situation.

   3.2 Identify potential for use of deficient judgment heuristics.

   3.3 Use conjunctive and/or disjunctive scanning to eliminate deficient alternatives and retain alternatives meeting minimum acceptability criteria across attributes.

   3.4 Determine the maximum amount of domination information possible.

      3.4.1 Display domination digraph.

      3.4.2 Identify alternative courses of action that could not be among the N most preferred alternatives. Normally, these are deleted from further consideration.

      3.4.3 If the decision maker can select an alternative for implementation by wholistic judgment, or prioritize the remaining alternative set through heuristic elimination, then go to step 3.6 of evaluation and interpretation.

      3.4.4 If a choice cannot be made, assess further information about values of imprecisely known parameters by iterating back to steps 2.6 through 2.12 of analysis, then return to step 1 of the evaluation and interpretation. Many possibilities exist for obtaining greater alternative evaluation specificity, such as

        3.4.4.1 Setting higher aspiration levels or aspects.

        3.4.4.2 Moving up the attribute tree by determination of a subset of attribute trade-off weights.

        3.4.4.3 Tightening bounds on event outcome probabilities, possibly through information-processing updates.

        3.4.4.4 Tightening bounds on the event outcome probabilities, possibly through information-processing updates.

        3.4.4.5 Tightening bounds on values or preference functions.

   3.5 If the decision maker has provided (partial) wholistic preferences as part of the analysis effort, use these with the inverse aiding feature of the aid to determine bounds on attribute weights implied by these preferences such as to provide learning feedback to decision maker.

   3.6 Conduct sensitivity analysis. Provide the decision maker with an indication of how sensitive the optimal action alternative, or prioritization of alternatives, is with respect to changes in values and information about impacts.

3.7 Evaluate validity and veracity of the approach. Encourage judgment concerning whether the formulation, analysis, and interpretation are sound. If not, encourage appropriate modification to structure and parameters associated with the decision situation, including identification of additional attributes and alternative courses of action. Then, iterate back to an appropriate step and continue.

There are some realistic behavioral considerations that appear to warrant a MBMS of this sort. Among the behavioral characteristics of the decision maker that strongly influence aiding requirements and considerations are the facts that the decision maker

1. Is often impatient with time-consuming and stressful assessment procedures that seem unrelated to the decision task at hand.
2. Wants to see some preliminary results promptly if these are needed or wanted.*
3. May lack interest in interacting directly with complex quantitative procedures for decision aiding that do not seem tailored to the specific contingency task structure of the issue at hand; and, as a consequence,
4. Requires a decision aiding approach that adapts to the decision-making style appropriate for the decision maker in the given contingency task structure.

For each of these reasons, use of an interactive approach that allows imprecise and incomplete information is desirable.

A number of considerations influence the most desirable interaction between the decision maker and the support system.† The interaction here is such that there results a list of objectives and an objectives hierarchy, a list of alternatives, and a list of outcomes for each alternative. The extent of the need for the use of these identified lists will vary greatly with the "expertise" of the decision maker. A major task in the formulation and analysis portion of the aiding effort is to assist the decision maker in identifying these lists in a behaviorally relevant and realistic manner. It should also be possible to ensure, to the extent possible, that

1. The foregoing lists are reasonably complete.
2. The lowest level objectives are additively independent.
3. The alternatives are mutually exclusive.
4. The outcomes that follow from each alternative are mutually exclusive and exhaustive.

This simplification of conditional dependencies, while not absolutely necessary to use the procedure, reduces the complexity associated with combining evidence and produces results whose trustworthiness is reasonably well assured. The nature of the interactive process is such that iterative changes can be made in terms of addition or

---

*Most decision analytic approaches produce no output until completion of all of the analysis.
†The support system may consist of the DSS and an analyst as needed to provide for effective use of the system.

deletion of alternatives and attributes. Nevertheless, there are significant advantages in attempting to be reasonably complete at the start of the interpretation portion of the process.

The result of the process should be such that the decision maker is able to provide, following behaviorally realistic elicitation procedures, information regarding

1. Alternative scores on lowest-level attributes
2. Trade-off weights
3. Probabilities
4. Relative risk-aversion coefficients

Alternatively, if precise values for this is difficult to obtain, the approach described here permits use of appropriate ratios or bounds on these quantities that represent the precision that the decision maker believes suitable or is capable of providing for the given decision situation.

When implemented in a DSS, the DGMS presentation to the decision maker should be such that the decision maker is able to respond to the question: *Has sufficient preference and structural information been elicited from and provided to the decision maker for alternative selection, or is more information required for identification of a dominance structure that is relevant and appropriate for quality decision support?*

If the decision maker feels that an alternative can be selected for action implementation at any stage in the interactive aiding effort, the analyst must be able to encourage decision-maker judgment concerning whether the issue formulation, analysis, and interpretation are sound. If these three items are not perceived as sound by the decision maker, the analyst must be able to encourage appropriate structural and parameter value modification, typically by means of sensitivity analysis, to ensure effective, explicable, and valid decision support. If the decision maker cannot choose an alternative from among those considered, the analyst must be capable of eliciting further structural and/or parameter information to enhance suitable selection of alternative courses of action.

Figure 3.9 presents some salient features of this dominance process model for search, discovery, judgment, and choice. The support system design paradigm is based on a process model of decision making in which a person perceives an issue that may require a change in the existing course of action. On the basis of a framing of the decision situation, one or more alternative courses of action, in addition to the present option which may be continued, are identified. A preliminary screening of the alternatives, using conjunctive and disjunctive scanning, may eliminate all but one alternative course of action. Unconflicted adherence to the present course of action or unconflicted change to a new option may well be the meta-strategy for judgment and choice that is adopted if the decision maker perceives that the decision situation is a familiar one and that the stakes are not so high that a more thorough search and deliberation are needed.* Figure 3.10 presents several two-dimensional attribute score graphs and associated dominance digraphs.

---

*This is a time–stress–experiential familiarity based model to decision making. It will be discussed further in Chapter 6.

3.2 DECISION MODELS   111

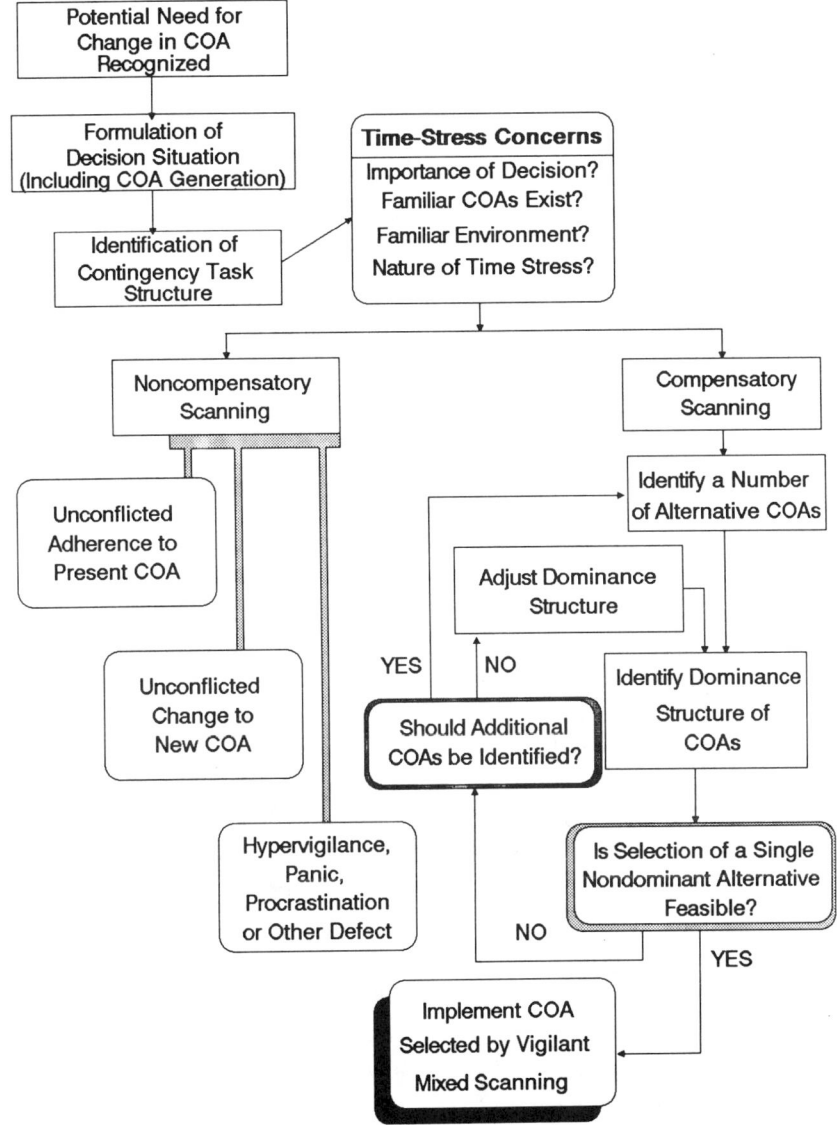

Figure 3.9 Mixed scanning through dominance structuring.

A realistic decision support process is necessarily iterative and the MBMS must then support iterative use of a DSS. There appear to be two primary implications with respect to the interpretation efforts achieved by the MBMS described here. The MBMS allows for revision in the elicited structure of the decision situation and for the identification of new options as awareness of the decision situation grows. Also, there is no requirement for the decision maker to quantify parameters beyond the level felt appropriate for the situation at hand. If the decision maker feels comfortable

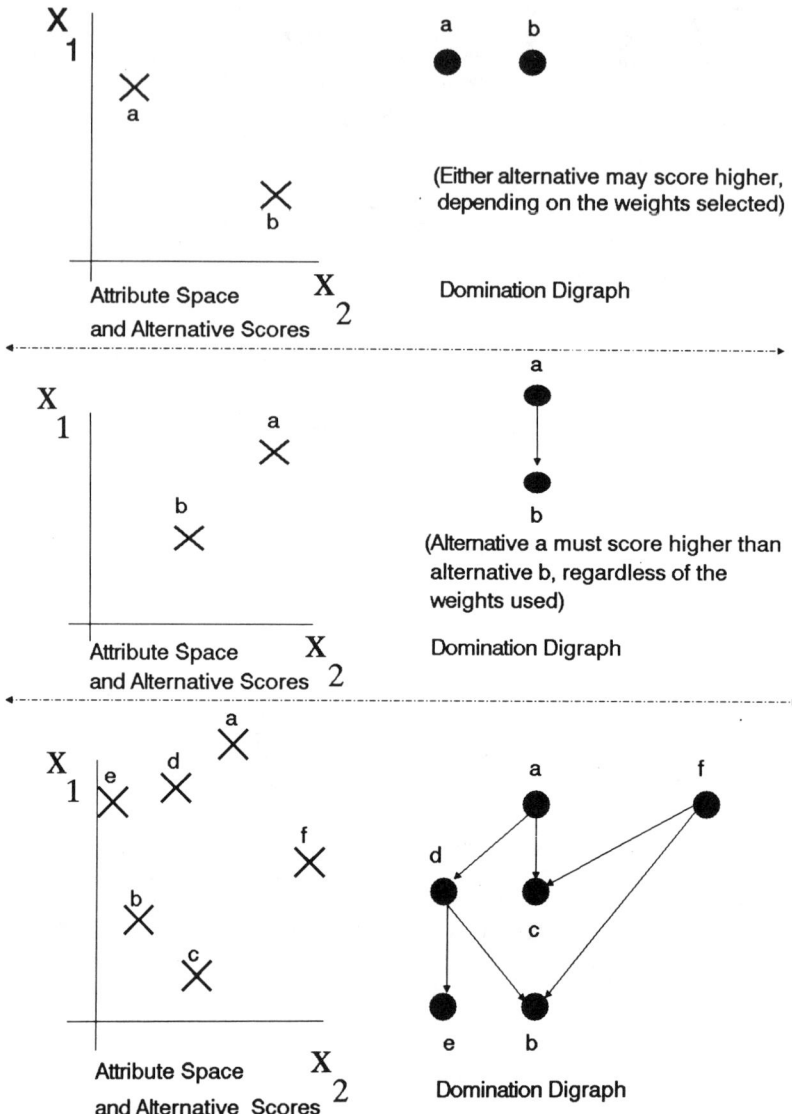

Figure 3.10 Two dimensional alternative scores and associated domination digraphs.

in exercising precision with respect to factual outcomes, this is perfectly acceptable and desirable, but parameter imprecision should be allowed in a behaviorally realistic support process.

ARIADNE permits parameter imprecision in order to satisfy this quantification relevancy requirement. The decision maker is encouraged to specify precise values or numerical ranges for facts and values. Thus, we allow, for instance, expressions for alternative scores on attributes in the form $0.2 \leq v_i(a) \leq 0.5$, weights associated with attributes in the form $0.2 \le w_i \le 0.4$, and probabilities resulting from an alternative in the form $0.3 \le P_i(A) \le 0.45n$. We allow ordinal representations in the linear forms $v_i(a) \le v_i(b) \le v_i(c)$, $2w_i < w_j < w_k$, $p_j \le p_i(a) \le 3p_k(a)$, or in similar forms. Quantification of imprecision in the form of numerical bounds on parameters is always such that it leads to behaviorally consistent information sets (BCIS). Sometimes, totally ordinal information may need further quantification in order to make the precision and rigidity of the mathematics correspond to the intentions of the decision maker in making a purely ordinal specification. This is generally not needed to obtain solutions but rather to obtain parametric models that are faithful to the understandings of the decision maker. For example, the ordinal alternative value score inequalities $0 \le v_i(a) \le v_i(b) \le v_i(c) \le 1$ are satisfied by the relations $0 \le v_i(a) \le 1 - 2t$, $w \le v_i(b) \le 1 - t$, $2w \le v_i(c) \le 1$ for small positive t and w, which in the limit become zero. It will usually not be the case that the decision maker would express this much imprecision and would wish to see it more fully quantified to reflect generally subjective beliefs. It is, therefore, important that a simple and informative display of value scores, weights, and probabilities be provided to the decision maker. This will enhance interactive use of the support system and will enable learning of the impact of these parameters, and associated imprecision, on decisions. Accordingly, we see that a well-designed DGMS is very supportive of effective use of a MBMS.

The Attribute Tree and Decisions Under Certainty. It is possible to use either a hierarchical tree structure or a single-level structure of attributes, each of which is shown in Figure 3.11. Fortunately, the relations between the weights associated with the tree structure and the single-level structure are easily determined and are also given in Figure 3.11. Linear inequalities in terms of hierarchical weights or weight ratios w_j^i become linear inequalities in terms of single-level weights p_i. It is this fact that allows us to use the single-level representation and still make assessment in terms of the hierarchical weights w_j^i at any level of the hierarchy.

For the case of decision making under outcome certainty, we know that the ith outcome x_i follows from the ith alternative. We thus have for the value of the ith alternative, $v(a_i)$, the expression

$$v(a_i) = \sum_{k=1}^{N} \sigma_k v_k(a_i)$$

We say that alternative i has a higher value score than alternative j when

$$\delta v_{ij\,min} = \min_\Gamma \delta v_{ij} = \min_\Gamma \sum_{k=1}^{N} \sigma_k [v_k(a_i) - v_k(a_j)]$$

$$= \min_\Gamma \sigma^T [v(a_i) - v(a_j)] \ge 0$$

where Γ denotes the set of imprecise parameters over which the extremization is conducted. σ and $\mathbf{v}$ are vectors with components σ_k and v_k. For the case where weights and attribute scores for each attribute are functionally independent, this expression becomes quite easy to evaluate. In many cases, the $v_k(a_i)$ are elicited so as to be functionally independent of the $v_k(a_j)$, and then we have

114 MODEL-BASE MANAGEMENT SYSTEMS

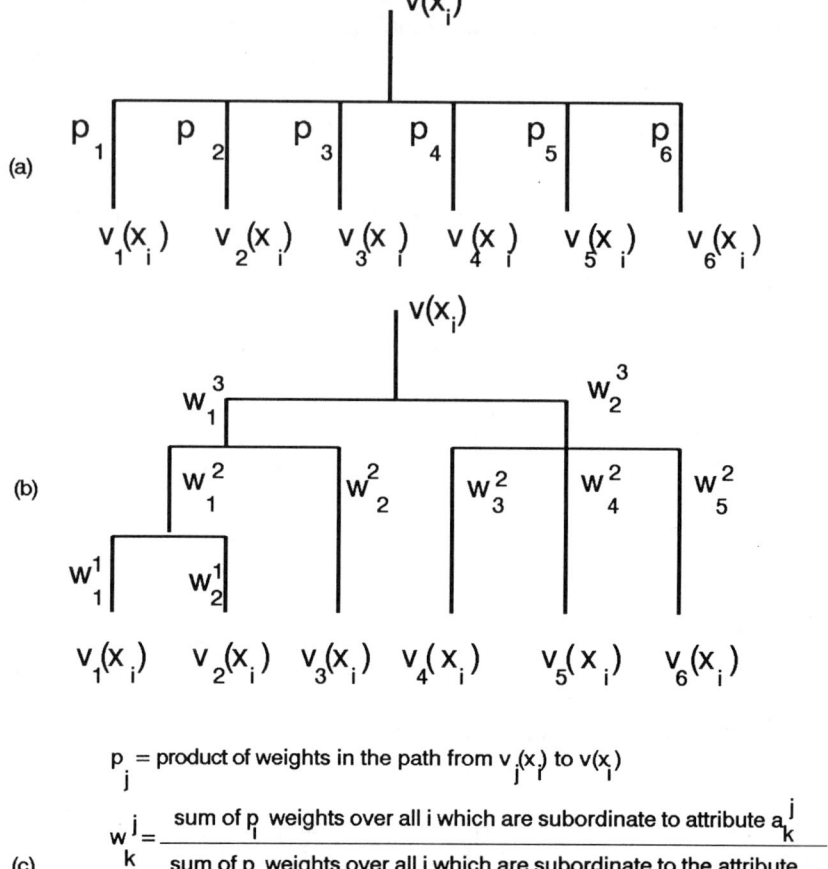

Figure 3.11 (a) Single- and (b) multiple-level attribute structure, and (c) weight relations.

$$\delta v_{ij \, min} = \min_\sigma \sigma^T [v(i, j)] \geq 0$$

where $v(i, j)$ is a vector given by

$$v(i, j) = \min v(a_i) - \max v(a_j) = v^-(a_i) - v^+(a_j)$$

where v^- and v^+ denote the minimum and maximum values of the value-score vector on the specified alternative. Determination of the solution for $v(i, j)$ requires a solution of a linear program (LP) for each ij pair. If A alternatives exist, we will need to solve no more that $A(A - 1)$ LPs to determine $\mathbf{v}(i, j)$. We may need to solve fewer LPs in many cases. Generally, these linear programs are extraordinarily simple to solve and result in necessary and sufficient conditions for $a_i > a_j$.

Example. As one simple example, let us consider the alternative-score matrix on the lowest-level attributes as shown in Figure 3.12. We assume that the decision maker specified a single-level attribute tree and is able to estimate the weights $0.1 \leq \sigma_1 \leq 0.2$, $0.2 \leq \sigma_2\ 0.4$, and $0.3 \leq \sigma_3 \leq 0.7$. Of course, these weights must sum to one, and so we have $\sigma_1 + \sigma_2 + \sigma_3 = 1$. We have already specified utilities in the max–min form $\mathbf{v}^+\ \mathbf{v}^-$. Therefore, we can use these values directly. To see whether $a > b$, we need to see whether $\delta v_{ab(\min)} \geq 0$ is satisfied. Consequently, we examine (in component form)

$$\delta_{ab(\min)} = \min_\sigma \{[0\,|\,1\,|\,0] - [1\,|\,0\,|\,.8]\}\,[\sigma_1\,|\,\sigma_2\,|\,\sigma_3]^T \geq 0$$

This is an LP with bounded variables, a particularly simple form of linear program. We assign maximum weights to the most negative $V_a^+ - V_b^+$ components until we are all out of weight. The weights are found by setting all weights at their minimum value and then allocating additional weight where it will do the most good. So we use $r_1 = 0.2$, $r_3 = 0.6$, $r_2 = 0.2$ and get $\delta V_{ab(\min)} = -1(0.2) + 1(0.2) - 0.8(0.6) = -0.48$, which is not greater than zero. Thus, it is not possible to have $a > b$. To see if $b > a$, we examine

$$\delta_{ba(\min)} = \min_\sigma \{[1\,|\,0\,|\,.6] - [0\,|\,1\,|\,0]\}\,[\sigma_1\,|\,\sigma_2\,|\,\sigma_3]^T \geq 0$$

We use $\sigma_2 = 0.4$, $\sigma_3 = 0.5$, $\sigma_1 = 0.1$ and get $\delta V_{ba(\min)} \geq 0$. So we conclude that $b > a$. We determine that $c > b$ and $b > d$, using this same procedure but with the appropriate vectors for those alternatives, such that we have the dominance structure of Figure 3.13. Hence, c is the preferred alternative here.

It may well be, however, that the decision maker visualizes the attributes in a

Alternative	Attribute 1 Max Score	Attribute 1 Min Score	Attribute 2 Max Score	Attribute 2 Min Score	Attribute 3 Max Score	Attribute 3 Min Score
a	0	0	1	1	0	0
b	1	1	0	0	0.8	0.61
c	0.5	0.5	0.4	0.2	1	1
d	0.4	0.2	0.18	0.1	0.7	0.5

Figure 3.12 Alternative value score on attributes.

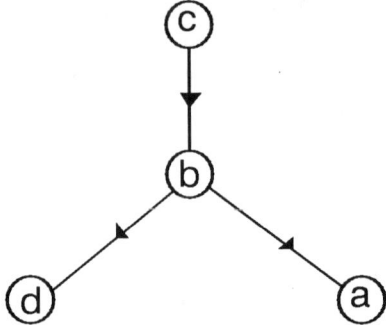

Figure 3.13 Dominance structure for example in text.

hierarchical form, as shown in Figure 3.14. The same alternative-score matrix used earlier is still appropriate here. If the decision maker feels comfortable in evaluating weights associated with attributes 1 and 2 but not the weight associated with attribute 3, then a multilevel hierarchy of attributes may be assumed. The analyst could attempt to assist by aggregating weights up the attribute tree. Alternatively, it could be determined whether or not the relationship between attributes 1 and 2 is sufficient to establish a single nondominated alternative by converting to the single-level weight form.

We will illustrate calculations using the first approach. Suppose that the decision maker says $\sigma_1^1 \leq \sigma_2^1$. Then, the analyst might use this ordinal expression or might convert to a cardinal representation and say that at level 1, the weights are such that

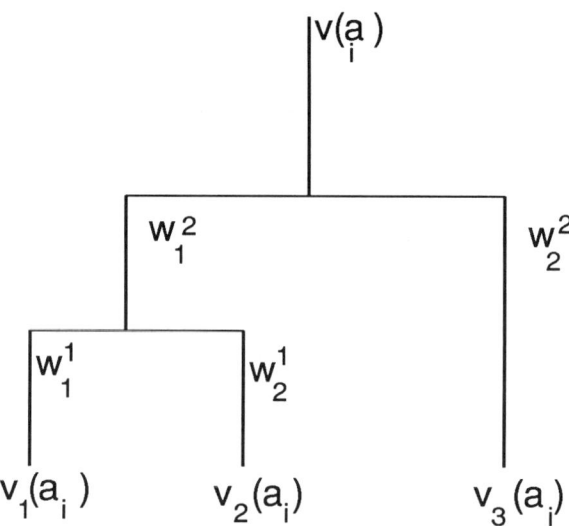

Figure 3.14 Hierarchical attribute tree.

$0 \le \sigma_1^1 \le 0.5$ and $0.5 < \sigma_2^1 \le 1.0$. Following a request to be more explicit, perhaps the decision maker indicates that $0.2 \le \sigma_1^1 \le 0.4$ and $0.6 \le \sigma_2^1 \le 0.8$. We now aggregate attributes 1 and 2. Based on this information, we can calculate a maximum and a minimum score for the utilities of the alternatives on the second-level attribute σ_1^2. We obtain the aggregated value-score matrix shown in Figure 3.15. No domination pattern exists at all with the information available thus far, so we must go further in our efforts to discover one.

As often occurs in problems of this sort, the level-2 alternative scores are not in proper 0–1 range. If the decision maker feels more comfortable in seeing these scaled over a 0–1 range, this can be easily done. Otherwise, the decision maker is asked to consider the difference in scores (0.8 on alternative a and 0.14 on alternative d) from maximum to minimum on weight σ_1^2 and express the importance weight of the difference on attribute 3 of the difference between the maximum and minimum scores on alternatives c and a. Suppose that inequalities in the form $0.2 \le \sigma_1^2 \le 0.35$ and $0.65 \le \sigma_2^2 \le 0.8$ finally result. We can then determine a table of maximum and minimum alternative scores, as shown in Figure 3.16. Thus, we have the preference digraph of Figure 3.17, which is slightly different from that obtained earlier. The conclusion is the same, however. Alternative c is the best alternative. This particular approach used to aggregate up the attribute tree yields only sufficient conditions for one alternative dominating another alternative. It has the advantage, though, of providing a display of maximum and minimum scores across alternatives after each aggregation up the tree. This is not obtained through use of the necessary and sufficient conditions, however.

One way to avoid the problem with the best and worst alternative scores on each attribute not being uniquely anchored on one and zero after aggregating up the attribute tree may be to define an ideal best and an ideal worst alternative. The ideal best alternative will have a score of one on each lowest-level attribute, and the ideal worst will have a score of zero on each lowest-level attribute. The decision maker should still specify the weight bounds $0.2 \le \sigma_1^1 \le 0.4$ and $0.6 \le \sigma_2^1 \le 0.8$ obtained

Alternative	Attribute w_1^2 Max Score	Attribute w_1^2 Min Score	Attribute w_2^2 Max Score	Attribute w_2^2 Min Score
a	0.8	0.6	0	0
b	0.4	0.2	0.8	0.6
c	0.44	0.24	1	1
d	0.268	0.14	0.7	0.5

Figure 3.15 Attribute-score ranges.

Alternative	Maximum Score	Minimum Score
a	0.28	0.12
b	0.72	0.46
c	0.888	0.734
d	0.6136	0.374

Figure 3.16 Final alternative-score ranges.

earlier. Now the aggregation up the attribute tree preserves the anchor over zero to one on alternative scores for the ideal alternative, and we obtain the result shown in Figure 3.18. Elicitation of swing weights might now be more comfortably accomplished than in the case where no pair of alternatives is uniquely anchored at zero and one on one or more aggregated attributes.

The question concerning whether the single-level attribute tree or the hierarchical tree is more suitable in a given situation is difficult to answer. If the decision maker is comfortable with the single-level tree and is willing to express information concerning all attribute weights, then this structure is certainly more convenient to use and very likely is more appropriate as well. We can easily convert from one representation to the other. The only essential difference between the two approaches is that it is "natural" when aggregating up the attribute tree to indicate maximum and minimum scores on each alternative. Use of these scores to determine preferences results in only sufficient conditions for preference determination.

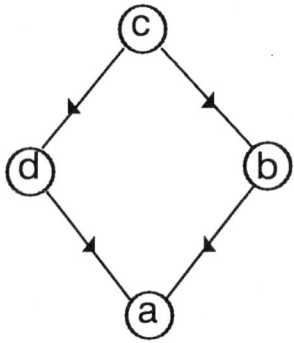

Figure 3.17 An example of a dominance stucture.

Alternative	Attribute w_1^2 Max Score	Attribute w_1^2 Min Score	Attribute w_2^2 Max Score	Attribute w_2^2 Min Score
a	0.8	0.6	0	0
b	0.4	0.2	0.8	0.6
c	0.44	0.24	1	1
d	0.268	0.14	0.7	0.5
ideal best	1	1	1	1
ideal worst	0	0	0	0

Figure 3.18 Attribute-score ranges.

Decisions Under Risk. For the decision-under-risk situation, we calculate the expected utility of alternative a from

$$U(a) = \sum_{i=1}^{M} p_i(a)\, U_i(a)$$

where M outcome states can result from alternative a. State x_i occurs with probability $p_i(a)$, and the utility of this state is $U_i(a)$. This utility function will generally be a multiattribute utility function. When additive independence conditions are satisfied, we have

$$U_i(a) = \sum_{j=1}^{N} \sigma_j\, U_{ji}(a)$$

where $U_{ji}(a)$ is the utility of the jth attribute of outcome state i associated with alternative a, and σ_j is the trade-off weight associated with the jth attribute. Generally, the decision situation should be structured so that the weights are alternative and outcome state independent. If this is not the case, there is probably a modeling deficiency in the framing of the decision situation structural model.

Combination of the latter two equations results in

$$U(a) = \sum_{i=1}^{M} \sum_{j=1}^{N} p_i(a)\, U_{ji}(a)\, \sigma_j = \mathbf{p}^T(a)\, \mathbf{U}(a)\, \sigma$$

where $\mathbf{p}^T(a)$ and σ are vectors of dimension M and N, and $\mathbf{U}(a)$ is an $M \times N$ von Neumann–Morgenstern cardinal utility function expressed as a matrix. Alternative a is guaranteed to be preferred to alternative b if

$$\min_\Theta\, [\mathbf{p}^T(a)\, \mathbf{U}(a) - \mathbf{p}^T(b)\, \mathbf{U}(b)]\, \sigma \geq 0$$

where Θ represents the set of all possible values that the various parameters can assume.

The simplest case occurs when probabilities and utilities are known precisely and when only the weights are imprecise. We will obtain $A(A - 1)$ linear programs to solve for all possible alternative preferences if the weight set inclusion is described by linear inequalities. We obtain necessary and sufficient conditions for preference inequalities. In a similar way, if only the probabilities or only the across attributes are imprecise, we may solve a set of $A(A - 1)$ linear programs to obtain necessary and sufficient conditions for alternative pair preferences if the precision is expressed as a set of linear inequalities.

If probabilities are known precisely, then we can obtain necessary and sufficient conditions for preferences. In all other cases,

- Utilities specified precisely, probabilities and weights imprecisely;
- Weights specified precisely, probabilities and utilities imprecisely; and
- Weights, probabilities, and utilities specified imprecisely,

obtaining necessary and sufficient conditions for optimality of linear programming solutions will generally not be possible unless the imprecision can be expressed by means of simple numerical inequalities, such as $0.2 \leq p_i(a) \leq 0.35$, in which case we can still make simple computations. The major conclusion is that it is a relatively straightforward matter to incorporate imprecision, in the form of numerical inequalities, into any combination of utility scores for lowest-level attributes, probabilities of event outcomes, and attribute weights. If probabilities and weights are not simultaneously imprecise and we have linear inequalities and do not have simple numerical inequalities, then we must solve quadratic programming problems and are no longer able to get necessary and sufficient conditions for preferences.

Additional research has been accomplished on this concept. A rather complete discussion of this simplest decision-under-certainty version of ARIADNE is contained in Ref. 41. Extensions to the stochastic case are presented in Refs. 42–44, and an evaluation of the approach is contained in Ref. 45. An extention to incorporate rule-based knowledge is presented in Ref. 46. This effort addresses the notion of a model as a set of rule-based statements about the world.

3.3 MODEL-BASE MANAGEMENT

As we have noted, an effective model-base management system (MBMS) will make the structural and algorithmic aspects of model organization and associated data processing transparent from users of the MBMS [1]. Such tasks as specifying explicit relationships between models to indicate formats for models and which model outputs are input to other models are not placed directly on the user of a MBMS but handled directly by the system. Figure 3.19 is a generic illustration of a MBMS. It shows a collection of models or model base, a model-base manager, a model dictionary,* and connections to the DBMS and the DGMS.

*That will perform essentially the same functions for a MBMS that a data dictionary performs for a DBMS.

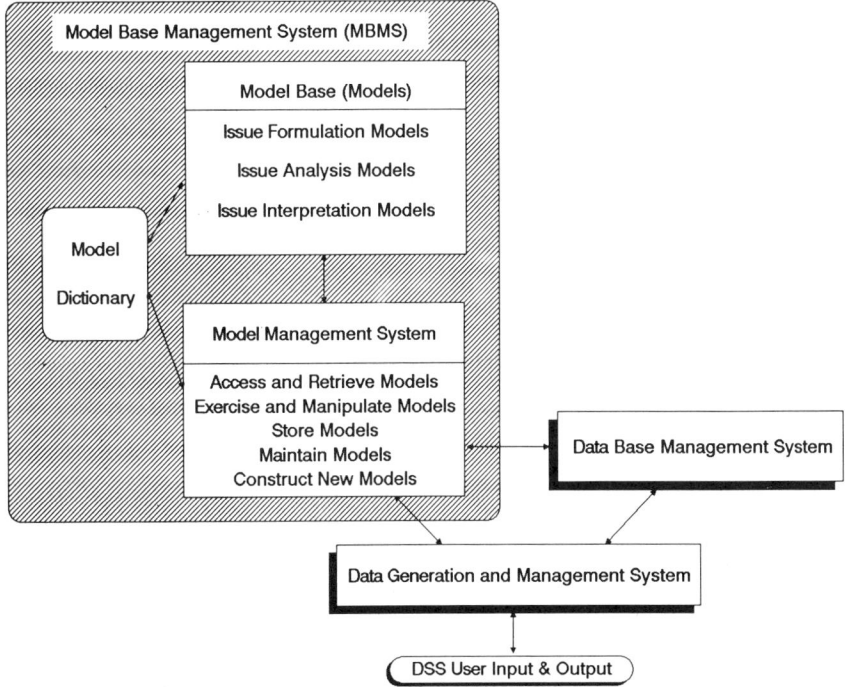

Figure 3.19 Prototypical structure of model management system.

There are a number of capabilities that should be provided by an integrated and shared MBMS of a DSS [47,48]. These include *model construction, model maintenance, model storage, model manipulation*, and *model access* [43]. There are several desirable MBMS attributes.

1. *Control*. The DSS user should be provided with a spectrum of control. The system should support both fully automated as well as manual selection of models that seem most useful to the user for an intended application. This will enable the user to proceed at the problem-solving pace that is most comfortable for the user's experiential familiarity with the task at hand. It should be possible for the user to introduce subjective information and to not have to provide full information. Also, the control mechanism should be such that the DSS user can obtain a recommendation for action with this partial information at essentially any point in the problem-solution process.
2. *Flexibility*. The DSS user should be able to develop part of the solution to the task at hand using one approach and then be able to switch to another modeling approach, if this appears preferable. Any change or modification in the model base will be made available to all DSS users.
3. *Feedback*. The MBMS of the DSS should provide sufficient feedback to enable the user to be aware of the state of the problem-solving process at any point in time.

4. *Interface.* The DSS user should feel comfortable with the specific model from the MBMS that is in use at any given time. The user should not have to laboriously supply inputs when he or she does not wish to do this.
5. *Redundancy Reduction.* This can be accomplished by use of shared models and associated elimination of redundant storage that would otherwise be needed.
6. *Increased Consistency.* This can be achieved through the ability of multiple decision makers to use the same model and the associated reduction of inconsistency that may result from use of different data or different versions of a model.

To provide these capabilities, it appears that a MBMS design must allow the DSS user to

1. *Access and retrieve existing models.*
2. *Exercise and manipulate existing models*—including model instantiation, model selection, and model synthesis, and the provision of suitable model outputs.
3. *Store existing models*—including model representation, model abstraction, and physical and logical model storage.
4. *Maintain existing models* as appropriate for changing conditions.
5. *Construct new models* with reasonable effort when they are needed, usually by building new models by using existing models as building blocks.

A number of auxiliary requirements must be achieved in order to provide these five capabilities. There must be, for example, appropriate communication and data changes among models that have been combined. It must also be possible to locate appropriate data from the DBMS and transmit it to the models that will use it.

In addition, it must be possible to analyze and interpret the results obtained from using a model. This can be accomplished in a number of ways. In this section, we will examine two of them: *relational MBMS*, and *expert system control of a MBMS*. The objective is to provide

1. A suitable set of models for the model base and appropriate software to manage the models in the model base, as illustrated in Figure 3.19.
2. Integration of the MBMS with the DBMS.
3. Integration of the MBMS with the DGMS.

We can expand further on each of these needs. Many of the technical capabilities needed for a MBMS will be analogous to those needed for a DBMS. These include *model generators* that will allow rapid building of specific models; *model modification* tools that will permit a model to be restructured easily on the basis of changes in the task to be accomplished; *update capability* that will enable changes in data to be input to the model; and *report generators* that will enable rapid preparation of results from using the system in a form appropriate for human use.

As is the case with a relational view of data, a relational view of models is based on a *mathematical theory of relations*. Thus, a model is viewed as a *virtual file* or *virtual relation*. It is a subset of the Cartesian product of the domain set that corresponds to these input and output attributes. This virtual file is, in principle, created by exercising the model with a wide spectrum (theoretically all) of inputs. These values of inputs and the associated outputs become records in the virtual file. The input data become *key attributes* and the model output data become *content attributes*.

Permissible data-base structures are very important in relational data bases. Elimination of possible data storage anomalies* through data-base organization according to the structure permitted by these normal forms is a major goal in relational data-base design. Model-base structuring and organization are critical for appropriate relational model management. Records in the *virtual file* of a model base are not individually updated, however, as they are in a relational data base. When a model change is made, all of the records that comprise the virtual file are changed. Nevertheless, there are possible processing anomalies in relational model management. Transitive dependencies in a relation, in the form of functional dependencies that affect only the output attributes, do occur and are eliminated by projecting into a suitable normal form.

Another issue of considerable significance relates to the contemporary need for usable *model-base query languages*, and needs within such languages for relational completeness. Three operations are needed for relational completeness in model management [49]:

1. *Execution*, which corresponds to selection and projection operations in relational data-base management.
2. *Optimization* of single-output attributes over one or more input attributes.
3. *Sensitivity analysis* to determine the change rates of output attributes relative to input attributes.

The implementation of *joins* is of concern in relational model-base management, just as it is in relational data-base management. For instance, if there is no redundancy in a relational model-base management system, the problem of *lossy joins*† does not occur. A relational model join is simply the result of using the output of one model as the input to another model. Therefore, joins will normally be implemented as part of the normal operation of software and a MBMS user will often not be aware that they are occurring. However, there can be cycles, since the output model 1 may be the input to model 2, which may become the input to model 1. Cycles such as this do not occur in DBMS.

An alternative to the use of relational model-base technology to implement model management approaches is that of structured modeling [50,51]. There are several potentially useful model management related objectives associated with this ap-

---

*It is vital that this be done in order that operations such as record deletion, record addition, or modifying the content of an existing record can be accomplished efficiently.
†In a relational data base, a join across two or more files results from linking the matching records in the file. The food supply at a given location would be obtained by linking the individual records for food items.

proach, which is intended to provide a foundation for computer-based modeling environments:

1. To nurture the entire modeling life cycle.
2. To be hospitable to decision makers, not just to modeling professionals.
3. To facilitate ongoing evolution of the models built with it.
4. To enable utilization by users of structured modeling approaches of the same language for model definition.
5. To facilitate good management of modeling resources.

The three principal steps associated with use of structured modeling are [51]

1. Identifying a suitable framework for conceptual modeling.
2. Designing an executable modeling language that supports this framework.
3. Establishing software integration approaches that can cope with the wide variety of elements and relations in a robust modeling environment.

Structured modeling, through use of graph theoretic based approaches, allows the user to describe models as acyclic attributed directed graphs. Structured modeling supports notions of user perceptions of a system or model. It is possible to specify different levels of abstraction quite easily, thereby permitting the user to interact with models at a meaningful level rather than being forced to a single prescribed view that is not easily changed. While related to relational models and earlier interpretive structural modeling approaches [4,5,14] structured modeling is more general and appears to easily adopt an entity–relationship, or object-oriented, perspective. Hence, structured modeling notions seem quite capable of integrating a variety of models as well as accommodating accessing and retrieval of existing models, exercising and manipulating existing models, storing existing models, maintaining existing models, and constructing new models.

Expert systems applications in MBMS represent another attractive possibility. Four different potential opportunities exist. It might be possible to utilize expert systems technology to considerable advantage in the construction of models [52,53], including decisions about whether or not to construct models* in terms of the cost and benefits associated with such decisions. Artificial intelligence (AI) and expert systems technology may potentially be used to integrate models. This model integration is needed to *join* models. AI and expert systems technology may prove useful in the validation of models. Finally, this technology might find application in the interpretation of the output of models. This would especially seem to be needed for large-scale models, such as large linear programming models [54].

While MBMS approaches based on a relational theory of models, structured modeling, and expert systems technology are new and operational as of this writing, they offer much promise for implementing model management notions in an effective

---

*This decision relates to the value of information, as discussed earlier for simple decision analysis problems.

manner. As has been noted, they offer the prospect of *data as models* [55] which may well prove much more useful than the conventional information systems perspective of "models as data."

3.4 SUMMARY

This chapter provided an overview of model-base management systems. First, we summarized some formal modeling efforts for the formulation, analysis, and interpretation of issues. Much of our effort was devoted to a discussion of decision analysis methods for issue interpretation as many DSS efforts are comprised of formal decision analytic efforts. We also presented an overview of issue interpretation with imperfect information and illustrated how linear programming algorithms could be useful for this purpose. Then, we turned to some more general concerns in implementation of the model management portion of a MBMS. The opportunity to view one particular software implementation of a relatively comprehensive MBMS will come in Chapter 5, when DSS evaluation is discussed.

PROBLEMS

3.1. Obtain one or more software modeling systems. For this software, idenitfy
  a. The model base
  b. The model management elements
  c. The associations between model and dialog
  d. The associations between model and data

3.2. How would the answers in problem 1 differ for a spreadsheet software package, and a program that would solve differential equations using the Runge–Kutta (or some other) numerical analysis method?

3.3. Prepare a discussion of the decision analysis approaches and the model management system that is found in Ref. 56.

3.4. It appears that dBase, or any other microcomputer data-base management system, is a DBMS. Also a spreadsheet, such as Lotus 123 or Supercalc, would be a model-base management system. Provide positive and negative arguments relative to these assertions. Since a data-base printout could certainly be in spreadsheet format, how does this affect the argument? How do *integrated packages*, such as Framework and Symphony, relate to this discussion of DBMS and MBMS?

3.5. Prepare of hypothetical dialog that might be used to describe an interpretation issue, with three alternatives and three attributes for which the ARIADNE concept described here might be suitable.

3.6. Draw the decision tree structure for either a prototypical lottery, or a government-sponsored lottery available for your purchase. Discuss the optimal decision, and how it is obtained.

3.7. A standard theory of the consumer relation would indicate that consumer demand for a product is inversely proportional to price. We might have

$$Q(p) = g(p) = \beta e^{-\alpha p}$$

The cost of purchasing products for sale can normally be expected to vary inversely with the number of products purchased. This cost also varies directly with the number of goods sold because of the marketing expenses. We might have

$$C(Q) = f(Q) = \Omega e^{-\Theta Q} + \phi e^{\tau Q}$$

where e is the standard exponential, and the parameters α, β, Ω, Θ, ϕ, and τ are constant and dependent upon the particular product in question. The object of the store if to maximize profit, or

$$\text{Max } \pi = \text{Max } [pQ(p) - C(Q)]$$

Discuss how this model might form the basic part of a MBMS for a DSS design. How would you extend this to the realistic case where the store markets more than one product. Expand on this for a large number of products. Discuss the DBMS. How would one go about validating the MBMS? (For details of microeconomic systems analysis, see ref. [19].)

References

[1] Will, H. J., "Model Management System," in Grochla, E., and Szyperski, N., *Information Systems and Organization Structure*, de Gruyter, Berlin, 1975, pp. 468–482.

[2] Sprague, R. H., and Carlson, E. D., *Building Effective Decision Support Systems*, Prentice-Hall, Englewood Cliffs, NJ, 1982.

[3] Applegate, L. M., Konsynski, B. R., and Nunamaker, J. F., "Model Management Systems: Design for Decision Support," *Decision Support Systems*, Vol. 2, No. 1, March 1986, pp. 81–91.

[4] Sage, A. P., *Methodology for Large Scale Systems*, McGraw-Hill, New York, 1977.

[5] Sage, A. P. (Ed.), *Systems Engineering: Methodology and Applications*, IEEE Press, New York, 1977.

[6] Sage, A. P., "Methodological Considerations in the Design of Large Scale Systems Engineering Processes," in Haimes, Y. (Ed.), *Large Scale Systems*, North-Holland, 1982, pp. 99–141.

[7] Sage, A. P. (Ed.), *Concise Encyclopedia of Information Processing in Systems and Organizations*, Pergamon Press, New York, 1990.

[8] Sage, A. P., *Systems Engineering*, Wiley, New York, 1991.

[9] Hall, A. D., "Three Dimensional Morphology of Systems Engineering," *IEEE Transactions on Systems Science and Cybernetics*, Vol. SSC-5, April 1969, pp. 156–160.

[10] Keller, L. R., and Ho, J. L., "Decision Problem Structuring," in Ref. 7, pp. 103–110.

[11] McGrath, J. E., *Groups: Interaction and Performance* Prentice-Hall, Englewood Cliffs, NJ, 1984.
[12] Van de Ven, A. H., and Delbecq, A. L., "The Effectiveness of Nominal, Delphi, and Interacting Group Decision Making Processes," *Academy of Management Journal*, Vol. 14, 1974, pp. 203–213.
[13] Delbecq, A. L., Van de Ven, A. H., and Gustafson, D. H., *Group Technology for Program Planning*, Scott, Foresman, Glenview, IL, 1974.
[14] Warfield, J. N., *Societal Systems: Planning, Policy, and Complexity*, Wiley, New York, 1976.
[15] Howard, R., and Matheson, J. E., "Influence Diagrams," in Howard, R., and Matheson, J. E. (Eds.), *The Principles and Applications of Decision Analysis*, Stanford University Press, Stanford, CA, 1984.
[16] Volkema, R. J., "Problem Formulation," in Ref. 7, pp. 377–382.
[17] Fraser, N. M., and Hipel, K. W., *Conflict Analysis: Models and Resolutions*, North-Holland, New York, 1984.
[18] Hipel, K. W., (Ed.), "Conflict Analysis Special Issue," *Information and Decision Technologies*, Vol. 16, Nos. 3 and 4, 1990, pp. 183–371.
[19] Sage, A. P., *Economic Systems Analysis: Microeconomics for Systems Engineering, Engineering Management, and Project Selection*, North-Holland, New York, 1983.
[20] Hillier, F. S., and Lieberman, G. J., *Operations Research*, 4th ed., Holden Day, San Francisco, 1986.
[21] Palmer, K. H., Boudwin, N. K., Patton, H. A., Rowland, A. J., Sammes, J. D., and Smith, D. M., *A Model Management Framework for Mathematical Programming*, Wiley, New York, 1984.
[22] Sage, A. P., and White, C. C., *Optimum Systems Control*, 2nd ed., Prentice-Hall, Englewood Cliffs, NJ, 1977.
[23] Raiffa, H., *Decision Analysis*, Addison-Wesley, Reading, MA, 1968.
[24] Kenney, R. L., and Raiffa, H., *Decisions with Multiple Objectives: Preferences and Value Tradeoffs*, Wiley, New York, 1976.
[25] Hammond, K. R., and Adelman, L., "Science, Values, and Human Judgment," *Science*, Vol. 194, 1976, pp. 389–396.
[26] Hammond, K. R., Stewart, T. R., Brehmer, B., and Steinmann, D. O., "Social Judgment Theory," in Kaplan, M. F., Schwartz, S. (Eds.), *Human Judgment and Decision Processes*, Academic, Orlando, FL, 1975.
[27] Tversky, A., "Elimination by Aspects: A Theory of Choice," *Psychological Review*, Vol. 76, 1969, pp. 31–48.
[28] Blanchard, B. S., and Fabrycky, W. J., *Systems Engineering and Analysis*, 2nd ed., Prentice-Hall, Englewood Cliffs, NJ, 1990.
[29] Sage, A. P., and White, E. B., "Decision and Information Structures in Regret Models of Judgment and Choice," *IEEE Transactions on Systems, Man and Cybernetics*, Vol. SMC-13, No. 2. March 1983, pp. 136–145.
[30] Luce, R. D., and Raiffa, H., *Games and Decisions: Introduction and Critical Survey*, Wiley, New York, 1957.
[31] von Winterfeldt, D., and Edwards, W., *Decision Analysis and Behavioral Research*, Cambridge University Press, 1986.

[32] von Neumann, J. and Morgenstern, O., *Theory of Games and Economic Behavior*, 3rd ed., Wiley, New York, 1964.

[33] Edwards, W., "How to Use Multiattribute Utility Measurement for Social Decisionmaking," *IEEE Transactions on Systems, Man, and Cybernetics*, Vol. SMC-7, May 1977, pp. 326–340.

[34] Dawes, R. M., "A Case Study of Graduate Admissions: Applications of Three Principles of Human Decision Making," *American Psychologist*, Vol. 26, 1971, pp. 180–188.

[35] Fishburn, P. C., "Analysis of Decisions with Incomplete Knowledge of Probabilities," *Operations Research*, Vol. 13, No. 2, March–April 1965, pp. 217–237.

[36] Sarin, R. K., "Screening of Multiattribute Alternatives," *OMEGA*, Vol. 5, No. 4, 1977, pp. 481–489.

[37] Sage, A. P., and White, C. C., "ARIADNE: A Knowledge Based Interactive System for Planning and Decision Support," *IEEE Transactions on Systems, Man, and Cybernetics*, Vol. SMC-14, No. 1, January 1984, pp. 35–47.

[38] Pearl, J., Leal, A., and Saleh, J., "GODDESS: A Goal Directed Decision Structuring System," *IEEE Transactions on Pattern Analysis and Machine Intelligence*, Vol. PAMI-4, May 1982, pp. 250–262.

[39] Rajala, D. W., and Sage, A. P., "On Decision Situation Structural Modeling," *Policy Analysis and Information Sciences*, Vol. 4, July 1980, pp. 53–81.

[40] Sage, A. P., "On Sensitivity Analysis in Systems for Planning and Decision Support," *Journal of the Franklin Institute*, Vol. 312, September 1981, pp. 265–291.

[41] White, C. C., and Sage, A. P., "A Multiple Objective Optimization Based Approach to Choicemaking," *IEEE Transactions on Systems, Man and Cybernetics*, Vol. SMC-10, No. 4, June 1980, pp. 315–326.

[42] White, C. C., and Sage, A. P., "Multiple Objective Evaluation and Choicemaking Under Risk with Partial Preference Information," *International Journal of Systems Science*, Vol. 14, 1983, pp. 467–485.

[43] White, C. C., Sage, A. P., and Scherer, W. T., "Decision Support with Partially Identified Parameters," *Large Scale Systems*, Vol. 3, August 1982, pp. 177–190.

[44] White, C. C., Sage, A. P., and Dozono, S., "A Model of Multiattribute Decisionmaking and Trade-off Weight Determination Under Uncertainty," *IEEE Transactions on Systems, Man and Cybernetics*, Vol. 14, No. 2, March 1984, pp. 168–184.

[45] White, C. C., Sage, A. P., Dozono, S., and Scherer, W. T., "An Evaluation of ARIADNE," *Proceedings of the 6th MIT/ONR Workshop on Command and Control*, July 1983.

[46] White, C. C., and Sykes, E. A., "A User Preference Guided Approach to Conflict Resolution in Rule Based Expert Systems," *IEEE Transactions on Systems, Man and Cybernetics*, Vol. 16, 1986, pp. 276–278.

[47] Barbosa, L. C., and Hersko, R. G., "Integration of Algorithmic Aids into Decision Support Systems," *MIS Quarterly*, Vol. 4, No. 1, March 1980, pp. 1–12.

[48] Liang, T. P., "Integrating Model Management with Data Management in Decision Support Systems," *Decision Support Systems*, Vol. 1, No. 3, September 1985, pp. 221–232.

[49] Blanning, R. W., "Entity-Relationship Approach to Model Management," *Decision Support Systems*, Vol. 2, No. 1, March 1986, pp. 65–72.

[50] Geoffrion, A., "An Introduction to Structured Modeling," *Management Science*, Vol. 33, 1987, pp. 547–588.

[51] Geoffrion, A., "The Formal Aspects of Structured Modeling," *Operations Research*, Vol. 37, No. 1, January 1989, pp. 30–51.

[52] Hwang, S., "Automatic Model Building Systems: A Survey," *Proceedings DSS-85*, Atlanta, GA, 1985, pp. 22–32.

[53] Murphy, F. H., and Stohr, E. A., "An Intelligent System for Formulating Linear Programs," *Decision Support Systems*, Vol. 2, No. 1, March 1986, pp. 39–47.

[54] Greenberg, H. J., "A Natural Language Discourse Model to Explain Linear Programming Models and Solutions," *Decision Support Systems*, Vol. 3, No. 4, December 1987, pp. 333–342.

[55] Dolk, D. R., "Data as Models: An Approach to Implementing Model Management," *Decision Support Systems*, Vol. 2, No. 1, March 1986, pp. 73–80.

[56] Dyer, J. S., Lund, R. N., Larsen, J. B., Kumar, V., and Leone, R. P., "A Decision Support System for Prioritizing Oil and Gas Exploration Activities," *Operations Research*, Vol. 38, No. 3, May 1990, pp. 386–396.

Chapter **4**

Dialog Generation and Management Systems

In all of our efforts in this text, we envision a basic DSS structure of the form shown in Figure 4.1. This figure also shows many of the operational functions of the data-base management system (DBMS) and the model-base management system (MBMS). *The primary purpose of the dialog generation and management system (DGMS) is to enhance the propensity and ability of the system user to utilize and benefit from the DSS.* There are doubtlessly few users of a DSS who use it because of necessity. Most uses of a DSS are optional. There are a variety of ways in which this use can occur.* In all uses of a DSS, it is the DGMS that the user interacts with. In an early seminal text, Bennett [1] posed three questions to indicate this centrality:

1. What presentations is the user able to *see* at the DSS display terminal?
2. What must the user *know* about what is seen at the display terminal in order to use the DSS?
3. What can the DSS user *do* with the systems that will aid in accomplishing the intended purpose?

He refers to the enabling elements as the *presentation language*, the *knowledge base*, and the *action language*. It is generally felt that there are three types of languages or modes of communications: *words, mathematics,* and *graphics.* The presentation and action languages, and the knowledge base many contain any or all three language types. The mix of these that is suitable for any given DSS task will be a function of the task itself, the environment into which the task is embedded, and the nature of the

---

*In terms of *representations of information*, we may have tabular, graphical, iconic, and so on. In terms of *dialog styles*, we may have a question–answer framework, a menu framework, or any of several others. In regard to *user–system interactions*, we may have interaction through members of the staff, and so forth. And for *frequency of use*, we may have frequent or infrequent.

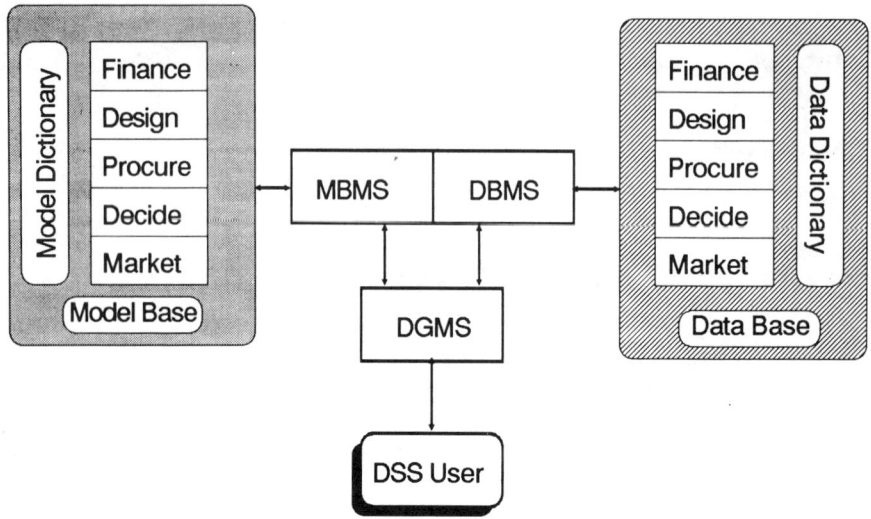

Figure 4.1 The DGMS as the user focused system in a DSS.

experiential familiarity of the person performing the task with it and the environment. The DSS, when one is used, becomes a fourth ingredient, although it is really much more of a vehicle supporting effective use of words, mathematics, and graphics. The DSS could simply be regarded as a component of the specific environment into which the task is embedded. Since we are focusing on DSS design, it is clearly appropriate to view it as another element. Of course, the DSS itself could be further disaggregated into subsystems, such as the DBMS, the MBMS, and the DGMS.

Notions of DGMS design are quite new, especially as a separately identified portion of the overall design effort. To be sure, user interface design is not at all new. However, the usual practice has been to assign the task of user interface design* to the design engineers responsible for the entire system. In the past, user interfaces have not been given special attention. They were merely viewed as another hardware and software component in the system. Often, system designers were not particularly familiar with, and perhaps not even especially interested in, the user-oriented design perspectives necessary to produce a successful interface design. As a result, many user interface designs have provided more of what the designer wanted, rather than what the user wanted and needed. Notions of dialog generation and dialog management extend far beyond that of interface issues, though the interface is a central concern in dialog generation and dialog management.

---

*For our purposes, the terms *user interface* and *dialog generation and management system* are essentially synonymous. The DGMS term is more recent, generally restricted to the DSS area, and more encompassing than user interface. A related generic term, that involves both DGMS and interface issues, is *human–computer interaction*. There are other terms, such as *user interface management systems* (UIMS) that appear similar in meaning to the term DGMS.

The DGMS is that DSS component that accommodates the various *information representations* identified during the requirements specification portion of the DSS design phase (to be discussed in the next chapter). The DGMS also accommodates the action languages or *control mechanisms* [2] which enable the user to manage the DSS outputs and inputs in the form of dialogs or processes. The DGMS provides an interface, as shown in Figure 4.1, between the system user and the rest of the DSS. There is much interest in the subject of human–computer interfaces at this time and an emerging literature on this subject [3, 4]. In particular, Ref. 3 presents a very useful taxonomy of the field. Some of this literature deals with such physiological issues as heights of work surfaces, clearances under work surfaces for legs, backrest heights, illumination, noise, temperature and humidity, and other issues that affect workplace design. Our concern is much more with cognitive and perceptive abilities. In this chapter, we will discuss those features of dialog generation, dialog management, and user interfaces most relevant to cognitive information processing issues of DSS design and use.

4.1 PRELIMINARY COMMENTS AND TERMINOLOGY FOR DGMS

It is appropriate to provide an informal definition of five concepts that will often be used in this chapter:

Dialog. A dialog (often spelled "dialogue") is a structured and observable series of interchanges of symbols (these symbols may be in the form of words, mathematics, and/or graphics) and actions between a computer and a human. Frequently, the terms *interface* and *dialog* are used as synonyms for one another. Occasionally, the term user interface management system [UIMS] is used as a synonym for DGMS.

Interface. An interface is the supporting hardware and software that enables a dialog, and all other aspects of human participation in the information-processing transactions of a DSS, to occur. The terms *interface* and *dialog* are commonly used as synonyms for one another, even though the meaning of the terms do not totally overlap.

Computation. Computation refers to calculation or algorithmic processing such as to enable functional transformation of inputs into outputs. While dialog and interface involve the interconnection between the computer and the external world, computation occurs uniquely within the computer itself. Normally, it is possible to distinguish computation and dialog, although this may at times be difficult. The term *action* is sometimes used as a synonym for computation in the dialog, interface, and DSS literature.

Dialog Management. Dialog management, user interface management, or human–computer interface management relates to the management of the computational aspects of the interface. User interface management systems (UIMS) are generally interactive tools that support the interface management activities of systems requirements representation, design, implementation, evaluation, and maintenance.

Model. A model is a representation, image, or perception of some entity. It is possible to speak of models in various ways, such as mental or computer models, or conceptual models. It is particularly important to distinguish between user models and designer models. A user model refers to the system image perceived by the user. This may be an idiosyncratic individual user model, or a generalized group model suitable for a *representative* DSS user. A designer model is the DSS designer's conceptual model of the DSS to be built.

4.2 INTERACTION STYLES

According to Ref. 5, there are at least two fundamental ways in which humans may interact with computers through a dialog or interface:

- The conversational world
- The graphical world

In the *conversational world** the user describes what it is that the user wishes to happen, typically through use of a *command language*. The dialog associated with the conversational world is generally a *sequential dialog* which progresses in a more or less predictable manner from one part of the dialog to the next. Navigation through menus, data entry, and request–response interactions are prototypical sequential dialogues. The user is able to illustrate what it is that is ultimately desired through manipulations. A mouse is the prototypical illustration of the model metaphor that is used for manipulations.

Schneiderman [6] identifies five primary interaction styles for human–computer interaction:

1. *Menu Selection*—in which the user reads a list of items and selects the one most appropriate to a particular task, applies a known syntax to initiate the selection, and then observes the effect. The major advantages to this approach are that there is a very distinct structure for decision making because of the limited number of choices available, and novice users can easily use menus. The use of function keys is one form of menu selection. This is commonly felt to be the simplest way for inexperienced users to use a computer.
2. *Command Language*—in which users who understand the associated syntax well can initiate complex procedures rapidly. However, error rates may be high, error diagnostics may be hard to provide, and training is necessary. Any

---

*The conversational world would be expected to include *words* and *mathematics*. Usually, most computer dialogs primarily use words for the conversational world.

high-level programming language, such as C or Pascal, could be used as a low-level command language. A special form of command language, known as a *query language*, may provide higher-level command forms that are more suitable than those provided by a lower-level command language.

3. *Forms*—in which data entry is required to fill in blanks, perhaps in a question–answer-like format. This is especially appropriate to satisfy intensive DBMS entry needs. Users must typically understand the logical structure of the DBMS to use this approach.
4. *Natural Language*—in which users are able to input ordinary conversational dialog and the system is able to understand such dialog.
5. *Direct Manipulation* —in which the user is able to use graphical representations that seem like those available in the *real world*.

The style used in the *graphical world* is called *direct manipulation* by Schneiderman [6]. A *direct manipulation interface* (DMI) is one that has the following properties [6]:

- Continuous representations of objects of interest.
- Physical actions, such as button press and movement of a mouse, instead of the complex syntax of computer language.
- Rapid incremental and reversible actions, whose impacts on object of interest is readily and visibly obvious.

Thus, a DMI is a hybrid syntactic–semantic model. In Schneiderman's view, semantic knowledge corresponds to the way in which a person understands a specific applications domain, and syntactic knowledge represents the conventional way in which an application might be described to others. Understanding is more associated with retention in long-term memory than is describing.

Norman [7] has described seven stages of user *cognitive* activity in performing a task:

1. *Establishing goals.*
2. *Forming intentions*, or internal mental characterizations of goals.
3. Specifying or *selecting the action sequence*, generally through review and evaluation of all identified actions.
4. *Executing actions.*
5. *Perceiving the resultant system state.*
6. *Interpreting this* with respect to the initially specified goals.
7. *Evaluating whether to continue* action or to accept the task as now accomplished.

In this model, the user first forms conceptual intent, reformulates this into action semantics, and ultimately produces a selected action. Errors occur in the process as intents are reformulated to lower and lower levels. Figure 4.2 illustrates these activities.

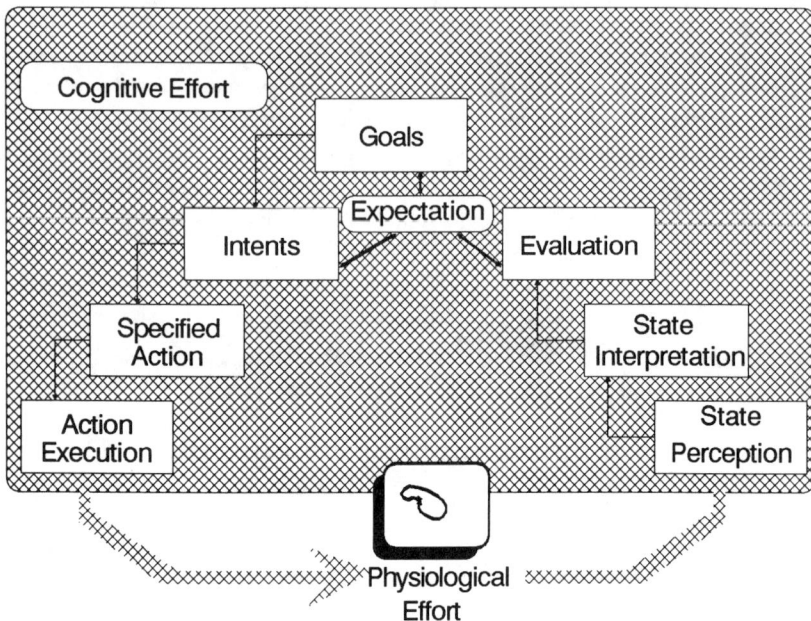

Figure 4.2 Norman's seven stages of user cognitive activity in task performance [7].

This model of cognitive activity has been used [5] to evaluate direct manipulation interfaces. These are interfaces with continuous representation of objects of interest, use of physical action, typically through object movement and button presses (i.e., use of a mouse) rather than potentially complex syntax, and rapid potentially reversible operations with immediate visibility of movement of the object of interest. The thrust of Schneiderman's argument [6] is that direct manipulation results in a more satisfactory interface than do other types. In part, this is because novices can learn basic functionality quickly, often through demonstrations by more experienced users.* It is also claimed that experts can work extremely rapidly through use of direct manipulation interfaces, and are aided in rapidly defining new functions and features. These claims are made, in part, because users can immediately see if their actions are furthering their intended goals. If they are not, actions can presumably

---

*Six claims are actually made:
1. Novices learn functionality quickly, often through learning from more experienced users.
2. Experts are enabled to work extremely rapidly, and are able to create new features.
3. Intermittent users learn, and are able to retain operational capabilities, despite the intermittent use.
4. Error messages are needed very infrequently.
5. Users are easily able to visualize progress toward achieving goals and alter activities if progress is not occurring.
6. Users anxiety is reduced because of the comprehensibility of the system and the ease with which activities may be changed.

be changed with relative ease. Therefore, users have reduced stress and anxiety both because the system is visibly comprehensible and because actions are readily reversible.

Norman [7] associates a *gulf of execution* and a *gulf of evaluation* with this model of user activity in terms of direct manipulation interfaces. The gulf of execution is reduced by making system commands and mechanisms match the thoughts and goals of the user as much as possible. The gulf of evaluation is reduced by making the output display present a conceptual model of the system that is easily perceived and evaluated. Two properties of an interface language, which are particularly appropriate for direct manipulation, may be defined: *articulatory directness* and *semantic directness*. An interface language is necessarily comprised of *form* of the expressions in the interface language and *meaning* of the expressions. Articulatory distance is that distance that exists between the physical form, or syntax, of expressions in the interface language and the meaning of the expressions. The articulatory distance is small when it is easy to go from appearance or form of the input or output, to the meaning of the input or output. The semantic distance relates to the difference between the meaning of the input or output expressions in the user interface language and the intentions or goals of the user. Figure 4.3 illustrates these concepts.

As noted, these notions were used [5] to evaluate Schneiderman's claims for superiority of direct manipulation interfaces over other types. For the most part, the claims are supported. The primary nonsupported claim is the one that indicates improvement in the ability of experts. In general, this claim appears not to be correct. Experts at using computer systems do not improve their ability to work rapidly and create new features through use of these interfaces (the second of Schneiderman's six claims listed before). We speculate that this is so because experts do not need the guidance provided by direct manipulation interfaces, and may regard the generally increased effort to use them as counterproductive. (This speculation follows directly from many of the observations that we will make in Chapter 6.)

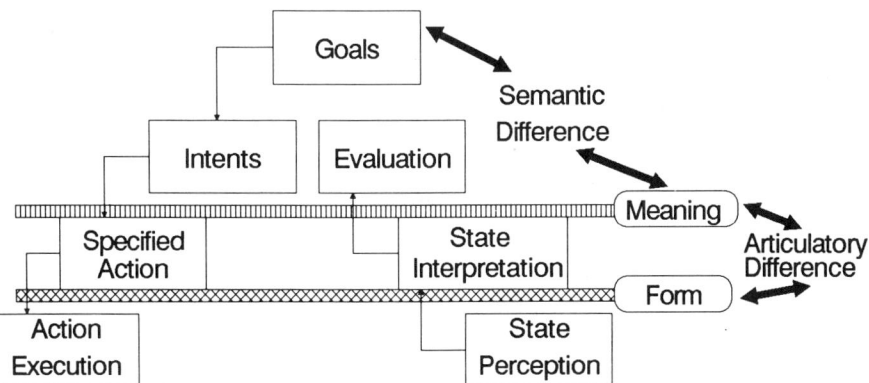

Figure 4.3 Illustration of semantic and articulatory differences between goals, meaning of expressions, and form of expressions.

We will now describe some design strategies for DGMS design. The major elements that influence system design are the hardware and software designs that are implemented. These influence the user of the DSS and the decision process that is used. Each of these can be further disaggregated such that it becomes possible to develop an attribute template that is potentially useful for evaluation of a DGMS. Carlson [8], for example, discusses many elements in the following template:

Hardware selection
    Output media
    Input media
Software selection
    Available software
    Software to be developed
User–system interaction characteristics
    Interaction style
    Training constraints
    Control style
    Experiential familiarity with issue
    Experiential familiarity with environment
    Experiential familiarity with DSS usage
Decision process
    Type of decision
    Importance of decision
    Number of participants
    Distributed nature of process

Much of our effort in what is to follow in this chapter will be concerned with developing a taxonomy for design and evaluation of DGMS.

Each of these elements, or variables or attributes, can be further disaggregated. We can, for example, identify six attributes that are related to input or output media [9]:

Input media
    Effective—serves intended purpose
    Ease of use—functionally appropriate for DSS user
    Accuracy—provides appropriate inputs
    Timeliness—provides timely inputs
    Consistent—provides veridicality check on input values
    Attractiveness—enables choice of suitable input format
Output media
    Effective—serves intended purpose
    Ease of use—functionally appropriate for DSS user

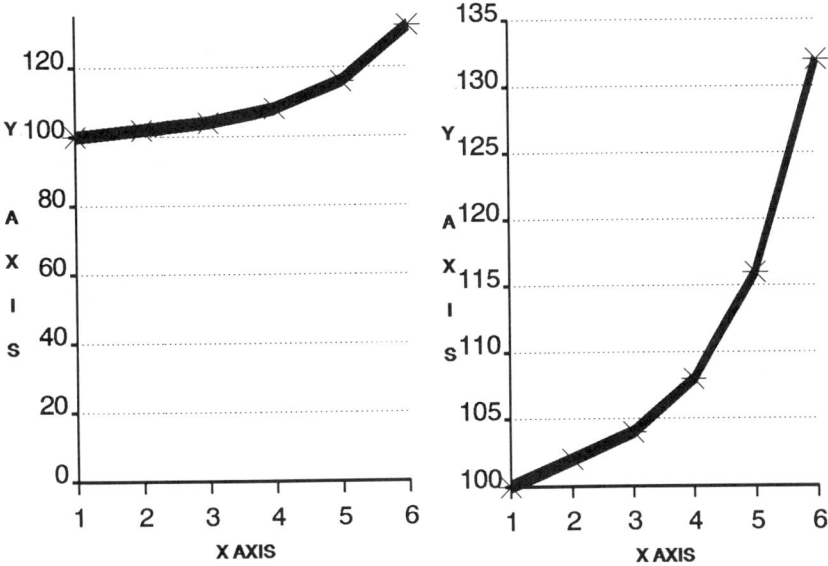

Figure 4.4 Potential bias issues in interpreting two graphs with the same information.

    Accuracy—provides suitable outputs
    Timeliness—provides timely outputs
    Consistent—provides proper output spatial distribution
    Attractiveness—enables choice of appropriate output format

All of this relates to notions of input and output *usability*, as broadly defined. There are many possible input and output devices: video monitors, mice, printers, plotters, magnetic storage, scanners, and even devices that emit noises and odors. There are a number of factors to consider here. One of the potential difficulties to avoid is that of output bias. Figure 4.4 presents two graphical plots of identical data. For the graph on the left, it is easy to conclude that the output is relatively constant over time. For the graph on the right, it is relatively easy to conclude that rapid change is occurring. We will comment further on some of these *bias* issues in Chapters 6 and 7.

4.3 DIALOG GENERATION OBJECTIVES

In this brief section, we will discuss some basic issues relative to models of user knowledge and associated dialog issues. Perhaps the most fundamental concern relates to the distinctions between semantics and syntax, or semantic level and syntactic level. *Semantic concerns* are conceptually based and may relate either to the task at hand or to DSS representations of these in terms of objects and actions. *Syntactic concerns* relate to the operational representation of semantic issues. Most computer programming languages are constructed to separate semantics from syntax. This independence is, of course, desirable for the many reasons that we have already noted.

It is possible to identify other levels. For instance, we could identify a *lexical level* that denotes the specific mechanisms that a person uses to specify syntax. In a similar way, we could identify a semantic meta-level that would represent a user's model of the decision concerning how to decide relative to choice of semantic representations. Moran [10] has identified six levels in his framework of user interface design which is denoted as *command language grammar* (CLG):

Task level
Semantic level
Syntactic level
Lexical level
Spatial layout level
Device level

and these are clearly related in a hierarchical manner. Additional levels can easily be defined. For example, we can distinguish between high-level and low-level tasks. These additional levels do not appear to add materially to the present discussion of dialog generation and management.

Semantic knowledge, which generally resides in long-term human memory, may be associated with the task to be performed, or the computer system that may potentially assist in performance of the task. There are a number of ways in which semantic knowledge may be represented or transferred from one person to another. Often, people deal with large, complex issues by hierarchically structuring them so that the resulting decomposition contains issues that are of manageable size. This refers primarily to semantic knowledge. Syntactic knowledge is usually quite specific to a given task or computer system. It may involve knowledge about what the *escape* key on the keyboard does, or what will happen if one dials 911 on a telephone in a given location. This knowledge is typically very system dependent and commonly needs to be modified considerably for it to be applicable to a different computer or task issue than one for which it is known to be applicable. Frequently, syntactic knowledge is stored in short-term memory only and, unless continually used, disappears from memory.

As indicated, there are at least five basic dialog generation approaches. Combinations of these are certainly possible and desirable. Further commentary on each of these is appropriate and useful here.

Menu Selection. Figure 4.5 shows the range of menu systems that are possible. Tree-structured menus are perhaps the most common. There can, naturally, be variations within each type, such as to allow pull-down and pop-up menus. A primary objective in menu design is to be able to move through menus correctly and quickly. Titles, placement of items, instructions, error messages, and status report concerns are each of importance in menu design. Menu selection encourages a short learning time,

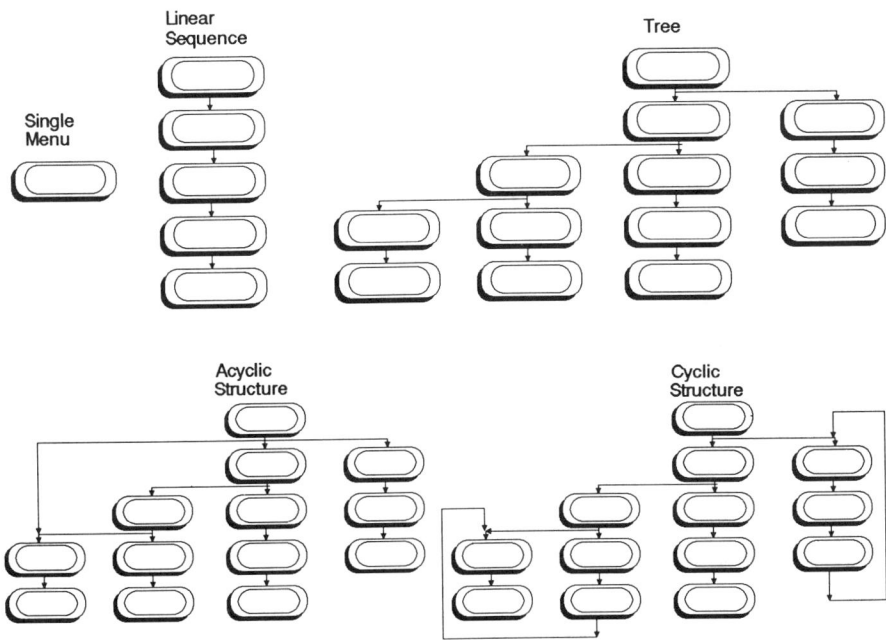

Figure 4.5 Types of menu systems.

structured decision making, and allows use of dialog management tools. Error handling is easily supported. There is a danger inherent in too many menus, and menus may slow the expert system user. Hence, there should be an *expert menu selection* which is, in effect, no menu at all.

Command Language. The basic goals of language design include precision, compactness, reading ease, writing ease, learning ease, error detection and correction, flexibility, expressiveness, visual appearance, and effectiveness in carrying out specified manipulations. The constraints on a command language include the capacity for humans to learn and retain the ability to use the language, and its ease and functionality of use. There are many benefits to structure, especially consistent structures, and benefits to use of very high level languages that are specifically designed for given tasks, such as data-base query languages. There are many general guidelines and, typically, these incorporate the desiderata presented here. Command languages are usually quite flexible and they are convenient for creation of *macros* or shorthand commands for *power* users. (The term *power user* is computer jargon for a very experienced user. *Heavy hitter* is, probably, an equivalent term.) Unfortunately, error handling is often poor and considerable user education and training may be needed.

Forms. Forms, including question and answer forms, are quite close to menus in terms of user characteristics. Data entry is normally quite simple, although perhaps time-consuming.

Natural Language. This is an ultimate form of command language in which there is no burden associated with learning the syntax, since the syntax is just that of normal oral and written expression. However, these advantages are also disadvantages in that the computer must interpret this natural dialog. Precision may pose a problem, as may context issues.*

Direct Manipulation. This heavily graphics- and mouse-oriented mode may be relatively easy to learn. However, an appropriate direct manipulation interface may be very difficult to develop.

The most extensive and detailed taxonomy or set of guidelines for the design of user interface software now available is doubtlessly that of Smith and Mosier [11]. They identify five high-level goals for *data entry*:

1. Consistency of data entry transactions
2. Minimal user input actions
3. Minimal user memory load
4. Data entry and data display compatibility
5. Flexible user control of data entry

These authors also identify five high-level goals for associated *information display:*

1. *Consistent Data Displays*—so that standardized terminology, abbreviations, and so forth are provided by a dictionary that is available to all system users.
2. *Efficient Information Assimilation*—so that the system user quickly associates the data format with the tasks required.
3. *Minimal Human Memory Burden*—such that the user is not required to remember information from one screen to another and such that the possibility of omitting required steps is minimized.
4. *Data Display and Data Entry Compatibility*—such that users can easily put information into a convenient form for the task on which they are working.
5. *Flexible User Control of Data Display*—such that system users can easily put information into a structural representation that is convenient and suitable for the task at hand.

Other actions of importance include sequence control, user guidance, data transmission, and data protection. There are many objectives identified to support each of these five primary functions of a user interface. Here, we only indicate the primary objectives identified in this insightful study.

---

*At the time of this writing, natural language dialogs exist only in very highly structured and constrained formats, and for very domain-specific applications.

Sequence Control refers to initiation, termination, and interruption of transactions that result from user actions and associated computer logic. Objectives for sequence control include

1. Consistency of control actions
2. Minimal control actions by user
3. Minimal memory load on user
4. Compatibility with task requirements
5. Sequence control flexibility

User Guidance refers to those aids provided to support the user's interaction with the computer. These include error messages, alarms, labels, prompts, and other instructional material. Efficient memory use with minimal memory load is the primary objective here. User guidance supports more efficient task performance, and error reduction, and greater user satisfaction with the system. The five primary objectives suggested by Smith and Mosier [11] for user guidance include

1. Consistency of operational procedures
2. Efficient use of full system capabilities
3. Minimal memory load on user
4. Minimal learning time
5. Flexibility in support of different users

Data Transmission refers to a variety of computer-arbitrated communications between the various system users. The five primary objectives identified here support effective data transmission (information transmission would have been a perhaps more appropriate term here):

1. Consistency of data transmission
2. Minimal user actions
3. Minimal memory load on user
4. Compatibility with other information-handling elements
5. User control flexibility in data transmission

Data Protection is concerned with ensuring the security of computer-processed data and information from unauthorized access, either of an intentional or unintentional nature, and computer failure. The five top-level objectives that support data protection, is identified by Smith and Mosier [11], include

1. Effective data security
2. Minimal entry of bad data
3. Minimal erroneous changes to stored data

4. Minimal loss of needed data
5. Minimal interference with normal information-processing tasks

A large number of lower-level performance attributes exist for each of these. It should be possible to do a thorough multiple-attribute evaluation of user interface designs using these.

An attribute tree for interface design based on this work is shown in Figure 4.6. This attribute tree can be used, in conjunction with the evaluation methods discussed in Chapters 2 and 5, to evaluate the effectiveness of interface designs.

There are other descriptions of interface attributes, some of which are less capable of instrumental measurement than these. On the basis of a thorough study of much of the human–computer interface and dialog design literature, Schneiderman [6] has identified eight primary objectives (often called the "golden rules for dialog design") for dialog design:

1. *Strive for consistency* of terminology, menus, prompts, commands and help screens.
2. *Enable frequent users to use shortcuts* that take advantage of their experiential familiarity with the computer system.
3. *Offer informative feedback* for every operator action that is proportional to the significance of the action.
4. *Design dialogs to yield closure* such that the system user is aware that specific actions have been concluded and that planning for the next set of activities may now take place.
5. *Offer simple error handling* so that, to the extent possible, the user is unable to make a mistake. Even when mistakes are made, the user should not have to, for example, retype an entire command entry line but, rather, just edit the incorrect portion.
6. *Permit easy reversal of action* so that the user is able to interrupt and then cancel wrong commands rather than having to wait for them to be fully executed.
7. *Support internal locus of control* such that users are always the initiators of actions rather than the reactors to computer actions.
8. *Reduce short-term memory load* so that users are able to master the dialog activities that they perform.

Clearly, all of these will have specific interpretations in different DGMS environments and need to be sustained in and capable of extension for a variety of environments.

It is not surprising that there have been a number of recent approaches to human–computer interaction, and associated interface design, issues. Some of these are almost totally empirical. Some involve almost totally theoretical and formal models [12]. Others attempt approximate predictive models that are potentially useful for design purposes [13]. The formative efforts of Card, Moran, and Newell [13] in this

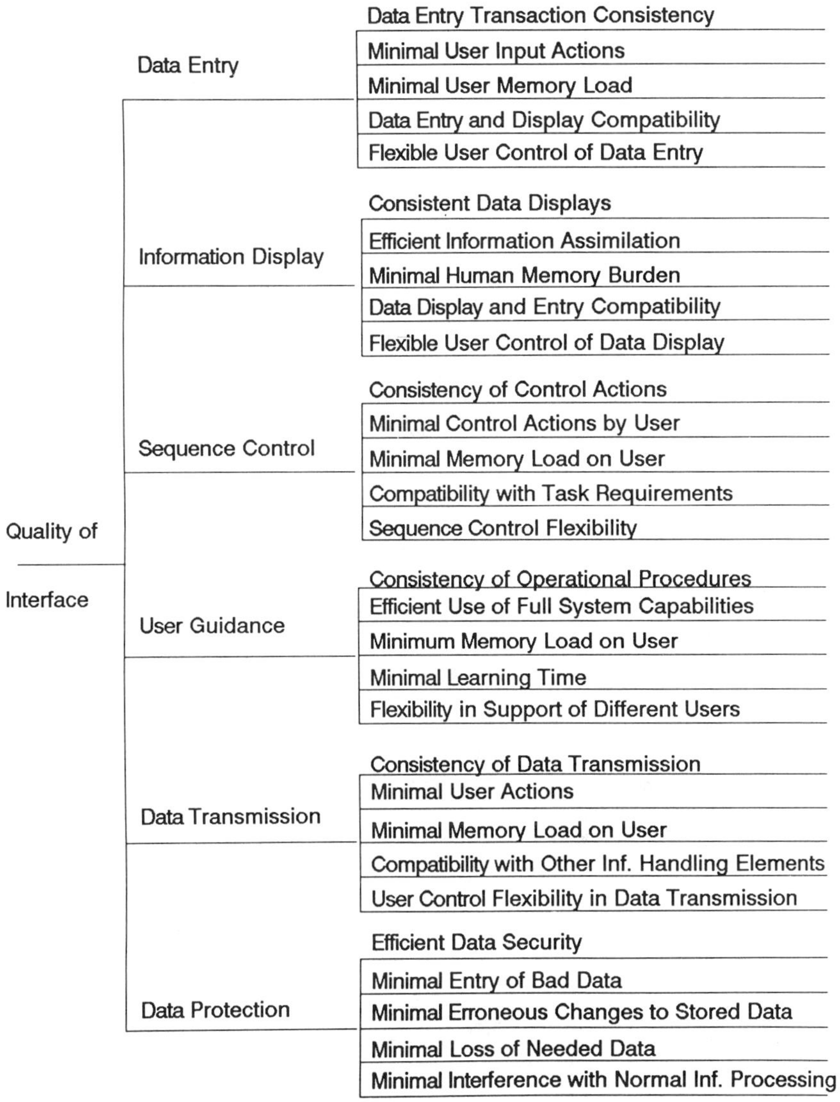

4.3 DIALOG GENERATION OBJECTIVES **145**

Quality of Interface		
	Data Entry	Data Entry Transaction Consistency
		Minimal User Input Actions
		Minimal User Memory Load
	Information Display	Data Entry and Display Compatibility
		Flexible User Control of Data Entry
		Consistent Data Displays
		Efficient Information Assimilation
		Minimal Human Memory Burden
	Sequence Control	Data Display and Entry Compatibility
		Flexible User Control of Data Display
		Consistency of Control Actions
		Minimal Control Actions by User
		Minimal Memory Load on User
	User Guidance	Compatibility with Task Requirements
		Sequence Control Flexibility
		Consistency of Operational Procedures
		Efficient Use of Full System Capabilities
		Minimum Memory Load on User
	Data Transmission	Minimal Learning Time
		Flexibility in Support of Different Users
		Consistency of Data Transmission
		Minimal User Actions
		Minimal Memory Load on User
	Data Protection	Compatibility with Other Inf. Handling Elements
		User Control Flexibility in Data Transmission
		Efficient Data Security
		Minimal Entry of Bad Data
		Minimal Erroneous Changes to Stored Data
		Minimal Loss of Needed Data
		Minimal Interference with Normal Inf. Processing

Figure 4.6 Attribute tree of Smith and Mosier [11] elements.

area have evolved a specific information-processing architecture called *the model human information processor*. Sensory, cognitive, and effector processors are included in the model, as well as a long-term memory and a working memory. Each are assigned such appropriate parameters as storage capacity and cycle processing time. A general-purpose model such as this might well be capable of describing the way one goes about such low-level lexical functions as keystroke entry. But it may not be as relevant to modeling how one goes about syntactic or semantic tasks.

These same authors recognize this, and also propose [14] a *goals, operators, methods, and selection* (GOMS) model that is intended to represent higher-level information-processing perspectives. In this model, goals provide a representation of the user's ultimate purposeful intent in performing a task ("edit paper" or "delete paragraph" are examples of intent here). Operations provide the system user's representation of elementary physiological actions (pressing the delete key, or entering today's date, or storing a specific file are examples of these). Methods are operational sequences that are designed to accomplish some intermediate-level objective (methods are generally complex, and may include such operations as deleting a paragraph or going to another menu). Selection rules are used to specify conditions that must be fulfilled in order to execute a method. Usually, these representations are based on complex pieces of experiential knowledge concerning the computer system being used and the application domain in which the interface is to be used.

This GOMS model is based on user decomposition of a task into subtasks. The decomposition also specifies the sequencing of tasks required to achieve the overall goal. For instance, manuscript editing [12] is decomposed into subtasks that involve

Locating the next edit in the marked manuscript
Making the indicated change and
Verifying that the change has been correctly made

Thus, the edit goal is decomposed into locating, changing, and verifying subgoals.

Norman's model for interface use and related design [7], discussed earlier, divides tasks up into even finer components based on the interactive production of action and the monitoring of the results of this action. This yields seven phases of action:

Formulating the goal
Framing the intention
Identifying an action
Executing the action
Perception of the resultant system state
Interpretation of the system state
Final evaluation of the outcome

which are not unlike the analogous phases in the systems life cycle.

There are a number of other suggested life cycles. For example, Polson [15] has evolved a four-phase methodology:

1. *System Definition.* User requirements, task environment, and basic structure needs for the user interface are identified. Functionality is defined in terms of the diversity of applications to be supported by the resulting system.
2. *Task Analysis.* The top and middle levels of the goal structure of the user are identified through decomposition of the system requirements. The interface design team develops methods that accomplish these decomposed tasks.

3. *Detailed Design.* The details of the user interface are specified. This includes such elements as menus, command languages, and so forth. A *test suite*, which specifies the tasks and associated characteristics that are to be utilized in design evaluation, is identified.
4. *Evaluation.* The design is evaluated, generally using simulation approaches. Rapid prototyping is suggested as an alternative to simulation-based evaluation.

We will have much more to say about design and evaluation of DGMS, and DSS as well, in the next chapter.

One word that has appeared many times in our discussions so far in this chapter is *consistency*. This is Schneiderman's first "Golden Rule of Dialog Design," and many other authors advocate this as well. A notable exception to this advocacy of consistency appears in the writing of Grudin [16]. While he surely does not advocate randomness in interface design, he argues that issues associated with consistency should be placed in a very broad context. Three types of consistency are defined:

1. *Internal Consistency.* The physical and graphic layout of the computer system, the command naming and use, dialog forms, and the like are consistent if these *internal features of the interface are the same across applications.*
2. *External Consistency.* If an interface has unchanging use features when compared to another interface with which the user is familiar, it is said to be externally consistent.
3. *Applications Consistency.* If the user interface uses metaphors or analogous representations of objects that correspond to those of the real-world application, then the interface may be said to correspond to experientially familiar features of the world and to be applications consistent.

Grudin makes several relevant observations. *Ease of learning can conflict with ease of use* (especially as experiential familiarity with the interface grows) and *Consistency can work against both ease of use and learning* are the two most relevant to interface consistency. On the basis of some experiments illustrating these hypotheses, he establishes some *appropriate dimensions for consistency*. These are generally based on the six levels for interface design of Moran [10], which we discussed earlier. The general conclusion is that the *higher-level (task) considerations can override consistency considerations at lower levels.** Accordingly, the system designer is encouraged to consider global aspects of the user work environment, rather than to focus on consistency as a design requirement, in and of itself and solely for the sake of consistency.

---

*Semantic aspects of a user task might justify what are otherwise good consistency choices relative to syntactic choices regarding menu defaulting. The general thrust might seem to be to optimize low-level interactions even at the expense of consistency but to maintain consistency at higher levels. This is *not* advocated, however. An overall study of the interface design, considering all three levels of design, is suggested.

4.4 DIALOG INDEPENDENCE

As has been noted, dialog independence suggests isolation of the design decisions that affect human–computer dialog from those design decisions that affect the structure and computational software for the application system. This is virtually essential to easy modification of interfaces and to use of the same DGMS for multiple applications. Without dialog independence, the design of an appropriate and flexible DGMS would be difficult indeed.

Thus, we envision dialog software and nondialog software. The dialog software can be further disaggregated into *internal dialog software* and *external dialog software*. The external dialog software would be at the interface between the DGMS and the user; the internal dialog software would communicate between the DGMS and the MBMS and DBMS. Essentially, the nondialog software (also called *computational software* and *action software* in different segments of the literature on this subject) is contained in the DBMS and the MBMS, and the DGMS contains primarily dialog software.

The developer of DGMS software needs to be concerned primarily with human cognitive factor concerns that relate to form, style, content, and presentation framework for the resulting dialog. For this reason, DGMS design concerns must be addressed throughout the DSS design life cycle, especially in phases that involve user requirements identification.

4.5 REPRESENTATIONS OF THE HUMAN–COMPUTER INTERFACE (HCI)

Representations are needed that support human–computer interface design issues. Initially, written computer programs and associated documentation were the usual representation formats. More recently, graphical and structured representation languages have emerged. On the horizon now are automated system for dialog development that permit interactive production of interface representations and, in some instances, actual interface code. Certainly, *prototyping* * is of major value in DGMS and HCI systems design. We shall examine some of these HCI representations in this section.

Three modeling representations of the user interface are common [3]:

1. *Interface Function Models (IFM)*. These are functional models used to describe and analyze details of particular user tasks. They are often very computing-device and dialog dependent, including such specific details as keyboard layout.
2. *Interface Structural Models (ISM)*. These describe the general process, or structure, of human–computer interaction, including the variety of exchanges or dialogs that humans and computers may have.

---

*Sometimes *prototyping* is called *rapid prototyping* (sometimes rabid prototyping!), but the term *rapid* seems to be redundant.

3. *Interface Purposeful Models (IPMs)*. These purposeful representation models depict strategies for representation of particular instances of human–computer interaction. They are concerned with forms, contents, and time-sequencing matters affecting interface design.

Combinations of these representations are certainly possible. A variety of representations can be used, and many of them (menus, command languages, etc.) have been identified in our earlier discussions. Various tools are available that support these representations. We can also view a modeling representation from three perspectives. The six levels of Moran's command language grammer (CLG) [10] involve *task* or physical functionality modeling components, *structural* or communication modeling components, and *representation* or purposeful modeling components:

Purposeful models
    Task level
    Semantic level
Structural models
    Syntactic level
    Lexical level
Functional models
    Spatial layout level
    Device level

From a linguistic perspective, the CLG provides a structural representation of the user interface. From a cognitive psychology perspective, CLG is, or at least should be, a purposeful representation of user knowledge about the computer system. From a design perspective, the CLG is a functionally operational representation of these. It would be highly desirable to make the specific implementation of the CLG adaptive such that the following objectives are realized [17]:

- A number of different dialog modes are potentially supported.
- The user is able potentially to switch between dialog modes at any time, even in the middle of a command.
- The transition between dialog modes is facile and natural.
- It is easy for the user to learn how to use all of the different dialog modes.

Kuo and Karimi [18] have developed an *adaptive user interface* (AUI) methodology. A *data flow diagram* (DFD) is used to represent functional requirements of the dialog system. This, together with real-time operation considerations is used to generate specifications for the user interface. In this approach, the user–system interactions are viewed as events that occur in a real-time environment. A control process coordinates process activations and deactivations during the course of user–

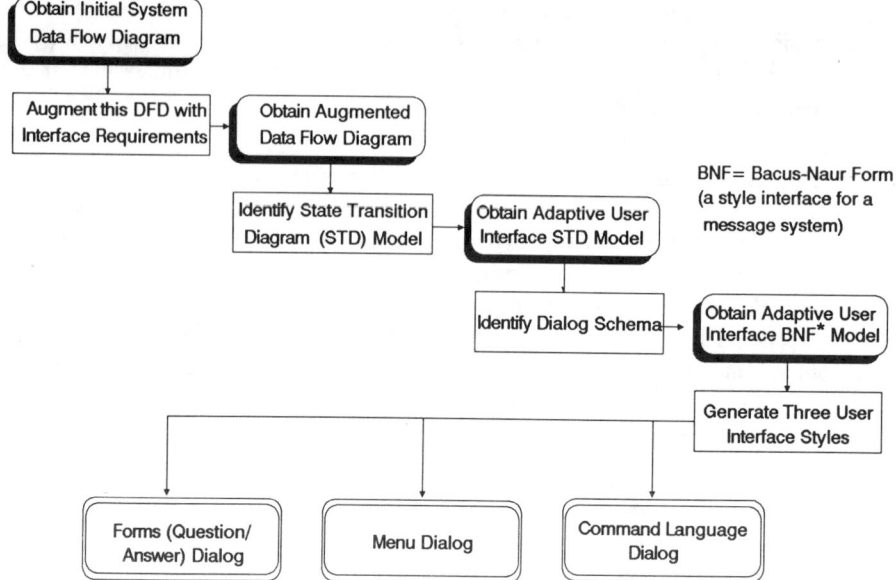

Figure 4.7 Phases in design of the Kuo-Karimi adaptive user interface (AUI).

computer interactions. Three DFD-based techniques are utilized, as illustrated in Figure 4.7, to design the user interface. These allow the extraction of objects and object operations, and in augmenting timing and condition requirements. As shown in the figure, three types of user interfaces are generated by the AUI approach. The user interface is denoted adaptive because three functionally equivalent but stylistically different interfaces result. The extent to which the resulting interface satisfies the preceding four success factors for an adaptive interface has yet to be determined.

4.6 EVALUATION OF INTERFACES, INTERFACE DEVELOPMENT TOOLS, AND HUMAN-COMPUTER DIALOGS

There are a number of desirable characteristics for user interfaces. Roberts and Moran [19] identify functionality of the editor, learning time required, time required to perform tasks, and errors committed as the most important attributes of text editors. To this might be added the cost of the system. Harrison and Hix [3] identify usability, completeness, extensibility, escapability, integration, locality of definition, structured guidance, and direct manipulation as well in their more general study of user interfaces. They also note a number of tools useful for interface development, as does Lee [20].

Evaluating the usability of human-computer interfaces is the subject of a recently published monograph by Ravden and Johnson [21]. Nine top-level attributes or criteria, whose definition and meaning is generally inferred from the attributes themselves, are identified in this effort:

Visual clarity
Consistency
Compatibility
Informative feedback
Explicitness
Appropriate functionality
Flexibility and control
Error prevention and correction
User guidance and support

These are each divided into a number of more measurable attributes. These attributes can be used as part of the evaluation strategy described in Chapter 2 and the considerably more expanded discussion to follow in Chapter 5.

Molich and Nielsen [4] also suggest nine top-level attributes to be used for evaluation of human–computer dialogs. Expressed in the form of guidelines, these are

1. *Use simple and natural dialog*, in which needed information appears in natural and logical order, and which does not contain irrelevant or rarely needed information.
2. *Speak the user's language*, such that the user obtains words, phrases, and concepts that are familiar and in common usage in the domain-specific area of the user, as contrasted with software- and interface-technology-specific terms.
3. *Minimize the user's memory load*, to recognize short-term memory limits and to enable the retrieval of simply stated and appropriate instructions.
4. *Be consistent*, so that users do not have to be concerned that the meaning of terms has changed from one subsystem to another.
5. *Provide feedback*, such that the system continually informs the user with needed and timely information about happenings.
6. *Provide clearly marked exits*, so that users are always and easily able to back out of undesired states and conditions.
7. *Provide shortcuts*, such that users are truly able to improve their performance as their experiential familiarity with the dialog increases.
8. *Provide good error messages*, so that the user obtains precise information about problems and their causes, and meaningful suggestions about what to do next.
9. *Practice error prevention*, such that as many problems as possible are prevented from occurring in the first place.

The conclusion of this study is that industrial designers and programmers have unfortunate difficulties in recognizing human–computer dialog deficiencies. The experimental portion of this study utilized traditional text based interfaces. Nielsen [22] has applied the same nine usability heuristics to evaluate modern graphical user interfaces, and they were found to be generally quite applicable.

This study by Molich and Nielsen [4] proposes a set of overarching dialog design principles similar to those of Gould and Lewis [23]. These, expressed in the form of requirements, are

Early focus on users and their tasks
Empirical measurements
Iterative design

Also encouraged is a focus on the *design product* itself, in terms of the nine requirements listed above.

While attributes of this sort are potentially useful for evaluation of existing interfaces, they do not provide a proactive guide to system design. There are many of these, of course. We have just outlined one set of three important design provisions [23]. The 10 principles, or prescriptions, in Ref. 13 are as valid today as when they were first written. They serve as an important linkage between the reactive and interactive efforts involved in evaluation of existing interface designs, and the proactive effort that should be involved in the design of interfaces. Also, they provide a useful concluding note for this section:

1. Consider the psychology of the user *and* the designer of the user interface.
2. Identify interface performance requirements.
3. Identify the user group.
4. Identify generic applications to be performed and associated user interface tasks.
5. Specify appropriate methods with which to accomplish the tasks.
6. Match the methods to the task and interface performance requirements and design process commitment.
7. Design the interface such that it can be used appropriately by people with greatly differing experiential familiarity with the computer system.
8. Design a set of alternative interface use strategies, and provide clear guidance concerning how to select an appropriate interface.
9. Identify, design, and implement a set of error detection, diagnosis, and correction methods.
10. Determine the sensitivity of the performance of the interface to design assumptions.

A goal in DGMS design is to define an abstract user interface that can be implemented on specific operating systems in different ways. The purpose of this is to allow for device independence such that, for example, switching from a command line interface to a mouse-driven pull-down-menu interface can be easily accom-

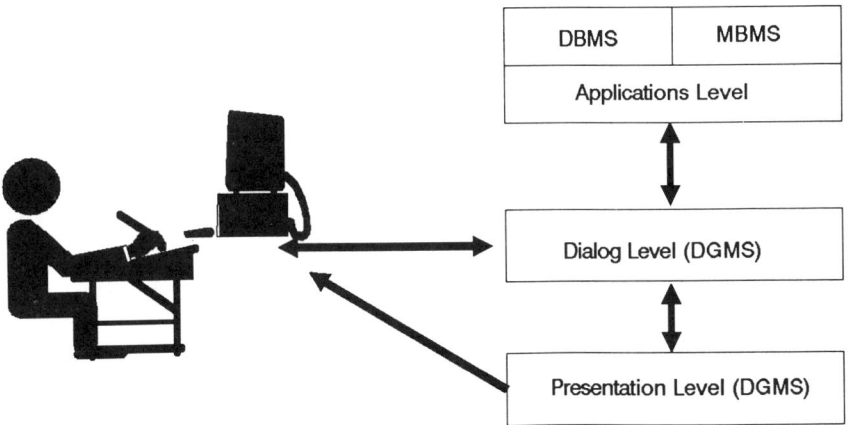

Figure 4.8 Dialog generation and management system architecture.

plished. Separating the application from the user interface should do much toward ensuring portability across operating systems and hardware platforms without modifying the MBMS and the DBMS that, together, comprise the applications software portions of the DSS.

Figure 4.8 illustrates this concept. The *dialog level* and *presentation level* in the figure comprise the dialog generation and management system. The *application level* consists of both the MBMS and the DBMS. The DBMS and MBMS comprise the substance of specific applications called for use in the DSS. The presentation level of the DGMS consists of a variety of interaction devices suitable for the given user interface that has been designed. The dialog level portion of the DGMS permits insertion and removal of interaction devices in a manner independent of the specific application. A variety of user interface types are supported, such as direct manipulation interfaces, pull-down menus, and so on. A *user interface definition language* (UIDL) might be used to aid in this, as might such approaches as rapid prototyping. Design procedures and processes for a *user interface management system* (UIMS) [24, 25]. Major objectives in UIMS design include ease of initial design, including installation and maintenance, and portability of DSS application software across multiple platforms.

4.7 ERRORS IN INTERFACE DESIGN

A major claim in recent efforts in interface design is that human errors are just simply not probabilistic random events that might be removed either through improved operator training, or through better interface design alone [26, 27]. Supporting this is the observation that errors are due to two generally more important sources.:

- Errors represent systematic interference and incongruities among models, rules, and procedures.

- Errors represent some disfunctionality of the effects of adaptive learning mechanisms. From this outlook, trustworthy human–system interactions are achieved through the design of interfaces that minimize and correct for these difficulties that cannot be eliminated through error-recovery or correction approaches. Four categories of error are identified and appropriate design guidelines are developed. These four error categories are also associated with the type of cognitive control, that is a function of user experiential familiarity with task and environment, brought to bear on the task at hand. We will discuss this cognitive control model [28] in some detail in Chapter 6, and refer to it again relative to group interface issues in Chapter 7.*

The following are among the relevant observations and suggestions [26, 27]:

1. *Errors related to learning and interaction* cannot and should not be removed totally in that occasional errors may play a valuable role in the skill-based developments. Four basic design guidelines are postulated:
   1.1 Experiments are necessary to enable interface users to optimize their *skills*, and appropriate interface design should make acceptable performance limits visible while their effects are still both observable and reversible.
   1.2 System operators should be provided with feedback on the effects of actions potentially taken such that they are able to cope with necessary time delays between execution of an action and the observation of its effect. This expedites error recovery through the support provided to functional understanding and knowledge-based monitoring of *rules* and constraints associated with the applicability of rules, particularly when these constraints are originated by another person, such as another decision maker or the system designer.
   1.3 Displays should be designed so that the *rule-based* mappings from the signs that define cues for action and symbols that describe how processes function are consistent and unique.
   1.4 System users should be provided with the ability (which could be accomplished through appropriate models in the MBMS) to perform *formal reasoning based* simulation experiments, such as to test hypotheses, without the necessity to apply the associated decisions or controls on a possibly irreversible system or process. This is especially needed in initially unforeseen situations.
2. *Interference among competing cognitive control structures* should be reduced to the extent possible.† Three design guidelines are conjectured:

---

*It might be well to read these now and again after some of the cognitive control background of Chapter 6 has been read.
†This relates to the fact that experiential familiarity with a task will change the type of cognitive control used for task performance. Interference may exist owing to improper judgment at the meta-level of decisions concerning how to decide. These two statements will, hopefully, be much more meaningful after reading Chapter 6.

2.1 Provide "overview of the entire situation" displays in order to support *skill-based* reasoning.

2.2 Use integrated patterns for symbolic representations and functional monitoring of performance that are based on defined *rules* in such a way as to avoid inadvertent activation of familiar task actions when these are inappropriate.

2.3 Support *formal knowledge based reason* by formalizing mental models such as to avoid undesired interference among models.

3. The effect of *lack of cognitive and physiological resources* should be ameliorated through automation of human information-processing tasks, whenever appropriate. Two guidelines are developed to support this:

    3.1 Enable effective data and information integration by using available data to develop consistent information conversion notions so as to support design of an interface that will allow information presentation at the cognitive control level that is most appropriate for decision making in a specific situation.

    3.2 Present information in structured representations that are effective for the level of cognitive control adopted. Since the type of cognitive control adopted varies with the contingency task structure,* the information presentation framework should be adaptable to this.

4. Cope with *intrinsic human variability* by attempting to utilize this random behavior in application of *skills*, and occasionally *rules*, in an adaptive manner that is associated with and that supports learning. The 10 guidelines mentioned on page 152 are applicable here, also. One additional guideline is identified:

    4.1 Memory aids, and appropriate representations, are useful in coping with intrinsic human variability.

On the basis of this, Rasmussen and Vincente [27] propose a theoretical framework for designing interfaces. The purpose of the design is reduction of human error through improvement in systematic interactions among models, and improvements in adaptive learning. The two primary objectives of *ecological interface design* (EID) are support for all the levels of cognitive control and not forcing human information processing to a higher level, in terms of not being more cognitively demanding, than required. Therefore, an EID does not contribute to overall task difficulty. The EID concept is viewed as extending and enhancing, not replacing, the earlier direct manipulation interface (DMI) thinking.

Three principles are viewed as being of primary importance in interface design in order to avoid errors.†

---

*As we have noted, the contingency task structure is a function of the task, the environment into which the task is embedded, and the user experiential familiarity with task and environment.
†These are referred to *skill-based behavior, rule-based behavior,* and *formal knowledge based behavior*. These concepts are fundamental to the Rasmussen model of cognitive control. This model is described, as has been mentioned before, in Chapter 6.

1. In order to support interaction through *skill-based* time–space signals, the interface user should be able to directly act on the display itself. The structure of the displayed information should be commensurate with a wholistic or gestalt structure of the situation, and a potential view of the situation from several hierarchical levels of detail. The use of a mouse is much to be preferred to a command language here, as it is easier to retain spatial and temporal aspects of a situation.
2. A consistent one-to-one blueprint should be provided between invariant properties of the situation and the cues or signs that are provided by the system interface. This supports control at the level of *rules* and avoids the situation in which inappropriate rules are selected for application.
3. A display of the structure of an application domain is provided for the interface user. This provides the necessary support in structuring initially unstructured or semistructured problems such that formal knowledge based problem-solving strategies can be more effectively utilized in those situations where they are needed.

A theoretical foundations such as this provides a framework for designing interfaces for complex systems. It is, based on earlier work of E. Brunswik [29], called an ecological interface design. The design supports the three cognitive levels of knowledge: skill-based, rule-based, and formal reasoning based, and attempts to keep processing at the lowest cognitive level that the task (and presumably the human experiential familiarity with the task and environment, as well) requires. The ecological interface attempts to minimize the difficulty of controlling a complex system while supporting the entire range of activities that specific users require.

Rasmussen and Vicente suggest [27] that the usual approach to interface design, which results in a direct manipulation interface, fails to consider that

- Practical problem solving can take place at various levels of abstraction defined by a hierarchical problem domain representation.
- The same interface can be interpreted in different ways, and that the way in which information is interpreted triggers qualitatively different modes of information processing, each requiring a different type of computer support.

The ecological interface construct suggests that an interface design must take these factors into account if it is to be a viable aid for designers of high-technology work domains. Ecological interfaces are related to direct manipulation interfaces, direct perception interfaces, object displays, and graphics-based displays. This construct is based on *Ashby's law of requisite variety* [30], which indicates that in designing a human–computer system interface system, the complexity inherent in the process cannot be reduced below some minimum level if effective control is to be achieved.

The three fundamental requirements for a successful interface design, as based on Ashby's law, are as follows:

1. The complexity must be addressed in one way or another, by the designer, the system, or the user.

2. Physical systems can* be described by physical principles, such as the laws of thermodynamics or electrical circuits.
3. Every good controller (human supervisory controller, or machine) must possess a model of the system that is being controlled.

To ensure that these requirements are met satisfactorily, two questions must be addressed by interface designers:

- What is the best way of describing or representing the complexity of the applications domain?
- What is the best way of communicating this information to the DSS operator?

The problem of designing an interface can be presented from an ecological perspective of a duality between organism and the environment by addressing two related questions:

- The *problem side of domain*—What is the best way of presenting the complexity inherent in the domain?
- The *user side of domain*—What is the most effective resource that the operator has for coping with complexity?

While somewhat philosophical at this point, the EDI principles presented here appear most relevant to designing interfaces and dialogs of *appropriate* complexity.

4.8 SUMMARY

We have identified some design guidelines for the systems engineering of dialog generation and management systems, a simplified architecture of which is shown in Figure 4.8. One of the fundamental notions in these studies of information technology and human errors [31] is that there is a intimate association between human intent and human error. Realistic efforts to discuss human error and to design systems for human interaction that cope with human error possibilities will, therefore, consider the different types of human intentions and associated errors. In a very insightful work, Reason [32] indicates the importance of knowing whether human actions are directed by conscious intent, whether human actions proceeded as planned, and whether they achieved the desired result. Five types of actions result from this observation, as indicated in Figure 4.9. Successful interface and dialog designs will necessarily seek to create systems that encourage human intent and associated actions that result in successful act performance. Important in this regard are evaluation methods for dialog generation and management systems and human computer interface development and design tools [33, 34].

---

*And should, although this raises some concern as well as a way to realize possible support from expert systems in supporting the control of physical processes.

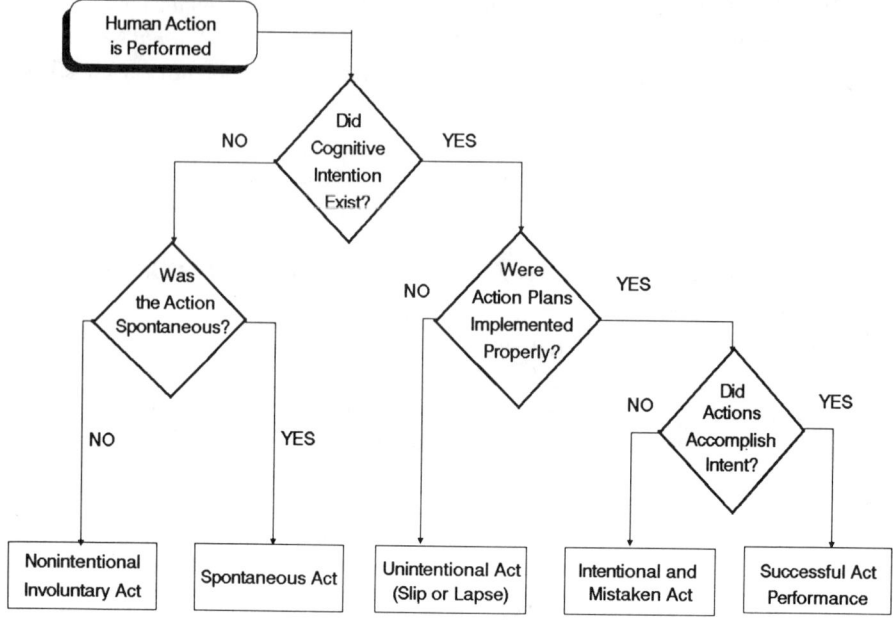

Figure 4.9 Reason's taxonomy of human actions and associated results [32].

We have attempted to focus our discussions at a conceptual level and have provided design guidelines for DGMS. This is a very active area of research at this time. Various hypertext and hypermedia systems are under development. The ultimate goal in all of this is more useful computer-based systems that support users in a variety of cognitive decision-related activities and greater contributions to *visualization*, broadly interpreted, of all relevant facets of decision-related activities involving human judgment and choice.

PROBLEMS

4.1. Identify the dialog styles that are used in four different word processors with which you are familiar.

4.2. How would you anticipate that improvements could be made to the dialog interface with the user for each of the word-processing packages identified in problem' 1? Why do you believe that these would represent improvements?

4.3. What are some trade-offs that might be made in deciding on an appropriate dialog style that is suitable for use in
   a. A programming language?
   b. A word processor?
   c. A DBMS?
   d. A DSS?

4.4. Often, it is claimed that menu interaction is the *favorite* user interface style. Write two paragraphs, one supporting and one contesting this opinion.

4.5. When will a command language be the preferred language for computer use?

4.6. How might hypertext and hypermedia be used as part of the DGMS for a DSS?

4.7. It is clearly true that every software system has a human–system interface. If this is so, why is it necessary, or is it, to study DGMS as a separate topic?

4.8. Prepare a discussion of DGMS or user interface evaluation using the approach outlined in Chapter 2 and with DGMS performance attributes identified in this chapter.

4.9. Prepare an evaluation methodology, similar to the ones developed in Chapter 2, for interface evaluation using the attributes identified by Smith and Mosier. Use this to evaluate a human–computer interface, or dialog, with which you are familiar.

References

[1] Bennett, J. L. (Ed.), *Building Decision Support Systems*, Addison-Wesley, Reading, MA, 1983.

[2] Sprague, R. H., Jr., and Carlson, E. D., *Building Effective Decision Support Systems*, Prentice-Hall, Englewood Cliffs, NJ, 1982.

[3] Harrison, H. R., and Hix, D., "Human-Computer Interface Development: Concepts and Systems for Its Management," *ACM Computing Surveys*, Vol. 21, No. 1, March 1989, pp. 5–92.

[4] Molich, R., and Nielsen, J., "Improving a Human-Computer Dialog," *Communications of the ACM*, Vol. 33, No. 3, March 1990, pp. 338–348.

[5] Hutchins, E. L., Hollan, J. D., and Norman, D. A., "Direct Manipulation Interfaces," in Norman, D. A., and Draper, S. W. (Eds.), *User Centered System Design*, Erlbaum, Hillsdale, NJ, 1986, pp. 87–124.

[6] Schneiderman, B., *Designing the User Interface: Strategies for Effective Human Computer Interaction*, Addison-Wesley, Reading, MA, 1987.

[7] Norman, D. A., "Cognitive Engineering," in Norman, D. A., and Draper, S. W. (Eds.), *User Centered System Design*, Erlbaum, Hillsdale, NJ, 1986, pp. 32–61.

[8] Carlson, E. D., "Developing the User Interface for Decisions Support Systems," in Bennett, J. L. (Ed.), *Building Decision Support Systems*, Addison-Wesley, Reading, MA, 1983, pp. 65–88.

[9] Kendall, K. E., and Kendall, K. E., *Systems Analysis and Design*, Prentice-Hall, Englewood Cliffs, NJ, 1988.

[10] Moran, T. P., "The Command Language Grammar: A Representation of the User Interface of Interactive Computer Systems," *International Journal of Man-Machine Studies*, Vol. 15, 1981, pp. 3–50.

[11] Smith, S. L., and Mosier, J. N., *Guidelines for Designing User Interface Software*, MITRE Corporation Technical Report MTR-10090, ESD-TR-86-278, Bedford, MA, 1986.

[12] Harrison, M., and Thimbleby, (Eds.), *Formal Methods in Human Computer Interaction*, Cambridge University Press, 1990.

[13] Card, S. K., Moran, T. P., and Newell, A., *The Psychology of Human Computer Interaction*, Erlbaum, Hillsdale, NJ, 1983.

[14] Card, S., Moran, T., and Newell, A., *Applied Information Processing Psychology*, Erlbaum, Hillsdale, NJ, 1983.

[15] Polson, P. G., "A Quantitative Theory of Human-Computer Interaction," in Carroll, J. M. (Ed), *Interfacing Thought: Cognitive Aspects of Human-Computer Interaction*, MIT Press, Boston, 1987, pp. 184–235.

[16] Grudin, J., "The Case Against User Interface Consistency," *Communications of the ACM*, Vol. 32, No. 10, October 1989, pp. 1164–1173.

[17] Kantorowitz, E., and Sudarsky, O., "The Adaptable User Interface," *Communications of the ACM*, Vol. 32, No. 11, November 1989, pp. 1352–1358.

[18] Kuo, F. Y., and Karimi, J., "User Interface Design from a Real Time Perspective," *Communications of the ACM*, Vol. 31, No. 12, December 1988, pp. 1456–1466.

[19] Roberts, T. L., and Moran, T. P., "A Methodology for Evaluating Text Editors," in Curtis, B. (Ed.), *Proceedings of the IEEE Conference on Human Factors in Software Development*, Gaithersburg, MD, 1982.

[20] Lee, E., "User-Interface Development Tools," *IEEE Software*, Vol. 7, No. 3, May 1990, pp. 31–36.

[21] Ravden, S., and Johnson, G., *Evaluating Usability of Human-Computer Interfaces: A Practical Method*, Wiley, New York, 1989.

[22] Nielsen, J., "Traditional Dialogue Design Applied to Modern User Interfaces," *Communications of the ACM*, Vol. 33, No. 10, October 1990, pp. 109–118.

[23] Gould, J. D., and Lewis, C., "Designing for Usability: Key Principles and What Designers Think," *Communications of the ACM*, Vol. 28, No. 3, March 1985, pp. 3001–3011.

[24] Thomas, J. J., and Hamlin, G., "Graphical Input Interaction Technique Workshop Summary," *Computer Graphics*, Vol. 17, No. 1, January 1983, pp. 5–30.

[25] Seacord, R. C., "User Interface Management Systems and Application Portability," *IEEE Computer*, Vol. 23, No. 10, October 1990, pp. 73–75.

[26] Rasmussen, J., Duncan, K., and Leplat, J. (Eds.), *New Technology and Human Error*, Wiley, New York, 1987.

[27] Rasmussen, J., and Vicente, K. J., "Coping with Human Error Through System Design: Implications for Ecological Interface Design," *International Journal of Man-Machine Studies*, Vol. 31, 1989, pp. 517–534.

[28] Rasmussen, J., *Information Processing and Human Machine Interaction: An Approach to Cognitive Engineering*, North-Holland, New York, 1986.

[29] Hammond, K. R. (Ed.), *The Psychology of Egon Brunswick*, Holt, Rinehart & Winston, New York, 1966.

[30] W. R. Ashby, *Introduction to Cybernetics*, Wiley, New York, 1956.

[31] Rasmussen, J., Duncan, K., and Leplat, J. (Eds.) *New Technology and Human Error*, Wiley, Chichester, 1987.

[32] Reason, J., *Human Error*, Cambridge University Press, Cambridge, 1990.

[33] Hix, D., and Schulman, R. S. "Human Computer Interface Development Tools: A Methodology for their Evaluation," *Communications of the ACM*, Vol. 34, No. 3, March 1991, pp. 74–87.

[34] Thimbleby, H., *User Interface Design* Addison Wesley, Reading MA, 1990.

Chapter **5**

Design and Evaluation of Decision Support Systems

In the three preceding chapters, we examined characteristics of the important three subsystems of a decision support system (DSS). These are the data-base management system (DBMS), the model-base management system (MBMS), and the dialog generation and management system (DGMS). In this chapter, we will discuss salient features associated with the integration of these three subsystems to form a complete DSS. The focus will be on the *design process* that leads to an acceptable DSS. A fairly detailed discussion of a DSS design and development life cycle will be presented. The chapter concludes with a discussion of operational test and evaluation of DSS. This supports the final phase of the life cycle, operational deployment, and associated support activities that involve maintenance and retrofit potentially needed to continually adapt the DSS the evolving needs.

There are three major *functional objectives for systems design:*

1. Formulating the design issue correctly
2. Developing an appropriate design
3. Operationalizing the design to enable performance of some desired task

These are associated with three *purposeful objectives for systems design* [1]:

1. Enhancing human abilities
2. Overcoming human limitations
3. Fostering user acceptance of the resultant product, process, or service

Four factors need to be strongly considered in determining what constitutes an appropriate design. The first of these relate to the system and the users of the system.

They are:

1. *Task.* The specific task to be performed obviously influences the nature of the system design that might best accomplish the task.
2. *Environment.* The environment into which the task is embedded, which includes internal organizational issues and the broad milieu of external issues surrounding the organization, strongly influences the characteristics of appropriate designs for task achievement.
3. *User Experiential Familiarity.* The DSS user or problem solver's familiarity with the task at hand and the environment into which this task is embedded influences whether the problems or issues to be ameliorated or tasks to be achieved are initially structured or unstructured. Thus, this is a major design ingredient.

These three factors or elements comprise the *contingency task structural variables* of an issue. Associated with this, we have the characteristics of the design team, which constitute an important factor as well.

4. *Designer Characteristics.* The extent of designer knowledge and availability, and the extent to which there is a group within the organization that might potentially use a DSS and that acts as advocates or champions for the DSS, also influence the nature of a suitable DSS design* process.

We may use a *one-quick-shot* approach to design, or a *complete phased approach.* Either is appropriate depending on the situation at hand, including the four factors just mentioned. For the most part, our emphasis will be on a complete phased life cycle approach. Either of these approaches to DSS development may involve purchase of an existing system, or designing† a system. To enable DSS design and use, there must be a plan for system design and development, a group to execute the plan, and resources to support the design and development effort.

The design group may function in one of two fundamental modes of operation. They may attempt to directly use tools for DSS design to produce a specific DSS design. They may use a *DSS generator* that will produce an operational DSS from a set of system-level *requirements specifications.* Figure 5.1 illustrates each of these concepts. For a number of reasons, the DSS generator approach will commonly be the preferred one. One reason is that it lends itself more easily to a rapid prototyping design mode in which the user is able to interact with the designer in production of a suitable DSS. A second reason is that the people that interact with the system user in the DSS-generator-based design process will naturally tend to be more oriented toward systems management and technical direction than the detail code specialists that would often be needed in the specific DSS design approach. This suggests that using the DSS generator approach will result in better facilitation of user-designer interaction than will the tool-based development approach.

---

*A full set of DSS design options should always include a *non-DSS-design* alternative.
†Either internal design within the user organization itself, or contracting with an external vendor to design the DSS, is possible.

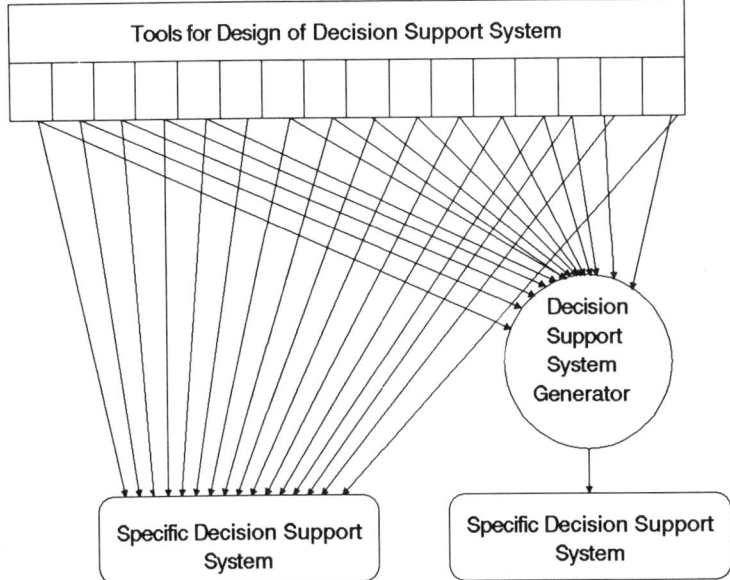

Figure 5.1 Two generic approaches to DSS design.

Figure 5.2 illustrates the phased life-cycle approach to decision support systems engineering that is discussed in some detail in the next section. A hierarchical approach to the DSS development life cycle evolves naturally from this, as suggested in Figure 5.3. Having a candidate DSS produced directly from the user-level or system-level requirements specifications will substantially enhance completion of the code production process that needs necessarily to occur at phase 4 in the phased life-cycle model of Figure 5.2. This encourages the use of such important software systems notions as software reusability [2] and will generally be associated with a number of economic advantages. It is essentially a high-level *computer-aided software engineering* (CASE) tool approach to DSS development, and we might call it a *computer-aided decision support software systems engineering* (CADSSE) development approach.

We will first look at some historical and philosophical issues concerning system design. This is critical here because it illustrates why systems design for human interaction is so important. Then, we examine a phased life-cycle for DSS design. We will first do this in a generic fashion that applies to system design in general, and therefore to DSS design. Subsequently, we shall explore some specific requirements for DSS design. Finally, we will address some operational evaluation issues.

5.1 THE EMERGENCE OF SYSTEMS DESIGN ENGINEERING

Throughout history, the development of more sophisticated tools has invariably been associated with a decrease in our dependence on human physical energy as a source

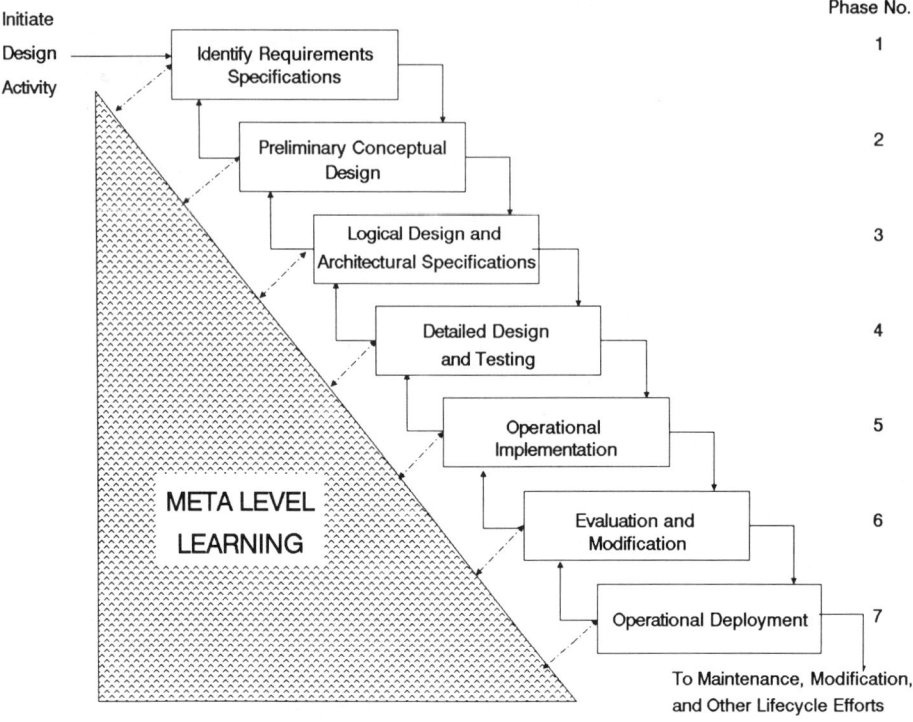

Figure 5.2 The decision support systems design process life cycle.

of effort. The Industrial Revolution represented a major thrust in this direction. In most cases, a new tool or machine has made it possible to perform a familiar task in a somewhat new and different way. In a smaller number of cases, a new tool has made it possible to do something entirely new and different—something that could not be done before. Clearly, the success of a design will depend greatly on whether the design issue was *formulated* correctly, whether the resulting design problem was *solved appropriately*, and whether the solution was operationalized in a manner that assured user satisfaction and performed well.

Concerns associated with the *design* of tools such that they can be used efficiently have always been addressed, but frequently on an implicit and *"trial-and-error"* basis. When tool designers were also tool users, which was more often than not the case for the simple tools and machines of the past, the resulting designs were often good initially, or soon evolved into good designs that did perform well and assured user satisfaction.

When physical tools, machines, and systems become so complex that it is no longer possible to design them by this single individual who also uses them, and a design team is necessary to produce a design for a different group of users, then a host of new problems emerge. This is the situation today. To cope with this, a number of methodologies associated with *systems design engineering* have evolved. Through these, it has been possible to decompose large design issues into smaller component subsystem design issues, design the subsystems, and build the complete system as a collection of these then-integrated subsystems.

Even so, problems remain. Just simply connecting together the individual subsystems often did not result in a system that performed acceptably, either from a technological efficiency perspective, or from a effectiveness perspective. This has led to the realization that *systems integration engineering* and *systems management* throughout an entire system life cycle will be necessary. Therefore, it is that contemporary efforts in *systems engineering* contain a focus on the tools, and methods that support the application of the principals of the physical and material sciences for the betterment of humankind, as well as on systems methodology and management

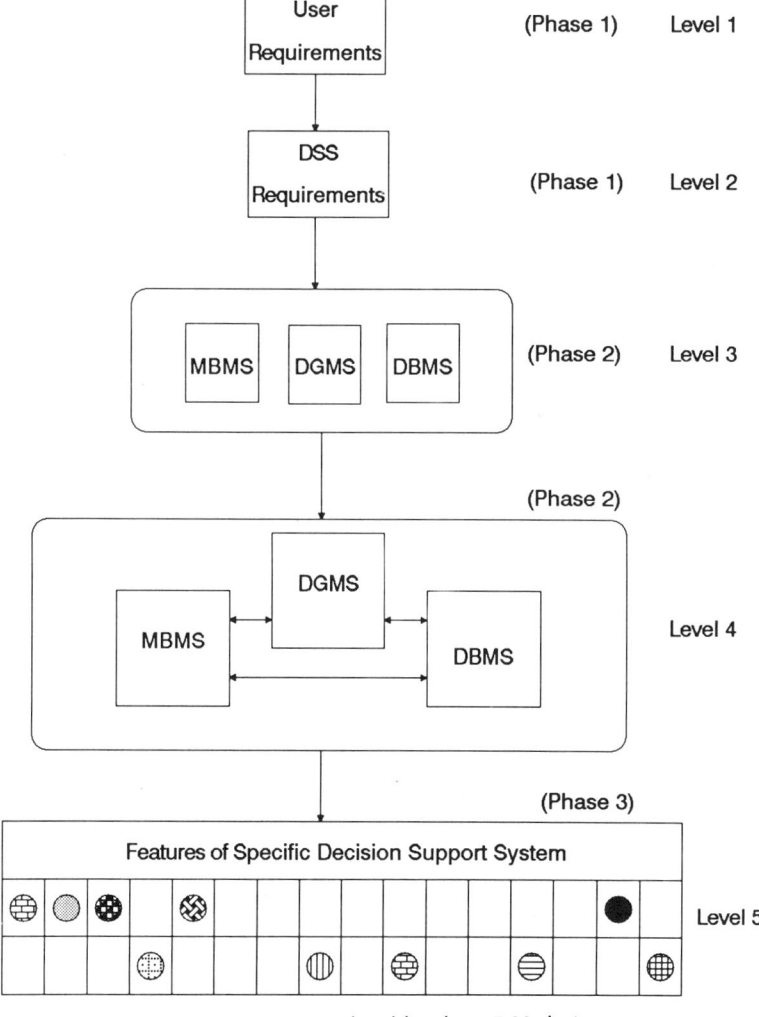

Figure 5.3 Hierarchical levels in DSS design.

constructs, that enable *system design for more efficient and effective human interaction*.

The *information technology revolution* is having and will have major impacts on design. While system designs have, in the past, relied most heavily on the mathematics of optimization and the physical and materials products that were being optimized, this can no longer be the case. Human behavioral and cognitive concerns now play a dominant role relative to the success or failure of system designs. They must be considered throughout all phases of system design. System management and integration issues are additionally of major importance in determining both the effectiveness and efficiency, and the overall *functionality* of system designs. To achieve a high measure of functionality, it must be possible for a system design to be *produced, used, maintained, retrofitted, and retired* throughout all phases of a life cycle: from need conceptualization and identification, through specification of system requirements and architectural structures, to ultimate system installation and evaluation, and ultimate operational implementation. This is a simple view of the phases of the system engineering life cycle, as illustrated in Figure 5.2.

5.2 THE NATURE OF SYSTEMS DESIGN ENGINEERING

Design is the creative process through which products, processes, or systems presumed to be responsive to client needs and requirements are conceptualized or specified. There are four primary ingredients in this not uncommon definition:

1. *Design results in specifications or architecture* for a product, process, or system.
2. *Design is a creative process.*
3. *Design activity is conceptual in nature.*
4. *A successful design must be responsive to client needs and requirements.*

Good design practice requires that the designer be responsive to each of these four ingredients for quality design effort. The fourth ingredient results in the mandate to obtain, from the client for a design effort, a set of needs and requirements for the product, process, or system that is to result from the design effort. This *information* requirement serves as the input to the design process. Design is creative, and it is a process that is conceptual in nature. The result of this creative and conceptual process is information concerning the specifications or architecture for the product, process, or service that will ultimately be manufactured, implemented, installed, or brought to fruition in some other way.

DSS users and DSS designers have needs and requirements that should be satisfied by the results of a successful design process. Information requirements determination as well as the associated identification of user requirements for a successful DSS design is, therefore, a multifaceted need for successful systems design. In a very real sense, this will often be the most important need for successful design. Without appropriate information, it is highly likely that functionality of the resulting design will be lacking and this may well be noticed only after expensive resources are allocated to a design that turns out to be immature. This concern naturally turns to important issues relative to the knowledge base for design, and how this knowledge base might best be employed and exercised in a support system that assists in decision and design processes that result in a successful DSS. To accomplish this, we need a data base and a model base for DSS design support that allows a purposeful interplay of the characteristics of successful DSS design.

5.3 SYSTEMS DESIGN METHODOLOGY

In systems design engineering practice there is, more frequently than not, some effort to first conduct a system design effort in a preliminary way in order to obtain several concepts that might work in accordance with identified user requirements. Several potential option alternatives are identified and the resulting options are subjected to at least a preliminary evaluation in order to eliminate clearly unacceptable alternatives. The surviving alternatives are then subjected to more detailed design efforts, and more complete architectures or specifications are obtained. The result of this is a system that can be subject to detailed design, testing, and at least preliminary operational implementation. Once this has occurred, operational evaluation and test of the implemented system, product, or process can occur. The system design may be modified as a result of this evaluation and this will, hopefully, lead to an ultimately improved system and operational implementation.

This leads us to a systems design engineering methodology, and a framework for this methodology, that consists of seven phases* [3]:

1. Requirements specifications identification
2. Preliminary conceptual design
3. Logical design and architectural specification identification
4. Detailed design and testing
5. Operational implementation
6. Operational evaluation and modification
7. Operational deployment

which are sequenced in an iterative manner, as shown in Figure 5.2. There are many descriptions of systems design engineering methodology and associated frameworks [4, 5], and we outline only one of them here. It is easy to see how we might redo Figure 5.2 in any number of relevant ways. For example, we could easily distinguish between user-level requirements and system-level requirements specifications. User-level requirements would represent information requirements concerning user needs,

---

*As has been noted earlier, the number of phases is somewhat arbitrary, as it is easily possible to aggregate or disaggregate any given listing of life-cycle phases into a smaller or larger number.

and system-level requirements would represent a translation of these requirements into technical requirements specifications that would be implementable in the form of hardware and software.

The requirements specification phase of our system design methodology has as its goal the identification of client needs, activities, and objectives to be achieved by implementation of the resulting DSS. As just noted, these user-level requirements are then transitioned into system-level (technical) requirements specifications. The efforts in this phase of the system design life cycle should, therefore, result in the identification and description of preliminary conceptual design considerations that are appropriate for the next phase. It is important to note that it is necessary to translate operational deployment needs into requirements specifications in order that these needs be addressed by the system design efforts. Hence, we see that information requirements specifications are affected by, and effect, each of the other phases of this DSS development life cycle.

As a result of the requirements specifications phase, there should exist a clear definition of design issues such that it becomes possible to make a decision concerning whether to undertake preliminary conceptual design of the DSS. If the result of the requirements specifications effort indicates that client needs can be satisfied in a functionally satisfactory manner, then documentation of the technical-level requirements specifications is typically prepared. This documentation concerns specifications for the preliminary conceptual design phase. Initial specifications for the following three phases of effort are typically also prepared and a concept design team is selected to implement the next phase of the design effort.

Preliminary conceptual design usually includes and results in more detailed specification of the content and associated architecture and general algorithms for the DSS that should result from the effort. The primary goal of this phase is to develop conceptualization of a *prototype* that is responsive to the requirements identified in the previous phase. Preliminary concept design according to the requirements specifications should be obtained. Rapid prototyping of the conceptual design is clearly desirable for a great many, if not almost all, applications. This can potentially be achieved by having a relatively high level DSS generator that will produce at least a prototype DSS from the technical-level requirements specifications, and potentially even from the user-level requirements specifications if there is some automatic translation mechanism that will produce system-level requirements specifications from user-level requirements.

The desired product of the next, or third, phase of design activity is a set of detailed design and architectural specifications that should result in a useful product, process, or system, and the result of the prototype design. There should be a sufficiently high degree of user confidence that a useful product will result from detailed design, or the entire design effort should be redone or possibly abandoned. Another product of this phase is a refined set of specifications for the evaluation and operational deployment phases of the design process.

An operational DSS is produced in the fourth phase of design. This is not the final design, but rather the result of implementation of the prototype design that results from the architectural specifications effort of the last phase. User guides for the DSS should be produced, such that realistic operational test and evaluation of the implemented DSS can be conducted in life-cycle phase 5. It is generally in this stage that a DSS generator can be most useful in eliminating the need for much detailed coding at the moment of specific DSS production. Operational implementation and test of this detailed design follow in the fifth phase of the design and development life cycle.

Operational evaluation of the design and the resulting operational DSS is achieved in the sixth phase of the design process. Preliminary evaluation criteria are obtained as a part of requirements specifications and modified during the following two phases of the design effort. The evaluation effort must be adapted to other phases of the design effort so that it becomes an integral and functional part of the overall design process. Generally, the critical issues for evaluation are adaptations of the elements present in the requirements specifications phase of the design process. A set of specific evaluation test requirements and tests are evolved from the objectives and needs determined in requirements specifications. These should be such that each objective measure and critical evaluation issue component can be measured from at least one evaluation test instrument. We will examine DSS evaluation in Section 5.6.

If it is determined that the DSS cannot meet user needs, the systemic design process reverts iteratively back to an earlier phase and effort continues. An important by-product of evaluation is determination of ultimate performance limitations for an operationally realizable system, and identification of those protocols and procedures for use of the result of the DSS design effort that enables maximum user satisfaction. Often, operational evaluation is the only realistic way to establish meaningful information concerning functional effectiveness of the result of a design effort. Successful evaluation is dependent on an explicit evaluation plan as developed before initiation of the evaluation effort. Clearly, rapid prototyping and automatic DSS generators will be of major assistance in allowing formal user evaluation to become a closely interactive part of the overall system design process.

The last phase of a complete system design engineering effort concerns final acceptance and operational deployment. This could involve a number of related efforts, such as the development and implementation of maintenance strategies and plans for evolution of the system over time (this would include such efforts as integration of the DSS with other operational information technology based systems, and transitioning to a new DSS design), and implementation of possible plans for marketing and sales of the DSS.

Our description of the DSS design methodology contains a strong *process* flavor. For our purposes, a process is the integration of a methodology with the behavioral concerns of human judgment in a realistic operational environment. The description of DSS design in this section has emphasized the methodological concerns and, perhaps to a lesser extent, operational environment concerns. We now turn our attention to some of the human and behavioral concerns in DSS design.

Regardless of the way in which the design process is portrayed, all characterizations will necessarily involve a number of phases, such as the seven that we have just described (additional and more detailed discussions of each of these seven phases are provided a bit later), and a number of steps within each phase. In a formal sense at least, there will be three principal steps [6] in each phase of a systems engineering life cycle:

1. *Formulation of the DSS design problem*—in which the needs and objectives of a particular phase in the life cycle are identified, and potentially acceptable alternatives, or options, are identified or generated.
2. *Analysis of the alternative designs*—in which the impacts of the identified options are evaluated at each particular life-cycle phase.
3. *Interpretation and selection*—in which the options are compared by means of an evaluation of the impacts of the alternatives at each life-cycle phase. The most acceptable alternative is selected for implementation or further study in a subsequent phase of the DSS development effort.

Without question, this is a formal rational model of the way in which DSS engineering might be accomplished. Even within this formal framework, there is the need for

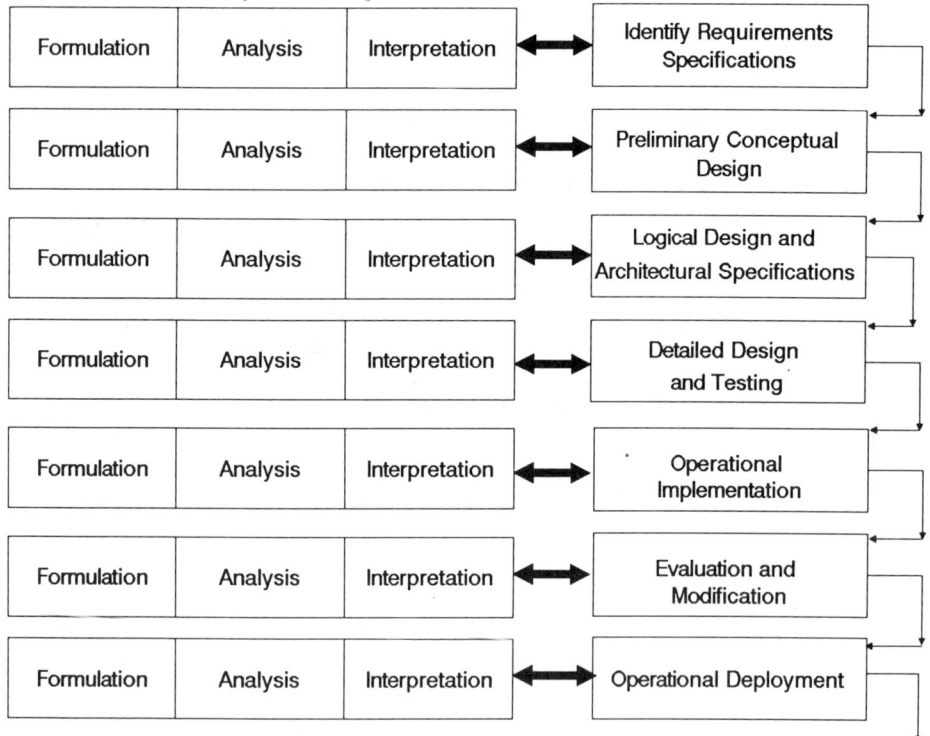

Figure 5.4 The DSS design process life cycle as a set of steps and phases.

much iteration from one step back to an earlier step when it is discovered that improvements in the results of an earlier step are needed in order to obtain a quality result at a later step. Further, this description does not emphasize the key role of information and information requirements determination, which is concentrated in the formulation step but which exists throughout all steps of the process [7]. In a similar way, information requirements determination is extraordinarily significant at the first phase of the system engineering life cycle but cannot be neglected at any phase. Figure 5.4 is a modification of Figure 5.2 to show the steps within each phase of the life cycle.

5.4 INFORMATION REQUIREMENTS FOR DESIGN

Judgments, at least prudent design judgments, are seldom made without information. For it is only through information that one becomes aware of the need for judgment and choice activities and the result of these, a decision. Information is often defined as data of value in decision making. The activities of data acquisition, representation, storage, distribution, and use are generally involved in information processing. The task of information requirements determination is necessarily involved with all of these, although formally it is concerned with determination of what information is to be acquired. This cannot be done, however, without some perceptions concerning what will be done with information after it has been acquired in order to convert it to useful knowledge. Human and organizational concerns are critical in this, as appropriate system design must be based on a satisfactory conceptual model for the decision situation (this is often called *situation assessment*).

It is possible to define information at several levels [8]. Shannon's model has been used as a meta-model of communication associated information processing. Within the syntactic delivery level of Shannon's model, the transmitter, channel, and receiver each treat messages simply as data. At this *technical level* or *syntactic level*, information and associated measures are concerned with the transmission quality of information over a channel. The syntactic or technical level encodes a message, sends the resulting signals over the channel, and decodes the signals in order to reproduce the syntax of the message. Communication is deemed successful if the message produced by the source is exactly recreated at the destination, regardless of semantic or functional ambiguity contained in the message.

Thus, design of a communication system that allows the human and a DSS to exchange knowledge about some task resolution or problem-solving issue requires that differences between the two human and the computer be recognized and that some sort of *human–computer communication architecture* be developed. The foundation for this is Shannon's information theory model [8], illustrated in Figure 5.5. As can be seen, Shannon's communication system consists of five components: the *source* of the information or producer of the messages; a *transmitter*, which operates on the message to produce a signal suitable for transmission; a *channel* , which is the medium used to transmit the signal from the transmitter to the receiver; the *receiver* itself, which performs the inverse operation of the transmitter, thereby, reconstructing

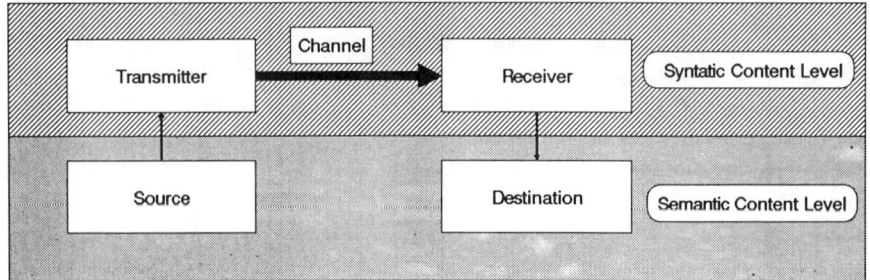

Figure 5.5 Semantic and syntactic content in electronic communications.

the message from the signal; and the *destination*, which interprets and acts on the message. The technological–or semantic-level approach to information is best exemplified by the seminal "information theory" work of Shannon. While these concepts are appropriate for maximizing channel capacity or otherwise enabling the optimization of technology components to best transmit the *data* that is in a given message, they do not directly concern whether the information that is transmitted is appropriate. That is, of course, our major concern here.

Shannon, who was completely concerned with the technical or syntactic level of communication, make the rather strong statement that *"semantic aspects of communication are irrelevant to the engineering problem."* Today, we recognize that higher-level concerns in information processing are of great importance. At the *semantic level*, concern is with the meaning and efficiency of various messages. As in Chapter 4, we could define other levels, higher and lower (e.g., information is valued in terms of its effectiveness in accomplishing an intended purpose at the *pragmatic level* or *task level*).

The four requirements for a decision support system, as identified by Sprague and Carlson [9], are

1. The ability to present information to a decision maker in ways that are clear and familiar, and that permit rapid comprehension.
2. Ease of use in terms of operations and commands to enable information acquisition and presentation.
3. Explication capability in terms of retention of results and how the results were obtained.
4. Management control in terms of enabling the decision maker, rather than the decision support system, to guide the process of judgement and choice.

These requirements are, for example, much more appropriate at the semantic and higher levels than they are at the syntactic and lower levels. It is also noteworthy here that although the four requirements are concerns at the implementation phase of DSS design, lack of attention to them at the information requirements determination stage of the requirements specifications phase of the systems design engineering life cycle is a cause of many poorly designed systems. This indicates, again, that it is vital to consider the major influence that effort at one phase of the life cycle has on other phases.

The now-classic *value of information* concept, described in most texts on systems engineering and decision making [4], does just this, but primarily from the standpoint of efficiency. From this perspective, information can only have positive value as long as it is "free," since the statistics that describe the information are assumed known, as is the structure of the decision situation. Various possible information-gathering activities that are possible are evaluated in terms of the expected (economic) benefit that will be expected from them. If the benefits in obtaining a particular item of information exceed the cost that must be paid to obtain it, then the information should be purchased according to the value-of-information concept. The biggest impediments to exclusively using this approach to determine the value of information are that

1. The requirements for a very detailed structural model of the decision situation will frequently not be met in practice.
2. Sensitivity analysis to determine the effects of imprecise parameters and knowledge is not at all easy to perform.
3. The major concern in the classic value of information approach is primarily with efficiency of information use, as contrasted with overall decision effectiveness.

In addition, it is difficult to interpret information sets that are structurally or parametrically inconsistent, in whole or in part, since the basis for derivation of the value-of-information concept assumes consistency and economic rationality. Nevertheless, the economic efficiency value of information is a significant concept and is of much potential value in information technology system design in general and DSS design in particular.

A number of other approaches have been described in the literature for determination of information needs in decision making. Taggart and Thorpe [10] have developed an approach called *"management information requirements analysis"* that is based on the realization that human communication needs and information complexity are important components of a DSS design. The result of using this approach is a set of information elements that are based on a thorough examination of pertinent reports and management responsibilities. These elements are then translated into a set of information requirements. The approach is based on a careful definition of what is that the decision maker does, determining a set of elements from this, and examining them for verb and noun indicators of information needs.

There has been some development of programming languages to assist in information requirements determination [11, 12]. The "problem statement language/ problem statement analyzer" language of Tiechroew and Hershey [12] is typical of several general-purpose languages for specifying requirements. These identified requirements are translated into system inputs that are stored in a data base for later recall and possible updating. Software tools produce a report directly from the identified data base. A top-down approach is used and this permits development of criteria, and definition of system boundaries through examination of the internal and external problem environment. After this is accomplished, as many as 22 objects may be utilized to define the conceptual qualities of the proposed system. Relations between each of the identified objects are identified next. These are stored in a centralized data base for later use in responding to queries. The efforts of Yadav [13] are concerned with these same notions and an expert modeling DSS is proposed to study information requirements.

Rockart [14] has developed an approach to information requirements determination that is based on "critical success factors." To determine these key indicators requires identification of a set of factors important to the success of the organization. There are a number of contemporary management science applications that make use of critical success factors, or success attributes [15].

The methodology of Davis [16, 17] represents a thorough and definitive approach to information requirements determination. In many respects, it is a complete synthesis of much earlier research on this subject. We will describe it here.

Davis has developed a framework for choosing one or more of four strategies for determining information requirements. According to this author, two levels of information requirements are necessary for the design of an information support system. *Organizational-level requirements* specify the information system structure, portfolios of applications, and boundaries for individual decisions. *Application-level requirements* determine specific information-processing needs to be implemented in a specific application. Although the uses of information in these two levels are different, the generic procedures for determining information requirements are the same for each. The specific procedures most useful at a given level will depend on several factors, as will be seen.

Davis identified four strategies for determining information requirements. These are designed to ameliorate the effect of three human limitations:

- Limited information-processing ability
- Bias in the selection and use of information
- Limited knowledge of appropriate problem-solving behavior

The first strategy is to *simply ask people for their requirements.* The appropriateness and completeness of the information needs assessed by this approach will be determined by the extent to which the people in question can define and structure their problem space and can compensate for their biases. This approach can be further subdivided into interacting-group and nominal-group approaches.

The second strategy is to *elicit information requirements from existing systems* that are similar in nature and purpose to the one in question. Properly executed anchoring and adjustment strategies, or perhaps analogous reasoning strategies, are useful here, since a starting point can be determined from the existing system and extrapolation of this can then be made. Examination of existing plans and reports represents one approach of identifying information requirements from an existing, or conceptualized, system.

The third strategy identified by Davis for determining information requirements consists of *synthesizing information requirements from characteristics of the utilizing system*. This permits an analytic structure for the problem space to be defined, from which information requirements can be determined. This strategy would be appropriate when the system in question is in a state of change and thus cannot be compared to an existing system. Techniques applicable in this strategy include input process–output analysis, decision analysis, and critical success factors approaches. *Process tracing* of DSS users in their present efforts is also of value.

The fourth strategy consists of *discovering needed items of information by experimentation*. Additional information can be requested as the system is employed in an operational, or simulated operational, setting and problem areas are encountered. The initial set of requirements for the system provides an anchor point for the experimentation. This represents an expensive approach, but is often the only alternative when the experience base to use one of the other approaches is lacking.

Each of the four strategies that comprise this approach has value in enhancing the abilities of systems users to specify requirements, as well as the abilities of systems design engineers to elicit and evaluate requirements. To this end, it is desirable to be able to select the best mix of these four strategies for information requirements determination at the two levels—specific problem level and meta-problem level—identified by Davis. The method of selecting the most suitable strategy is based primarily on deciding the amount of uncertainty involved in the set of information requirements that result from the use of each strategy. Here, *uncertainty* is used in a very general context to imply general information imperfection. Five steps are potentially useful in selecting an appropriate information requirements determination strategy in terms of the amount of uncertainty involved in a particular problem:

1. Identifying characteristics of the utilizing system elements, information technology system elements, users, and designers associated with system development as they affect uncertainty of information requirements determination.
2. Evaluating the effect of the characteristics of these four elements on three types of information requirements determination uncertainties:
   2.1 Availability of a set of requirements
   2.2 Ability of users to specify requirements
   2.3 Ability of system designers to elicit and specify requirements
3. Evaluating the combined effect of the information requirements determination process uncertainties on overall requirements uncertainty.
4. Selecting a primary information requirements determination strategy.
5. Selecting a set of specific methods to implement the primary requirements determination strategy.

Figure 5.6 illustrates the use of these steps to identify an appropriate mix of information requirements identification strategies. The information requirements determination process uncertainty—that is to say, the amount of information imperfection that exists in the environment for the particular task—influences the selection from among

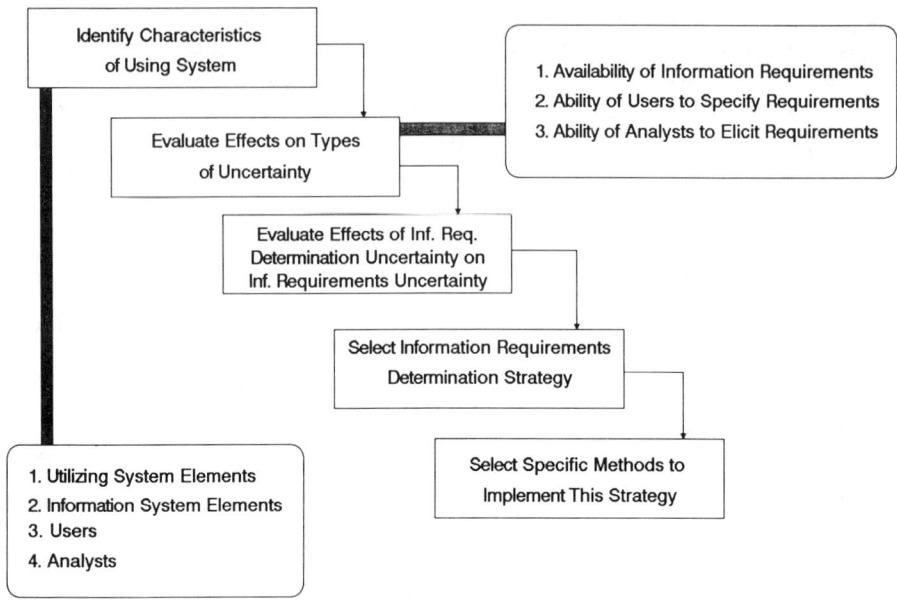

Figure 5.6 Identification of information requirements determination strategies.

the four basic strategies, as indicated in Figure 5.7. In terms of the organizational-level elements, the factors that primarily influence or effect information imperfection include stability of the environment; stability of organizational management; experience with planning, design, and use of information systems; and the extent to which the present information system is appropriate. Taken together, these enable selection of a set of information requirements determination approaches that considers the three essential contingency-dependent variables relating to uncertainties relative to information determination.

Information obtained from any approach to information requirements determination, or from a combination of approaches, must be capable of representation in a support system to aid the systems designer, including the designer of a DSS. A purpose of a DSS should be to determine possibilities of insufficient and/or inappropriate information; that is, information that is sufficiently imperfect such as to make the likelihood of an acceptable design high. The support system should then be able to determine the nature of the missing or otherwise imperfect information, and suggest steps to the user to remedy this deficiency. This suggests that a DSS should be capable of detection, diagnosis, and correction of faults in a set of information obtained for an issue. The type of information that the user of a particular support system will wish to, or should, use is very much contingency-task-structure dependent. Another information associated requirement for a support system is that of identifying the information, and judgment and choice, perspectives that a designer will and should wish to use, and to be capable of coping with requirements for design support from this multiple-perspectives viewpoint. Satisfactorily coping with these

Uncertainty	Desirable Strategy
Low	Asking
Low to Moderate	Derive from Existing System
Moderate to High	Synthesize from Existing System
High	Discovery through Experimentation

Figure 5.7 Influence of information imperfections on desirable information determination strategy.

needs should result in truly innovative and useful support systems for design processes.

Information requirements determination has also been a subject of much interest in software systems engineering [2, 18–20] and other areas [21–23]. Researchers in this area have come to much the same conclusions as systems analysts: that humans have great difficulty in specifying requirements in terms of verbal discourse or unstructured paragraphs of natural language. Consequently, support systems for requirements determination, including information requirements determination, appear quite needed.

5.5 THE ENVIRONMENT FOR DSS DESIGN AND CHARACTERISTICS OF SUCCESSFUL DESIGNS

There are many contemporary issues that may result in the need for systems design [24], including the design of decisions support systems. These issues are invariably complex. They typically involve a number of competing concerns, contain much uncertainty, and require expertise from a number of different disciplines for resolution. A systems design procedure must be specifically related to the operational environment [25] for which the final system is intended. Control-group testing and evaluation may serve many useful purposes with respect to the determination of aspects of algorithmic and behavioral efficacy of a system. Ultimate effectiveness involves user acceptability of the resulting system, and evaluation of this process effectiveness will often involve testing and evaluation in the environment, or at least a closely simulated model of the environment, in which the system would be potentially deployed.

The potential benefits of systems engineering approaches to design can be interpreted as attributes or criteria for evaluation of the design approach itself. Achievement of many of these attributes may often not be experimentally measured except by inference, anecdotal, or testimonial and case-study evidence taken in the operational environment for which the system is designed. Explicit evaluation of attribute achievement is a critical part of the overall systemic design process.

A number of characteristics of effective systems efforts can be identified. These form the basis for determining the attributes of systems and systemic design procedures. Some of these attributes will be more important for a given environment than others. Effective design must typically include an operational evaluation component that will consider the strong interaction between the system and the situational issues that led to the system design requirement. This operational environment evaluation is needed in order to determine whether a system or a systemic process for incorporation into a physical system consisting of humans and machines

- Is logically sound.
- Is matched to the operational and organizational situation and environment extant.
- Supports a variety of cognitive skills, styles, and knowledge of the humans who must use the system.
- Assists users of the system to develop and use their own cognitive skills, styles, and knowledge.
- Is sufficiently flexible to allow use and adaptation by users with differing experiential knowledge.
- Encourages more effective solution of unstructured and unfamiliar issues, allowing the application of job-specific experiences in a way compatible with various acceptability constraints.
- Promotes effective long-term management.

In their discussion of environments and frameworks for DSS design, Sprague and Carlson [9] describe DSS design perspectives from three levels; users, DSS designers, and "toolsmiths." To a considerable extent, these perspectives are those of purpose, function, and structure. They identify a four-phase design methodology, as illustrated in Figure 5.8. The specific DSS called for in phases 3 and 4 may be obtained directly from the "toolsmiths," or through use of a DSS generator.

These studies have additionally led to the identification, on the basis of requirements satisfaction within the constraint of capabilities that are necessarily limited by available resources, of four DSS characteristics that also represent capabilities or attributes of the specific DSS that will ultimately be realized. These four characteristics, which strongly influence dialog generation and management system design, may be described as follows:

1. *Representations.* It is highly desirable that a DSS provide presentations or representations that support appropriate conceptualization of the decision situation and possible alternative courses of action and their impacts. In other words, appropriate representations should be available that support the formulation, analysis, and interpretation steps of decision making.* The representations that

---

*Clearly, this applies also to other taxonometric descriptions of the steps of decision making or problem solving. In our earlier discussions, we identified a seven-step approach, for example. Simon's three-step framework, comprised of *intelligence, design,* and *choice,* is the model actually cited and used by Sprague and Carlson [9] in their study.

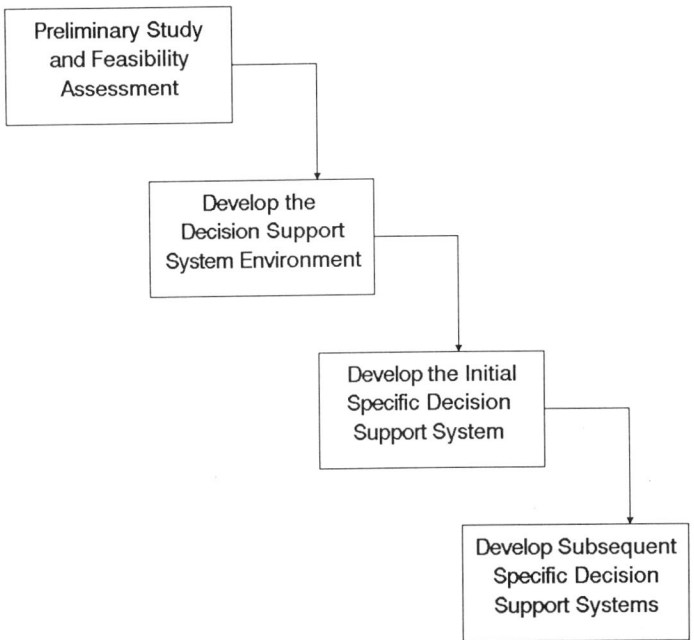

Figure 5.8 Sprague and Carlson's four DSS design phases [9].

are used in a DSS are used in the DGMS. Typical representations include PERT charts, maps, organization charts, and so forth.

2. *Operations.* Not only should a DSS properly support representations of the decision situation, it should also support cognitive activities and operations associated with the steps of formulation, analysis, and interpretation. These operations should be integrated and are *primarily* associated with the model-base management system.

3. *Memory Aids.* Long-term and short-term memory aids should be provided. Memory aids should also be provided to cope with the additional requirements imposed by use of a specific DSS. The memory aids available in a DSS are associated with capabilities provided by the DGMS and the MBMS.

4. *Control Mechanisms.* Whereas the representations, operations, and memory aids in a DSS provide support to various decision processes, the control mechanisms aid the decision maker to use these. Control mechanisms are quite critical in a DSS, since they assist the user of the DSS in adapting and integrating human problem-solving abilities and perspectives with the perspectives provided through use of the DSS. Hence, control mechanisms are also *control aids* in that they enhance the ability of the DSS user to interact with and control, or direct, the course of problem solving and decision making.

Figure 5.9 is a simplified illustration of the linkage of these four characteristics—ROMC for short—with the technological components in a DSS.

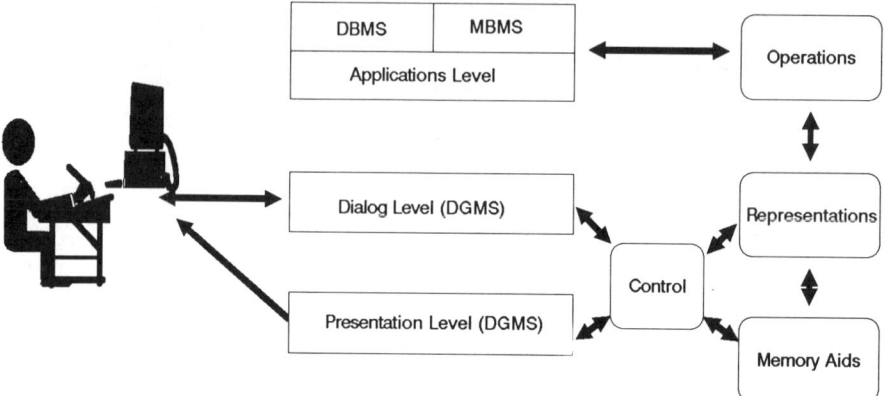

Figure 5.9 Illustration of DSS subsystems in terms of ROMC dialog design elements.

Not all of the performance objectives for quality systems design engineering will be, or need be, fully attained in all design instances, but it is generally true that quality of a system, or of a system design process, necessarily improves as more and more of these objectives are obtained. Measures of quality of the resulting system, and thus systemic process design quality, may be obtained by assessing the degree of achievement of these performance criteria by the resulting system. Generally this will need to be accomplished in an operational environment.

A taxonomy based on operational environments is necessary to describe particular situation models through which decision support is achieved. With these, we are able to evolve test instruments to establish quantitative and qualitative evaluations of a system within an operational environment. The structural and functional properties of a system, or a systemic process, must be described if a purposeful evaluation is to be accomplished. This purposeful evaluation effort also allows iteration and feedback to ultimately improve the overall systems design process. The evaluation methodology to be described in our next section is useful, therefore, as a part or phase of the design process. Also it is useful, in and of itself, to evaluate an implemented DSS, thereby providing a methodological framework both for the design and evaluation.

As we have noted, there are seven phases in the design of decision support systems. These phases serve as a guide not only for the sound design and development of systems for decision support, but for their evaluation and ultimate operational deployment as well. Although the phases were described as if they are to be sequenced in a chronological fashion, sound design practice will generally necessitate iteration and feedback from a given phase to earlier phases.

5.5.1 Requirements Specifications

Among the many objectives of the requirements specifications phase of decision support systems design are the following:

1. To define the problem to be solved, or range of problems to be solved, or issue to be resolved or ameliorated: including identification of needs, constraints, alterables, and stakeholder groups associated with operational deployment of the decision support system.
2. To determine objectives for operational system or the operational aids for decision support.
3. To obtain commitment for prototype DSS design from user group and management.
4. To search the literature and seek other expert opinions concerning the approach that is most suitable for the particular decision support design situation.
5. To assess the estimated frequency and extent of need for the DSS.
6. To determine the possible need to modify the initial design and operational DSS to meet changed requirements.
7. To identify the degree and type of accuracy expected from the DSS.
8. To estimate expected effectiveness improvement or benefits due to the use of the DSS.
9. To calculate the expected costs of using the DSS, including those pertaining to design and development as well as operation and maintenance.
10. To determine typical planning horizons and periods to which DSS support process must be responsive.
11. To assess the extent of tolerable operational environment alteration owing to use of the DSS.
12. To decide what particular decision process appears best and the formulation, analysis, and interpretation algorithms that best support this need.
13. To determine the most appropriate roles for the DSS to play within the context of the decision situation and operational environment under consideration.
14. To estimate potential leadership requirements for use of the final DSS.
15. To estimate user-group training requirements for use of the DSS.
16. To estimate the qualifications required of the design team that will design the DSS.
17. To determine preliminary operational evaluation plans and criteria for the DSS.
18. To evaluate political acceptability and institutional constraints affecting use of the DSS.
19. To document analytical and behavioral specifications to be satisfied by the DSS support process and the DSS itself.
20. To evaluate the extent to which the user group can and will likely require changes during and after DSS development.
21. To determine potential requirements for contractor availability after completion of development and operational tests of the DSS.

22. To develop the system-level requirements specifications for prototype design of the DSS support process and the operational DSS itself.

Many of those objectives relate to user-level requirements specifications. Others relate to the system-, or technical-, level requirements specifications. The primary products of this phase are a set of user-level requirements specifications for a DSS, and a set of system-level specifications.

The identified user requirements should enable the design team to have appropriate information concerning the use characteristics associated with use of the DSS. These include

1. Frequency of occurrence of need for the DSS.
2. Time available from recognition of need for a decision to identification of an appropriate decision.
3. Time available from determination of an appropriate decision to implementation of the decision.
4. Value of time.
5. Possible interactions with the decisions of others.
6. Value of information of various types.
7. Organizational structure.
8. Management support for the resulting decision support system or process.

As a result of this phase, there should be a clear definition of typical decision issues or problems requiring support and other requirements specifications, such that it is possible to make a decision concerning whether to undertake preliminary conceptual design of the DSS. If the result of this phase indicates that the user group or client needs can potentially be satisfied in a cost-effective manner by a DSS, then documentation should be prepared concerning detailed specifications for the next, preliminary conceptual design, phase. This documentation is a written embodiment of the system-level requirements specifications. Initial specifications for the last five phases of effort are also prepared, at least in a preliminary way. If the information obtained relative to system effectiveness up to this point is sufficiently positive, a *go* decision is made (this decision should be the joint responsibility of the DSS design team and the user group) and development proceeds to the next phase. A specific design team is then selected to implement the next phase of the system life cycle. This discussion emphasizes the inherently coupled nature of these phases of the system life cycle, and illustrates why it is not reasonable to consider the phases as if they are uncoupled.

5.5.2 Preliminary Conceptual Design

The preliminary conceptual design phase includes specification of the mathematical and behavioral content and associated algorithms for the decision support system and process that should ultimately result from the effort, as well as the needed software

5.5 THE ENVIRONMENT FOR DSS DESIGN AND CHARACTERISITCS OF SUCCESSFUL DESIGNS

and hardware computer support to implement these. The primary goal of this phase is to develop conceptualization of a prototype system or process in response to the technical- or system-level requirements specifications developed in the previous phase. Preliminary design according to the requirements specifications should be achieved. Objectives for preliminary conceptual design include

1. Searching the literature and seeking expert opinion concerning the particular approach to design and implementation that is likely to be most responsive to requirements specifications.
2. Determining the general class of analytic algorithms to be implemented by the DSS.
3. Determining the specific behavioral situation and operational environment in which the DSS and DSS process are to operate.
4. Deciding on the specific leadership requirements for DSS in the operational environment extant.
5. Determining specific hardware and software implementation requirements, including type of computer programming language, input devices, and so on.
6. Identifying specific information input requirements for the operational DSS.
7. Determining the specific type of output, and interpretation of the output, to be obtained from the system or process that will result from the design procedure.
8. Reevaluating objectives obtained in the previous phase, to provide documentation of minor changes, and to conduct an extensive reexamination of the effort if major changes are detected that could result in major modification and iteration through requirements specification or even termination effort.
9. Developing a preliminary conceptual design of a prototype DSS that is responsive to the requirements specification.
10. Identifying conceptual specifications for the DBMS, MBMS, and DGMS that will ultimately involve from preliminary conceptual design.

The expected product of this phase is a set of detailed design and testing specifications which, if followed, should result in a usable prototype system or process. User-group confidence that an ultimately useful product should result from detailed design should be above some threshold, or the entire design effort should be redone (or possibly even *scrapped*, the extreme meaning of "redone,"). Another product of this phase is a refined set of evaluation guidelines for the evaluation phases. Generally, these result from the conceptual architectural specifications obtained at this phase.

It should be emphasized that this second phase of the life cycle is *conceptual* in nature, and that the result of it is specification of a conceptual architecture for the DSS. If the result of this phase is successful, so that a continued *go* decision is made, the logical design phase is initiated. This third phase is then followed by a fourth phase, which is devoted to the detailed design, testing, and implementation of the DSS. These two phases, logical design and detailed design, may be quite different depending on whether a DSS is being produced directly from low-level DSS design tools or whether a DSS generator is being used.

The logical design phase, and the detailed design phase that follows it, are based on the products of the preliminary conceptual design phase which should result in a common understanding—among all parties at interest in the DSS design effort—concerning

1. Who the user group of responsive stakeholder is.
2. The structure of the operational environment in which the DSS is to be used.
3. What constitutes a plan, a design, or a decision.
4. How plans, designs, and decisions are made without the DSS and DSS process, and how they will be made with it.
5. What implementation, political acceptability, and institutional constraints affect the use of the DSS.
6. What specific DSS architectural structure will comprise the DSS; what will be contained in the DBMS, the MBMS, and the DGMS; what algorithms will be used; and how these algorithms will be interconnected to form the methodological construction of the DSS.

5.5.3 Detailed Design and Testing Phase, and Implementation Phase

In the fourth phase of design, the DSS that is presumably useful in the operational environment is produced. Among the objectives to be attained in this phase are

- To obtain and design appropriate physical facilities (physical hardware, computer hardware, output device, situation room, etc.).
- To prepare computer software for the DSS.
- To document computer software.
- To prepare a user's guide to the system and the process into which the system is embedded.
- To conduct control-group tests (including such efforts as design reviews, design walk-throughs, unit testing, integration testing, verification, validation, and other technical detailed design activities) of the DSS and make minor changes in the DSS as a result of the tests, and to document the test results.
- To complete detailed design and associated testing of the DSS based on the results of the previous phase.

Following satisfactory detailed design and testing, the DSS is implemented in the operational environment. This is generally a preliminary implementation. After implementation, operational test and evaluation occurs and this may well lead to modification of the system to improve its responsiveness to user needs.

5.5.4 The Operational Test and Evaluation Phase

Evaluation of the operational DSS is accomplished in accordance with evaluation criteria that are initially determined in the requirements specification phase and

5.5 THE ENVIRONMENT FOR DSS DESIGN AND CHARACTERISTICS OF SUCCESSFUL DESIGNS

potentially modified in subsequent phases. This evaluation should always be assisted to the extent possible by all parties at interest in the DSS design effort and the resulting DSS and DSS process. The evaluation effort must be adapted to other phases of the design effort such that it becomes an integral part of the overall design process. It is, of course, necessary for there to be some evaluation of the efficacy of the requirements specifications themselves in terms of appropriate capturing of user requirements. As noted (we provided an evaluation of DBMS software in Chapter 2 in accordance with this) evaluation may well be an effort distinct from design that is used to determine usefulness, or suitability for specified purposes, of one or more previously designed systems. Among the objectives of DSS evaluation are

1. Identifying a methodology for evaluation.
2. Identifying criteria on which the success of the system or process may be judged.
3. Determining effectiveness of the DSS in terms of success criteria.
4. Deciding on an appropriate balance between the operational environment evaluation, which is generally a purposeful and a functional evaluation, and the control-group evaluation that occurs in phases 3 and 4, which is generally a structural evaluation.
5. Determining the functional performance objective achievement of the DSS.
6. Identifying human factors or behavioral effectiveness of the DSS.
7. Deciding on the most useful strategy for employment of the DSS.
8. Assessing user-group acceptance of the DSS.
9. Evaluating the purposeful effectiveness of the resulting integrated DSS system and DSS process.
10. Based on the results of the above inquiries, suggesting refinements in the existing DSS design that will enable greater effectiveness of the DSS and DSS process.

These objectives are obtained from critical evaluation issue specifications, or evaluation need specifications. This is the first, or issue formulation, step of the evaluation phase of the DSS design life cycle. Generally, the critical issues for evaluation are minor adaptations of the elements that are present in the user-level portion of the requirements specifications phase of the systems engineering life cycle. A set of specific evaluation test requirements and tests are evolved from these objectives and needs. These must be such that each objective measure and critical evaluation issue component can be determined from at least one evaluation test instrument.

If it is determined that the operational DSS system and the resulting DSS support process cannot meet user needs, the DSS design process iterates to an earlier phase and design and development continues. An important by-product of operational evaluation is the determination of ultimate performance limitations for a specific DSS, and the establishment of a protocol and procedure for use of the system which results in greater user-group satisfaction. A report is written concerning results of the operational evaluation process, especially those factors relating to user-group satisfaction with the designed system. The evaluation process should result in suggestions for improvement in design and in better methodologies for future evaluations.

Operational evaluation of a system or process that involves human interaction appears the only realistic way to extract truly meaningful information concerning process effectiveness of a given system design. This must necessarily include leadership and training requirements to use the system. There are necessary trade-offs associated with leadership and training for use of a system and these are addressed in operational evaluation.

Successful evaluation, especially operational evaluation, strongly depends on a plan for evaluation having already been explicitly developed and in place. Our next section will deal with the development of a methodological framework for operational DSS evaluation. Objectives for evaluation of a DSS include

- Identifying a methodology for operational evaluation.
- Establishing criteria by which the success of the DSS may be judged.
- Assessing the effectiveness of the support in terms of these criteria.
- Determining the most useful strategy for employment of the existing specific DSS and potential improvements so that effectiveness might be improved.

Operational evaluation [26] of a system, which is primarily a functional and purposeful evaluation, should be based on the performance objectives for the system identified as part of the requirements specifications effort. These objectives form pertinent criteria, as they involve the algorithmic effectiveness or performance-objective achievement of the system, the behavioral or human-factor effectiveness of the system in the operational environment, and system efficacy.

Many effectiveness questions will likely arise as an evaluation of a system, or system design, proceeds. One of the critical considerations in evaluation is that of those parts of the efficacy evaluation that deal with various "abilities" of a system. These include producibility, reliability, maintainability, and marketability. Questions specific to a given evaluation are determined after study of the particular situation and the system being evaluated. It is, however, important to have an initial set of questions to guide the evaluation investigation and a purpose of this subsection is to provide a framework for accomplishing this.

5.5.5 Operational Deployment

The last phase of DSS design concerns operational deployment and final implementation. This must be accomplished in such a way that all user groups obtain adequate instructions in use of the system and complete operating and maintenance documentation. Specific objectives for the operational deployment phase of a DSS design effort are

1. To enhance operational deployment of the DSS.
2. To accomplish final design of the DSS.
3. To provide for continuous monitoring of postimplementation effectiveness of the DSS system and the support process into which the DSS is embedded.
4. To provide for retrofit or retrodesign of the DSS as indicated by the operational effectiveness evaluation.
5. To provide proper training and leadership for successful continued operational use of the DSS.
6. To identify barriers to successful implementation of the final DSS design, and strategies that will overcome these.
7. To provide for "maintenance" of the DSS.*

5.5.6 The Value of System Design and the System Design Life Cycle

The actual use of a system, as contrasted with potential usefulness, directly depends on the value that the user group of stakeholders associates with use of the system and the resulting process in an operational environment. This is dependent, in part, on how well the system satisfies performance objectives and on how well it is able to cope with one or more of the pathologies or pitfalls of planning, design, and/or decision making under potentially stressful operational environment conditions.

Quality decision support is very dependent on being able to obtain relatively complete identification of pertinent factors that influence the range of decisions that are expected to be encountered in the operational environment of the DSS. The careful comprehensive formulation of issues and associated requirements for issue resolution will lead to identification of pertinent critical factors for DSS design. These factors are ideally illuminated in a relatively easy-to-understand fashion that facilitates the interpretation necessary to evaluate and subsequently select a DSS design for implementation.

It is generally not fully meaningful to talk only of an algorithm or even a complete decision support system, which is typically a piece of hardware and software but which may well be a carefully written set of protocols and procedures, as useful by itself. It is meaningful to talk of a particular decision support process as being useful. This process involves the interaction of a methodology with systems management at the cognitive process or human judgment level. *A DSS process depends on the system, the operational environment, and leadership associated with use of the DSS.* A process involves design integration of a methodology with the behavioral concerns of human cognitive judgment in an operational environment. For all of these reasons, DSS design and DSS evaluation must necessarily be concerned with the algorithmic, behavioral, and process nature of DSS use.

*Including *reactive maintenance*, or bug fixes; *interactive maintenance*, or maintenance that better supports present user interaction with the system; and *proactive maintenance*, or maintenance that will enable the DSS to keep abreast of needs and technology as each evolves over time.

5.6 OPERATIONAL EVALUATION OF DECISION SUPPORT SYSTEMS

It is very important that DSS designers support potential effectiveness by means of an operational evaluation, or field evaluation. Without this, there is little but speculation concerning the value of a DSS. Also, without an evaluation, there is little information available that might suggest modifications to the DSS design that would make it more appropriate.

Much could be said on the subject of evaluation, and the reader is encouraged to consult Adelman [27] for an expanded treatment. In general, there are three perspectives from which an evaluation could be conducted—structural, functional, and purposeful. We will be much more concerned with the last two here. First, we will discuss some philosophical issues relative to empirical approaches to evaluation. Then, we will reexamine some of our previous discussions of multiple-attribute evaluation from an empirical operations evaluation perspective.

5.6.1 Empirical Evaluation of Decision Support Systems

This subsection, based to some extent on Tien [28, 29] and Adelman [30], provides an overview and perspective on approaches to DSS evaluation. Our efforts will be based on empirical or experientially based approaches to evaluation. Generally, empirical approaches are the approaches of choice for purposeful and functional evaluations. Empirical methods are especially suitable for testing a DSS against purposeful performance criteria. They are less useful for functional evaluation, and considerably less useful still for structural evaluation. Functional evaluation would generally correspond to validation, and structural evaluation to verification. There are many software validation and verification methods for assessing how well the hardware and software in a DSS perform. Beizer [31] provides a detailed account of software verification and testing. A discussion of software testing is also contained in Ref. 2 as well as in a number of contemporary references. In this section, we will consider operational test and evaluation or phase 6 of the life cycle. Usually, all structural evaluation and testing and most functional evaluation and test is accomplished at earlier phases in the system life cycle. At phase 6, we are primarily concerned with determining the extent to which purposeful requirements, or user requirements, are satisfied by the DSS.

We consider empirical evaluation based on observations from experiments and/or case studies. These two empirical approaches are considered because they represent a spectrum of evaluation information that ranges from fully reproducible and fully controlled laboratory like formal studies to opportunistic, uncontrolled, spontaneous studies. Generally, formal experiments will be quite convenient during the early stages of the design and development life cycle. They may also be quite useful when we wish to evaluate the performance acceptability of system functions or features, such as a specific model base, MBMS, user interface, or DGMS. Case-study evaluations will normally be most feasible in the operational environment, where control laboratory-based experiments will usually be difficult, if not impossible, to implement. Evaluation methods will vary in their appropriateness across different environmental settings. Furthermore, a combination of approaches may be best in any given situation to evaluate reliability and validity claims.

The information, or observations, obtained in an empirical evaluation may be processed using objective or subjective approaches. Experimental tests lend themselves to formal objective evaluation, often using statistical methods. Case-study observations will often, but not always, need to be processed using subjective approaches.

Without question, experiments are the most commonly used empirical evaluation approach. They are especially suitable for use when a number of people may use the operational DSS. The results of formal experiments are often generalizable from a test sample to a larger population and can, in principle, be used to indicate how a variety of people can best use a DSS [32, 33]. The typical experiment design is a *factorial design* where

- There are a number of independent variables which are systematically varied.
- There are a number of quantitative dependent variables that represent presumably objective measures of system performance.

Most *factorial experiments* contain five basic elements:

1. *Subjects*, or participants in the experiment.
2. The *task* that the subjects perform.
3. *Experimental conditions* or independent variables, such as whether or not the subjects perform an assigned task with or without use of the DSS.
4. *Dependent variables* of interest, which may relate to such purposeful measures as decision quality, or decision process quality.*
5. *Execution guidelines*, which influence the specific conduct of the experiment.

A number of detailed suggestions can also be given. For example, the evaluation team should exercise care to ensure accurate representation of the unaided, as well as DSS-aided, situation in order to conduct a fair evaluation. If performance is better in the DSS-aided situation, we want to be able to meaningfully conclude that it is due to the DSS and not to some other extraneous factor. To do so, we need to control conceivable competing hypotheses that might also explain the observed results. Also, task difficulty should be as characteristic of the operational environment as possible, or else equivalent to the presumed performance capabilities of the DSS.

*The DSS evaluation team should use either *ground truth* or *collective judgment* for measurement of decision quality. Ground truth is the *correct answer*, which may not always be known. If ground truth is not available, the collective judgment of experts should be used as correct. If expert judgment is used as a surrogate for ground truth, the experts should be uninformed concerning which experimental conditions produced particular solutions, so that the evaluations of the experts are not prejudiced.

Several attributes of an operational evaluation suggest themselves. These include

Reliability
Internal validity
External validity
Construct validity
Statistical conclusion validity
Conduct conclusion validity

The last five of these were initially identified as *threats to validity* in the classic work of Campbell and Stanley* [34]. They are certainly threats to validity in the sense that the lack of achievement of any one of these attributes of evaluation will certainly threaten the validity of an evaluation.

A *reliable* evaluation is one in which the various activities performed during the evaluation can be repeated and the same result obtained. Faithful replication is the key concept in reliability. By *valid*, we mean that conclusions of an experiment can be accepted as correct because of sound evidence. Sadly, it is possible for an experiment to be reliable, but to result in invalid conclusions for any of several reasons. But, we cannot say that an experiment will result in valid conclusions if it is unreliable. (This simply says that we cannot conclude that the results of an experiment are valid if the evidence on which this conclusion is based is unreliable.) Thus, the foundation for good evaluation results is reliable evaluation procedures and guidelines. Reliability is often possible in laboratory experiments because of rigid experimenter control of the experimental conditions. However, a number of threats to experimental validity exist regardless of experimental reliability.

Definitions of these five types of validity that need to be considered when performing experiments, are important:

1. *Internal validity* involves being able to conclude that the independent variables, and not other spurious or uncontrolled factors, caused the effects observed on the dependent variables.
2. *External validity* is concerned with generalizability. (We are concerned therefore with other organizations, decision situations, and the like for which an observed effect can be generalized.) With respect to DSS evaluations, external validity deals with the extent to which the results obtained also apply to cases not specifically examined.†

---

*The original 12 threats to validity identified by Campbell and Stanley have been expanded by Tien [28] to 20 threats, which can be aggregated into the six given here.
†With respect to a DSS evaluation, external validity also deals with the extent to which the results obtained in an experiment conducted in a simulated or laboratory setting will generalize to an operational setting. The substitute environment, the substitute decision making organization, and even the surrogate user in a laboratory based evaluation can yield results that translate over to operational results that vary between being only superficially dependable to being very dependable.

3. *Construct validity* involves determining good operational measures for the notions being evaluated. It implies that we measure only that that we want to measure.
4. *Statistical conclusion validity* deals with sources of random error and with the appropriate use of statistics in DSS evaluation. (Thus, concern is with whether or not an operational evaluation result justifies statistically defensible statements concerning covariation between independent and dependent variables, and the statistical tests that are needed to determine this.)
5. *Conduct conclusion validity* relates to the extent that any intervention in normal operations, which *may* be necessary in order to obtain information to conduct an evaluation, will be successful in that the test does not distort the normal operation* without the test.

The lack of reliability or repeatability can also be viewed as a potential threat to validity. Each of these six attributes, the lack of which becomes a threat, can also be regarded as *plausible rival hypotheses* that may also explain results obtained, or not obtained, from an evaluation. (This simply means that the test hypotheses, or causal relationships being evaluated, are potentially vulnerable to incorrect interpretation by these rival explanations of obtained results.)

Some further commentary on these types of validity is appropriate here. *Spurious factors* represent *rival hypotheses* that may be used to explain the results of an experiment. Two general approaches for control of rival hypotheses are

- Use an experimental design that will explicitly permit the DSS evaluator to test the effect of spurious factors on performance. Unfortunately, doing this requires that the evaluators can identify all plausible rival hypotheses. This is generally not possible, as there may always be alternative hypotheses for explaining observed effects. It is for this reason that the philosophy of science concentrates on disconfirmation, and not on confirmation, of hypotheses. From this perspective, a successful hypothesis is one that has been tested many times and that has continually escaped being disconfirmed.
- Eliminate any possibility that rival hypotheses can effect observed results. This generally necessitates randomization, such as achieved by arbitrarily assigning subjects to the DSS-aided and DSS-unaided portions of an experiment.

The notion of *placebos* is used in medical research to avoid problems with construct validity caused by *confounded variables*. Once we identify confounded variables that potentially may be confounded with experimental conditions, then we may choose to

- Take steps to eliminate or at least minimize their adverse influence on the DSS evaluation.

---

*This relates to nondestructive testing, and to testing that does not produce the equivalent of *self-fulfilling prophecies.*

- Methodically incorporate them into our experimental design so that we can analyze their impact.
- Measure them so that we can perform a post hoc assessment of their impact.

In the latter two approaches, we desire to measure the effects of potential correctness of the rival hypotheses or spurious factors in order to assess which hypotheses have been potentially falsified. For instance, we wish to determine whether the seemingly positive effect of use of a DSS is due to some inherent features associated with the DSS, or the support for use of the DSS by senior-level management. If subjects evaluate a DSS positively only because of the latter factor, performance may deteriorate once the DSS has been operationally deployed and the subjects in the evaluation are no longer directed to like it by senior-level management.

As is well known, there are two classical types of potential errors when performing statistical tests. The first of these is called a *Type-I error* and represents the probability of incorrectly rejecting the null hypothesis that there is no differential effect of the experimental conditions. For DSS evaluation, this is the probability of incorrectly concluding that there is a difference in the performance levels obtained with and without use of a DSS when there is no difference. Often, a Type-I error is called a *false alarm*. The second type of error is called a *Type-II error*, or *miss*. A Type-II error is that of saying there is no problem when there is a problem. A Type-I error is that of saying there is a problem when there is no problem. More formally, a Type-II error, or miss, represents the probability of incorrectly accepting the null hypothesis. In a DSS evaluation, the miss probability is the probability of concluding that there is no difference in the performance obtained with and without the DSS when a difference does exist. There are a number of other related measures. For example, the *statistical power* of a test is the complement of its Type-II error or 1 minus the miss probability. The statistical power of a test is the probability that the test will correctly reject the null hypothesis. Increasing the statistical power of a test will increase the statistical conclusion validity of an evaluation. This can be done in several ways, including

1. *Increasing the sample size*, which in general increases the precision of the sample estimate of the values on the dependent variable.
2. *Increasing the experimental reliability* by increasing the reliability of the measurement instruments that are used in the experiment.
3. *Improving the research design* by including only those factors that are truly essential to the evaluation issue under investigation. Any inclusion of low-relevance factors will always decrease the statistical power of the evaluation test if this decrease is not compensated for by a sample size increase.
4. *Selecting appropriate trade-offs among misses and false alarms* by determining which of these two types of error are most important in the evaluation. A trade-off is required because the miss and statistical power values are constrained by the value set for the false-alarm probability. Often, Type-I errors are regarded as more serious than Type-II errors, but this may not always be so.

There is also a third type of error, often called a *Type-III error*. Whereas Type-I and Type-II errors result from incorrect problem solution, Type-III errors result from wrong problem definition. Volkema [35] provides an excellent overview of approaches to avoid Type-III errors. For the most part, this is an issue for the requirements specifications phase of the DSS design life cycle. Unquestionably, poor requirements specifications will almost certainly* result in a poor DSS. It is often easier to detect Type-III, or *wrong-problem*, errors with case-study evaluations than with experimental evaluations.

Accurate characterization of the operational environment of a DSS is particularly important if initial evaluations of a DSS are to conform to the operational situation that will exist in the later stages of DSS design and development. Generally, it is less expensive to accomplish activities at the earlier life-cycle phases than at the later phases. Clearly, this is the case, since the early stages of DSS design involve conceptual models and simulated architectures, and other proofs of concept. The actual operational evaluation will be concerned with actual organizational structures, decision processes, and communication patterns that relate to task performance. Hence, an operational evaluation will necessarily attempt to emulate realistic time-stress pressures, interruptions, organizational reward structures, and the actual person or group that will eventually operate the DSS. Obviously, there will be cases where this realism is not totally possible and a realistic simulated operational environment must be used for the evaluation.

In many cases, formal experimentation will not be appropriate and perhaps not even possible in an operational setting. In this case, *case-study evaluation* is appropriate. A case study is an empirical investigation that probes and examines responses of a system to coincident influences within the real operational environment of the task, user, and system. Generally, not all variables in the operational environment can be controlled.

Two major difficulties exist in case-study-based research, including case-study-based evaluations. The first is that there is presently no really good methodological framework for conduct of case studies or use of case-study research. Also, lack of experimental control normally makes it much more difficult to minimize possible confounding of variables effects than in a formal experiment. In addition, it may be more difficult to measure such dependent variables as decision quality, since the evaluation team cannot create *correct* solutions to the problem. Accordingly, there is need for a two-step procedure, as we have noted before:

1. Since there is no ground truth, there is need for multiple experts who rate the decision quality of solution(s) obtained with and without use of the DSS.
2. Disagreements in the ratings of the experts must be resolved in some agreed-upon manner, such as by having them reach a consensus position on decision-quality ratings, or by computing some sort of average ratings.

---

*There is the possibility of dumb luck acting to produce a good DSS design, but it is generally not wise to count on this happening.

Construct validity assures that the evaluators are measuring variables they wish to measure. It does not indicate whether there are causal or covariant relations between these variables. To determine causality of relations, we need to consider statistical conclusion validity and internal validity. Statistical conclusion validity is generally impossible to assure in case-study research, since a single case will almost always have more variables than data points. Therefore, the controls normally associated with statistical experiments are not possible [36]. It is still possible, however, to determine internal validity of a test.

Two modes of data analysis for case-study research emphasized in Yin [37] appear particularly suitable for DSS case-study research.*

1. *Pattern matching* may be used for identification of potentially competing assumptions. The significant characteristic of these assumptions is that each involves a pattern of independent variables that are ideally mutually exclusive. Then, if one explanation is valid, no other can be also valid. Ideally, the identified assumptions or patterns or templates are also collectively exhaustive such that one of the patterns must be valid. In practice, this will be difficult to achieve.

2. *Explanation building* is also appropriate. Explanation building relies on iteration, in which an initial set of alternative suppositions are compared to observed data and thereafter revised. The finally selected supposition is generally not identified at the start of the effort, except in very simple cases. It usually evolves as information about the situation is processed from different perspectives. There are dangers in the approach, as it is generally never possible to confirm the truth of a hypothesis explicitly and scientifically. Thus, falsification of hypotheses, and not confirmation, should be sought. This naturally leads to pitting one rival plausible hypothesis against another.

A case study [38] on resistance to management information system implementation is a good example of the use of pattern matching. First, Markus proposed three alternative propositions to explain MIS implementation resistance. Each of the propositions led to the prediction of a different pattern of events. These events pitted the proposed propositions against each other. Patterns of information collected relative to each event supported one of the propositions. In this case study, implementation resistance was due to human–system interaction issues, and not to the alternative human-only or system-only propositions. Bourgeois and Eisenhardt [39] and Kaplan and Duchon [40] provide illustrative examples of explanation-building case studies. Reference 41 also discusses DSS evaluation from essentially this perspective.

Tien [29] has identified a five-step approach to empirical evaluation. Figure 5.10 indicates the flow of activities suggested for such evaluation.

1. *Identify Test Hypotheses.* Test hypotheses are related to the purposeful and functional objectives for the DSS and the DSS process. Each suitable hypoth-

---

Time series analysis, in which group performance is measured frequently, both before and after use of a DSS, was identified as a third mode for data analysis in case-study research. The relevance of this approach for DSS evaluation does not appear as direct as for the other two modes discussed here.

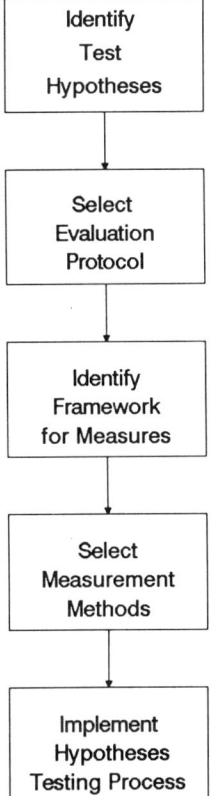

Figure 5.10 Steps in hypothesis testing for DSS evaluation [29].

esis should express a causal relationship between dependent, or output, and independent, or input, variables. The functional *purpose* of the evaluation is to test the validity of the hypotheses. Ideally, each hypothesis should be expressed in terms of quantifiable measures. It should express specific relationships that can be recognized from among other relationships, and should also be tractable using the analysis techniques that will be used for the evaluation.

2. *Select an Evaluation Protocol.* The evaluation scheme or protocol selection step includes the selection of test groups, control groups, placebos, decision process intervention techniques, and appropriate randomization and sampling techniques. Selection of an experimental design, or a nonexperimental or case-study design, is accomplished here.* Many authors favor use of experimental designs over case-study or nonexperimental designs. Often, but *not always*, they are better, since better is a context-dependent expression.

---

*When an experimental design is used, it is highly desirable to use equivalent designs for *pretest* and *posttest*. This lack of an equivalent or comparable test group and control group, and associated randomization, has led to use of the name *quasi-experimental design* to describe the departure from ideal experimental designs.

3. *Select a Measures Framework.* It is necessary to select a specific set of evaluation measures to be used in a specific evaluation. Usually, it is also necessary to construct a model that reflects the inevitable linkages and interconnections among these measures. The three basic categories for measurement—structural, functional, and purposeful—are related to the DSS input, output, technical configuration, and management process. There can be no question but that the multiple-attribute utility approach is the most-used measures framework for evaluation purposes. We have described this approach in some detail in Chapter 3 and will provide several needed extensions in our next subsection that are particularly relevant to the evaluation of DSS.
4. *Select Measurement Methods.* This involves both the selection of methods themselves, such as questionnaires, brainstorming, and nominal-group or other approaches, and the selection of such measurement methods aspects as measurement time frame, scales, instruments, procedures, and security.
5. *Implement Analysis Process.* Analytic techniques are employed to yield evaluation results, obtained from testing of the identified hypotheses. There are a plethora of statistical and other systems analysis techniques available for this purpose.

Use of these sequenced steps—especially when there are provisions for return to earlier steps to correct deficiencies in them that are only observed while accomplishing the activities of later steps—should result in appropriate evaluations of DSS. One of the major concerns in accomplishing an evaluation is to be sure that a suitable measurement framework, specified in step 3 of this framework for evaluation, has been established. Our discussions in this chapter conclude with an examination of this topic.

5.6.2 Measurement Frameworks for DSS Evaluation

This brief subsection will contain some relevant discussion of measurement frameworks, especially multiattribute utility theory frameworks, for DSS evaluation. We have already discussed MAUT in Chapters 2 and 3, and so this will focus on attribute templates for evaluation.

If DSS evaluation of design support systems is an important issue, then selection of an appropriate measures framework for evaluation is equally important. It will not generally be possible to select this framework without a reasonable knowledge of the purposes for DSS evaluation, and the ends to which DSS evaluation information will be put. In our preceding discussions, we have emphasized the contingency task structural elements of

Task
Task performer or system user
Environment
Support system potentially used
Experiential familiarity of user with task, environment, and support system

An appropriate set of evaluation measures should be capable of yielding pertinent information about relevant aspects of performance along these dimensions with and without the use of one or more support systems. These contingency task structural variables can easily be expanded. We can, for example, also consider organizational issues that impact, and that are impacted by, the DSS and the DSS user. In our discussions, we assume that the term *task performer* refers to all organizational members that impact, or are impacted by, the DSS and use of a support process. (In later chapters, we will specifically consider organizational issues, distributed DSS issues, group DSS, and other concerns relevant to support in *collective* situations.)

We have commented on purposes for DSS and DSS design in the previous section. A number of researchers have identified purposes for DSS themselves. Metersky [42], for instance has indicated that a *process* evaluation methodology should, at minimum

1. Provide a meaningful measure of decision quality.
2. Allow different decision process designs to be compared.
3. Be *acceptable* to both developer group and project sponsor.
4. Include consideration of major *environmental* factors, behavioral and physical.
5. Be adaptable across a variety of uses or missions for the support process.

Riedel and Pitz [43], in their evaluation research overview, identify three important dimensions for evaluation:

Appropriateness for task
Appropriateness for users
    Organizational user (manager or organization to whom DSS user reports)
    End user (specific DSS user)
Appropriateness for environment

Figure 5.11 is an attribute tree or template of evaluation measures based on these dimensions.

White et al. [41] suggest DSS evaluation along the dimensions of

- Algorithmic effectiveness in achievement of DSS performance objectives
- Behavioral, organizational, and human factors
- Efficacy in support of decision and decision process quality

The research reported on in this paper [41] compares the decision aid ARIADNE, mentioned in Chapter 3, to a standard MAUT-based approach to plan evaluation and to no aid at all. Eight hypotheses are identified and evaluated.

Sprague and Carlson [9] suggest measures for DSS evaluation along the lines of

1. *Productivity measures*, which relate to efficiency measures in terms of time and cost to reach or make a decision.

Category	Criterion	Criterion
Task	Logical Soundness	Options Generated - Number
	Decision Process Changes	Options Generated - Quality
Organization	Political Acceptability	Attributes Generated - Number
		Attributes Generated - Quality
	Institutional Constraints	Information Used
User	Time Requirements	Procedural Changes
	Personnel Requirements	Precision
		Flexibility
End User	Skill Level Needed	Implementation Consistency
	Effort Level Needed	Correct Answers
	Convenience of Access	Ground Truth
	Documentation Adequacy	Rationale for Decision
	Training and Leadership	Learnability
	Satisfaction with Results	Transfer
	Ease of Use	Retention
	Errors	Proneness
		Detection
		Recovery
		Criticality
	User Acceptance	Attractiveness
	Satisfaction with Results	Convenience
	Ease of Use	Confidence
		Decision Model
	Understandability	DSS Recommendation
Environment	Implementability	
	Reliability	
	Security	
	Level of Development	
	Expandability	
	Existing System Compatibility	
	Level of Funding Needed	
	Hardware and Software Support Needed	
	Integratibility with Existing System	

Figure 5.11 Decision aid evaluation criteria of Riedel and Pitz [43].

2. *Process measures*, which relate to the quality of the procedures used to reach a decision, such as number of alternatives generated and examined.
3. *Perception measures*, which relate to DSS usefulness, friendliness, and confidence in results obtained.
4. *Product measures*, which relate to the more technical features of the DSS, such as response time, reliability, maintainability, and other measures of technical trustworthiness.

Several specific tools to aid in obtaining these evaluation measures are also suggested.

5.6 OPERATIONAL EVALUATION OF DECISION SUPPORT SYSTEMS

Kumar [44] is very concerned in his research with postimplementation evaluations. The survey respondents used here were apparently all commercial firms that has installed information systems. Certainly, not all of these would be classed as DSS. The results of the study appear, however, generally applicable to DSS. He found that about 21 percent of organizations do not evaluate their information systems at all, and that 30 percent evaluate at least three-quarters of their information systems. More than 50 percent of organizations evaluate less than 50 percent of their systems. On the other hand, 79 percent are evaluating at least some of their systems. Kumar identifies three generic sets of measure criteria used for evaluation: *information criteria, system facilitating criteria*, and *system impact criteria*. A fourth factor, *quality of programs*, was also identified.

Figure 5.12 illustrates a performance evaluation attribute tree, or template, that results from the 17 lowest-level evaluation criteria used in Kumar's study. These evaluation criteria, and their relative weights (which were very close to one another) may, of course, be used to evaluate specific systems. The evaluation results so obtained will naturally be matched to the importance of various purposeful uses for the evaluation. In this study, the rank ordering of these purposeful uses was found to be as follows:

1. Verify that installed system meets system requirements,
2. Provide feedback to system design and development team,
3. Justify adoption, continuation, modification, or termination of installed system,
4. Clarify and set priorities for modification of existing system,

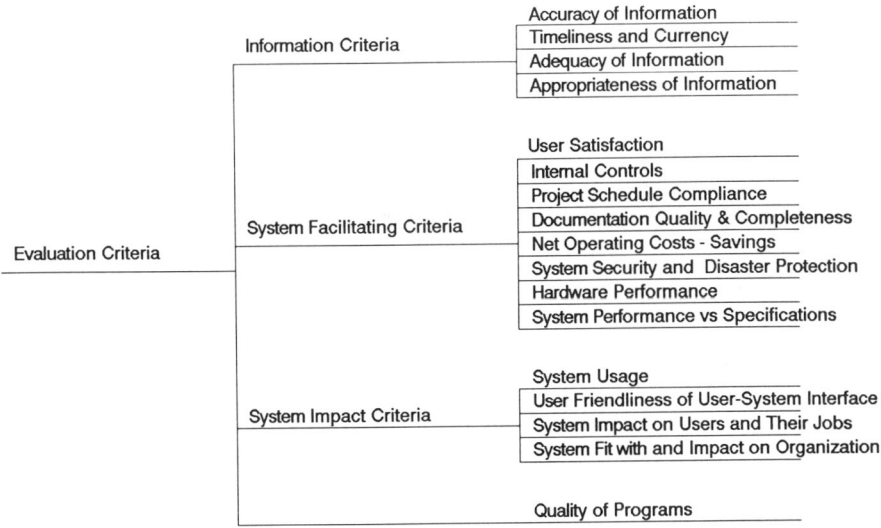

Figure 5.12 Information system evaluation criteria of Kumar [44].

5. Transfer system responsibility from design and development group to user group,
6. Report on system effectiveness to user-group management,
7. Evaluate and refine system controls,
8. Provide feedback for modification of design and development methods,
9. Verify economic payoff of system,
10. Close out system design and development process,
11. Provide feedback for modification of system use management, and
12. Evaluate system design and development personnel.

The key issues and features involved in a DSS may also be used directly as attributes for evaluation. Keen and Scott-Morton [45] suggest eight of these. Figure 5.13 illustrates these in the form of an attribute tree. A major issue in DSS evaluation is that of understanding and determining the impact of a specific DSS on both decision quality and the decision process. A major secondary goal is that of learning how to design more appropriate DSS through the learning that occurs in the evaluation process itself.

In this subsection, we have been concerned with illustrating some of the templates and evaluation criteria that may be useful for DSS evaluation. We have intentionally not discussed the many methods, such as surveys and processing tracing [46]. To some extent, overviews of many suitable methods are discussed in the initial portions of Chapter 3.

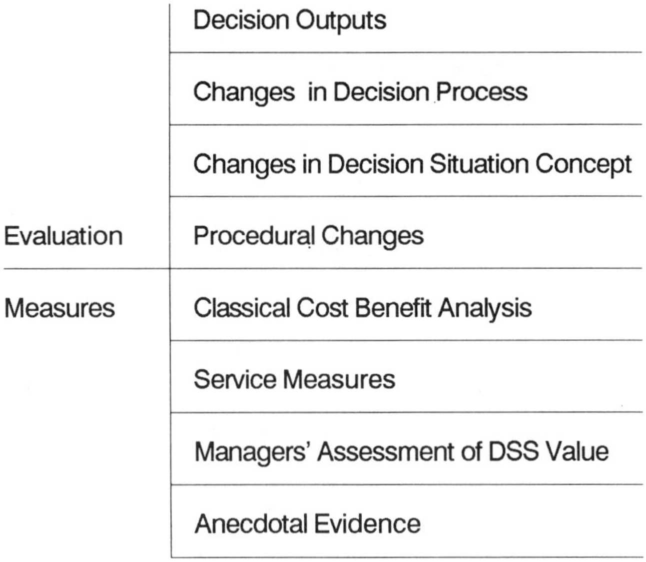

Evaluation Measures	
	Decision Outputs
	Changes in Decision Process
	Changes in Decision Situation Concept
	Procedural Changes
	Classical Cost Benefit Analysis
	Service Measures
	Managers' Assessment of DSS Value
	Anecdotal Evidence

Figure 5.13 DSS evaluation measures of Keen and Scott Morton [45].

5.7 SUMMARY

In this chapter, we have examined methods for the design and evaluation of decision support systems. In keeping with the tone of much of the rest of the book, our emphasis has been on design and evaluation principles and not on details of specific systems. The ultimate purpose of design and evaluation, as well as all other activities in the systems engineering design and development life cycle, is support for [47]:

- *DSS effectiveness*—that is, the DSS accomplishing its intended purposes.
- *DSS understandability*—that is, ease of comprehension for those who design, use, and manage the DSS.
- *DSS compatibility* with existing and likely future systems, of organizations and machines, which are potentially impacted by and that impact the DSS.

PROBLEMS

5.1. Provide a brief discussion of the potential design trade-offs involved in designing a specific DSS directly from tools, as contrasted with using a DSS generator. Approach the discussion from each of three perspectives: a toolsmith, a DSS engineer, and a DSS user group.

5.2. Identify a DSS with which you are familiar in your work environment. Describe the structure, function, and purpose of the DSS. How was the DSS developed and/or procured? Describe this in the form of a development life cycle. Contrast and compare it with the one that we have used here.

5.3. List at least six purposeful performance criteria that a DSS should possess. How do these purposeful performance criteria relate to possible functional performance criteria? How do they relate to the DBMS, MBMS, and DGMS components of a DSS? How do they relate to the ROMC aspects of dialog?

5.4. Describe some salient features of decision situations and decision makers that strongly influence the requirements specifications for a DSS.

5.5. Write a brief case-study scenario for cases where each of the four basic methods for information requirements determination is applicable.

5.6. You have been tasked, as president of DSSE Inc., to design a DSS for salespeople of the XYZ insurance company. The purpose of the DSS is to assist these salespeople and potential customers in evaluating options and selecting appropriate life insurance policy types and amounts. What now, President?

5.7. Rework the evaluation material in Chapter 2 such that is applicable to evaluation of a specific DSS software product.

5.8. Reexamine the interface design study of Smith and Mosier summarized in Chapter 4. Recast the numerous attributes or pitfalls provided in terms of the ROMC taxonomy. Write a few words about the notion of doing this. Was anything gained? What and why?

5.9. Contrast and compare the several operational evaluation measure sets described in Section 5.6.2.

References

[1] Rouse, W. B., *Design for Success: A Human Centered Approach to Designing Successful Products and Systems*, Wiley, New York, 1991.
[2] Sage, A. P., and Palmer, J. D., *Software Systems Engineering*, Wiley, New York, 1990.
[3] Sage, A. P., "A Methodological Framework for Systemic Design and Evaluation of Computer Aids for Planning and Decision Support," *Computers and Electrical Engineering*, Vol. 8, No. 2, 1981, pp. 87–102.
[4] Sage, A. P., *Methodology for Large Scale Systems*, McGraw-Hill, New York, 1977.
[5] Nadler, G., "Systems Methodology and Design," *IEEE Transactions on Systems, Man and Cybernetics*, Vol. 15, No. 6, November 1985, pp. 685–697.
[6] Sage, A. P., "Methodological Considerations in the Design of Large Scale Systems Engineering Processes," in Haimes, Y. Y. (Ed.), "Large Scale Systems," North-Holland, 1982, pp. 99–141.
[7] Sage, A. P., Galing, B., and Lagomasino, A., "Methodologies for the Determination of Information Requirements for Decision Support Systems," *Large Scale Systems*, Vol. 5, No. 2, 1983, pp. 131–167.
[8] Shannon, C. E., and Weaver, W., *The Mathematical Theory of Communication*, University of Illinois Press, Champaign, 1949.
[9] Sprague, Jr., R. H., and Carlson, E. D., *Building Effective Decision Support Systems*, Prentice-Hall, Englewood Cliffs, NJ, 1982.
[10] Taggart, W. M., and Tharp, M. O., A Survey of Information Requirements Analysis Techniques," *Computing Surveys*, Vol. 9, No. 4, December 1977, pp. 273–290.
[11] Tiechroew, D., "A Survey of Languages for Stating Requirements for Computer Based Information Systems," *Proceedings AFIPS National Computer Conference*, Vol. 41, 1972, pp. 1203–1224.
[12] Tiechroew, D., and Hershey, E. A., "PSL/PSA: A Computer Aided Technique for Structured Documentation and Analysis of Computer Based Information Systems," *IEEE Transactions on Software Engineering*, Vol. 3, No. 1, January 1977, pp. 41–48.
[13] Yadav, B. B., "Determining an Organization's Information Requirements: A State of the Art Survey," *Data Base*, Spring 1983, pp. 3–20.
[14] Rockart, J. F., "Chief Executives Define Their Own Data Needs: Critical Success Factors," *Harvard Business Review*, Vol. 57, No. 2, March/April 1979, pp. 81–93.
[15] Rockart, J. F., and Bullen, C. V. (Eds.), *The Rise of Managerial Computing*, Dow Jones–Irwin, Homewood, IL, 1986.
[16] Davis, G. B., "Strategies for Information Requirements Determination," *IBM Systems Journal*, Vol. 21, No. 1, 1982, pp. 4–30.
[17] Naumann, J. D., Davis, G. B., and McKeen, J. D., "Determining Information Requirements: A Contingency Method for Selection of a Requirements Assurance Strategy," *Journal of Systems and Software*, Vol. 1, 1980, pp. 273–281.
[18] Heninger, K. L., "Specifying Software Requirements for Complex Systems: New Techniques and Their Applications," *IEEE Transactions on Software Engineering*, Vol. 6, No. 1, January 1980, pp. 2–13.

[19] Sommerville, I., *Software Engineering*, Addison-Wesley, Reading, MA, 1982.
[20] Davis, A. M., *Software Requirements: Analysis and Specification*, Prentice-Hall, Englewood Cliffs, NJ, 1990.
[21] Ross, B. H., Ryan, W. J., and Tenpenny, P. L., "The Analysis of Relevant Information for Solving Problems," *Memory and Cognition*, Vol. 17, No. 5, 1989, pp. 639–651.
[22] Yadav, S. B., and Chand, D. R., "An Expert Modeling Support System for Modeling an Object System to Specify Its Information Requirements," *Decision Support Systems*, Vol. 5, 1989, pp. 29–45.
[23] Repo, A. J., "The Value of Information: Approaches in Economics, Accounting, and Management Science," *Journal of the American Society for Information Science*, Vol. 40, No. 2, 1989, pp. 68–85.
[24] Rouse, W. B., and Boff, K. R. (Eds.), *The Psychology of System Design*, North-Holland, New York, 1987.
[25] Wallace, R. H., Stockenberg, J. E., and Charette, R. N., *A Unified Methodology for Developing Systems*, McGraw-Hill, New York, 1987.
[26] Stevens, R. T., *Operational Test and Evaluation*, Wiley, New York, 1979.
[27] Adelman, L., *Evaluating Decision Support and Expert System Technology*, Wiley, New York, 1991.
[28] Tien, J. M., "Towards a Systematic Approach to Program Evaluation Design," *IEEE Transactions on Systems, Man and Cybernetics*, Vol. 9, No. 3, May 1979, pp. 494–515.
[29] Tien, J. M., "Evaluation Design: Systems and Models Approach," in Singh, M. (Ed.), *Systems and Controls Encyclopedia*, Pergamon Press, Oxford, 1987, pp. 1559–1566.
[30] Adelman, L., "Experiments, Quasi-Experiments, and Case Studies: Empirical Methods for Evaluating Decision Support Systems," *IEEE Transactions on Systems, Man and Cybernetics*, Vol. 21, No. 2, March 1991.
[31] Beizer, B., *Software System Testing and Quality Assurance*, Van Nostrand, New York, 1984.
[32] Cats-Baril, W. L., and Huber, G. P., "Decision Support Systems for Ill-structured Problems: An Empirical Study," *Decison Sciences*, Vol. 18, No. 2, 1977, pp. 350–372.
[33] Sharda, R., Barr, S. H., and McDonnell, J. C., "Decision Support System Effectiveness: A Review and an Empirical Test," *Management Science*, Vol. 34, No. 1, 1988, pp. 139–159.
[34] Campbell, D. T., and Stanley, J. C., *Experimental and Quasi-Experimental Design for Research*, Rand McNally, Chicago, 1966.
[35] Volkema, R. J., "Problem Formulation," in Sage, A. P. (Ed.), *Concise Encyclopedia of Information Processing in Systems and Organizations*, Pergamon Press, Oxford, UK, 1990, pp. 377–382.
[36] Lee, A. S., "A Scientific Methodology for MIS Case Studies," *MIS Quarterly*, Vol. 13, No. 1, 1989, pp. 33–50.
[37] Yin, R. K., *Case Study Research: Design and Methods*, Sage, Beverly Hills, CA, 1984.
[38] Markus, M. L., *Systems in Organizations: Bugs and Features*, Pitman, Marshfield, MA, 1984.
[39] Bourgeois, L. J., and Eisenhardt, K. M., "Strategic Decision Processes in High Velocity Environments: Four Cases in the Microcomputer Industry," *Management Science*, Vol. 34, 1988, pp. 816–835.

[40] Kaplan, B., and Duchon, D., "Combining Qualitative and Quantitative Methods in Information Systems Research: A Case Study," *MIS Quarterly*, Vol. 12, 1988, pp. 571–586.

[41] White, C. C., Sage, A. P., Dozono, S., and Scherer, W. T., "Performance Evaluation of a Decision Support System," *Large Scale Systems*, Vol. 6, No. 1, 1984, pp. 39–48.

[42] Metersky, M. L., "A C2 Process and an Approach to Design and Evaluation," *IEEE Transactions on Systems, Man and Cybernetics*, Vol. 16, No. 6, November 1986, pp. 880–889.

[43] Riedel, S. L., and Pitz, G. F., "Utilization-Oriented Evaluation of Decision Support Systems," *IEEE Transactions on Systems, Man and Cybernetics*, Vol. 16, No. 6, November 1986, pp. 980–996.

[44] Kumar, K., "Post Implementation Evaluation of Computer-Based Information Systems: Current Practices," *Communications of the ACM*, Vol. 33, No. 2, February 1990, pp. 203–212.

[45] Keen, P. G. W., and Scott-Morton, M. S., *Decision Support Systems: An Organizational Perspective*, Addison-Wesley, Reading, MA, 1978.

[46] Todd, P., and Benbasat, I., "Process Tracing Methods in Decision Support Systems Research: Exploring the Black Box," *MIS Quarterly*, Vol. 11, No. 4, December 1987, pp. 493–512.

[47] Rouse, W. B., "Design and Evaluation of Computer Based DSS," in Andriole, S. J. (Ed.), *Microcomputer Decision Support Systems: Design, Implementation and Evaluation*, QED Information Sciences, Wellesley MA, 1986, pp. 259–284.

Chapter **6**

Information Processing in Individuals and Organizations

In our efforts thus far, we have been primarily concerned with technological design issues associated with decision support systems. In this chapter, and in much of the rest of the book, we shift our interest to human and organizational issues that are critical for the successful design and use of DSS.

The designer of a DSS must be concerned both with normative models of decision and choice processes and with descriptive models of how individuals and organizations perform, and can perform, in given situations. In this chapter, we will be especially concerned with describing information-processing behavior in humans and organizations as they are influenced by the contingency structural elements of task, environment, and the human problem solver's experience with these. The contingency task structure model we first describe is related to Jean Piaget's theory of intellectual development. After a description of this model, we will indicate its implications for DSS design. Also, we will describe a number of more recent models that attempt to explain *how we decide how to process information and exercise judgment.*

There are several ways that might be used to describe how individuals and organizations acquire, represent, and use information with which to describe their perceptions of the world around them as well as issues and situations that are of importance. Rationality perspectives on knowledge will also be discussed here, since they are of considerable significance to the subject of information processing for decision support. In particular, they are a major determining force in the *decision concerning how to decide.* The roles of information, feedback, and individual and organizational learning in determining choice, and the organizational objectives that lead to choice and that are responsive to choice, are emphasized.

Unfortunately, not all human and organizational information processing is flawless. There have been a number of studies that have identified cognitive biases in human information processing. Some of these will be discussed in the concluding portions of this chapter. Some approaches that may lead to *debiasing* will also be examined.

In making a decision, the human decision maker is dealing, more often that not, with environments that are characterized by risks, hazards, uncertainty, complexity, changes over time, and conflict. Further, the quality of a decision depends on how well the decision maker is able to acquire, analyze, and evaluate and interpret information such as to discriminate between the relevant and irrelevant. Decision quality also depends on how well the decision maker assesses the situation at hand, and the process that is used to obtain a decision. We discuss these important issues for DSS design and management in this chapter. Much of our discussion is based on Ref. 1. Extensions and corollary discussions may be found in Ref. 2, and the references therein.

6.1 MOTIVATIONS FOR THE STUDY OF INFORMATION-PROCESSING MODELS

Human information processing is a vital and crucial ingredient in effective decision making. Information-processing theories of problem solving, judgment, and decision making are normally based on the assumption that individuals have

- An input mechanism for acquisition of information
- An output mechanism for interpretation and choice making
- Internal processes for filtering and other analysis efforts associated with information
- Memories for long- and short-term storage of information.

There are a large number of ways of representing human information processing. Many of these are described in texts in cognitive psychology, such as those of Anderson [3,4], Estes [5], Mayer [6], Eysenck [7], and Mandler [8], as well as in applied works in such areas as consumer choice [9].

Figure 6.1 presents some aspects of an engineering framework for human information processing. There are doubtlessly a number of components missing from this model. It does not show, for example, the essentially iterative nature of the information-processing process that enables learning. Nevertheless, it provides a useful point of departure and a physiological model structure for human information processing.

As shown in this figure, the key functions that determine how a specific problem or decision situation is cognized depend on an interaction of the memory and higher-order cognition of the problem solver with the environment that occurs through what we will denote as the contingency task structure. The various information analysis and interpretation processes of thinking, task performance objective identification, evaluation, and decision rule identification are called "higher-order"

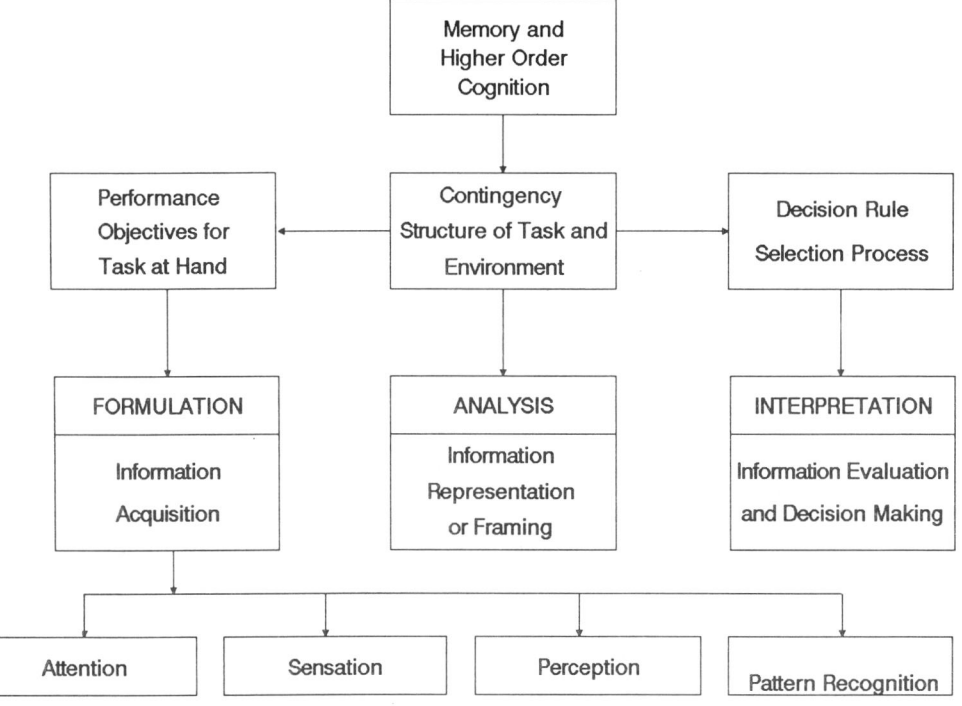

Figure 6.1 Model of human information processing.

cognition. This is not because they are somehow more important than the so-called "lower-order" cognition efforts of information acquisition that involve such efforts as sensation, attention, perception, and pattern recognition. They are called higher-order because they occur later in time in the overall information-processing effort.

Information-processing and decision-making efforts intimately involve memory. Memory influences human judgment in a number of ways. It will influence the perception of the contingency task structure associated with an issue as well as the decision rules used for evaluation of alternatives. Two characteristics of human memory are of special significance here. First, information will be encoded in more or less efficient and effective ways in terms of human abilities for recall. The coding process depends, also, on the interpretation attached to information and this strongly influences event recall, perceptions, and associated cognitive biases. The literature about memory and its components, and their relations and interaction with human perceptual experience and behavior, is vast and quite often rather speculative.* We will not be especially concerned here with details of these various related behavior therapies and will concentrate on just a few highlights.

---

*There have been many studies, for instance, dealing with the identification of the memory "engram," which is hypothesized to be the fundamental unit of memory.

Human memory is often claimed to be comprised of two major components, short-term and long term memory. The first plays a key role in immediate recall of actively rehearsed limited information. Unless conscious effort is put forth in recalling information from short-term memory, this cannot be done after a lapse of 30 to 60 seconds from initial presentation. Models of a working short-term memory involve a number of mechanisms, such as an articulatory rehearsal loop that has the capacity to retain short verbal sequences. This is just one mechanism by which short-term retention is possible. There are a number of other sensory registers. It is important to note that short-term memory is an integrated network of many mechanisms and is associated with a number of processes.

Shiffrin and Schneider [10], for example, incorporate concepts of attention, memory, and perceptual learning in their theory of short-term retention. They hypothesize that short-term storage enables such functions as active control of thinking, reasoning, and general memory processes. According to them, short-term storage is an activated subset of long-term storage. Transfer of information from short-term storage to long-term storage is dependent on attentional limitations, interference from strong external and internal stimuli, extent of analysis of information, and formation of associations in long-term storage. While seven, plus or minus two, unconnected items are believed to be the maximum amount of information that can be retained in short-term memory [11], long-term memory may contain a virtually limitless amount of information, which is generally symbolic in nature.

Thus, we see an enormous difference between human abilities and computer abilities. Because of its large long-term memory and ability for quick search and recall, a human mind easily reasons wholistically if it has an appropriate experiential basis for this. Wholistic or gestalt reasoning, such as reasoning by analogy, is not at all easy for a computer. Significant unaided computational effort would be difficult for a human, since computation must be done in short-term memory. Computers are quite agile at performing computational tasks. Therefore, we see the possibility of meaningful computer-based support to human information processing, as well as judgment and choice. A principal task of computer-aided support must be to augment human capabilities in need of augmentation, while not diminishing abilities in those areas in which human abilities generally exceed those of the computer.

Hence, pattern recognition processes involve memory and the other three components of information acquisition:

1. *Sensation,* or the initial experience of stimulation from the sensory modalities,
2. *Attention,* or the concentration of cognitive effort on sensory stimuli,
3. *Perception,* or the use of higher-order cognition to interpret sensory stimuli.

In *sensation,* information is acquired through the five major sense modalities, which are environmentally activated, in response to a specific array of stimulus energies. (These five are touch, taste, hearing, smell, and vision. They are often called *sensory stores.*) In a specific decision-making situation, the decision maker filters out bits of data believed to be irrelevant. The filtering process is based on task characteristics, experience, and motivation, as well as other features and demands of the specific decision-making situation. If such a filtering mechanism were not to exist, the decision maker would often encounter information overload. This would generally result in a form of cognitive saturation and the inability to process sufficient information for the task at hand.

Ultimately involved in *retention* processes is the notion of *attention*. For information to be transferred from short-term to long-term memory, constant conscious attention, in terms of rehearsal, is required. Information entering short-term memory that is not attended to, through specific conscious processes, is lost. Processing of information demands attending to relevant bits of incoming data and transfer of the data into long-term memory for future retrieval for making a decision. Interferences of various types may interrupt attention and thus hinder transfer and retention of relevant stimuli into long-term memory.

The process of *perception*, or pattern recognition, is also inherent in the processing of information acquisition. This process normally involves two phases: extraction and identification. A given stimulus is "coded" in terms of its features and may be received through any of the sense modalities. The meaning that a stimulus conveys to the decision maker, or the manner in which the decision maker perceives the stimulus, depends on the patterns extracted from the stimulus. In the identification phase, the sensory-perceptual system classifies the stimulus object. The way in which this is often assumed to occur is by a weighted matching of the current feature list against a likely set of prototypes in long-term memory with the input being classified according to the name of the best matching prototype. The quality or extent of the sensory information extracted determines the accuracy of identification.

Figure 6.2 illustrates the role of these in a commonly used model of human memory. This model illustrates a number of processes that lead to information acquisition and ultimate storage. Short-term and long-term memory components play key roles in the information acquisition process as the decision maker proceeds with efforts that ultimately culminate in choice. A response system couples the memory system to the sensory system and the environment. Thus, it controls or activates the sensory modalities on the basis of the actions taken. Through the response system, we close the information flow feedback loop. A model of the principal components of information flow might consist of the response, sensory, and memory systems, and the central processor. The central processor coordinates memorizing, thinking, evaluation of information, and final decision making.

We have just described what might be regarded as a component, or physiological, model of information processing. In such a stimulus response approach, behavior is seen as being initiated by the onset of stimuli. An apparent deficiency in approaches of this sort is that there is little consideration of how information bits are aggregated to influence choice and how the decision maker goes about the process of information formulation, or acquisition, analysis, and interpretation. These are needs in studies involving information processing in humans and organizations. Therefore, we would like to be able to transition from a model of physiological information processing, such as Figure 6.1 or 6.2, to a systems engineering model of various stages of information processing, such as shown in Figure 6.3.

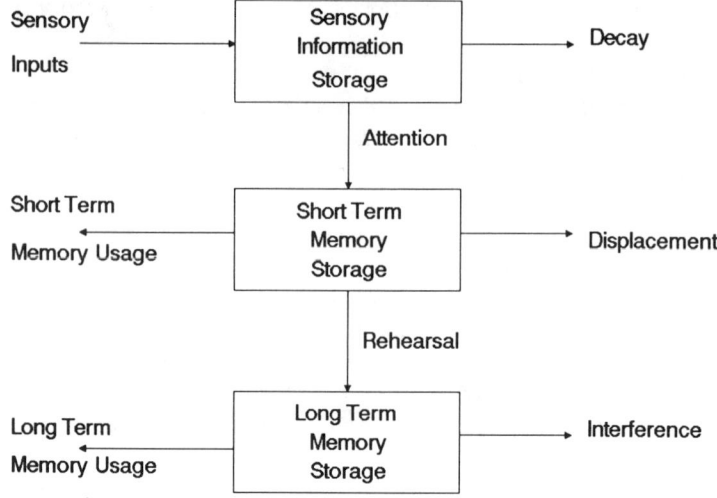

Figure 6.2 Model of human information sensory and memory storage.

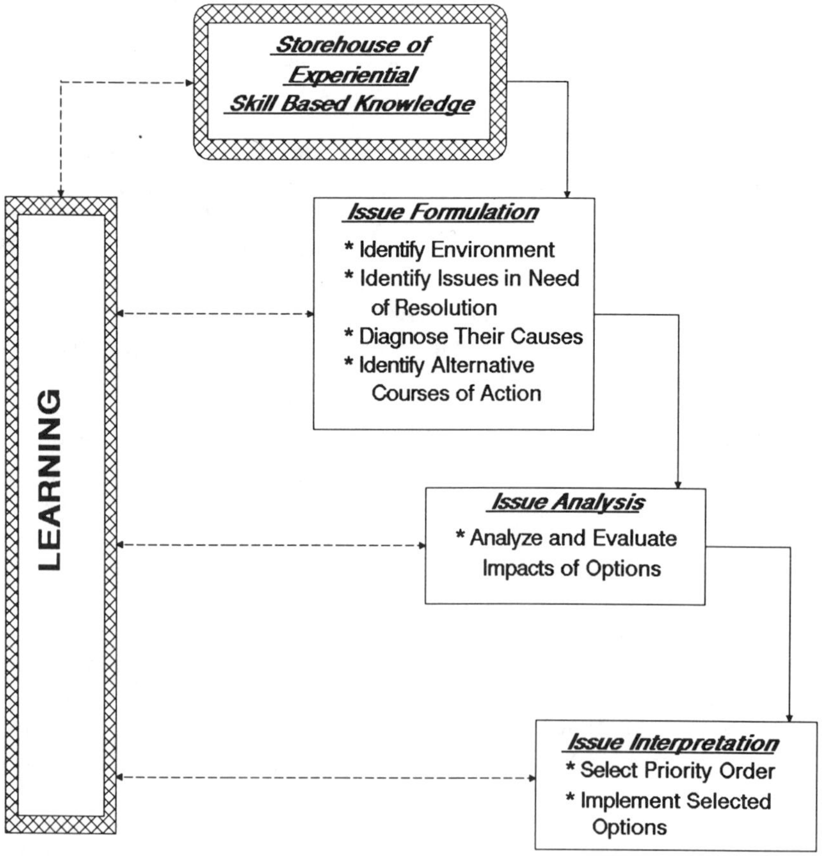

Figure 6.3 Illustration of the three formal steps in problem solving and decision making—with learning.

Two distinct phases can be identified in the process of information and knowledge acquisition. The first state is a *generative phase*, in which the need for knowledge acquisition is recognized and some requirements concerning the scope of this knowledge are identified. Next, there is a *cognitive validation phase*, which is concerned with degrees of validity and confidence that should be attributed to the present knowledge and level of expertise of decision makers relative to tasks at hand. This leads, among other things, to an assessment of the decision situation, including an identification of the (meta-level) decision concerning how to decide, a judgment concerning objectives to be achieved for the task at hand, and information needs for the issue being addressed.

During the various stages of a decision-making process, each of these generation and validation efforts may be repeated several times. Initially, a preliminary set of requirements concerning the scope of available information is identified. This set of requirements leads to an estimate of validity and confidence relative to the expertise associated with the task at hand. This, in turn, leads to the implicit identification of the decision perspective that will be used for selection of an alternative course of action. In some cases, the associated information-processing behavior is "open" in the sense that the decision-maker actively searches for potentially disconfirming information. At times, it will be "closed" in the sense that the decision-maker will ignore information that is potentially disconfirming to already-held beliefs. This open and closed information processing behavior has been observed by several researchers. Kruglanski and his colleagues [12–14] conceptualize these tendencies as consequences of epistemic motivations and use the terms *freezing* and *unfreezing* to describe them.

Examining conditions under which one of these information-processing behavior patterns is evoked should yield much insight into the variables that influence meta-level decisions concerning how to decide how to decide. In part, this might be accomplished by identifying classes of internal and external factors that influence various "freezing–unfreezing" tendencies. Three types of epistemic motivations that influence these tendencies have been suggested: fear of invalidity, sensed need for structure, and need for a desired conclusion. Several external or environmental factors that influence these may be identified: availability and saliency of information, time pressure, and group and organizational factors.

6.2 HUMAN INFORMATION-PROCESSING MODELS

In this section, we will present a number of models of human information processing. The first is the *genetic epistemology* model of Piaget. Then, we examine some other, and more contemporary, models.

6.2.1 Piaget's Model

Insights into the nature of cognitive development and into a conceptual model of cognitive activity are contained in the works of Piaget, who founded genetic epistemology in the 1930s, and recent accounts of this development [15–18]. According to Piaget, there are four stages of intellectual development:

1. Sensory motor
2. Preoperational
3. Concrete operational
4. Formal operational

The last two are particularly germane to our efforts here. In the writings of Piaget, intellectual development is seen as a function of four variables: maturation, experience, education, and self-regulation.* In Piaget's model of intellectual development, concrete operational thinkers can deal logically with empirical data, manipulate symbols, and organize facts toward the solution of well-structured and personally familiar problems. Formal operational thinkers can cope in this fashion also.

A major difference, however, is that those concrete thinkers who are not also capable of formal thought lack the capacity to reason hypothetically and to consider the effect of different variables or possibilities outside of personal experience. This suggests that concrete operational (only) thinkers may be capable of learning skills through the repeated use of rules to which they are exposed. It suggests that they will be unable to formally reason relative to such things as possible inapplicability of these rules in some situations.†

We wish to develop a model of higher-order cognitive processing that describes the mature adult decision maker. Such a decision maker will typically be capable of both formal and concrete operational thought. As will be argued, selection of a formal or concrete cognitive process will depend on the decision maker's diagnosis of need with respect to a particular task. That need will depend on a decision maker's maturity, experience, and education with respect to a particular problem. Each of these influences cognitive strain or stress, a subject discussed later in this section. Ordinarily, a decision maker will prefer a concrete operational thought process and will make use of a formal operational thought process only when concrete operational thought is perceived inappropriate. In general, a concrete operational thought process involves less stress and may well involve repetitive and previously learned behavioral patterns. Familiarity and experience, with the issue at hand or with issues perceived to be similar or analogous, play a vital role in concrete operational thought. In novel situations, which are initially unstructured and where new learning is required, formal operational thought is typically more appropriate than concrete operational thought.

*Self-regulation is a process of mental struggle with discomforting information until identification of a satisfactory mental construct allows intellectual growth or learning.
†Concrete operational *only* thinkers, for instance, will often have difficulty in responding "true" or "false" to the statement, "six is not equal to three plus four." As another example: "A card has a number on one side and a letter on the other; test the hypothesis that a card with a vowel on one side will have an even number on the other side." Concrete operational thinkers will have difficulty selecting cards for bottom-side examination if the top sides of four cards are a, b, 2, 3. However, failure to pick the cards with "a" and 3 on top may not indicate inability as a formal operational thinker but, rather, failure to properly diagnose the task and determine the need for formal operational thought.

It is of interest to describe some salient features of these two processes. In concrete operational thought, people use concepts that

- Are drawn directly from their personal experiences;
- Involve elementary classification and generalization concerning tangible and familiar objects;
- Involve direct cause-and-effect relationships, typically in simple two-variable situations;
- Can be taught or understood by analogy, algorithms, affect, standard operating, procedures or recipes; and
- Are "closed" in the sense of not demanding exploration of possibilities outside the known environment of the person and the given observed data.

In formal operational thought, however, people use concepts that may

- Be imagined, hypothetical, based on alternative scenarios, and/or contrary to fact;
- Be "open-ended," in the sense of requiring speculation about unstated possibilities;
- Require deductive reasoning using unverified and perhaps flawed hypotheses;
- Require definition by means of other concepts or abstractions that may have little or no obvious correlation with contemporary reality; and that may therefore
- Require the identification and structuring of intermediate concepts not initially specified.

Formal operational thought involves three principal stages:

1. Reversal of realities and possibilities
2. Hypothetico-deductive reasoning
3. Operations on operations

Figure 6.4 illustrates how these processes blend together, and how concrete operational thought may evolve from formal operational thought, or from training. The formal operational thought processes are accomplished through reflective observation, abstract conceptualization, and the testing of the resulting concept implications in new situations. It is in this way that the divergence produced by discomforting new experiences allows the learning of new developments and concepts to be "stored" in memory as part of one's concrete operational experiences. We will return to a discussion of this model after we introduce some contemporary related models of human judgment and choice.

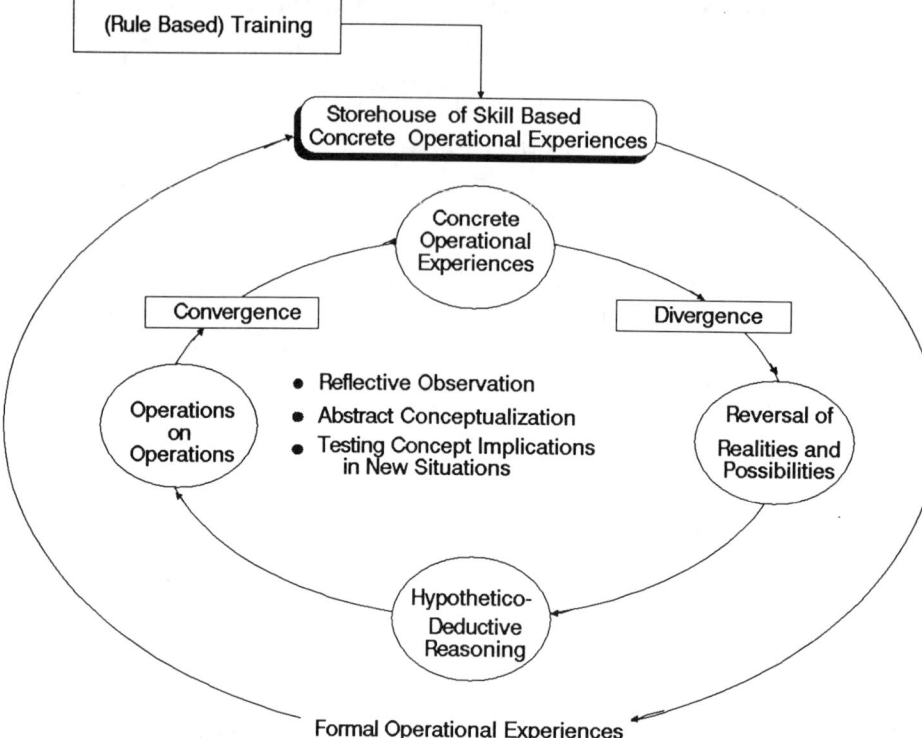

Figure 6.4 Learning through formal operational experiences (Piaget).

6.2.2 The Rasmussen Model of Judgment and Choice

One particularly useful taxonomy, due to Rasmussen [19, 20], conceptualizes three distinct types of problem-solving behavior, or reasoning:

1. Formal knowledge based behavior
2. Rule-based behavior
3. Skill-based behavior

The choice of which type of reasoning to employ is made by the problem solver on the basis of experiential familiarity with the task at hand, and the environment into which this task is embedded. Figure 6.5 presents an interpretation of the Rasmussen model, which was initially devised to describe the judgment and choice processes of process control operators. This figure does not explicitly show the dynamic learning over time that enables a person to transfer formal rule-based reasoning results to a set of rule-based judgments and then, in turn, to skill-based reasoning. These notions are much present in the works of Rasmussen.

6.2 HUMAN INFORMATION-PROCESSING MODELS

Rasmussen [21], with regard to nuclear plant operations, says that human data processes can be described in terms of: *data,* the mental representations on information describing the state; *models,* the mental representation of the system's anatomical or functional structure; and *strategies,* the higher-level structures of the mental processes that relate goals to sets of models, data, and tactical process rules. Tactical rules describe the control of the detailed processes within a formal strategy. Rasmussen says that a diagnostic search can be performed in two basic ways:

1. *Symptomatic search* uses a set of symptomatic observations as a search template for comparison with a library of symptomatic characterizations of different conditions to find a matching set. The search can be a parallel data driven *pattern recognition* or a sequential *decision table search,* as shown in Figure

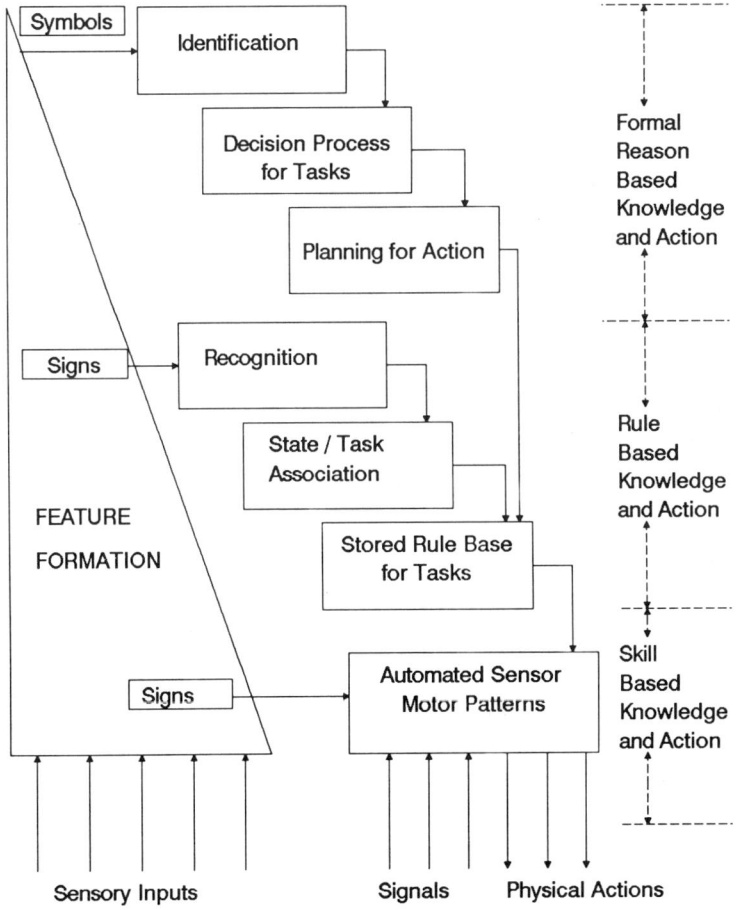

Figure 6.5 Three-level decision style model of Rasmussen [19, 21]. (The meta-level systems management for choice of style is not shown.)

6.5. A *hypothesis and test search strategy* uses reference patterns that are generated on-line by modifying a functional model to correspond to a postulated situation. This strategy is efficient if the method for generating hypotheses is efficient.

2. *Topographic search* is performed with reference to a cognitive template. This method is applied by comparing an actual situation with a template representing a *normal or desired situation*. A mismatch is observed. The template may depict the situations at several levels of abstraction. It is important for effective topographic search that the observational information be available in forms that correspond to the levels of the reference template that represent the desired situation.

Rasmussen concludes that topographic search is not economic in its use of information but uses simple data processing and small short-term memory load. Hence, it is basically unaided human search. On the other hand, search by hypothesis and test is economic in its use of information but uses complex data processing and high memory load. Accordingly, it might be more appropriate for mechanistic or computer-oriented search.

Rasmussen [22] discusses cognitive control domains in terms of skill-, rule-, and formal knowledge based behavior. This characterization is used to distinguish between the psychological mechanisms behind typical categories of errors considered as occurrences of human–task mismatches. The argument is that there are three levels of cognitive control that can be identified. These depend on different kinds of knowledge about the environment and different interpretation of the available information, that is, situation assessment. A model of the three levels of control is shown in Figure 6.5.

At the skill-based level, sensed information is perceived as time–space signals and performance is governed by schemata (stored patterns of preprogrammed instructions) represented as analog structures in a time–space domain. At the rule-based level, sensed information is perceived as signs that activate stored rules or productions, and performance is goal-driven. Signs cannot be used for functional reasoning, generating new rules, or predicting the response of an environment to unfamiliar conditions. Signs can only be used to trigger or modify rules controlling the sequencing of skilled programs. The formal knowledge based level is triggered by sensed information that indicates an unfamiliar situation.

Frequently, there is a mismatch between that problem-solving behavior that a particular human might wish to use in a given situation and the behavior that a machine designed to support a human in judgment and choice activities might be programmed to emulate. Expert systems often attempt, for example, to use rule-based representations of skill-based knowledge, or alternatively use rules when an experienced person would use a more skilled-based representation of knowledge. This knowledge may initially be expressed in any of several affective or intuitive forms that have been learned by the expert on the basis of much relevant experience. Although experts may well have learned how to be experts through formal means that require an absorbed and alert monitoring of the task components, they may no longer be formally aware of all of their monitoring actions, and may therefore give incomplete information concerning their activities. This simply reflects the view that expertise develops through perceptual learning *and* through the acquisition of a larger number of rules. Experts are not just faster and more accurate with their use of a larger number of rules, but can perceive situations, similarities, and task objectives with considerable clarity. Dreyfus and Dreyfus [23] and Klein [24, 25] have stated very useful models of human problem-solving activity that are based on their statements of the observations just made.

6.2.3 The Klein Model

Studies of information support for U.S. Air Force command and communication systems accomplished by Klein [24, 25] express a number of concerns regarding artificial intelligence and formal decision support based approaches to aid decision aiding. Specifically, these reservations involve potential inabilities and unwillingness of experts to disaggregate situations into components and to analyze these discrete components. Klein indicates that the proficient performance of experts may well be based more on reasoning by analogy than by representations in terms of set-by-step descriptions capable of traditional digital computer processing.

Further, expert proficient performers may not follow explicit, conscious rules. Requiring them to do so may reduce performance quality, and they will be unable to describe the rules that they do follow accurately. Klein views expertise as arising from perceptual abilities, including: recognitional capacity in terms of analogous situations; sensitivity to environmental context in the sense of appreciation of the significance of subtle variations; and sensitivity to intentional context by viewing the relevance and importance of task components as a whole by anticipating what has to occur to achieve a goal rather than just what will occur at the next time instant or step. He presents a comparison-guided model of proficient decision making. In this model, which is illustrated in Figure 6.6,

- A current decision situation is perceived in terms of objectives.
- The decision makers' experience allows recognition of a comparison situation.
- Similarities and differences between the comparison situation and the current situation are noted.
- This application suggests options, including evaluation of options and selection of a preferred option based on what worked in the comparison option.
- The way the objectives and the decision are perceived, possible further adjustments of options, generation of new options, and combination of options follow from this.

Klein strongly encourages development of decision aids to support the recognitional capacity of the expert. These aids will assist the expert in recognizing new situations in terms of analogous comparison cases and in using these to define options or alternatives. Such an aid would also keep track of options, assist in generation of new ones, and perform computations to assess the impacts of various options. It

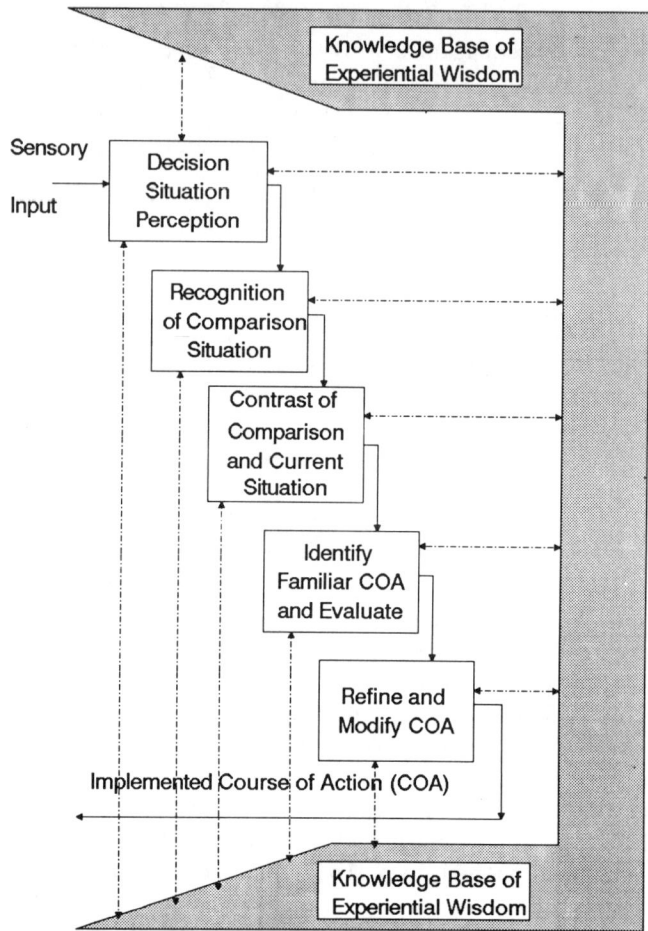

Figure 6.6 Interpretation of the Klein proficient decision style [24, 25].

certainly appears that this is a needed and necessary role for information technology systems for decision support. But it must be remembered that not all users of such a system will be proficient and expert in all of the tasks they are to perform. There will generally be a need also for provisions for formal operational thought type processes for those contingency task situations that have not been sufficiently cognized, such that appropriate use of concrete operational thought necessarily leads to efficient and effective performance.

6.2.4 The Dreyfus Model

Dreyfus and Dreyfus [23] also argue that experienced and expert human decision makers solve new problems primarily by seeing similarities to previously experienced situations in them. They argue strongly that, since similarity-based processes actually used by experienced and expert humans lead to better performance than formal approaches practiced by beginners, decision making based on proven expertise should not be replaced by formal computer-based models, which do not replicate the performance of experts.

They pose a model that contains six developmental stages through which a person passes in acquiring a skill such as to become a proficient expert. Their basic tenet is that people depend less and less on formal and abstract principles, and more and more on concrete experience, as they become proficient. The models proposed have evolved over time and as a function of the specific purpose to which the model is to be put. The six stages of development and suggested judgment characteristics or instructions at each stage are as follows:

1. *Novice.* Decompose the task environment into context-free nonsituational features that the beginner can recognize without experience. Give the beginner rules for determining action and provide monitoring and feedback to improve rule following. Expect the beginner to be consciously aware of monitoring their performance of the task, to have no perspective from which to judge their efforts, and to be detached relative to their commitment to the task.

2. *Advanced Beginner.* Decompose the task environment into context-free situationally dependent features. Except for now being able to view features from a situational perspective, other judgment features are those of a beginner, or novice.

3. *Competence.* Encourage aspect recognition not by calling attention to recurrent sets of features, but rather by singling out perspicuous examples. Encourage recognition of dangerous aspects and knowledge of guidelines to correct these conditions. Equal importance weights are typically associated with aspects at this stage. The competent person is also consciously aware of personal monitoring of their performance and is beginning to develop a perspective relative to the task at hand. There is still a detached commitment relative to understanding of the situation and deciding, but the competent person has become involved in the outcome of the decision.

4. *Proficiency.* This comes with increased practice that exposes one to a variety of whole situations. Aspects appear more or less important, depending on relevance to goal achievement. Contextual identification of similar features and aspects of the task is now possible and memorized principles, called maxims, are used to determine action. There is still a detached commitment relative to deciding, but the competent person has become involved in the outcome of the decision and understanding of the features and aspects of the task. The proficient person has developed an experienced perspective relative to the task.

5. *Expertise.* The repertoire of experienced situations is now vast, such that the occurrence of a specific situation triggers an intuitively appropriate action. The expert is consciously aware of monitoring of performance and has an involved commitment to all facets of the task.

6. *Mastery.* The master is absorbed and no longer needs to devote constant attention to performance. There is no need for self-monitoring of performance, and energy is devoted only to identifying the appropriate perspectives and suitable alternative actions.

It should be noted that the identification of six levels of capability is somewhat arbitrary. A larger or smaller number could be identified and the model presented here is somewhat of a composite of the evolving Dreyfus models. In the view of Dreyfus and Dreyfus [23], computers can, often with ease, emulate the performance of novices through capable levels of functionality. They are very strong in their arguments that the higher-level capabilities of the expert and the master will not be so easily emulated through machine intelligence.

Dreyfus and Dreyfus associate the development of these six skill categories with successive transformation of six mental functions. Figure 6.7 indicates how these transformations occur with increased stages of proficiency. While developed initially for training, this model contains much of value with respect to information systems design and general automated knowledge support. Three mental tasks occur in the judgment and choice process:

1. *Recollection of Similar Features.* This task describes the way in which a person is able to sense environmental characteristics and task needs. A novice

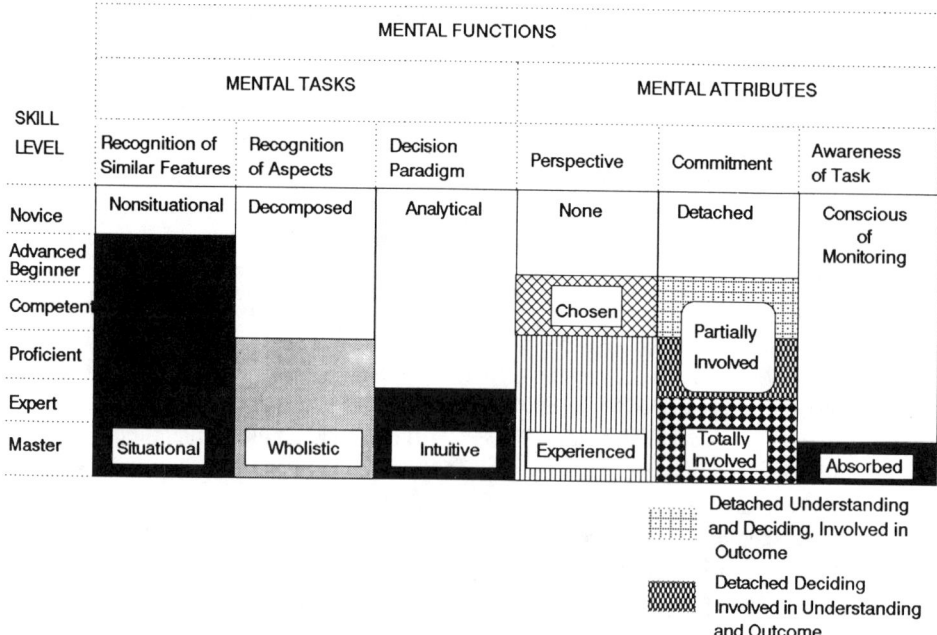

Figure 6.7 Interpretation of the Dreyfus decision style model [23].

can only view these in a nonsituational way, as the novice is, by definition, unfamiliar with the task at hand and the environment into which it is embedded.
2. *Recognition of Aspects.* This refers to the way in which the activities to resolve the task requirements are cognized. A novice and competent person must decompose these into component parts, such as the rules needed to make a left-hand turn while driving an automobile. Above the level of competence, a person is able to perceive necessary activities in a wholistic or gestalt fashion, without the necessity of decomposition of the activities that will constitute potential solutions to the identified problem or task.
3. *Decision Paradigm.* This refers to how one decides how to decide. Up to the level of expertise, people will generally use an analytical decision style. At and above the level of expertise, intuitive judgment will be the decision style of choice.

There are also three mental attributes that also vary across the six capability levels:

4. *Perspective.* A novice or advanced beginner will have no perspective relative to the unfamiliar task at hand. A person at the competent level will have a "chosen" perspective, and above the level of competent, an experienced perspective is developed.
5. *Commitment.* Novices and advanced beginners are detached relative to all mental functions. They can perform only by being given instructions from others. At the level of competence, a person becomes involved in the outcome to be achieved from a decision or task solution, but is detached in commitment to all other mental functions. The commitment increases with increasing mastery of the task, and experts and masters are involved in all facets of a task.
6. *Monitoring.* Up to the level of mastery, people are aware of some conscious task-monitoring efforts. At the level of mastery, a person becomes totally absorbed in performance of the task and is not consciously aware of monitoring efforts.

Very important concerns exist with respect to possible cognitive bias and value incoherencies in the concrete operational decision making of experts or masters. Questions related to the effects of changing environments on the judgment and decision quality of masters and novices alike are critical in all of these models. For it is possible that intuitive experience may not be a good guide for judgments and decisions in uncertain, unfamiliar, and/or rapidly changing environments. But quantitative or qualitative analysis-based efforts may well not be very good either, owing to changed decision situation and contingency task structural models. It is possible to become a "master," not only of a specific task, but unfortunately of the art of self-deception as well. The external behavior of the two "masters" may well be the same: situational, wholistic, intuitive, and absorbed. What is an appropriate style for one "master" may well be inappropriate for another. Figure 6.8 illustrates some of the effects of these potentially erroneous contingency task structure assessments.

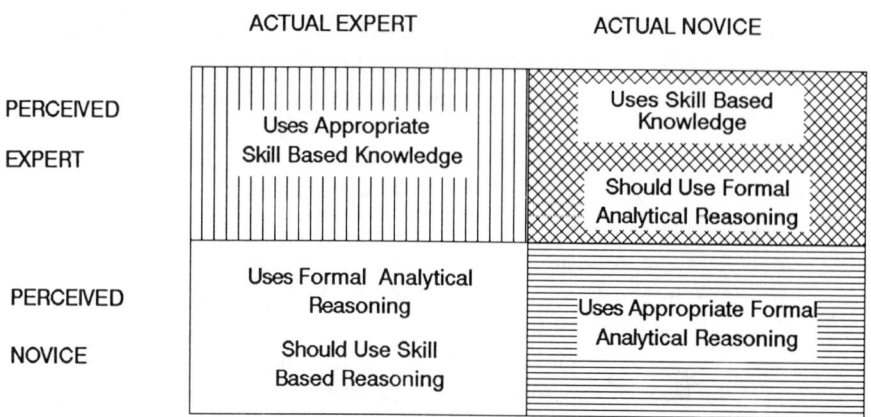

Figure 6.8 Actual knowledge perspective vs. appropriate knowledge level.

6.2.5 The Janis and Mann Model

Judgment and decision-making efforts are often characterized by intense emotion, stress, and conflict, especially when there are significant consequences likely to follow from decisions. As the decision maker becomes aware of various risks and uncertainties that may be associated with a course of action, this stress becomes all the more acute. Janis and Mann [26] have developed a conflict model of decision making that reflects this thinking. Here, conflict refers to *"simultaneous and opposing tendencies within the individual to accept and reject a given course of action."* Symptoms of conflicts may be hesitation, feelings of uncertainty, vacillation, and acute emotional stress with an unpleasant feeling of distress being, typically, the most prevalent of all characteristics associated with decision making [27]. For this reason, this model is often called a *stress-based model*, although, the term *time-stress based model* would seem more appropriate. The major elements associated with the conflict model are the concept of vigilant information processing, the distinction between hot and cold cognitions, and several coping patterns associated with judgments.

Cold cognitions are defined to be those made in a calm, detached environmental state. The changes in utility possible owing to different decisions are small and easy to determine. Hot cognitions are those associated with vital issues and concerns, and are associated with a high level of stress. Whether a cognition is, or should be, hot or cold depends on the task at hand and the experiential familiarity and expertness of the decision maker with respect to the task. The symptoms of stress include feelings of apprehensiveness, a desire to escape from the distressing choice dilemma, and self-blame for having allowed oneself to get into a predicament where one is forced to choose between unsatisfactory alternatives. Janis and Mann state that *psychological stress* is used as a generic term to designate unpleasant emotional states evoked by threatening environmental events or stimuli. They define a "stressful" event as "any change in the environment that typically induces a high degree of unpleasant emotion, such as anxiety, guilt, or shame, and which affects normal patterns of information processing" [26].

Janis and Mann describe several functional relationships between psychological time-stress and decision conflict:

1. The degree of time-stress generated by decision conflict is a function of those objectives that the decision maker expects to remain unsatisfied after implementing a decision.
2. Often, a person encounters new threats or opportunities that motivate consideration of a new course of action. The degree of decision stress is a function of the degree of commitment to adhere to the present course of action.
3. When the degree of time-stress is low, and there is satisfaction with the present course of action, *unconflicted adherence to the present course of action* will be the chosen decision. When the time-stress is low, and there is dissatisfaction with the present course of action and a single satisfactory alternative can be identified, the decision maker will implement a decision involving *unconflicted change to a new course of action*.
4. When decision conflict is severe because all identified alternatives pose serious risks, failure to identify a better decision than the least objectionable one will lead to *defensive avoidance*, or undue procrastination.
5. In severe decision conflict when the decision maker anticipates having insufficient time to identify an adequate alternative that will avoid serious losses, the level of stress remains extremely high. The likelihood that the dominant pattern of response will be *hypervigilance*, or panic, increases.
6. A moderate degree of stress, which results when there is sufficient time to identify acceptable alternatives, in response to a challenging situation, induces a *vigilant effort to scrutinize all identified alternative courses of action carefully and to select a good decision*.

Based on these relationships or propositions, Janis and Mann present five coping patterns that a decision maker would use as a function of the level of stress: unconflicted adherence or inertia, unconflicted change to a new course of action, defensive avoidance, hypervigilance or panic, and vigilance.

These five coping patterns are used by Janis and Mann [26] to devise their conflict model of decision making. This model postulates that each pattern of decision stress and associated coping strategy is associated with a characteristic mode of information processing. It is this mode of information processing that governs the type and amount of information the decision maker will prefer. Figure 6.9 presents an interpretation of this conflict model of decision making in terms of the contingency models discussed here. This model points to a number of markedly different tendencies which become dominant under particular conditions of time-stress. These include open-mindedness, indifference, active evasion of potentially disconfirming information, failure to assimilate new information, and other cognitive information-processing biases that are identified later in this chapter. A number of information-processing preferences and decision styles are potentially generated by this conflict model. Especially evident is the striking complexity entailed by the vigilant information-processing pattern in comparison to the other coping patterns. This vigilance pattern is characterized by seven key steps that require somewhat prolonged deliberation. The other four coping patterns require that only a few key steps be addressed. Just as with selection of a decision style, selection of a coping pattern may be made properly or unwisely. The steps of vigilant information processing identified in Figure 6.9 appear quite equivalent to the formulation, analysis, and interpretation steps for formal problem solving we have discussed here.

Janis and Mann [26] combine the hypotheses they present concerning the phases of decision making, the functional relation propositions of psychological stress, and the five stress-coping patterns. In addition, they present a decision balance sheet, an adaptation of the moral algebra of Benjamin Franklin, on which to construct a profile of the identified options together with various cost and benefit attributes of possible decision outcomes. They have shown that decision regret reduction and increased adherence to the adopted decision result from use of this balance sheet. Strategies for challenging outworn decisions and improving decision quality are also developed in this seminal work.

In this stress-based conflict-theory model, there are many activities connected with information processing and associated situation assessment:

- Evaluation of general input information to recognize that there is a potentially challenging opportunity.
- Obtaining additional information about losses if the present course of action is continued.
- Obtaining additional information about losses if a change is made to a new, but familiar course of action.
- Obtaining additional information to ascertain if it is reasonable to find a better course of action than the familiar ones already considered and dismissed.
- Obtaining still more information to ascertain if familiar courses of action not previously considered are acceptable.
- Obtaining information concerning whether the remaining time until the decision must be made is sufficient for a formal rational deliberation.
- Obtaining information to support a formal formulation, analysis, and interpretation of the issues and a vigilant search, processing, and deliberation.

It is of considerable interest and value to indicate the typical interactions between these basically contingency task structure models of decision style that we have discussed in this section. Each of these models is appropriate and to portray similar but still somewhat different relevant aspects and features of task evaluation, information-processing preference, and decision-rule selection in terms of contingency elements associated with the environment and the decision maker's prior experiences. We now turn to an expanded interpretation of these decision-style models and indicate their role in DSS design.

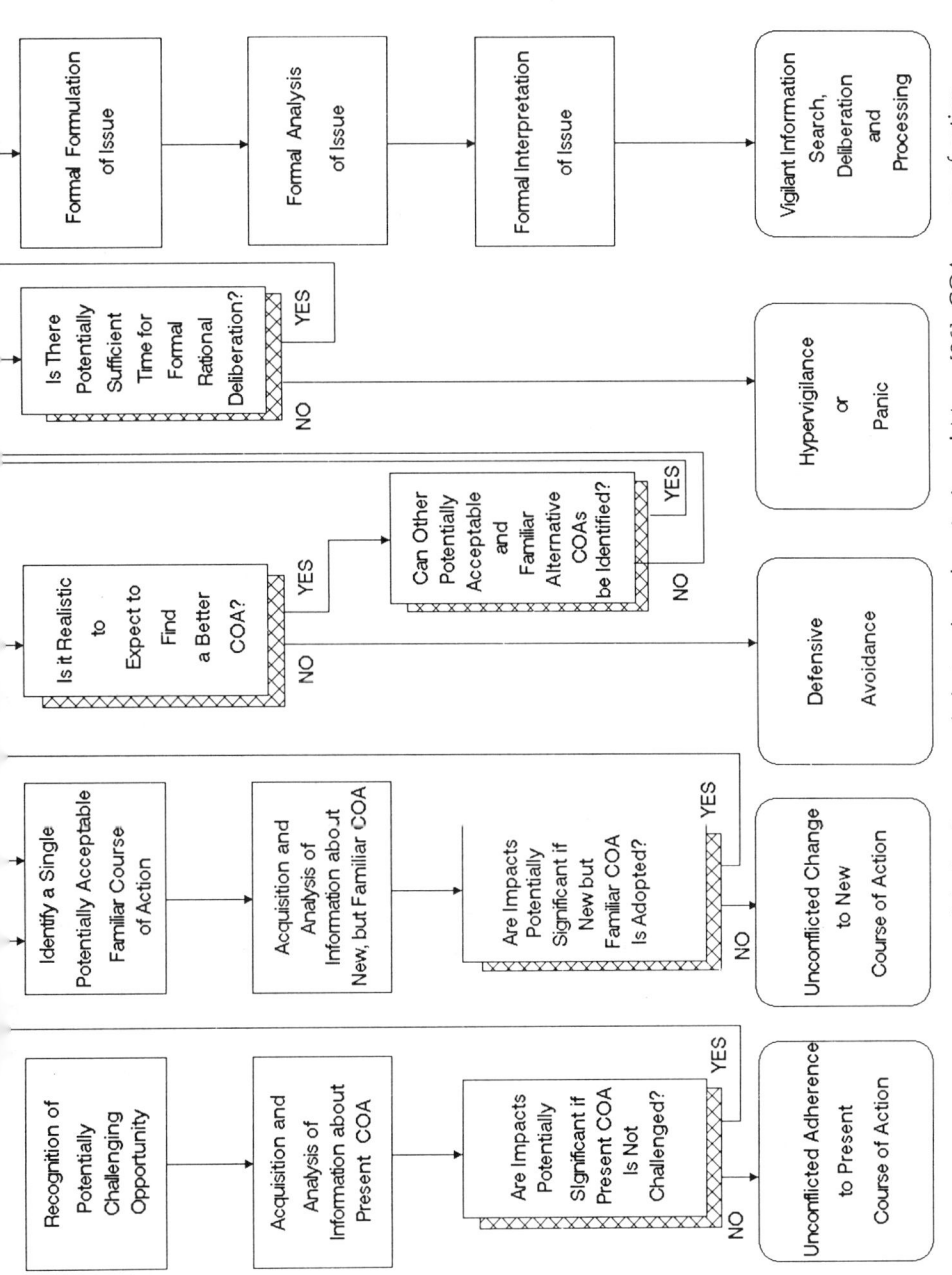

Figure 6.9 Contingency model of judgment and choice, based on Janis and Mann [26]. COA-course of action.

6.2.6 Interpretation of the Human Information-Processing Models

The concrete operational thinker does not necessarily have limited abilities to process or integrate information in a formal sense. In a similar way, the formal operational thinker is not necessarily incapable of concrete operational thought, which we see to be of a rule-based or skill-based nature. Our contingency task structural model for the mature, perhaps expert, adult decision maker is one in which the decision maker may use formal or concrete operational thought based primarily on diagnosis of the contingency structure of the decision situation, and the stress that is perceived to be associated with the decision situation. This election of a formal or concrete operational mode of thought may be appropriate or inappropriate.

Decision support systems design must be responsive to the observation that there are two fundamentally different thought or cognition processes. These are often and correctly associated physiologically with different halves of the brain[28–31]. One type of thought process is typically described by adjectives or attributes such as verbal, logical, sequenced, thinking, and analytical. The second type is described as nonverbal, intuitive, wholistic, feeling, and heuristic. The verbal process is generally viewed as superior in engineering and natural science, and the affective process is more often associated with the arts. But this static and stereotypical viewpoint on the unchanging nature of human thought processes appears unsatisfactory [32] and should be discouraged as potentially harmful, for the two thought processes are complementary and compatible. They are not competitive and incompatible in any meaningful way. One thought process may be deficient, in fact, if not supported by the other. (For example, a person may be taught rules and skills, or concrete operational thought relative to some specific task. They may be quite proficient as long as the task performance is occurring *naturally*. However, environmental or other changes may create the need for formal operational thought or vigilant information processing. If there is no capacity for this, major difficulties may ensue.) The nonverbal supports the verbal by suggesting ideas, alternatives, and so forth. The verbal supports the nonverbal by expressing, structuring, analyzing, and validating the creative ideas that occur in the nonverbal process. Appropriate information support for judgment and choice processes must provide for verbal and nonverbal support.

An appropriate support process must be tolerant and supportive of the cognitive thought processes of an individual or a group. These will usually vary across individuals and within the same individual as a function of the environment, the individual's previous experience with the environment, and those associated factors that introduce varying amounts of stress. Thus, a contingency task structural view of individuals and organizations in decision situations is needed, as contrasted with a stereotypical view in which individuals are assumed to process fixed, static, and unchanging cognitive characteristics which are uninfluenced by environmental and experiential considerations.

This view will encourage us not only to consider the evolution of future events over time as inherently uncertain and associated with much information imperfection, but also to consider value change over time. It is especially vital that we consider values as containing noncommensurate, ambiguous, and uncertain components, rather than as being absolute, consistent, precise, and exogenous with respect to choice [33].

A particularly important role for a DSS is to assist the user in minimizing errors between perceived knowledge level relative to a particular task, and the environment into which the task requirements are embedded, and their actual knowledge level relative to the task and environment. When both perceived and actual knowledge level are at the level of "master," for example, then skill-based experiential knowledge is generally suitable for judgment and choice tasks. When the perceived and actual knowledge level is that of "novice," then the support system user should be generally aware of the need for support. When the perceived knowledge level is that of "master" and the actual knowledge is that of "novice," perhaps due to an unrecognized change in environment, then it is likely that acts of judgment and choice will be associated with self-deception. This was illustrated in Figure 6.8. The task for a DSS, in this regard, would be to alert the decision maker to the potential difficulties of skill-based behavior in a suitable manner. A critical role for a DSS, therefore, is that of alerting decision makers to the information requirements appropriate to the task at hand, and the environment surrounding the task and task requirements.

An appropriate conceptual framework for human information processing and judgment must be set within the context of real decisions that are made by real people in real decision situations. This is one reason why operational testing and evaluation of DSS designs are so essential. The terms *judgment* and *choice* refer to human cognition over a continuum of perspectives that range from formal analytical thought at one end of the spectrum to wholistic intuitive thought based on concrete operational experiences at the other [34]. The difference between analytical and perceptual thought processes is rooted in the writings of many authors. Piaget's theory of intellectual development, briefly described earlier, was among the first to identify relevant variables that influence selection of judgment and choice style: maturation, experience, education, and "self-regulation." Brunswick [35, 36] describes perception as an intuitive, continuous, and rapid process—as contrasted with analytical reasoning, which is typically deterministic, discontinuous, and slow. Hammond [37] has provided definitive discussions on intuitive and analytical cognitions, as well.

A major conclusion from this is that it would be desirable to develop predictable interrelations between human cognitive processes for human information processing, and associated judgment and choice, and environmental characteristics. While these will depend on the contingency task structure of decision task, surrounding environment, and decision-maker experiential familiarity with these, it should be expected that *most* decision support processes will tend to encourage use of formal analytical thought processes by both novices and experts [38]. Also, people tend to test and potentially change their initially favored hypotheses when provided with relevant information feedback [39]. Without information feedback, it is possible for alternatives to be selected without a felt need to justify this selection.

A general underpinning for this is that we normally learn through experience. We should be rather cautious, however, in the apparently reasonable inference that we *always* learn correctly from experience. Important studies by Brehmer [40, 41] have shown that by no means do people always improve their judgment and decision-making ability on the basis of increased experience. Biases, such as the tendency to use or to associate more saliency with potentially confirming evidence—to the neglect of potentially disconfirming evidence—are the key culprits. Brehmer indicates how these biases can be understood in terms of available information. He concludes that truth is not manifest. It needs to be inferred in order to extract from experience information components that will truly lead to better judgments and decisions.

6.3 ORGANIZATIONAL INFORMATION PROCESSING AND DECISION MAKING

Many contemporary information technologies are major potential aids to organizational decision making. Sound design and implementation of information and knowledge-based support to organizational decision making require a knowledge of the ways in which organizations can acquire and process information; the ways in which they adapt to their internal and external environment; the ways in which they cope with conflict; the ways in which organizational references result from decisions as well as being determined by them; and the ways in which organizations learn and fail to learn.

There are a variety of definitions of an organization. These include

1. A system of consciously coordinated activities of two or more people [42].
2. Social units deliberately constructed to seek specific goals [43].
3. Collectives that have been established on a relatively continuous basis in an environment, with relatively fixed boundaries, a normative order, authority ranks, communication systems, and an incentive system designed to enable participants to engage in activities in general pursuit of a common set of goals [44].
4. A set of individuals with bounded rationality who are engaged in the decision-making process [45].

Organizations can be viewed from a closed-system perspective which views an organization as an instrument designed to enable pursuit of well-defined specified objectives. In this view, an organization will be concerned primarily with four objectives [46]:

- Efficiency
- Effectiveness
- Flexibility or adaptability to external environmental influences
- job satisfaction

Four organizational means or activities follow from this:

- Complexity and specialization of tasks
- Centralization or hierarchy of authority

- Formalization or standardization of jobs
- Stratification of employment levels

In this view, everything is functional and tuned such that all resource inputs are optimum and the associated responses fit into a well-defined master plan.

March and Simon [47] are among many who discuss the inherent shortcomings associated with this closed-system model of humans as machines. Not only is the *human-as-machine* view inappropriate, but there are pitfalls associated with viewing environmental influences as only *noise*. Cyert and Simon [48] describe *behavioral rules* as modes of behavior that an individual or an organization develop as guidelines for decision making in complex environments characterized by uncertainty and incomplete information. These rules incorporate the decision maker's assumptions about both the nature of the internal environment of the organization and the external environment of the world surrounding the environment. In this model, judgment is capable of being decomposed into a set of behavioral rules that change and move closer to those described by simple known situations as uncertainties give way to certainty and as knowledge increases.

In the open-system view of an organization, concern is not only with objectives but with suitable responses to a number of internal and external influences. Weick [49, 50] describes organizational activities of *enactment, selection,* and *retention* which assist in the processing of ambiguous information that results from an organization's interactions with ecological changes in the environment. The overall result of this process is the minimization of information equivocality* such that the organization is able to

1. Understand its environment
2. Recognize problems
3. Diagnose the causes of problems
4. Identify policies to potentially resolve problems
5. Evaluate efficacy of these policies
6. Select a priority order for problem resolution

Figure 6.10 presents a partial interpretation of Weick's social theory of organizing. Here, the result of the enactment activities of the organization is the enacted environment of the organization. This enacted environment contains an external part, which represents the activities of the organization in product markets, and an internal part, which is the result of organizing people into a structure to achieve organizational goals. Each of these environments is subject to uncontrollable ecological influences due to economic, social, and other changes. Selection activities allow perception framing, editing, and interpretation of the effects of the organization's actions on the external and internal environments so as to enable selection of a set of relationships believed of importance. Retention activities permit admission, rejection, and modifi-

---

*Earlier, we used Weick's definition of an organization from an information equivocality perspective.

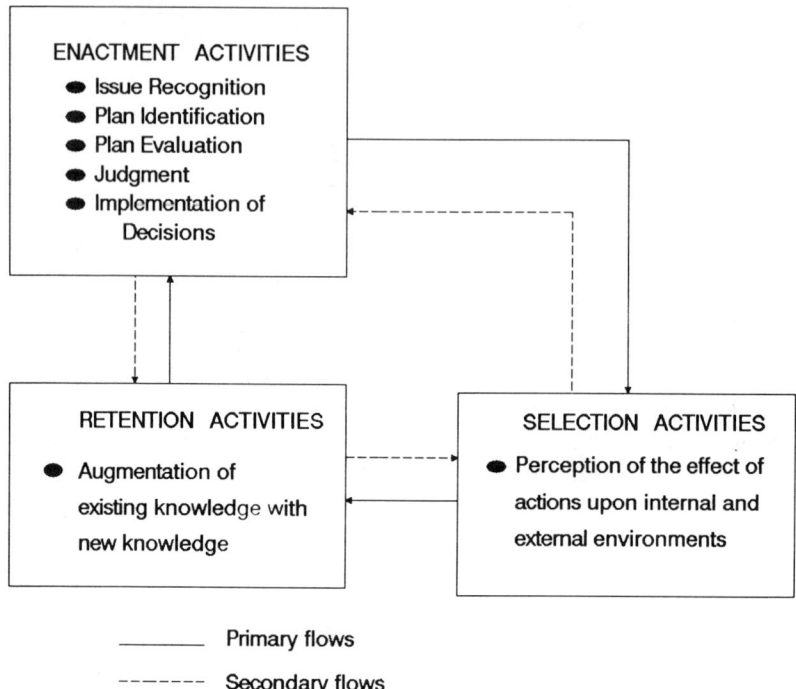

Figure 6.10 Interpretation of Weick's social theory of organizing [49, 50].

cation of the set of selected knowledge in accordance with existing retained knowledge and integration of previously retained organizational knowledge with new knowledge. A potentially large number of cycles may be associated with enactment, selection, and retention. These cycles generally minimize informational equivocality and allow for organizational learning such that the organization is able to cope with complex and changing environments.

A critical feature of many models of organizations is that of *organizational learning*. Much of the organizational learning that occurs in practice is not necessarily beneficial or appropriate in a descriptive sense. For example, there is much literature that shows that organizations and individuals use improperly simplified and often distorted models of causal and diagnostic inferences, and improperly simplified and distorted models of the contingency structure of environment and task in which these realities are embedded.

This surely occurs in group and organizational situations, as well as in individual information-processing and judgment situations. (We will identify a number of information processing biases in Section 6.5.) Individuals often join "groups" to enhance survival possibilities and to enable pursuit of career and other objectives. These coalitions of like-minded people pursue interests that result in emotional and intellectual fulfillment and pleasure. The activities that are perceived to result in need fulfillment become objectives for the group. Group cohesion, conformity, and reinforcing beliefs commonly lead to what has been called *groupthink* [51] and an information acquisition and analysis structure that facilitates processing only in accordance with the belief structure of the group. The resulting selective perceptions and neglect of potentially disconfirming information preclude change of beliefs.

Organizational learning results when members of the organization react to changes in the internal or external environment of the organization by detection and correction of errors [52–54]. An error is a feature of knowledge that makes action ineffective, and detection and correction of error produces learning. Individuals in an organization are agents of organizational action and organizational learning. In the studies cited in References 52–54, Argyris identifies two information-related factors that inhibit organizational learning:

- The degree to which information is distorted such that its value in influencing quality decisions is lessened.
- Lack of receptivity to corrective feedback.

Two types of organizational learning are defined. *Single-loop learning,* illustrated in Figure 6.11, is learning that does not question the fundamental objectives or actions of an organization. Members of the organization discover sources of error and identify new strategic activities that might correct the error. The activities are analyzed and evaluated and one or more selected for implementation. Environmental control and self-protection through control over others, primarily by imposition of power, are typical strategies. The consequences of this approach include defensive group dynamics and low production of valid information.

This lack of information does not result in disturbances to prevailing values. The resulting inefficiencies in decision making encourage frustration and an increase in secrecy and loyalty demands from decision makers. All of this is mutually self-

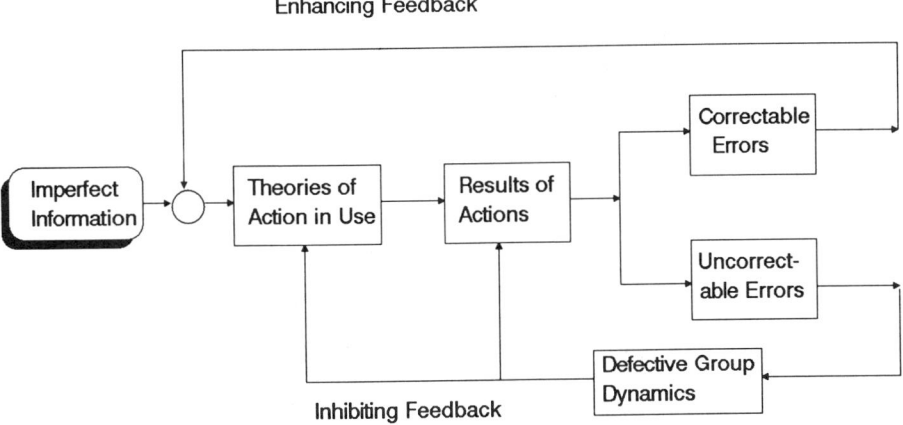

Figure 6.11 Interpretation of single loop learning.

reinforcing. It results in a stable autocratic state and a self-fulfilling prophecy with respect to the need for organizational control.

Double-loop learning, shown in Figure 6.12, involves identification of potential changes in organizational goals and of the particular approach to inquiry that allows confrontation with and resolution of conflict rather than the translation of incompatible objectives into intergroup conflict. Not all conflict resolution is the result of double-loop learning, however. Good examples of this are conflicts settled through imposition of power rather than inquiry. Thus, double-loop learning is seen to be the result of that organizational inquiry that resolves initially perceived incompatible organizational objectives through the restructuring and setting of new priorities and objectives. New understandings are developed that result in updated cognitive maps and scripts of organizational behavior. Organizations are claimed to learn primarily on the basis of single-loop learning and, typically, do not engage in a double-loop learning.

Individuals act as agents of organizational learning through the processing of initially inaccessible and obscure information and by resolving potential inadequacies associated with individual and organizational theories of action. All human action is said to be based on theories of action. There are two types:

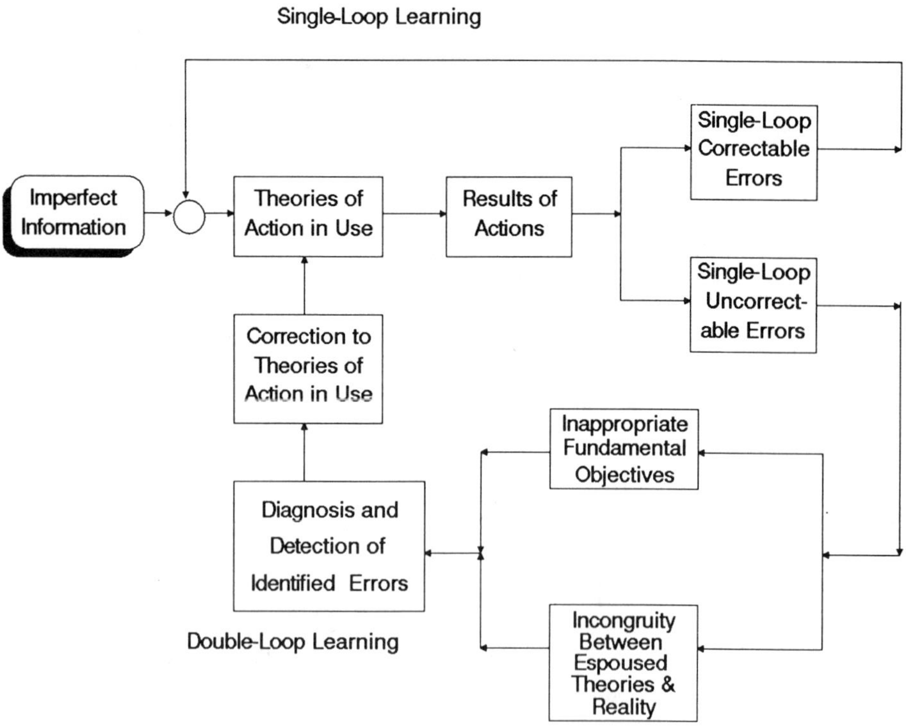

Figure 6.12 Interpretation of double-loop learning.

- *Espoused theories of action,* which are the "official" theories that people claim as a basis for action.
- *Theories in use,* which are the descriptive theories of action that may be inferred from actual behavior.

While people are often adept at identifying those discrepancies between espoused theories of action and theories in use that are related to the behavior of others, they are not equally capable of self-diagnosis. However, people are generally programmed with theories in use that suggest that this observed inconsistent behavior in others should not be reported to them by those who detect it. So we see again the presence of social exchanges and customs that inhibit double-loop learning.

There are several dilemmas connected with this theory of action building. Among these nonmutually exclusive dilemmas, which aggregate to result in conflicting and intolerable pressures, are

1. *Incongruity* between espoused theory and theory in use which is recognized but not corrected.
2. *Inconsistency* between theories in use.
3. *Ineffectiveness* as objectives associated with theories in use become less and less achievable over time.
4. *Disutility* as theories in use become less valued over time.
5. *Unobservability* as theories in use result in suppression of information by others such that evaluation of effectiveness becomes impossible.

Detection and correction of inappropriate espoused theories of action and theories in use are suggested as potentially leading to a reduction in those factors that inhibit double-loop learning. Of course, single-loop learning often will be appropriate and is encouraged. The result of double-loop learning, however, is a *new* set of goals and standard operating policies that become part of the organization's knowledge base. It is when the environment, or more generally the contingency task structure, changes that double-loop learning is called for. Inability to accommodate double-loop learning is a flaw. Ability to successfully integrate and utilize the appropriate blend of single- and double-loop learning is called deutero, or dialectic, learning. Of particular interest in Argyris' seminal work [52–54] are the several caveats given concerning difficulties in the design of management information and DSS such that they support double-loop learning rather than only single-loop learning.

Huber [55, 56] and Vroom and Yetton [57] have indicated a number of potential advantages and disadvantages to group or organizational participation in decision making. Since a group has more information and knowledge potentially available to it than any individual in the group, it should be capable of making a better decision than an individual. Group decisions are often more easily implemented than individual decisions, since participation will generally increase decision acceptance as well as understanding of the decision. Also, group participation increases the skills and information that members may need in making future organizational decisions. On the other hand, there are potential disadvantages to groups. They consume more time in decision making than individuals. Their decisions may not fully support higher organizational goals. Group participation may lead to unrealistic anticipations of involvement in future decisions and resentment by individuals toward subsequent decisions in which they have not participated. Finally, there is no guarantee that the group will reach consensus on a decision alternative.

Huber [55, 56] determines guidelines for selection of a particular form of group decision making. These forms include

Involving others
Encouraging group activities
Delegating authority to the group
Including the leader in the group

The responses to a set of questions determine an appropriate form of group decision making. For example, we may determine whether or not to involve others by posing questions involving decision quality, understanding and acceptance, personnel development and relationships, and time required.

Vroom and Yetton [57] deal with the issues of leadership and decision making. Their primary concern is with effective decision behaviors. They develop a number of clearly articulated normative models of leadership style for individual and group decisions. These should be of use to those attempting to structure normative or prescriptive models of the leadership-style portion of decision situations that are capable of operational implementation. It is the apparent goal of Vroom and Yetton to come to grips with, and use explicitly, leadership behavior and situational variables to enhance organizational effectiveness.

Keen [58] acknowledges four causes of inertia relative to organizational information systems. He indicates that

1. Information is only a small component task.
2. Human information processing is experiential and relies on simplification.
3. Organizational change is incremental and evolutionary, with large changes being avoided.
4. Data are a political resource of particular groups as well as being an intellectual commodity.

Each of these factors suggests the importance of a knowledge of the way in which information is processed by organizations.

Huber [55, 56] and Tushman and Nadler [59] have developed a number of propositions, based on their own research and that of others, reflecting various aspects of information processing in organizations. The general conclusion of these studies is that in an effort to enhance efficiency, organizational information processing typically requires selective routing of messages and summarization of messages. In the classical normative theory of decision making, it is easily shown that information about the consequences of alternative courses of action should be "purchased" only if the benefits of the information, in terms of precision, relevance, reliability, and other qualities, exceed the cost. Feldman and March [60] present a highly conjectural and alternative point of view in their descriptive portrait of information use in organizations. Their discussions of information incentives indicate systematic bias in estimating the benefits and costs of information due to the fact that the costs and benefits do not occur at the same place and at the same time such that one group has responsibility for information use, whereas another has responsibility for information availability. Further, people are prone to obtain more information than is needed, since under uncertainty conditions the postoutcome probabilities of events that do occur will be judged higher than the prior probabilities of these events. This will suggest that less information was obtained than should have been obtained and will, typically, lead to incentives to obtain too much information.

Feldman and March [60] also indicate that much of the information that is obtained is obtained for surveillance purposes to uncover potential surprises rather than to clarify uncertainties for decision making. Strategic misrepresentation of information, due to interpersonal conflicts and power struggles, is a third factor suggested as decoupling information gathering from decision making. This occurs since information is not innocent and must be suspected of bias. Finally, information is a symbol that indicates a commitment to rationality, and there are incentives to displaying the incentive even if it is not used.

Identification of other variables that influence information processing in and by organizations would represent a desirable activity. To determine how these information-processing variables are influences by the information-processing biases of individuals is especially desirable, both in its own right and in terms of the likely usefulness of the results and the need for an expanded theory of information-processing biases. (We examine many of these later in this chapter.) There appear to have been only limited results obtained in the area of cognitive information-processing biases and use of inferior heuristics on the part of groups. The development of suitable normative strategies for information requirements determination is especially important toward these ends.

6.4 RATIONALITY PERSPECTIVES AND MODELS OF INDIVIDUAL AND ORGANIZATIONAL INFORMATION PROCESSING

In this section, we describe some rationality perspectives concerning individual and organizational information processing. In the concluding portion of the section, we will attempt to relate these to the important subjects of information processing, and dialog and interface design.

The research of Diesing [61] and Steinbruner [62], and many others, have dealt with *rationality* as it pertains to human information processing and other judgment and choice activities. The various forms of rationality are very helpful in providing at least a partial explanation of why people seek the information they do. Understanding these reasons will help enable support system design such as to result in more effective ways to determine information needs. Although a variety of "rationality" forms may be defined, the following appear to be the most common ones.

6.4.1 Economic Rationality

Maximum goal achievement with respect to technical production of a single product, subject to a production cost constraint, is the typical desired end of economic rationality. Economic rationality extends this concept to a number of products. It seeks to maximize the overall worth, in an economic sense, of a number of investments [63]. This is possible if desired goals are well defined and measurable, the techniques employed to attain these goals are not limited in scope or hindered in application, supply and demand operates in a stable manner, and the interrelationships of supply and demand are known and available to all—in other words, if the requirements for a "perfectly competitive economy" are satisfied. Using this model of rationality, it is possible to maximize goal achievement should there be any constraints placed on the above requirements. Some goals can typically be achieved and this results in enhanced economic progress. Achievements of some goals become the means toward the achievement of other societally desirable goals. This process continues, and the continuation of economic progress itself becomes the top-level goal to be achieved. Over the long term, only as long as decisions do not adversely affect society as a whole will these decisions be acceptable. From an economic rationality perspective, those items of information not providing a basis for increasing the profit goals of an organization are to be avoided. Hence, this is a useful but incomplete form of rationality. It is generalized somewhat by *technical rationality*.

6.4.2 Technical Rationality

The activities of an individual are determined in such a way as to maximize the return, or benefit, to the individual from the investment cost of that activity. In a similar way, we can define technical rationality of an organization. All activities within an organization are formed in a manner so as to reach the goals set forth by the organization. Most traditional engineering and organizational analysis has presumed, at least implicitly, technical rationality. Systems are presumed to be designed such as to achieve "optimal attainment" of objectives. The presence of multidimensional and noncommensurate objectives will frequently prevent this sort of optimization from being easily accomplished. The need for coordination and communication among people in modern decentralized organizations also makes attaining technical rationality difficult. There are a number of other reasons as well. Implementation of technical rationality results in what is called *the rational actor model* (however, this is by no means *the* rational actor model, as our discussions here hopefully make quite clear).

Most formal decision analytic efforts are based on the *technically rational actor model*. In this model, the decision maker becomes aware of a problem, studies it, carefully weighs alternative means to a solution, and makes a choice or decision based on an objective set of values. At first glance, the rational actor model appears to contain much of value. It is especially well matched to the entrepreneurship and decision theory schools of thought as described by Mintzberg [45]. However, we must be aware that it is a normative substantive model. There may be any number of descriptive process realities that make prescriptive realization infeasible. In rational planning or decision making, the following steps are typically performed:

1. The decision maker is confronted with an issue that can be meaningfully isolated from other issues.
2. Objectives, which will result in need satisfaction, are identified.
3. Possible alternative activities to resolve needs are identified.
4. The impacts of action alternatives are determined.
5. The utility of each alternative is evaluated in terms of its impacts on needs.
6. The utilities of all alternatives are compared and the policy or activity with the highest utility is selected for action implementation.

From the perspective of a technical rational actor model, the decision maker becomes aware of a problem, structures the problem space, gathers information, identifies the impacts of alternatives, and implements the best alternative based on a set of values.* Since a complete identification of all needs, alterables, objectives, and so on, is not usually possible, one cannot be completely rational in the purest unconstrained sense. This observation, and the more important observation that, in a descriptive sense, humans often do not attempt, due to cognitive limitations, to follow the prescriptions of the rational actor model, led Simon [64–67] to develop the satisficing or bounded rationality framework.

6.4.3 Satisficing or Bounded Rationality

Decisions are implemented based on a minimum set of requirements to provide a degree of acceptable achievement over the short term. The decision maker does not attempt to extremize an objective function, not even in a substantive way, but rather attempts to achieve some aspiration level. The aspiration level may possibly change

---

*From a technically rational perspective, the effects of alternatives that are proposed for implementation, including the effects they have on the environment in which they are to be utilized, are determined in detail using the technologies of systems engineering. Cost-benefit analyses are determined, statistics are used, computer models are constructed, and other systems science and operations research methods are employed in order to ascertain the effects and results of a particular alternative that is being considered for implementation. That this perspective is very important is shown by the extensive use of polls and statistics by virtually all organizations. Of course, there are dangers in this. Often, the quantity that is being measured is not a quantity that is fundamentally of interest, but a surrogate for this. A danger with overuse, and improper use, of the technological perspective is that sublimation of objectives measures for objectives may easily occur. For example, the objective "to obtain a high school education that is a stepping-stone to college and an appropriate career" may be replaced by the instrumental objective "to obtain a high score on the Scholastic Achievement Test." There is ample evidence that this sublimation does occur.

due to the difficulty in searching for a solution. It may be lowered in this case, or raised if the goal or aspiration level is too easily achieved.

The satisficing, or bounded rationality, model of Simon [64–67] was perhaps the first to make use of the observation, about two decades ago, that unaided decision makers may not be able to make complete substantive use of the economic and technically rational actor model possible. In these situations, the concepts of bounded rationality and satisficing represent much more realistic substantive models of actual decision rules and practices. According to the satisficing or bounded rationality model, the decision maker looks for a course of action that is basically good enough to meet a minimum set of requirements. The goal, from an organizational perspective, is "do not shake the system" or "play it safe," by making decisions primarily on the basis of short-term acceptability rather than seeking a long-term optimum. Simon suggested that decision makers compensate for their limited abilities by constructing a simplified representation of the problem and then behaving rationally within the constraints imposed by this simplified model. We may satisfice by finding either optimum solutions in a simplified world or satisfactory solutions in a more realistic world. As Simon says, "neither approach dominates the other".

Satisficing is actually searching for a "good enough" choice. Simon suggested that the threshold for satisfaction, or aspiration level, may change according to the ease or difficulty of search. If many alternatives can be found, the conclusion is reached that the aspiration level is too low and needs to be increased. The converse is true if no satisfactory alternatives can be found. This may lead to a unique solution through iteration. The principle of bounded rationality and the resulting satisficing model suggest the simple heuristics may well be adequate for complex problem-solving situations. While satisficing strategies may well be excellent for repetitive problems by encouraging one to "do what we did last time if it worked last time and the opposite if it didn't," they may also lead to premature choices that result in unforeseen disastrous consequences; consequences that could have been foreseen by more careful analysis.

6.4.4 Social Rationality

Society functions as a unit seeking betterment for itself. All its energy is directed toward the realization of this goal. The social system is cohesive in that all its activities reinforce achievement of the desired goal. Present decisions are related to those of the past and are projected into the future. While these actions and decisions are usually not efficient and sometimes not even effective, the cohesiveness of society provides continuity for the system. The roles and structure of society are reinforced from previous results, both good and bad, lending credence to the fact that a social system is rather intractable. It maintains a conservative appearance and avoids risk. That it ought to be adaptive to change perhaps can be shown by sudden changes in the morality or consciousness of the members of the society through a violent opposition to the status quo, such as opposition to or blatant disregard of the law by leaders of the society.

6.4.5 Political Rationality

The decision-making structure is assumed to be influenced by embedded beliefs, values, and interpersonal relationships, the interaction of which define roles under which actions and decisions are based. The three characteristics of this rationality are that all actors remain independent regardless of the pressures to be dependent on one another, the work load is distributed among all members so as to balance and moderate actions of the group, and future decisions are chosen in such a way that the impacts of these decisions will act to bind the group further together and increase participation.

6.4.6 Legal Rationality

A system exhibiting this form of rationality operates on the basis of rules that are complex, consistent, precise, and detailed. As a result, no ambiguous conflict can occur. It is effective in preventing disputes even though the rules of this system apply differently, to some extent, to each person. The prevention of disputes is accomplished through a "legal" framework that provides a means for settlement of disputes that do result and that sets precedents to guide members of society.

Other approaches can be used to characterize rationality. Simon [68] has developed a two-element categorization of rationality as a function of whether an act is rational from an input–output perspective, or whether the internal components of the process used are rational. This leads to a description of substantive rationality and procedural rationality.

6.4.7 Substantive Rationality

This is the classic, input–output, or means–ends rationality of economics. This form of rationality is outcome-oriented in that behavior is considered acceptable when given goals are achieved. Given a set of goals, rational behavior is determined by the characteristics of the environment in which it takes place. For instance, use of the methods of optimum systems control will result in a system that achieves a goal (minimum cost, perhaps) while satisfying a set of constraint equations that governs the behavior of the physical system concerned. That there are several possible mathematical representations of a given input–output behavior is immaterial. Substantive rationality is not concerned with this.

6.4.8 Procedural Rationality

This is the prevalent rationality of descriptive decision making in which any decision-making process must necessarily correspond to the capabilities of the user. It must allow a person to make use of those knowledge components that make maximum use of that person's abilities (reasoning ability, managerial ability, etc.) and minimize use of those knowledge components concerning areas in which the decision maker is not able to perform effectively. Behavior is rational, in a procedural sense, when a person effectively uses existing cognitive powers to choose actions in order to alleviate some issue. It is the process of selecting procedures for resolution of issues that is the basis for and the justification of rationality, rather than the outcome of the decision. Procedural rationality is, therefore, the method of searching for information for solutions to problems.

6.4.9 Bureaucratic Politics, Incrementalism, or "Muddling-Through" Rationality

Bold changes to existing policies are avoided and decisions are based on a rather limited set of alternatives which basically are minor perturbations of existing policies. Long-range side effects are not dealt with, but rather are left to future decision makers who ameliorate these side effects with other incremental policies.

The bureaucratic politics, incrementalism, or muddling-through model represents another attempt to characterize individual and organizational behavior. After problems arise that require a change of policy, policymakers typically consider only a narrow range of alternatives differing a small degree from the existing policy. One alternative is selected and tried, with unforeseen consequences left to be discovered and treated by subsequent incremental policies. This is the incremental view.

In 1959, Lindblom postulated the approach called incrementalism, or muddling through [69–71], to cope with perceived limitations in the economically rational model. Marginal values of change only are considered—and these for only a few dimensions of value—whereas the rational approach calls for exhaustive analysis of each identified alternative along all identified dimensions of value. A number of authors have shown incrementalism to be the typical, common, and currently practiced decision process of groups in pluralistic societies. Coalitions of special-interest groups make cumulative decisions and arrive at workable compromise through a give-and-take process that Lindblom calls "partisan mutual adjustment." He indicates that ideological and other value differences do not influence marginal decisions as much as they influence major changes and that, in fact, considering marginal values subject to practical constraints will lead to agreement on marginal programs. Further, incrementalism can result in agreement on decisions and plans even by those who are in fundamental disagreement on values. However, incrementalism appears based on keeping the masses marginally content and thus may not be able to do much to help the greatly underprivileged and unrepresented. A number of studies have indicated incrementalism to be an often-used approach in practice. Without doubt, this is a realistic process-oriented descriptive model of judgment and choice, especially in political environments.

Lindblom rejects economic or technical rationality even as a normatively useful model. He proposes incrementalism as a normative approach, and indicates that systems analysis and economic rationality will often lead to ill-considered, often accidental incompleteness. He offers the following "inevitable limitations" to analysis. It is fallible, never rises to infallibility, and can be poorly informed, superficial, biased, or mendacious. It cannot wholly resolve conflicts of value and interest. Sustained analysis may be too slow and too costly compared with realistic needs.

Issue formulation questions call for acts of choice or will, and suggest that analysis must allow room for politics.

The main features of the model proposed by Lindblom are as follows. Ends and means are viewed as not distinct. Consequently, means–ends analysis is viewed as often inappropriate. Identification of values and goals is not distinct from the analysis of alternative actions. Rather, the two processes are confounded. The test for a good policy is typically that various decision makers, or analysts, agree on a policy as suitable without necessarily agreeing that it is the most appropriate means to an end. Analysis is drastically limited, significant policy options are neglected, and important outcomes are not considered. By proceeding incrementally and comparing the results of each new policy with the old, decision makers reduce or eliminate reliance on theory. There is a greater preoccupation with ills to be remedied rather than positive goals to be sought. Incremental analysis is a good description of political decision making and is sometimes referred to as the *political rationality* or *political process* model.

6.4.10 Organizational Processes Rationality

In the purest form of the organization, everyone in it is aware of how it functions, because these functions are spelled out in a well-communicated set of standard operating procedures. Decisions to be made are structured around, and evaluated in terms of, these procedures. Information needs are determined through discovery of how these standard operating policies or rules affected previous problems.

From the perspective of the *organizational process model,* or organizational rationality, plans and decisions are the result of interpretation of standard operating procedures. Improvements are obtained by careful identification of existing standard operating procedures and associated organizational structures and determination of improvements in these procedures and structures. The organizational process model, originally due to Cyert and March [72], functions by relying on standard operating procedures, which constitute the memory or intelligence bank of the organization. Only if the standard operating procedures fail will the organization attempt to develop new standard procedures.

The organizational process model may be viewed as an extension of the concept of bounded rationality to organizations. There are four main concepts of the behavioral theory of the firm that are suggested as descriptive models of actual choice-making in organizations:

1. *Quasi-resolution of Conflict.* Decision makers avoid conflicts arising from noncommensurate and conflicting goals. Major problems are disaggregated and each subproblem is attacked locally by a department. An acceptable conflict resolution between the efforts of different departments is reached through sequential attention to departmental goals and through the formulation of coalitions which seek power and status. When resources are scarce and there must then be unsatisfied objectives, decisions concerning allocations will be met largely on political grounds.

2. *Uncertainty avoidance* is achieved by reacting to external feedback, by emphasizing short-term choices, and by advocating negotiated futures. Typically, there will be uncertainties about the future, including those associated with future impacts of alternatives and future preferences. Generally, deficient information-processing heuristics and cognitive biases are used to avoid uncertainties. The effects are, of course, suboptimal.
3. *Problem search* is stimulated by encountering issues, and not before issues are surfaced. A form of "satisficing" is used as a decision rule. Search in the neighborhood of the status quo only is attempted and only incremental solutions are considered.
4. *Organization Learning.* Organizations adapt on the basis of experience. They often pay considerable attention to one part of their environment at the expense of another.

The organizational process model may be viewed as suggesting that decisions at time t may be forecasted with almost complete certainty, from knowledge of decisions at time t-T where T is the planning or forecasting period. Standard operating procedures or "programs," and education motivation and experience or "programming" of management are the critical determinants of behavior for the organizational process model. Cohen and March [73] recommend a strategy of management leadership to cope with organizational process realities. Managers are encouraged to be intimately involved in organizations such that they will be able to strongly influence decisions; to become widely informed so that they will be highly valued in the information-poor organization; to be extraordinarily persistent, since unmitigated chutzpa will often have entirely undeserved rewards; to encourage those with opposing views to participate; and to overload organizational systems such as to make themselves more necessary. In this view, the descriptive characteristics of the organization are seen as performance-inhibiting factors. They are factors not to be overcome, but to be understood and used to the advantage of the manager.

6.4.11 Garbage Can Rationality

Of course, an organization is also a mechanism for problem solving and decision making. When the realities of ambiguity are associated with organizational problem solving and decision making, the result is what is termed a *garbage can model* of organizational choice [74]. In this model, which has generated much recent interest, there are five fundamental elements:

Issues or problems
Organizational structure
Participants, actors, or agents
Choice opportunities and actions
Solutions or products of the choice process

The problems, solutions, and choice opportunities are assumed to be quasi-independent, exogenous *"streams"* that are *linked* in a fashion that is determined by organizational structure constraints. There are several of these. The most important are *access structure,* or the access of problems to choice opportunities, *decision structure,* or the access of choice opportunities to solutions, and *energy structure,* which evolves in a dynamic fashion in terms of the number of problems or solutions that are linked to choice opportunities at a particular time.

The participants in the process can also be regarded as variables, since they "come and go" over time, and devote varying amounts of time and energy to problems, solutions, and choice opportunities owing to other competing demands on their time. This relatively new organizational decision model views organizational decision making as resulting from four variables: problems, solutions, choice opportunities, and people.

Decisions result from the interaction of solutions looking for problems, problems looking for solutions, decision opportunities, and participants in the problem-solving process. The model allows for these variables being selected more or less at random from a garbage can. The interaction of these variables provides the opportunity for decision making. Generally, these interactions are not controlled. Rather, they occur in an almost random fashion owing to the vexing equivocality associated with problematic preferences, unclear procedures, and fluid participants. The major reason for the garbage can approach is the chronic ambiguity and considerable equivocality that is present in the environment.

In a "garbage can" environment, decisions generally occur through rational problem solving, through ignoring the problem until it goes away or resolves itself (this often-used method of decision making is sometimes called *decision flight*), or through having the problem solved, inadvertently, by having another related problem solved. Doubtlessly, this is a realistic descriptive model. It has been used to analyze a number of existing decision situations, especially in a university decision context [73]. Examination of garbage can decision environments have led to conclusions concerning normative strategies to maximize decision effectiveness [75]. It has been shown, for instance, that a chief executive officer can maximize success through using a personal hands-off policy, and by hiring very conservative people to manage high-criticality projects, and very liberal people to manage low-criticality projects.

Three areas of equivocality are generally present in a garbage can environment:

1. *Problematic preferences*—in that different decision-making units have different objectives, and these generally evolve over time in an imprecise and unpredictable manner.
2. *Unclear procedures for making decisions*—in that responsibility and authority are usually separated and fragmented.
3. *Fluid decision participation*—in that the members of the decision-making units change over time, in an often unpredictable manner.

In the garbage can model, the problems, solutions, and choice opportunities are mixed together in "garbage cans." The division of human effort among problems, solutions, and choices is fuzzy and not fixed in any highly organized way. Problems, solutions, and choice opportunities may not coalesce in the right way at the right time so as to lead to a "rational" solution to a problem.

There are many unanswered questions relative to descriptive and normative use of this interesting model, and there is much study in progress at this time concerning extensions of this model. A recent book edited by March and Weissinger-Baylon [76] describes application of the garbage can model to military decision making. There have been a considerable number of earlier studies in which university decision making, especially that of faculty search committees, is represented by a garbage can model. Among the necessary and appropriate questions are

1. How are the number of garbage cans determined and what choice situations do they represent?
2. Who participates and how do they participate in the various choices?
3. What structures and flows represent the various problems, solutions, and choice opportunities?
4. How does the relative structure of the problems, solutions, choice opportunities, and participants evolve over time?
5. How is the interaction and information interchange among the various garbage cans determined?
6. What influences situation interpretation, and variables that represent situation interpretation, in the various garbage cans?
7. What is the appropriate role for models, such as this, in the normative design of information systems that support enhanced organizational efficiency and effectiveness?
8. How can such designs be evaluated in an operational context, and the resulting information used to enhance systems designs and organizational effectiveness?

One of the most potentially useful features of the garbage can model, or garbage can rationality, is that it is a definitive approach for relating social structure to cognitive structure. Not only does it have this descriptive appeal, but it is a potentially serviceable organizational model that can cope with such potential crisis situations as breakdown in organizational communications [77, 78].

6.4.12 Comparison of Approaches

These rationalities are all related to one another. For example, technical rationality is necessary for, and is also part of, economic rationality. Social and political rationality are each concerned with internal processes and procedures. Generally, one would exhibit substantive rationality in an environment of technical or economic rationality. In the environments of social or political rationality, we would expect procedural rationality to be the dominant form. Legal rationality would typically be a hybrid of the two in that the initial development of codes would be based on procedural concerns, but the actual functioning of an established code is substantive.

All of these models, or frameworks, for decision making have both desirable and undesirable characteristics and any of them may be relevant in specific circumstances for individuals and/or for organizations. If we accept the facts that

- Decision makers use a variety of methods to select among alternatives for action implementation;
- These methods are frequently suboptimal; and
- Most decision makers want to enhance their decision-making efficiency and effectiveness;

then we must conclude that there is much more motivation and need for research and ultimate design and development of DSS that incorporate rationality perspectives. These models make it quite obvious that improved decision-making efficiency and effectiveness, and DSS aids to this end, can only be accomplished if we understand human and organizational decision making as it is as well as how it might be and allow for incorporation of this understanding in the design of DSSs. One of the requirements imposed will be relevance to the individual and organizational decision-making structure. Another is relevance to the information requirements of the decision maker. Especially important also is accommodation of organizational learning, a topic that we have addressed here as well.

A number of other frameworks have been proposed from which to view decision situations [79]. Steinbruner [62], for instance, uses three situation models—analytic, cybernetic, and cognitive—in his study of political actions. The analytic model is mush like the rational actor model, and the cognitive model is much like the bounded rationality framework. The cybernetic model appears to be a blend of the rational actor and organizational processes models. It is a dynamic feedback oriented model in which both energy and information flow into the system from outside. Learning occurs through the error control and feedback mechanisms. In a similar way, a social framework or model could be defined. Doubtlessly, this decision framework would have much in common with the garbage can framework. Linstone [80, 81] has proposed several perspectives that extend these concepts by providing a more pragmatic view of how people may view issues that are of concern to them. Based on a study of the literature, Linstone has chosen to define three perspectives: technical, organizational, and personal.

In the many studies that have been performed, models other than the rational actor model are normally selected as the decision framework actually used. Allison's study of the Cuban missile crisis [82] evaluated the rational actor, organizational processes, and bureaucratic politics frameworks as best candidates for explaining the events surrounding this crisis. The bureaucratic politics model provided the best fit.

One potential use for these various rationality perspectives is in the construction of an *inquiry system* for a dialog generation and management system (DGMS) that provides for enhanced decision relevance. Churchman [83] has described several inquiry systems that represent the various modes of inquiry that may be used by an individual. The inquiry systems are based on the teachings of several philosophers and Churchman has translated these teachings into a modern systems theory format.

Mitroff and his colleagues [84–89] express the belief that existing implementations of these inquiry systems, in general, do not query the user enough, and/or are insensitive to dangers of information misinterpretation. According to Mitroff, inquiry systems need to be able to determine whether what the decision maker perceives as information is actually information that is relevant to the task at hand.

An inquiring system should be capable of recognizing the goals of the decision maker, determining what information is relevant to the task at hand and what is not, and summarizing this information in a form that is suitable for the decision maker and in the sense of being compatible with various contingency-related elements of the task, such as time available for judgment and choice. Such an inquiry system might be of use in understanding reasons why a decision maker disregards what should be regarded as decision relevant information. Thus, for example, there exists the potential to build an aid for information requirements determination based on the somewhat philosophical concepts of inquiry systems.

A *dialectical inquiry system* has been described by Mitroff [89] as representing the solution to many of the aforementioned deficiencies of inquiry systems. A dialectical inquirer is basically an "intelligent" management information system that presents alternative, or pro–con arguments concerning specific items of importance to the decision maker. Data by itself is unintelligible until it is joined to a person's image of reality or frame of the decision situation. For, it is at this point that data becomes information and knowledge. Hence, we again see the heavily context-dependent nature of information-processing tasks that involve judgment and choice. Until one is able to place measurements or observed data into some context that is presumed relevant and meaningful to the task at hand, the data has little, if any, meaning. Input data changes in character, interpretation, and meaning when joined with a decision maker's own theories and hypotheses.

The dialectical inquirer presents the strongest possible debate and/or disagreement concerning problems. The disagreement is not over the data, but rather the underlying views of what the data represents. There can always be found (or created) two experts having opposing and diverging opinions on any issue. After witnessing the debate by the two experts, one should, according to the prescriptions of the dialectical inquirer, be in a better position to understand the issue in question and the relation of relevant information to the issue. An implied assumption in all of this is that out of two fundamentally different, opposing, and perhaps artificially exaggerated positions, an observer will somehow be able to understand the "truth" as lying somewhere between the two extremes. There have been a number of interesting applications of dialectic inquiry systems in the aforementioned references.

We might also attempt to describe human information seeking and decision behavior in terms of the type of "rationality" that a person employs to guide this search and evaluation. In general terms, a person may be said to be rational if he or she acts in a way that is sensible in terms of the existing environment, the task requirements, and the experiential familiarity or state of knowledge of the person with respect to these. According to this informal definition, rationality is an instrumental way of thinking and a person may be said to be rational if they choose those activities most likely to lead to achievement of their goals. We immediately see that this is a multidimensional or multiobjective problem, and that there will be no simple unique determination of what is "rational" that is independent of the contingencies of the particular decision situation, especially since the dimensions involved include the technical, economic, organizational, social, legal, and political.

In a sense, the advocate of formal economic and technical rationality can rejoice in that a large number of the decisions studied in these cases were often ones where very flawed results occurred. They might, therefore, speculate that much better decisions could have resulted had an economic or technical rationality based approach been used. This might well be the case. However, the fact that the prescriptions of this framework were not used cannot be a cause for rejoicing, but a clear indication of the need to study human information processing as a prescriptive and as a descriptive effort. It is an effort that is especially needed for the design of DSS, as well as in any area in which there are interactions between human cognition and physical tasks. After addressing some of the observed information-processing biases, we will discuss some of these issues.

6.5 HUMAN INFORMATION-PROCESSING BIASES

We will now examine the ways in which humans actually process information that is acquired. After this, we provide some guidelines that potentially enable better information processing.

A large number of contemporary studies in cognitive psychology indicate that the attempts of people, including experts, to apply various intuitive strategies in order to acquire and analyze information for purposes such as prediction, forecasting, and planning are often flawed. Many studies have been conducted to describe and explain the way information is acquired and analyzed and the results of faulty acquisition and analysis. Usually, the descriptive behavior of subjects in tasks involving information acquisition and analysis is compared to the normative results that would prevail if people followed an "optimal" procedure. Most of these information-processing biases involve the processing of statistical information, and a Bayesian framework is usually assumed in order to obtain normative results. There have been a number of recent discussions, from several perspectives, of cognitive biases. The text by Hogarth [90] concerning strategies and biases associated with judgment and choice is especially noteworthy, as is the collection edited by Kahneman, Slovic, and Tversky [91], the text by Bazerman [92] and an overview paper by Einhorn and Hogarth [93].

We will describe only a single bias in any detail here. It is known as the *base rate bias* or *base rate fallacy*. Suppose that it is known that 7.69 percent of the cards in a standard 52-card deck are aces. A single card is drawn, face down, and we are asked the question: *What is the probability that the card drawn is not an ace?* It turns out that almost everyone will say 0.9231, or 92.31 percent. In almost all cases like this, the base rate information is used as representative information, and a particular sample is assumed to have the same statistical properties as the entire set of items.

Now suppose that we are allowed to ask the opinion of a spy. The spy says that it was an ace. But, spies have been known to be inaccurate. So, a vision test is given the spy. The vision test is precise and it determines that the spy can correctly identify the face value of a card 95 percent of the time. This means that the probability that the card will be identified as an ace given that it is an ace is 0.95, that is, $P(SA|A) = 0.95$. The visual ability of the spy also means that the probability that the spy will say that it is not an ace, given that it is not an ace, is also 0.95, that is, $P(SNA|NA) = 0.95$. The other two conditional probabilities are, of course, $P(SNA|A) = 0.05$ and $P(SNA|A) = 0.05$. Often, the last two sentences are not initially provided the subject; in many cases they will be, and they would generally be provided if requested by the subject.

The question now posed to the subjects is: *Given the uncertainty associated with the response of the spy, what is the probability that the card is an ace, given that the spy says that it is an ace?* Most people will reason that: *Since the spy says it is an ace and since the spy is accurate 95 percent of the time, the probability that the card drawn from the deck is actually an ace is 0.95, or 95%!*

There is a significant problem associated with this answer, as the subjects have ignored base rates. What we really wish to know is the probability of the event "*card is an ace, given that the spy says that it is an ace.*" It is quite possible that the subjects misinterpret the conditional probabilities that are given, and perceive these as probabilities of the actual number of the card given the claimed number seen by the spy. The experimenter is generally very explicit in indicating to the subjects that this is not the case and that the spy is really telling the number that the spy actually believes was observed.

The actual probability of the card being an ace, conditioned upon the observation by the spy that it was an ace, may be obtained from Bayes rule as

$$P(A|SA) = P(SA|A)P(A)/P(SA)$$

We compute

$$P(SA) = P(SA|A)P(A) + P(SA|NA)P(NA)$$
$$P(SA) = 0.95(0.0769) + 0.05(0.9231) = 0.1192$$

So, we see that

$$P(A|SA) = 0.95(0.0769)/(0.1192) = 0.61$$

Rather than the spy being correct, in that the card is an ace, with probably 0.95, the spy is only correct with probability 0.61. The difficulty here, usually unrecognized by those who do not do the calculation, is that the spy has a lot of *false alarms,* that is to say, misdiagnoses a large percentage of non-aces as aces. However, it appears that not only do subjects not do calculations like this, they neglect base rates completely when they are given such individuating information as the fact that the spy said the card was an ace.

This is a prototypical illustration of the sort of information-processing bias that is observed, generally in experimentally controlled laboratory settings. The many studies that have been made suggest that the errors that occur are systemic errors and not just random errors that might be due to factors such as guessing. Kahneman and Tversky [94] indicate that there are three primary reasons for study of these systematic errors and human inferential biases:

1. They expose human intellectual limitations and suggest ways to improve the quality of human reasoning and information processing.
2. They reveal the psychological processes that govern human inference and judgment.
3. They indicate those portions of statistical theory that are nonintuitive or counterintuitive.

Let us now look at a summary list of some of these identified cognitive biases.

6.5.1 A Summary of Identified Biases

Anchoring and Adjustment. Often a person finds that difficulty in problem solving is due not to the lack of data and information, but rather to the existence of excess data and information. In such situations, the person often resorts to heuristics which may reduce the mental efforts required to arrive at a solution. In using the anchoring and adjustment heuristic when confronted with a large amount of data, the person selects a particular datum, such as the mean, as an initial or starting point, or anchor, and then adjusts that value improperly in order to incorporate the rest of the data such as to result in flawed information.

Availability. The decision maker uses only easily available information and ignores not easily available sources of significant information. An event is believed to occur frequently—that is, with high probability—if it is easy to recall similar events.

Base Rate. The likelihood of occurrence of two events is commonly compared by contrasting the number of times the two events occur and ignoring the rate of occurrence of each event. This bias often occurs when the decision maker has concrete experience with one event but only statistical or abstract information on the other. In general, abstract information will be ignored at the expense of concrete information. A base rate determined primarily from concrete information may be called a causal base rate, whereas that determined from abstract information is an incidental base rate. When information updates occur, this individuating information frequently is given much more weight than it deserves. It is much easier for individuating information to override incidental base rates than causal base rates.

Confirmation Bias. People are more prone to utilize information that is likely to validate currently held beliefs than information that might disconfirm or falsify these beliefs.

Conservatism. The failure to revise estimates as much as they should be revised, based on receipt of new significant information, is known as conservatism. This is related to data saturation and regression effects biases.

Data Presentation Context. The impact of summarized data, for example, may be much greater than that of the same data presented in detail, nonsummarized form. In addition, different scales may be used to change the impact of the same data considerably.

Data Saturation. People often reach premature conclusions on the basis of too small a sample of information while ignoring the rest of the data that is received later on, or stopping acquisition of data prematurely.

Desire for Self-fulfilling Prophecies. The decision maker values a certain outcome, interpretation, or conclusion and acquires and analyzes only information that supports this conclusion. This is another form of selective perception.

Ease of Recall. Data that can easily be recalled or assessed will affect perception of the likelihood of similar events occurring again. People typically weigh easily recalled data more in decision making than those data that cannot easily be recalled.

Expectations. People often remember and attach higher validity to information that confirms their previously held beliefs and expectations than they do to disconfirming information. Thus, the presence of large amounts of information make it easier for one to selectively ignore disconfirming information such as to reach any conclusion and thereby prove anything that one desires.

Fact-Value Confusion. Strongly held values may frequently be regarded and presented as facts. That type of information is sought that confirms or lends credibility to one's views and values. Information contradicting one's views or values is ignored. This is related to wishful thinking in that both are forms of selective perception.

Fundamental Attribution Error (Success/Failure Error). The decision maker associates success with personal inherent ability and associates failure with poor luck in chance events. This is related to availability and representativeness.

Gamblers' Fallacy. The decision maker falsely assumes that unexpected occurrence of a "run" of some events enhances the probability of occurrence of an event that has not occurred.

Habit. Familiarity with a particular rule for solving a problem may result in reutilization of the same procedure and selection of the same alternative when confronted with a similar type of problem and similar information. We choose an alternative because it has previously been acceptable for a perceived similar purpose, or because of superstition.

Hindsight. People are often unable to think objectively if they receive information that an outcome has occurred and they are told to ignore this information.

Illusion of Control. A good outcome in a chance situation may well have resulted from a poor decision. The decision maker may assume a feeling of control over events that is not reasonable.

Illusion of Correlation. A mistaken belief that two events covary when they do not covary is known as the illusion of correlation.

Law of Small Numbers. People are insufficiently sensitive to the available quantity and quality of evidence. They commonly express greater confidence in predictions based on small samples of data with nondisconfirming evidence than in much larger samples with minor disconfirming evidence. Sample size and reliability frequently have little influence on confidence.

Order Effects. The order in which information is presented affects information retention in memory. Typically, the first piece of information presented (primacy effect) and the last presented (recency effect) assume undue importance in the mind of the decision maker.

Outcome-Irrelevant Learning System. Use of an inferior information processing or decision rule can lead to poor results, and the decision maker can believe that these are good because of inability to evaluate the impacts of the choices not selected and the hypotheses not tested.

Overconfidence. People generally ascribe more credibility to data than is warranted and hence overestimate the probability of success merely owing to the presence of an abundance of data. The greater the amount of data, the more confident the person is in the accuracy of the data.

Redundancy. The more redundancy in the data, the more confidence people often have in their predictions, although this overconfidence is usually unwarranted.

Reference Effect. People normally perceive and evaluate stimuli in accordance with their present and past experiential level for the stimuli. They sense a reference level in accordance with past experience. Therefore, reactions to stimuli, such as a comment from an associate, are interpreted favorably or unfavorably in accordance with our previous expectations and experiences. A reference point defines an operating point in the space of outcomes. Changes in perceptions, due to changes in the reference point, are called reference effects. These changes may not be based on proper, statistically relevant computations.

Regression Effects. The largest observed values of observations are used without regressing toward the mean to consider the effects of noisy measurements. In effect, this ignores uncertainties.

Representativeness. When making inference from data, too much weight is given to results of small samples. As sample size is increased, the results of small samples are taken to be representative of the larger population. The "laws" of representativeness differ considerably from the laws of probability and violations of the conjunction rule, $P(A|B) < P(A)$, are often observed.

Selective Perceptions. People often seek only information that confirms their views and values. They disregard or ignore disconfirming evidence. Issues are structured on the basis of personal experience and wishful thinking. There are many illustrations of selective perception. One is "reading between the lines" such as, for example, to deny antecedent statements and, as a consequence, accept "if you don't promote me, I won't perform well" as following inferentially from "I will perform well if you promote me."

Spurious Cues. Frequently, cues appear only by occurrence of a low-probability event, but they are accepted by the decision maker as commonly occurring.

Substitution of Correlation for Causation. Often, we assume that because two events are correlated, there must also be some causative relation between them. Causation must imply correlation. However, correlation does not infer any necessary causative relationships.

Wishful Thinking. The preference of the decision maker for particular outcomes and particular decisions can lead the decision maker to choose an alternative that the decision maker would like to have associated with a desirable outcome. This implies a confounding of facts and values and is a form of selective perception.

There a number of related biases, many of which may be derived from this list. For example, the conjunctive fallacy, $P(A,B) > P(A)P(B)$, is similar to representativeness.

Of particular interest are circumstances under which these biases occur; and appropriate styles that might result in debiasing or amelioration of their effects. Many of the cognitive biases that have been found to exist have been found in the unfamiliar surroundings (unfamiliar to the subjects on whom the experiments were performed, that is) of the experimental laboratory, and generalization of this work to real-world situations is a contemporary research area of much interest. However, most of the laboratory experiments have concerned very simple, if unfamiliar tasks.

An especially cogent summary of those principles that encourage use of proper information processing, particularly in the statistical settings in which many of the information-processing biases have been developed, is contained in Nisbett et al. [95]. Three task variables are identified as being most important in influencing adults, capable of formal operational thought in the sense of Piaget, to reason correctly in a statistical sense. These include

- The degree to which randomness in data-sensing devices is evident.
- Experiential familiarity with analogous situations.
- Cultural disposition for statistical reasoning in the particular task being considered.

The results of much of this work, while there is some controversy, show that simple quantitative models perform better in human judgment and decision-making tasks, including information processing, than wholistic expert performance in similar tasks. This would appear to have major implications and to sound major caveats for such areas as *"expert forecasting."* This caution is strongly emphasized in the works of Makridakis and Wheelwright [96], Beyth-Marom and Dekel [97], and Einhorn and Hogarth [98], who provide guidelines that should be useful in assisting people to process statistical information better. Klayman and Ha [99, 100] are particularly concerned with the provision of appropriate feedback, such that humans can process information more correctly in stochastic environments. Some of these approaches will now be briefly examined.

6.5.2 Debiasing

A number of prescriptions might be given to encourage avoidance of possible cognitive biases and to debias those that do occur. Some suggestions to avoid cognitive bias are

1. Sample information from a broad data base and be especially careful to include data bases that might contain disconfirming information.
2. Include sample size, confidence intervals, and other measures of information validity in addition to mean values.
3. Encourage use of models and quantitative aids to improve on information analysis through proper aggregation of acquired information.
4. Avoid the hindsight bias by providing access to information at critical past times.
5. Encourage decision makers to distinguish good and bad decisions from good and bad outcomes in order to avoid various forms of selective perception such as, for instance, the illusion of control.
6. Encourage effective learning from experience. Foster understanding of the decision situation, and methods and rules used in practice to process information and make decisions, such as to avoid outcome-irrelevant learning systems.
7. Use structured frameworks based on logical reasoning in order to avoid confusing facts and values, and wishful thinking; and to assist in processing information updates.
8. Collect both qualitative and quantitative data, and be sure that all data is regarded with "appropriate" emphasis. None of the data should be overweighted or underweighted in accordance with personal views, beliefs, or values only.
9. People should be reminded, from time to time, about what type or size of sample from which data are being gathered, so as to avoid the representativeness bias.
10. Information should be presented in several orderings so as to avoid recency and primacy order effects, and the data presentation context and data saturation biases.

Kahneman and Tversky [94] discuss a systemic procedure to enhance debiasing of information-processing activities. A five-step procedure, designed to produce properly regressive procedures by experts who are familiar with the subject area of the investigation, is proposed:

1. Select a proper reference class,
2. Make a statistical estimate of the distribution of the reference class,
3. Make an intuitive, generally nonregressive, estimate,
4. Assess probabilities, and
5. Correct the intuitive estimate.

A definitive discussion of debiasing methods for hindsight and overconfidence is presented by Fischhoff in Kahneman, Slovic, and Tversky [91]. He suggests identifying faulty judges, faulty tasks, and mismatches between judges and tasks. Strategies for each of these situations are given.

6.5.3 Contrasting Views

Not everyone agrees with conclusions just reached about cognitive human information processing and inferential behavior. Several arguments have been advanced for a decidedly less pessimistic view of human inference and decision. In one of these, Jonathan Cohen [101, 102] argues that all of this research is based on a conventional model for probabilistic reasoning, which he calls the *"Pascalian"* probability calculus. He expresses the view that human behavior does not appear "biased" at all when it is viewed in terms of other equally appropriate schemes for probabilistic reasoning, such as his own *"inductive probability"* system. Cohen states that human irrationality can never be demonstrated in laboratory experiments, especially experiments that are based on the use of what he calls *"probabilistic conundrums."* There are a number of other contrasting viewpoints as well.

In their definitive study of behavioral and normative decision analysis, von Winterfeldt and Edwards [103] refer to these information-processing biases as *cognitive illusions*. They indicate that there are four fundamental elements to every cognitive illusion:

1. A *formal operational* rule that determines *the* correct solution to an intellectual question.
2. An intellectual question that *almost invariably* includes all of the information required to obtain *the* correct answer through use of the formal rule.
3. A human judgment, generally made without the use of these analytical tools, that is intended to answer the posed question.
4. A *systematic* and generally large and unforgivable discrepancy between the correct answer and the human judgment.

There are several current perspectives relative to probability and inference that do not depend on conventional Bayesian logic, or that are extensions of it [104]. Other concerns are based on what are believed to be inadequacies of the studies on which the conclusions are based. Von Winterfeldt and Edwards [103] and Phillips [105] describe some of the ways in which subjects might have been put at a disadvantage in this research on cognitive heuristics and information-processing biases. Much of this centers around the fact that the subjects have little experiential familiarity with the tasks they are asked to perform.

As inference tasks are decomposed and better structured, it is likely that a large number of information-processing biases will disappear. Accordingly, concern should be expressed about the structuring of inference and decision problems and the learning that is reflected by revisions of problem structure in the light of new knowledge. The real task for the designer of a DSS is how to provide data and model bases and the means for humans to interact with these in ways that facilitate appropriate problem structuring.

6.6 INFORMATION-PROCESSING CONCERNS IN DECISION SUPPORT SYSTEMS DESIGN

Many contemporary decision-making studies attempt to integrate a *descriptive* and personalized behavioral model of the decision maker in conjunction with a *normative* and often quantitative decision model. The descriptive model illustrates the manner in which a real person goes about making a decision in a variety of situations. Frequently, descriptive decision-making behavior is very flawed. The normative model describes what decision a person *should* make if they follow certain axioms. Some authors speak of a third type of decision model, a *prescriptive* model. This is basically the normative model as modified to fit a real human in a real decision situation, as contrasted with a hypothetical human in a hypothetical situation who is able to follow the mathematical prescriptions of axiomatic behavior. Some authors do not distinguish between normative and prescriptive decision studies, although it appears to be a growing trend to do this [106].

Morris [107] conjectures that it is the abilities of the decision aid to improve the intuitive capabilities, as opposed to the logical/mathematical capabilities, that are the more important and useful for the decision maker. It must be recognized that decision makers develop personal styles of their own, and that these styles are dependent on the *contingency task structure* of the issue at hand. This contingency task structure is composed of the task to be accomplished, the environmental context into which the task is embedded, and the decision maker's experiential familiarity with task and environment. Morris's *personal style hypothesis* states that one can gain more from attempts to apply natural enhancements to the decision maker's personal style than from equivalent efforts to radically reformulate and externalize it in the normative image of some axiomatic model.

Information processing is fundamentally a hypothesis identification and testing effort. Schum [108] has identified five criteria for evaluating the usefulness or satisfaction level of a hypotheses: relevance, testability, explanatory and predictive power, compatibility with other knowledge, and simplicity. These criteria may be described as follows:

1. *Relevance.* Hypotheses should be relevant to matters concerning the inferential problem. When this rule is violated, we have what is sometimes called

a Type-III error (an error that comes about by solving the wrong problem). Often, these are unexpected as people generally expect Type-I and Type-II errors (which occur from rejecting a true hypothesis as being false, and accepting a false hypothesis as being true, respectively).

2. *Testability.* The utility of a hypothesis, in most practical cases, depends on whether or not there is some form of evidence that would tend to confirm or disconfirm the hypothesis. Hypotheses about some person's behavior, motivations, or intentions are frequently very difficult to confirm.

3. *Explanatory and Predictive Power.* The extent to which a hypothesis allows one to deduce evidentiary consequences is a very significant criterion in retaining one hypothesis and rejecting another. The issue here concerns the ability to anticipate relevant evidence. In a defense of a stated hypothesis, one must give attention to the sufficiency of the evidence, and the sufficiency of the evidence depends heavily on the ability to judge its relevance. The success one enjoys in the discovery of relevant evidence is quite dependent on the hypotheses one generates. In other words, some hypotheses permit the user to request information whose answers or values involve potentially relevant evidence. It is possible that a particularly well-formed hypothesis may allow the user to deduce truly novel consequences whose occurrence may be unanticipated under other, less adequate, hypotheses.

4. *Compatibility with Other Knowledge.* The extent to which hypotheses are compatible with established knowledge is critical. A hypothesis that ignores established information will be easily rejected by a devil's advocate in a dialectic inquiring system, for example. This points out the importance of having coordination and cooperation among the different analytic disciplines and inquiry systems.

5. *Simplicity.* If possible, one should choose a simpler hypothesis over a more complicated hypothesis. Because of environmental and situational complexities concerning a particular problem, hypotheses may not be simple, but certainly one can be simpler than another in explaining a specific set of information or evidential data. When hypotheses involve the conjunction of many levels of evidence, a decision about how much detail is required will likely be difficult.

These would also seem appropriate attributes to use in the design and evaluation of decision support aids that enhance human information-processing activities.

6.7 SUMMARY

We have discussed some important models of how humans, as individuals and in organizations, process information for judgment and choice. Some rationality perspectives were examined. Finally, we presented an overview of human information-processing biases and an outline of how these topics relate to the design of DSS. This is an area of much importance as evidenced by diverse recent works addressed to the layperson [109], and the engineer and policy analyst [110].

PROBLEMS

6.1. Contrast and compare the Janis–Mann model of decision making with the Dreyfus model. In what ways are the two models similar and dissimilar?

6.2. Contrast and compare the Klein model of decision making with the Dreyfus model. In what ways are the two models similar and dissimilar?

6.3. Contrast and compare the Rasmussen model of decision making with the Dreycus model. In what ways are the two models similar and dissimilar?

6.4. Contrast and compare the various models of decision making with the rationality perspectives that we discussed. In what ways are models and rationality perspective approaches similar and dissimilar?

6.5. A not-uncommon situation for a civil defense emergency preparedness effort might read as follows:

A civil defense committee in a large metropolitan area met recently to discuss emergency plans in the event of various crisis situations. One emergency under discussion was the following: *A train carrying a very toxic chemical substance derails and the storage tanks begin to leak. The threat of explosion and lethal discharge of poisonous chemicals is imminent.* Two possible actions were considered by the committee. Indicate your opinion about the relative merits of each.

Option A: carries with it a 0.5 probability of containing the threat without any loss of life and a 0.5 probability of losing 100 lives.

Option B: would produce a certain loss of 50 lives.

Which option is preferred? How would this issue be resolved using the various decision models and rationality perspectives discussed in this chapter? Provide a brief discussion in your commentary concerning how an interface design might support, or might have difficulty in supporting, each of these.

6.6. Identify one human-information processing bias that appears to be of interest and write a case-study-type scenario of how a human might process or misprocess information using it.

References

[1] Sage, A. P., "Behavioral and Organizational Considerations in the Design of Information Systems and Processes for Planning and Decision Support," *IEEE Transactions on Systems, Man and Cybernetics,* Vol. 11, No. 9, September 1981, pp. 640–678.

[2] Sage, A. P. (Ed.), *Concise Encyclopedia of Information Processing in Systems and Organizations,* Pergamon Press, Oxford, UK, 1990.

[3] Anderson, J. R., *Cognitive Psychology and Its Implications,* Freeman, San Francisco, 1980.

[4] Anderson, J. R., *The Architecture of Cognition,* Harvard University Press, Cambridge, 1983.
[5] Estes, W. K., *Handbook of Learning and Cognitive Processes,* Vol. 1–6, Erlbaum, Hillsdale, NJ, 1975–1979.
[6] Mayer, R. E., *Thinking, Problem Solving, Cognition,* Freeman, San Francisco, 1983.
[7] Eysenck, M. W., *A Handbook of Cognitive Psychology,* Erlbaum, Hillsdale, NJ, 1984.
[8] Mandler, G., *Cognitive Psychology,* Erlbaum, Hillsdale, NJ, 1985.
[9] Bettman, J. R., *An Information Processing Theory of Consumer Choice,* Addison-Wesley, Reading, MA, 1979.
[10] Shiffrin, R. M., and Schneider, W., "Controlled and Automatic Human Information Processing: I Perceptual Learning, Automatic Attending and a General Theory," *Psychological Review,* Vol. 84, 1977, pp. 127–190.
[11] Miller, G. A., "The Magical Number Seven, Plus or Minus Two: Some Limits on Our Capacity for Processing Information," *Psychological Review,* Vol. 63, 1956, pp. 81–97.
[12] Kruglanski, A. W., "Lay-Epistemic Logic—Process and Content: Another Look at Attribution Theory," *Psychological Review,* Vol. 87, 1980, pp. 70–87.
[13] Kruglanski, A. W., and Ajzen, I., "Bias and Error in Human Judgment," *European Journal of Social Psychology,* Vol. 13, 1983, pp. 1–44.
[14] Kruglanski, A. W., and Freund, T., "The Freezing and Unfreezing of Lay-Inferences: Effects on Impressionable Primacy, Ethnic Stereotyping, and Numerical Anchoring," *Journal of Experimental Social Psychology,* Vol. 19, 1983, pp. 448–468.
[15] Brainerd, C. J., *Piaget's Theory of Intelligence,* Prentice-Hall, Englewood Cliffs, NJ, 1978.
[16] Flavell, J. H., *Cognitive Development,* Prentice-Hall, Englewood Cliffs, NJ, 1977.
[17] Ginsburg, H., and Opper, S., *Piaget's Theory of Intellectual Development,* Prentice-Hall, Englewood Cliffs, NJ, 1979.
[18] Stone, C. A. and Day, M. C., "Competence and Performance Models and the Characterization of Formal Operational Skills," *Human Development,* Vol. 28, 1980, pp. 323–353.
[19] Rasmussen, J., "Skills, Rules, Knowledge; Signals, Signs, and Symbols; and Other Distinctions in Human Performance Models," *IEEE Transactions on Systems, Man and Cybernetics,* Vol. SMC 13, No. 3, May 1983, pp. 257–266.
[20] Rasmussen, J., *On Information Processing and Human-Machine Interaction: An Approach to Cognitive Engineering,* North-Holland, New York, 1986.
[21] Rasmussen, J., "Models of Mental Strategies in Process Plant Diagnosis," in Rasmussen, J., and Rouse, W. B. (Eds.), *Human Detection and Diagnosis of System Failures,* Plenum, New York, 1980, pp. 241–258.
[22] Rasmussen, J., "Use of Computer Games to Test Experimental Techniques and Cognitive Models," in Rasmussen, J. and Zunde, P. (Eds.), *Empirical Foundations of Information and Software Science III,* Plenum, New York, 1987, pp. 187–195.
[23] Dreyfus, H. L., and Dreyfus, S. E., *Mind Over Machine: The Power of Human Intuition and Expertise in the Era of the Computer,* Free Press, New York, 1986.
[24] Klein, G. A., and Weitzenfeld, J., "Improvement of Skills for Solving Ill-Defined Problems," *Educational Psychology,* Vol. 13, 1978, pp. 31–41.
[25] Klein, G. A., "Automated Aids for the Proficient Decision Maker," *Proceedings of the 1980 IEEE Systems, Man and Cybernetics Conference,* October 1980, pp. 301–304.

[26] Janis, I. L., and Mann, L., *Decision Making: A Psychological Analysis of Conflict, Choice, and Commitment,* Free Press, New York, 1977.
[27] Broadbent, D. W., *Decision and Stress,* Academic, London, 1971.
[28] Blakeslee, T. R., *The Right Brain,* Anchor Press, New York, 1980.
[29] Craik, F. I. M., "Human Memory," *Annual Review of Psychology,* Vol. 30, 1979, pp. 63–102.
[30] Fishbein, M., and Azjin, I., *Belief, Attitude, Intention, and Behavior,* Addison-Wesley, Reading, MA, 1975.
[31] Gregory, R. L. (Ed.), *The Oxford Companion to the Mind,* Oxford University Press, 1987.
[32] Huber, G. P., "Cognitive Style as a Basis for MIS and DSS Designs: Much Ado About Nothing," *Management Science,* Vol. 29, No. 5, May 1983, pp. 567–579.
[33] March, J. G., "Bounded Rationality, Ambiguity, and the Engineering of Choice," *The Bell Journal of Economics,* Vol. 10, 1978, pp. 587–608.
[34] Hammond, K. R., "Intuitive and Analytical Cognition: Information Models," in Sage, A. P. (Ed.), *Concise Encyclopedia of Information Processing in Systems and Organizations,* Pergamon Press, Oxford, UK, 1990, pp. 306–312.
[35] Brunswick, E., "The Conceptual Framework of Psychology," in *International Encyclopedia of Unified Science,* Vol. 1, No. 10, University of Chicago Press, 1952.
[36] Brunswick, E., *Perception and the Representative Design of Psychological Experiments,* University of California Press, Berkeley, 1956.
[37] Hammond, K. R., "Information Models for Intuitive and Analytical Cognition," in Ref. 2, pp. 306–323.
[38] Hagafors, R., and Brehmer, B., "Does Having to Justify One's Judgments Change the Nature of the Judgment Process," *Organizational Behavior and Human Performance,* Vol. 31, 1983, pp. 223–232.
[39] Crocker, J., Fiske, S. T., and Taylor, S. E., "Schematic Basis for Belief Change," in Eiser, J. R. (Ed.), *Additudional Judgment,* Springer Verlag, New York, 1984.
[40] Brehmer, B., "Response Consistency in Probabilistic Inference Tasks," *Organizational Behavior and Human Performance,* Vol. 22, 1978, pp. 103–115.
[41] Brehmer, B., "In One Word: Not from Experience," *Acta Psychologica,* Vol. 45, 1980, pp. 223–241.
[42] Barnard, C. I., *The Functions of the Executive,* Harvard University Press, Cambridge, 1938.
[43] Etzioni, A., *Modern Organizations,* Prentice-Hall, Englewood Cliffs, NJ, 1964.
[44] Hall, R. H., *Organizations: Structure and Process,* Prentice-Hall, Englewood Cliffs, NJ, 1977.
[45] Mintzberg, H., *The Nature of Managerial Work,* Harper & Row, New York, 1973.
[46] Haye, J., "An Axiomatic Theory of Organizations," *Administrative Science Quarterly,* Vol. 10, No. 3, December 1965, pp. 289–320.
[47] March, J. G., and Simon, H. A., *Organizations,* Wiley, New York, 1958.
[48] Cyert, R. M., and Simon, H. A., "The Behavioral Approach: With Emphasis on Economics," *Behavioral Science,* Vol. 28, 1983, pp. 95–108.
[49] Weick, K. E., *The Social Psychology of Organizing,* Addison-Wesley, Reading, MA, 1979.

[50] Weick, K. E., "Cosmos versus Chaos: Sense and Nonsense in Electronic Contexts," *Organizational Dynamics,* Vol. 14, No. 3, 1985, pp. 50–64.

[51] Janis, I. L., *Groupthink,* Free Press, New York, 1982.

[52] Argyris, C., and Schon, D. A., *Organizational Learning: A Theory of Action Perspective,* Addison-Wesley, Reading, MA, 1978.

[53] Argyris, C., and Schon, D. A., *Theory in Practice: Increasing Professional Effectiveness,* Jossey-Bass, San Francisco, 1974.

[54] Argyris, C., *Reasoning, Learning, and Action: Individual and Organizational,* Jossey-Bass, San Francisco, 1982.

[55] Huber, G. P., "Organizational Decision Making and the Design of Decision Support Systems," *Management Information Systems Quarterly,* Vol. 5, No. 2, 1981, pp. 1–10.

[56] Huber, G. P., "Organizational Information Systems: Determinants of Their Performance and Behavior," *Management Science,* Vol. 28, No. 2, 1982, pp. 138–155.

[57] Vroom, V. H., and Yetton, P. W., *Leadership and Decision Making,* University of Pittsburgh, Pittsburgh, PA, 1973.

[58] Keen, P. G. W., "Information Systems and Organizational Change." *Communications of the Association for Computing Machinery,* Vol. 24, No. 1, January 1981, pp. 24–33.

[59] Tushman, M. L., and Nadler, D. A., "Information Processing as an Integrating Concept in Organizational Design," *Academy of Management Review,* Vol. 3, No. 3, July 1978, pp. 613–624.

[60] Feldman, M. S., and March, J. G., "Information in Organizations as Signal and Symbol," *Administrative Science Quarterly,* Vol. 26, 1981, pp. 171–186.

[61] Diesing, P., *Reason in Society,* University of Illinois Press, Urbana, IL, 1962.

[62] Steinbruner, J. D., *The Cybernetic Theory of Decision,* Princeton University, Princeton, NJ, 1974.

[63] Sage, A. P., *Economic Systems Analysis: Microeconomics for Systems Engineering, Engineering Management, and Project Selection,* Elsevier North-Holland, New York, 1983.

[64] Simon, H. A., "From Substantive to Procedural Rationality," in Latsis, S. J. (Ed.), *Method and Appraisal in Economics,* Cambridge University Press, 1976, pp. 129–148.

[65] Simon, H. A., *Models of Thought,* Yale University Press, New Haven, CT, 1979.

[66] Simon, H. A., "Rational Decision Making in Business Organization," *American Economic Review,* Vol. 69, No. 4, September 1979, pp. 493–513.

[67] Simon, H. A., "The Behavioral and Social Scienses," *Science,* Vol. 209, July 1980, pp. 72–78.

[68] Simon, H. A., "Rationality as Process and as Product of Thought," *American Economic Review,* Vol. 68, May 1978, 1–16.

[69] Lindblom, C. E., "The Science of 'Muddling Through'," *Public Administrative Review,* Vol. 19, Spring 1959, pp. 155–169.

[70] Lindblom, C. E., *The Intelligence of Democracy: Decision Making Through Mutual Adjustment,* Free Press, New York, 1965.

[71] Lindblom, C. E., *The Policy Making Process,* Prentice-Hall, Englewood Cliffs, NJ, 1980.

[72] Cyert, R. M., and March, J. G., *A Behavioral Theory of the Firm,* Prentice-Hall, Englewood Cliffs, NJ, 1963.

[73] Cohen, M. D., and March, J. G., *Leadership and Ambiguity*, Second Edition, Harvard Business School Press, Cambridge, MA, 1986.

[74] Cohen, M. D., March, J. B., and Olsen, J. P., "A Garbage Can Model of Organizational Choice," *Administrative Science Quarterly*, Vol. 17, No. 1, 1972, pp. 1–25.

[75] Padgett, J., "Managing Garbage Can Hierarchies," *Administrative Science Quarterly*, Vol. 25, No. 4, 1980, pp. 583–604.

[76] March, J., and Wessinger-Baylon, T. (Eds.), *Ambiguity and Command: Organizational Perspectives on Military Decisionmaking*, Pitman, Boston, 1986.

[77] Carley, K., "An Approach for Relating Social Structure to Cognitive Structure," *Journal of Mathematical Sociology*, Vol. 12, No. 2, 1986, pp. 137–189.

[78] Carley, K., "Designing Organizational Structures to Cope with Communications Breakdowns: A Simulation Model," working paper, Carnegie Mellon University, September 1990.

[79] Axelrod, R. M. (Ed.), *Structure of Decision: The Cognitive Maps of Political Elites*, Princeton University Press, Princeton, NJ, 1976.

[80] Linstone, H. A., "The Multiple Perspective Concept," *Technological Forecasting and Social Change*, Vol. 20, 1981, pp. 275–325.

[81] Linstone, H. A., *Multiple Perspectives for Decision Making*, North-Holland, New York, 1984.

[82] Allison, G., *Essence of Decision*, Little, Brown, Boston, 1971.

[83] Churchman, C. W., *Design of Inquiring Systems*, Basic Books, New York, 1971.

[84] Mason, R. O., and Mitroff, I. I., *Challenging Strategic Planning Assumptions*, Wiley, New York, 1981.

[85] Mason, R.O., and Mitroff, I., "A Program for Research on Management Information Systems," *Management Science*, Vol. 19, January 1973, pp. 475–487.

[86] Mitroff, I. I., and Mason, R. O., "Business Policy and Metaphysics: Some Philosophical Considerations," *Academy of Management Review*, Vol. 7, No. 3, 1982, pp. 361–371.

[87] Mitroff, I., Quinton, H., and Mason, R. O., "Beyond Contradiction and Consistency, A Design for Dialectical Policy Systems," *Theory and Decision*, Vol. 15, 1983, pp. 107–120.

[88] Mitroff, I. I., and Emshoff, J. R., "On Strategic Assumption Making: A Dialectical Approach to Policy and Planning," *Academy of Management Review*, Vol. 4, 1979, pp. 1–12.

[89] Mitroff, I., "A Communication Model of Dialectical Inquiring Systems—A Strategy for Strategic Planning," *Management Science*, Vol. 17, June 1971, pp. 634–648.

[90] Hogarth, R. M., *Judgment and Choice*, 2nd ed., Wiley, New York, 1987.

[91] Kahneman, D., Slovic, P., and Tversky, A. (Eds.), *Judgment Under Uncertainty: Heuristics and Biases*, Cambridge University Press, New York, 1981.

[92] Bazerman, M. H., *Judgment in Managerial Decision Making*, Wiley, New York, 1986.

[93] Einhorn, H. J., and Hogarth, R. M., "Behavioral Decision Theory: Processes of Judgment and Choice," *Annual Review of Psychology*, Vol. 32, 1981, pp. 53–88.

[94] Kahneman, D. and Tversky, A., "Intuitive Prediction, Biases and Corrective Procedures," in Makridakis, S., and Wheelwright, S. C. (Eds.), *Forecasting*, North-Holland, New York, 1979, pp. 313–327.

[95] Nisbett, R. E., Krantz, D. H. Jepson, C., and Kunda, Z., "The Use of Satistical Heuristics in Everyday Reasoning," *Psychological Review,* Vol. 90, No. 4, 1983, pp. 339–363.

[96] Makridakis, S. and Wheelwright, S. C. (Eds.), *Forecasting,* North-Holland, New York, 1979.

[97] Beyth-Marom, R., and Dekel, S., *An Elementary Approach to Thinking Under Uncertainty,* Erlbaum, Hillsdale, NJ, 1985.

[98] Einhorn, H. J., and Hogarth, R. M., "Decision Making Under Ambiguity," in Hogarth, R. M., and Reder, M. W. (Eds.), *Rational Choice,* University of Chicago Press, 1987.

[99] Klayman, J., "Learning from Feedback in Probabilistic Environments," *Acta Psychologica,* Vol. 56, 1984, pp. 81–92.

[100] Klayman, J. and Ha, Y. W., "Confirmation, Disconfirmation, and Information in Hypothesis-Testing," *Psychological Review,* Vol. 94, No. 2, 1987, pp. 211–228.

[101] Cohen, L. J., "On the Psychology of Prediction: Whose is the Fallacy," *Cognition,* Vol. 7, No. 4, 1979, pp. 385–407.

[102] Cohen, L. J., "Can Human Irrationality Be Experimentally Demonstrated?," *The Behavioral and Brain Sciences,* Vol. 4, 1981, pp. 317–370.

[103] Von Winterfeldt, D., and Edwards, W., *Decision Analysis and Behavioral Research,* Cambridge University Press, 1986.

[104] Shafer, G., and Pearl, J. (Eds.), *Readings in Uncertain Reasoning,* Morgan Kaufman, San Mateo, CA, 1990.

[105] Phillips, L., "Theoretical Perspectives on Heuristics and Biases in Probabilistic Thinking," in Humphries, P. C., Svenson, O., and Vari, O. (Eds.), *Analyzing and Aiding Decision Problems,* North-Holland, New York, 1984.

[106] Keller, L. R., "The Role of Generalized Utility Theories in Descriptive, Prescriptive, and Normative Decision Analysis," *Information and Decision Technologies,* Vol. 15, No. 4, 1989, pp. 259–272.

[107] Morris, W., "Matching Decision Aids with Intuitive Styles," in Brinkers, H. (Ed.), *Decision-Making: Creativity, Judgment, and Systems,* Ohio State University Press, Columbus, 1972.

[108] Schum, D., *Evidence and Inference for the Intelligence Analyst,* Vol. I and II, University Press of America, Lanham, MD, 1987.

[109] Norman, D. A. *The Psychology of Everyday Things,* Basic Books, NY, 1988.

[110] Morgan, M. G., and Henrion, M. *Uncertainty,* Cambridge University Press, Cambridge, 1990.

Chapter 7

Group and Organizational Decision Support Systems

The term *group decision support system* (GDSS) is defined as an information technology based support system designed to provide decision-making support to groups and/or organizations. This could refer to a group meeting occurring at one physical location at which judgments and decisions are made that affect an organization or group. Alternatively, it could refer to a spectrum of *meetings* of one or more individuals that occur at distributed locations, or distributed in time, or distributed spatially and temporally. Frequently, these are called *organizational decision support systems* (ODSS). There are other terms often used. These include *executive support systems* (ESS), which are information technology based systems designed to support executives and managers, and *command and control systems*, a term commonly used in the military for a decision support system. We will generally use the term GDSS to describe all of these, and will provide some additional commentary on these distinctions later in this chapter.

Managers and other *knowledge workers* spend considerable time in meetings. Much research into meeting effectiveness suggests that it is low, and there have been proposals to increase this through information technology support [1]. Specific components of this information technology based support might include computer hardware and software, audio and video technology, and communications media. There are three fundamental ingredients in this support concept: technological support facilities, the support processes provided, and the environment. The environment for support would include the humans supported, the tasks in which they are engaged, and their experiential familiarity with these tasks and the environment in which they are embedded. A most compelling commentary supporting the need for group efforts was provided by Kraemer and King [2] in their overview of GDSS efforts, where they indicate that *group activities are economically necessary, efficient as a means of production, and reinforcing of democratic values.*

There are a number of predecessors for group decision support technology. Certainly, *decision rooms*, or *situation rooms*, where managers and boards meet to select from among alternative plans or courses of action, are very common. The first *computer-based* decision support facility for group use is reported to be one due to Douglas C. Engelbart, the inventor of the (computer) mouse, at Stanford in the 1960s. A discussion of this and other early support facilities is contained in Ref. 1.

The *electronic boardroom* type design of Engelbart is acknowledged to be the first type of information technology based GDSS. The electronic format was, however, preceded by a number of nonelectronic formats. The *cabinet war room* of Winston Churchill is perhaps the most famous of these. Maps placed on the wall and tables for military decision makers were the primary ingredients of this room. The early 1970s saw the introduction of a number of simple computer-based support aids into situation rooms. The first system that resembles that of the GDSS in use today is often attributed to Gerald Wagner, the chief executive officer of Execucom, who implemented a *planning laboratory*, which was comprised of a U-shaped table around which people sat, a projection TV system for use as a public viewing screen, individual small terminals and keyboards available to participants, and a minicomputer to which the terminals and keyboards were connected. This enabled participants to vote and to conduct simple spreadsheetlike exercises. Figure 7.1 illustrates the essential features of this concept. Most present-day GDSS centralized facilities appear much like the conceptual illustration of a support room, or situation room, shown in the figure.

As with a single-user DSS, appropriate questions for a GDSS that have major implications for design are questions that concern the perceptions and insights that the group obtains through use of the GDSS, and the activities that can be carried out through its use. Also, additional concerns arise regarding the public screen, interactions between the public screen and individual screens, the characteristics of individual workscreens, and contingency task structural variables associated with the individuals in the group using the GDSS [3].

Huber [4] has indicated both the needs for GDSS and how an appropriately designed GDSS can meet these needs. There are four interacting and complicating concerns identified by Huber.

1. Effective decision making requires not only obtaining an appropriate decision, but also assuring that participants are happy with the process used to reach the decision and that they will be willing to meet and work cooperatively in the future.
2. Productivity losses occur because of dominant individuals and group pressures that lead to conformity of thought, or *groupthink*.
3. Miscommunications are common in group situations.
4. Insufficient time is often spent in situation assessment, problem exploration, and generation of alternative courses of action.

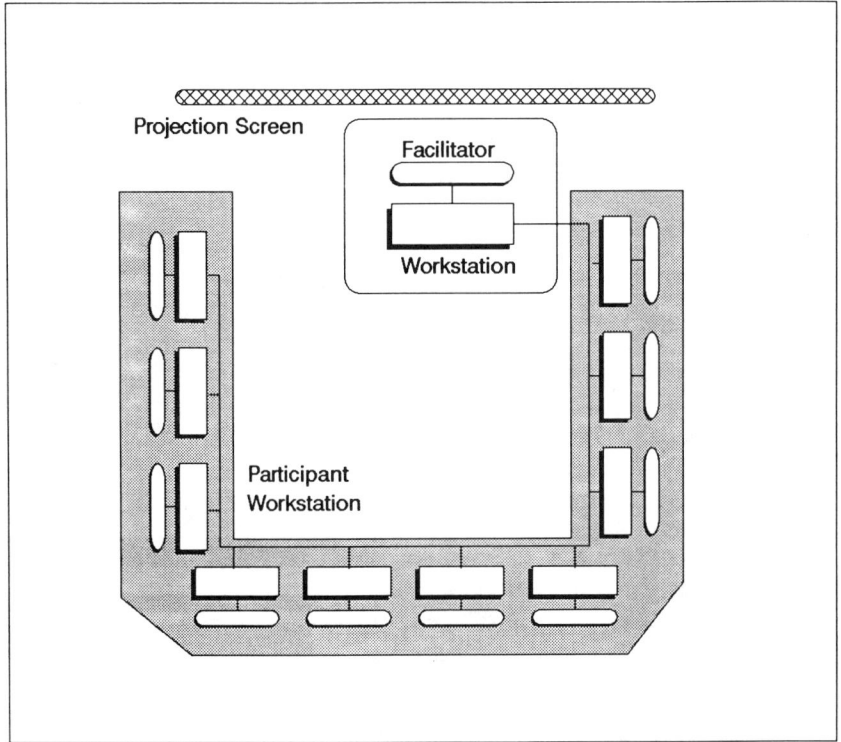

Figure 7.1 Early group decision support system (GDSS) situation room.

Huber further indicates that a GDSS can help improve the unaided decision situation, which often suffers from imperfect information processing and suboptimal decision selection.

A GDSS is comprised of

- *Technological components*—in terms of computer hardware and software, and communication equipment.
- *Environmental components*—in terms of the people involved, their locations in time and space, and their experiential familiarity with the task at hand.
- *Process components*—or variables that are comprised of the conventions used to support task performance, and to enable the other components of decision making to function appropriately.

We have already described the technological design features of DSS. Thus, commentary on this can be brief here. We do need to provide a perspective on groups and organizations and will do this in the next two sections. It will largely be based on discussions in the last chapter. Then, we will turn to some architectural considerations specifically relevant to GDSS.

7.1 CHARACTERISTICS OF ORGANIZATIONS

There have been many definitions of an organization. A large number of them infer a *group of individuals, established on a relatively continuous and stable basis, in an environment with changing characteristics.* The organization contains *relatively fixed boundaries, a normative order for management and authority, a communication system, and a set of incentives that encourage engagement in activities that are in general pursuit of a common and accepted set of goals.* As is known from earlier chapters, four top-level attributes or success factors are critical to the functionality of an organization: efficiency, effectiveness, adaptability to external environmental changes, and job satisfaction. Each contributes to the primary goals of organizational management, and information technology supports each of these four factors. Two of the most important of these goals are to improve the products and services of the organization, and to increase productivity in managing the organization. This chapter is primarily concerned with characterization of the design and development requirements and features of GDSS to effectively support the decision-making functions by humans in organizations such as to enable attainment of these goals.

Management is vitally concerned with the processing of information* in the organization. Generally, high-quality information is well recognized as a vital strategic resource for organizational well-being, since organizational success depends on management quality, management quality depends on decision quality, and decision quality depends on information quality. Naturally, many ingredients other than quality information influence organizational success. Nevertheless, one of the major tasks of management is that of minimizing the equivocality or ambiguity of the information that results from the organization's interaction with its external environment.† This is accomplished in order to better enable the organization to understand its environment; to detect or identify problems in need of resolution, to diagnose their causes; to identify alternative courses of action or policies to correct or resolve problems; to evaluate the potential efficacy of these policies; to select an appropriate priority order for problem resolution; to select suitable policies for implementation; and to augment existing knowledge with the new knowledge obtained in this implementation such that *organizational learning* occurs.

---

*Information processing may be broadly defined to include acquisition, representation, transmission, and use of information. Information is, as we defined previously, data of value for use in decision making.
†This relates directly to notions of separation of management functions. Equivocality cannot be eliminated, of course. It can be minimized. It is a task of top management to accomplish this and to create an environment in which those reporting to top management do not deal with the equivocality that remains, this being a task of top management.

7.2 INFORMATION NEEDS FOR GROUP AND ORGANIZATIONAL DECISION MAKING

There have been many attempts to classify different types of decisions. Among the classifications of particular interest here is the decision-type taxonomy, identified more than 25 years ago by Robert Anthony [5], in which four types of decisions are identified: strategic planning decisions, management control decisions, operational control decisions, and operational performance decisions. These decisions are not unrelated.* Clearly, strategic planning decisions lead to management control decisions. These in turn lead to operational control decisions which, in turn, lead to operational performance decisions. There exists the opportunity for a DSS at each of these hierarchical levels. *Ideally*, information flow is bilateral to and from each of these levels; and there is, also *ideally*, organizational learning that occurs at each level, as suggested in Figure 1.1.

The nature of the decisions, and the type of information that is required, differ across each of these four levels. Generally, operational activities occur much more frequently than strategic planning activities. In addition, there is a difference in the degree to which the knowledge required for each of these levels is *structured*. In 1960, Herbert Simon [6] described decisions as structured or unstructured depending on whether or not the decision-making process could be explicitly described prior to the time when it is necessary to make a decision. This taxonomy would seem to lead directly to that in which expert skills (wholistic reasoning), rules (heuristics), or formal reasoning (holistic analysis) are normatively used for judgment. (Descriptions for these are generally provided in Chapter 6 in terms of each of the relative expertise models discussed there.) Generally, operational performance decisions are more likely than strategic planning decisions to be prestructured.† This gives rise to a number of questions concerning efficiency and effectiveness trade-offs between training and aiding [7] support for these levels; as we will discuss in the next chapter.

There are several human abilities that a GDSS should augment:

1. It should help the decision maker to *formulate*, frame, or assess the decision situation. This includes identifying the salient features of the environment, recognizing needs, identifying appropriate objectives by which to measure successful resolution of an issue, and generating alternative courses of action that will resolve the needs and satisfy objectives.

---

*There are many taxonomies or typologies of types of decisions. *Objectives, strategies,* and *tactics* represent often-used descriptors of organizational or individual decision types. Objectives are at a level above the four identified by Anthony, and tactics would appear to correspond to levels three and four. Level two in the Anthony typology appears to be a blend of low-level strategies and high-level tactics.

†Expert systems would usually be expected to be more suitable for operational performance and operational control decisions than they are for strategic planning and management planning decisions. Prestructured knowledge is usually more amenable to operationalization in an expert system, more often than not in the form of production rules, than unstructured and semistructured knowledge.

2. It should provide support in enhancing the abilities of the decision maker to obtain and *analyze* the possible impacts of the alternative courses of action.
3. There should be the capability to enhance the ability of the decision maker to *interpret* these impacts in terms of objectives. This interpretation capability will lead to evaluation of the alternatives and selection of a preferred alternative option.

Associated with each of these three formal steps* of *formulation, analysis,* and *interpretation* must be the ability to acquire, represent, and utilize information or knowledge[†], and the ability to implement the chosen alternative course of action.

Many attributes will affect the quality and usefulness of the information that is, or should be, obtained relative to any given decision situation. These variables are clearly contingency task dependent. Included among them are [8]:

*Inherent and Required **Accuracy** of Available Information.* Operational control and performance situations will commonly deal with information that is relatively accurate. The information in strategic planning and management control situations is often inaccurate.

*Inherent **Precision** of Available Information.* Generally, information available for strategic planning and management control decisions is very imprecise.

*Inherent **Relevancy** of Available Information.* Operational control and performance situations will frequently deal with information that is relatively relevant to the task at hand because it has been prepared that way by management. The information in strategic planning and management control situations is often obtained from the external environment and may be irrelevant to the strategic tasks at hand, although it may not initially appear this way.

*Inherent and Required **Completeness** of Available Information.* Operational control and performance situations will commonly deal with information that is relatively complete and sufficient for operational performance. The information in strategic planning and management control situations is often very incomplete and insufficient to enable great confidence in strategic planning and management control.

*Inherent and Required **Verifiability** of Available Information.* Operational control and performance situations will frequently deal with information that is relatively verifiable to determine correctness for the intended purpose. The information in strategic planning and management control situations is often

---

*This does not imply that an experienced human decision maker necessarily is consciously aware of monitoring activities associated with these three formal steps. But it does imply that issues are resolved *as if* the decision maker used these three formal steps. The discussions in Chapter 6 are especially relevant to this point.

[†]Information is data of value for decision making. Knowledge refers to something that has been learned, either by a human or by a computer. Essentially, the terms are synonymous, except for the somewhat more personal association implied by knowledge.

unverifiable, or relatively so, and this gives rise to a potential lack of confidence in strategic planning and management control decisions.

Inherent and Required **Consistency and Coherency** *of Available Information.* Operational control and performance situations will often deal with information that is relatively consistent and coherent. The information in strategic planning and management control situations is commonly inconsistent and perhaps even contradictory or incoherent, especially when it comes from multiple external sources.

Information Scope. Usually, (but not always), operational decisions are made on the basis of narrow-scope information related to well-defined events that are internal to the organizations. Strategic decisions are generally based on broad-scope information and a wide range of factors that often cannot be fully anticipated prior to the need for the decision.

Information Quantifiability. In strategic planning, information is likely to be highly qualitative, at least initially. For operational decisions, the available information is often highly quantified.

Information Currency. In strategic planning, information is frequently rather old, and it is commonly difficult to obtain current information about the external environment. For operational control decisions, extremely current information is often needed and is generally present.

Needed Level of Detail. Frequently, quite detailed information is needed for operational-type decisions. Highly aggregated information is often desired for strategic decisions. There are many difficulties associated with information summarization that need attention.

Time Horizon for Information Needed. Operational decisions are typically based on information over a short time horizon, and the nature of the control may be changed very frequently. Strategic decisions are predicated on information and predictions based on a long time horizon.

Frequency of Use. Strategic decisions are made infrequently, although they are perhaps refined fairly often. Operational decisions are made quite frequently, and are relatively easily changed.

Internal or External Information Source. Operational decisions are commonly based on information that is available internally to the organization, whereas strategic decisions are much more likely to be dependent on information content that can only be obtained external to the organization.

These attributes, and others, could be used to form the basis for an evaluation of information quality in a DSS or GDSS.

Information is used in a DSS for a variety of purposes. In general, it is equivalent to, or is used as, evidence. Often, information is used directly as a basis for testing an hypothesis. Sometimes, it is used indirectly for this purpose. According to Schum [9], there are three different conditions for describing hypotheses:

1. Different alternative hypotheses or assessments are possible if evidence is imperfect in any way. An hypothesis may be imperfect if it is based on imperfect information—that is to say, information that is incomplete, inconclusive, unreliable, inconsistent, or uncertain. Any or all of these alternative hypotheses may or may not be true.
2. Hypotheses may refer to past, present, or future events.
3. Hypotheses may be sharp (i.e., specific) or diffuse (i.e., unspecific). Sharp hypotheses are usually based on specific evidence rather than earlier diffuse hypotheses. An overly sharp hypothesis may contain irrelevant detail and invite invalidation by obtaining disconfirming evidence on a single issue in the hypothesis. An overly diffuse hypothesis may be judged too vague and uninteresting by those who must make a decision based on the hypothesis.

The support for any hypothesis can always be improved by either revising a portion of the hypothesis to accommodate new evidence or by gathering more evidence that infers the hypothesis.

Hypotheses can arise be of potentially significant use in each of the following situations [9]:

Explanations. An explanation usually involves a model, which can be elaborate or simple. The explanation consists of the rationale for why certain events occurred.

Event Predictions. In this case, the hypothesis is proposed for a possible future event. It may include the date or period when the possible event will occur.

Forecasting and Estimation. This involves the generation of a hypothesis based on data that does not exist, or that is inaccessible.

Categorization. Sometimes, it is useful to place persons, objects, or events into certain categories based on inconclusive evidence linking the persons, objects, or events to these categories. In this case, the categories represent hypotheses about category membership.

Assessment of the validity of a given hypothesis is inductive in nature. The generation of hypotheses and the determination of evidence relevant to these hypotheses involve deductive and abductive reasoning. Hypotheses may be generated on the basis of the experience and prior knowledge that leads to analogous representations and recognitional decision making, as has been noted by Klein [10] and discussed in Chapter 6. The different rationality perspectives of decision makers can result in different hypotheses given the same evidential information set.

Schum [9] has also identified five criteria for evaluating the usefulness or satisfaction level of a hypotheses: relevance, testability, explanatory and predictive power, compatibility with other knowledge, and simplicity. These were discussed in Chapter 6. Although no widely accepted theory on how to quantify the value of evidence has been developed, it is important to be able to support an hypothesis in some logical manner. Usually, there is a major hypothesis that is inferred by supporting hypotheses, and each of these supporting hypotheses is inferred by its supporting hypothesis, and so on. ***Evidence*** is relevant to the extent that it causes one to increase or decrease the likeliness of an existing hypothesis, or causes one to modify an existing hypothesis, or causes one to create a new hypothesis. Evidence is ***direct*** if it has a straightforward bearing on the validity of the main hypothesis. It is ***indirect*** if its effect on the main hypothesis is inferred through at least one other level of supporting hypothesis.

We can obtain information by making observations of an activity or event through an *internal observation* (the person or system accomplishes self-observation or self measurement) or through an *external observation* (the system or person is observed by an external observer). Assumptions are necessary in determining which information to observe for purposes such as developing an inference task. These should be explicitly stated if there is any doubt as to the general acceptability of the assumptions. Many times, assumptions are stated in the hypothesis itself.

Rasmussen [11] says that human information processing can be described in terms of

- *Data*, the mental representations on information describing the state.
- *Models*, the mental representation of the system's anatomical or functional structure.
- *Strategies*, the higher-level structures of the mental processes that relate goals to sets of models, data, and tactical process rules.

Tactical rules describe the control of the detailed processes within a formal strategy. Assessment of a situation can be performed in two basic ways, topographic search and symptomatic search, as noted in Chapter 6.

A number of human information-processing capabilities and limitations interact with organizational arrangements and task requirements to strongly influence resource allocations for organizational problem solving. Needs in this area have led to the development of GDSS. The purpose of these computerized aids to planning, problem solving, and decision making includes

- Removing a number of common communication barriers in groups and organizations.
- Providing techniques for the formulation, analysis, and interpretation of decisions.
- Systematically directing the discussion process, and associated problem solving and decision making, in terms of the patterns, timing, and content of the information that influences these actions.

As is soon discussed, a number of variations and permutations are possible in the provision of group and organizational decision support. These are associated with specific realization or architectural format for a GDSS to support a set of GDSS performance objectives for a particular task in a particular environment.

The same maladies that affect individual decision-making and problem-solving behavior, as well as many others, can result from group and organizational limitations. There is a considerable body of knowledge, generally qualitative, relative to organizational structure, effectiveness, and decision making in organizations. Some of this was discussed in Chapter 6. The majority of such studies suggest that a bounded rationality or satisficing perspective, often heavily influenced by bureaucratic political considerations, will generally be the decision perspective adopted in actual decision-making practice in organizations. To cope with this effectively requires the ability to deal *concurrently* with technological, environmental, and process concerns as they each, separately and collectively, motivate group and organizational problem-solving issues.

The influencers of decision and decision process quality are especially important in this. At this point, we should sound a note of caution relative to some possibly overly simplistic notions relative to this. Welch [12] identifies possible imperfections in organizational decision making and discusses their relationship to decision process quality. In part, these are based on an application of seven symptoms identified in Ref. 13 to the Cuban missile crisis of 1962. The Janis and Mann decision model discussed in Chapter 6 is the basis for study of this crisis. These potential imperfections include

1. Omissions in surveying alternative courses of action.
2. Omissions in surveying objectives.
3. Failure to examine major costs and risks of the selected course of action (COA).
4. Poor information search, resulting in imperfect information. (Information is *imperfect* if it is too uncertain, imprecise, unreliable, inconsistent, or otherwise untrustworthy for use for an intended purpose.)
5. Selective bias in processing available information.
6. Failure to reconsider alternatives initially rejected, potentially by discounting favorable information and overweighting unfavorable information.
7. Failure to work out detailed implementation, monitoring, and contingency plans.

The central thrust of this study is that the relationship between the quality of the decision-making process and the quality of the outcome is difficult to establish.* This suggests strongly the usefulness of the contingency task structural model, and the need for approaches that evaluate the quality of processes, and not just decisions.

Organizational **ambiguity** is a primary reason why much observed "*bounded rationality*" behavior is asserted as being so pervasive in Chapter 6. March [14] and

---

*We know that this is indeed the case because of our studies in Chapter 3, in which we learned that probabilistic randomness can well lead to a poor outcome from a good decision and a good outcome from a bad decision. Here though, the discussion is about decision *process* and not just the decision. Welch's claim in Ref. 12 is that *adaptation to circumstances* is a primary factor in determining the choice of which decision process to use. This is in accordance with the contingency task structural model we visualize for situations such as this, and provides strong rationale for use of boundedly rational approaches, especially in dynamically evolving situations in which information may not be available in the right place at the right time.

March and Wessinger–Baylon [15] show that this is very often the case, even in situations when formal rational thought or *"vigilant information processing"* might be thought to be a preferred decision style. March [14] indicates that there are at least four kinds of ambiguity, opaqueness, or equivocality in organizations:

Ambiguity of intention
Ambiguity of understanding
Ambiguity of history
Ambiguity of human participation

These four ambiguities relate to an organization's structure, function, and purpose, as well as to the perception of the decision-making agents in an organization. They influence the information that is communicated in an organization, and generally introduce one or more forms of information imperfection. The notions of organizational management and organizational information processing are, indeed, inseparable. In the context of human information processing, it would not be incorrect to define the central purpose of management as development of a consensual grammar to ameliorate the effects of equivocality or ambiguity. This is the perspective taken by Karl Weick [16,17] in his noteworthy efforts concerning organizations.

Weick [17] has studied five human activities that assist in people's understanding of issues: *enactment, triangulation, interaction, deliberation,* and *abstraction. Enactment* is the process through which people learn more about situations by probative and prodding efforts. *Triangulation* involves the systematic use of alternative sources of information. Weick uses the term *future perfect thinking* to characterize this. The benefits of triangularization include the use of potentially disconfirming information and multiple perspectives. There are trade-offs between triangularization and enactment in the sense that the time required for triangularization may inhibit enactment. Related to triangularization is the notion of *social interaction*, which is the process of learning about situations by comparing people's perceptions of them with those of others and then negotiating a communal view of the situation. *Deliberation* involves slow, careful, and formal systemic reasoning. This is a fundamental basis for most decision aids, of course. Weick suggests strong encouragement for deliberation under stress, including time pressure, since stress has such a major effect on human and organizational information processing and often results in flawed decision making. *Abstraction* leads to situation understanding by the process of building environmental contexts around situations and, through this, moving to higher levels of abstraction. As this involves studies of portfolios of similar situations, the process of abstraction would seem closely related to that of *analogous reasoning* in that both involve the use of larger, more comprehensive cases in which the special case at hand is embedded.

Starbuck [18] notes that much direct action is a form of deliberation. He indicates that action should often be introduced earlier in the process of deliberation and that action and thought should be integrated and interspersed with one another. The rational behind this argument is that probative actions generate information and tangible results that modify potential thoughts. Naturally, any approach that involves *act now, think later* type behavior should be applied with considerable caution.

It is apparently Weick's view that a large number of conventional computerized decision aids frequently inhibit incorporation of situation understanding activities. Situation assessment, which includes situation understanding and interpretation, is therefore seen as a vital part of decision making and problem solving; often neglected [19, 20], it needs to be a major determinant of the architecture of DSS. After we examine some design issues for GDSS, architectural considerations will be explored.

Much of the discussion to be found in the judgment, choice, and decision literature concentrates on what may be called *formal reasoning and decision selection* efforts. These involve the issue resolution efforts that follow as part of the problem-solving efforts of issue *formulation, analysis*, and *interpretation* that we have often discussed. There are other decision-making activities, or decision-associated activities, as well. Critical among them are activities allowing perception, framing, editing, and interpretation of the effects of actions on the internal and external environments of a decision situation. These might be called *information selection* activities. There will also be *information-retention* activities that permit admission, rejection, and modification of the set of selected information or knowledge such as to result in short-term learning through reduction of incongruities, and long-term learning through the acquisition of new information that reflects enhanced understanding. Although the basic GDSS design effort may well be concerned with the short-term effects of various problem-solving, decision-making, and information presentation formats, the actual knowledge that a person brings to bear on a given problem is a function of the accumulated experience that the person possesses, and hence long-term effects need to be considered, at least as a matter of secondary importance.

It was remarked earlier that a principal purpose of a GDSS is to enhance the value of information and, through this, to also enhance group and organizational decision making. Three attributes of information appear dominant in the discussion thus far relative to value for problem-solving purposes and in the literature in general:

1. **Task Relevance.** Of course, information must be relevant to the task at hand. It must allow the decision maker to know what needs to be known in order to make an effective decision. This is not as trivial a statement as might initially be suspected. Relevance varies considerably across individuals, as a function of the contingency task structure, and in time as well.
2. **Representational Appropriateness.** In addition to the need that information be relevant to the task at hand, it must be represented in a form that is suitable for use by the person who needs the information.
3. **Equivocality Reduction.** It is generally accepted that high-quality information may reduce imperfection or equivocality. This equivocality commonly takes the form of uncertainty, imprecision, inconsistency, or incompleteness. It is essential to note that it is neither necessary nor desirable to obtain decision information that is unequivocal or totally "perfect." Information need be only sufficiently unequivocal or unambiguous for the task at hand. To make it better may well be a waste of resources!

Each of these top-level attributes may be decomposed into attributes at a lower level. Each is needed as fundamental metrics for valuation of information quality. We have indicated that some of the components of equivocality or imperfection are uncertainty, imprecision, inconsistency, and incompleteness. A few of the attributes of representational appropriateness include naturalness, transformability to naturalness, and conciseness. These attributes of information presentation system effectiveness relate strongly to overall value of information concerns and should be measured as a part of the DSS and GDSS evaluation effort even though any one of them may appear to be a secondary theme.

There are many ways in which we can characterize information. Among attributes that we noted earlier and that we might use are accuracy, precision, completeness, sufficiency, understandability, relevancy, reliability, redundancy, verifiability, consistency, freedom from bias, frequency of use, age, timeliness, and uncertainty. Our concerns with information involve at least five desiderata [21]:

1. Information should be presented in clear and familiar ways, such as to enable rapid comprehension.
2. Information should be such as to improve the precision of understanding of the task situation.
3. Information that contains an advice or decision recommendation component should contain an explication facility that enables the user to determine how and why results and advice are obtained.
4. Information needs should be based on identification of the information requirements for the particular situation.
5. Information presentations and all other associated management control aspects of the support process should be such that the decision maker, rather than a computerized support system, guides the process of judgment and choice.

It will generally be necessary to evaluate a GDSS to determine the extent to which these relevant characteristics are present. We will briefly examine GDSS evaluation in the concluding section of this chapter. First, we will discuss some design considerations and some architectural considerations. These also allow us to draw some important conclusions about GDSS evaluation metrics.

7.3 GDSS DESIGN CONSTRUCTS

In an organization, there are two fundamental types of decision making: individual, and group or organizational. Individual decisions are decisions made by a single person, and group or organizational decisions are those made by a collection of two or more people. It is, of course, possible to disaggregate this still further. An individual decision may, for example, be based on the value system of one or more people, and the individual making the decision may or may not have their values included. In a multistage decision process, the various decisions may be made by different people (with the same or different objectives). Some authors will attempt to differentiate between group and organizational decisions [22], but we see no need for this here even though this may be warranted in some contexts. There can be no doubt at all, however, of the fact that a GDSS needs to be carefully matched to an organization that may use it. Surely, our discussions emphasize this reality!

Often, groups make decisions differently from the way an individual does. Groups need protocols that allow effective inputs by individuals in the group or organization, a method for mediating a discussion of issues and inputs, and algorithms for resolution of disagreements and reaching a group consensus. Acquisition and elicitation of inputs and mediation of issues are usually local to a specific group, that is informed of personalities, status, and contingencies of the members of the group. Members of the group are usually desirous of cooperating in reaching a consensus on conflicting issues or preferences. The support for individual vs. group decisions is different and hence DSS and GDSS may require different designs. Because members of a group have different personalities, motivations, and experiential familiarities with the situation at hand, a GDSS must assist in supporting a wide range of judgment and choice perspectives.

It is important to note that the group of people may be centralized at one spot, or decentralized in space and/or time. Also, the decision considered by each individual in a decision-making group may or may not be the *ultimate* decision. The decision being considered may be sequential over time and may involve many component decisions. Alternatively, or in addition, many members in a decision-making group may be formulating and/or analyzing options, and preparing a short list of these for review by a person with greater authority or responsibility over a different portion of the decision-making effort.

Consequently, the number of possible types of GDSS may be relatively extensive. Johansen [1] has identified no less than 17 approaches for computer support in groups in his discussion of *groupware*. It is of value to describe these here:

1. *Face-to-Face Meeting Facilitation Services.* This is little more than office automation support in the preparation of reports, overheads, videos, and the like that will be used in a group meeting. The person making the presentation is called a *facilitator* or *chauffeur*.
2. *Group Decision Support Systems.* By this, Johansen essentially infers the GDSS structure shown in Figure 7.1 except that there is but a single video monitor under the control of a facilitator or chauffeur.
3. *Computer-Based Extensions of Telephony for Use by Work Groups.* This involves use either of commercial telephone services, or private branch exchanges (PBXs). These services exist now and Northern Telecom Meridian is an example of a conference calling service.
4. *Presentation Support Software.* This approach is not unlike that of approach 1, except that computer software is used to enable the presentation to be contained within a computer. Often, the presentation material is prepared by those who will present it, and this may be done in an interactive manner to the group receiving the presentation.

5. *Project Management Software.* This is software that is receptive to presentation team input over time and that has capabilities to organize and structure the tasks associated with the group, often in the form of a Gantt chart. This is very specialized software and would be potentially useful for a team interested primarily in obtaining typical project management results in terms of PERT charts and the like.

6. *Calendar Management for Groups.* Frequently, individuals in a group need to coordinate times with one another. They indicate times that are available, potentially with weights to indicate schedule adjustment flexibility in the event that it is not possible to determine an acceptable meeting time.

7. *Group Authoring Software.* This allows members of a group to suggest changes in a document stored in the system, without changing the original. A lead person can then make document revisions. It is possible for the group to view alternative revisions to drafts as well. The overall objective is to encourage group writing, and to improve the quality and efficiency of ·gorup writing. It seems quite clear that there needs to be overall structuring and format guidance that, while possibly group determined, must be agreed on before filling out the structure with report details.

8. *Computer-Supported Face-to-Face Meetings.* Here, individual members of the group work directly with a workstation and monitor, rather than having just a single computer system and monitor. A large screen video may, however, be included. This is the sort of DSS envisioned in Figure 7.1. Although there are a number of such systems in existence, the Colab system at the Xerox Palo Alto Research Center (XEROX PARC) [23] is probably the most sophisticated.* There are also facilities at the University of Minnesota, the University of Arizona, Claremont University, and elsewhere. A simple sketch of these would appear somewhat as in Figure 7.1. Normally, there are both public and private information contained in these systems. The public information is shared, and the private information, or a portion of it, may be converted to public programs as shown in Figure 7.2. The private screens normally start with a menu screen from which participants can select activities in which they engage, potentially under the direction of a facilitator.

---

*Colab meetings can involve two to eight people in a small room. The context for the meeting is decision in the domain of system design (of AI-based systems). In the room are
- A large touch-sensitive display, called an *electronic chalkboard* or *Liveboard*
- An automated podium, called *ELECTERN*
- Four workstations with 19-inch displays and a mouse input, each located on a semicircle
- A local-area Ethernet that connects the workstations and the Liveboard
- A conventional chalkboard or whiteboard

A basic philosophy of Colab is *"what you see is what I see"* in that images on the large screen are seen by all participants. Thus, there is provision for information sharing among group participants. This does not necessarily result in the same image appearing in the same place on all screens, as there are private windows and public windows. Two primary software tools used in Colab have been developed. These include *COGNOTER*, a form of idea-generating software for *Cognition Noting and Knowing Together* that consists of brainstorming, ordering, and evaluation. The other software product is called *ARGNOTER* and is a computer-based scratchpad for *Argument Noting.*

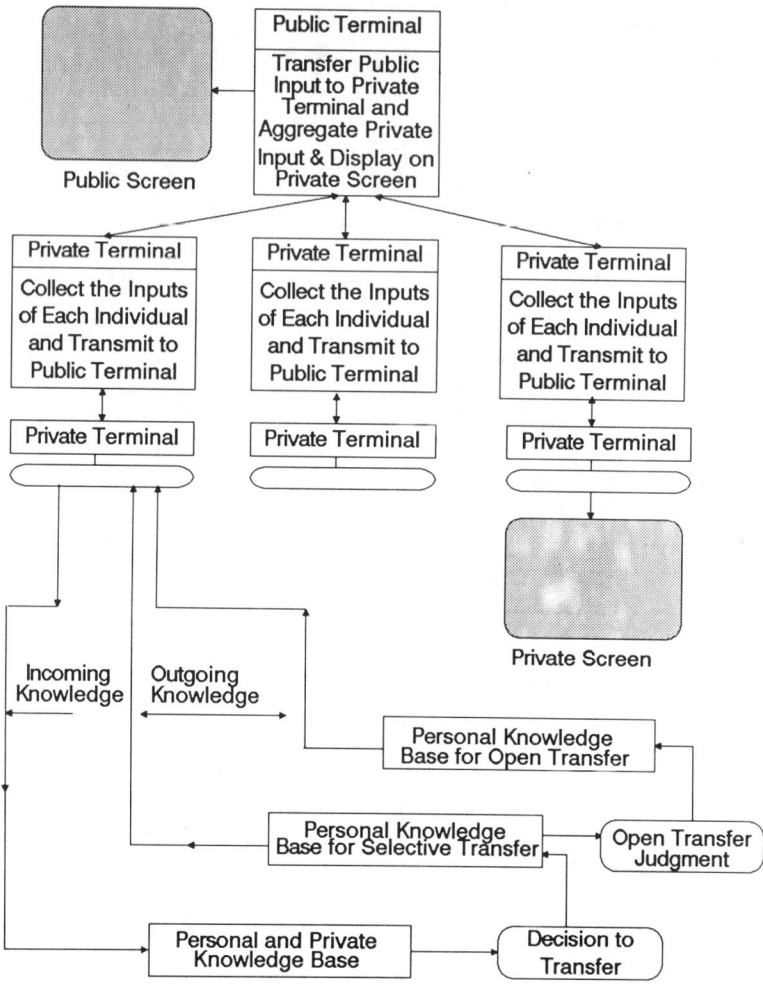

Figure 7.2 Public and private portions of a GDSS.

9. *Screen-Sharing Software.* This software enables one member of a group to share screens with other group members selectively. There are clearly advantages and pitfalls in this. The primary advantage to this approach is that of sharing information with those who have a reason to know specific information and not having to bother others who do not need it. The disadvantage is just this also, and it may lead to a feeling of *ganging up* by one subgroup on another subgroup.

10. *Computer-Conferencing Systems.* This is the group version of electronic mail. Figure 1.8 illustrates a generic GDSS in a group conferencing mode. Basically, what we have shown is a collection of DSS with some means of

communications among the individuals that comprise the group. This form of communication might be regarded as a *product hierarchy* in which people communicate. Normally, communication across the lowest levels in a product hierarchy does not occur, although communication in this way is shown in Figure 1.8. We may identify six coordination structures, as patterns of decision making and communication among a set of actors in order to achieve goals [24]. In these structures, actors are either task processors, product managers, or function managers. The six coordination structures indicated in Figure 7.3 can also be adapted to local area network (LAN) linkage of a GDSS according to the various coordination structures. Therefore, Figure 1.8 should be regarded as a generic distributed GDSS, and not the architecture for a specific implementation. It is easy to recognize that systems such as these create channels of communication that may not be in conformity with organizational charts, unless these are considered when accomplishing the system design.

11. *Text-Filtering Software.* This allows system users to search normal or semi-structured text through the specification of search criteria that are used by the filtering software to select relevant portions of text. The name of the original system to accomplish this was *electronic mail filter* [25], although there is now also emphasis on an *information lens* that will enable the system to obtain information-matching rules that are specified by the system user.

12. *Computer-Supported Audio or Video Conferences.* This is simply the standard telephone or video conferencing, as augmented by each participant having access to a computer and appropriate software.

13. *Conversational Structuring.* This involves identification and use of a structure for conversations that is presumably in close relationship to the task, environment, and their experiential familiarity to the group participants [26]. While highly structured conversations might provide for enhanced efficiency and effectiveness, there may be a perception of unwarranted intrusions that can defeat the possible advantages.

14. *Group Memory Management.* This refers to the provision of support between group meetings such that individual members of a group can search a computer memory in personally preferred ways through the use of flexible indexing structures. The term *hypertext* [27] is generally given to this flexible information storage and retrieval. One potential difficulty with hypertext is the need for a good theory of how to prepare the text and associated index so that it can be indexed and used as we now use a thesaurus. An extension of hypertext to include other than textual material is known as *hypermedia*.

15. *Computer-Supported Spontaneous Interaction.* The purpose of these systems is to encourage the sort of impromptu and extemporaneous interaction that often occurs at unscheduled meetings between colleagues in an informal setting, such as a hallway. The need for this could occur, for example, when it is necessary for two physically separated groups to communicate relative to some detailed design issue [28].

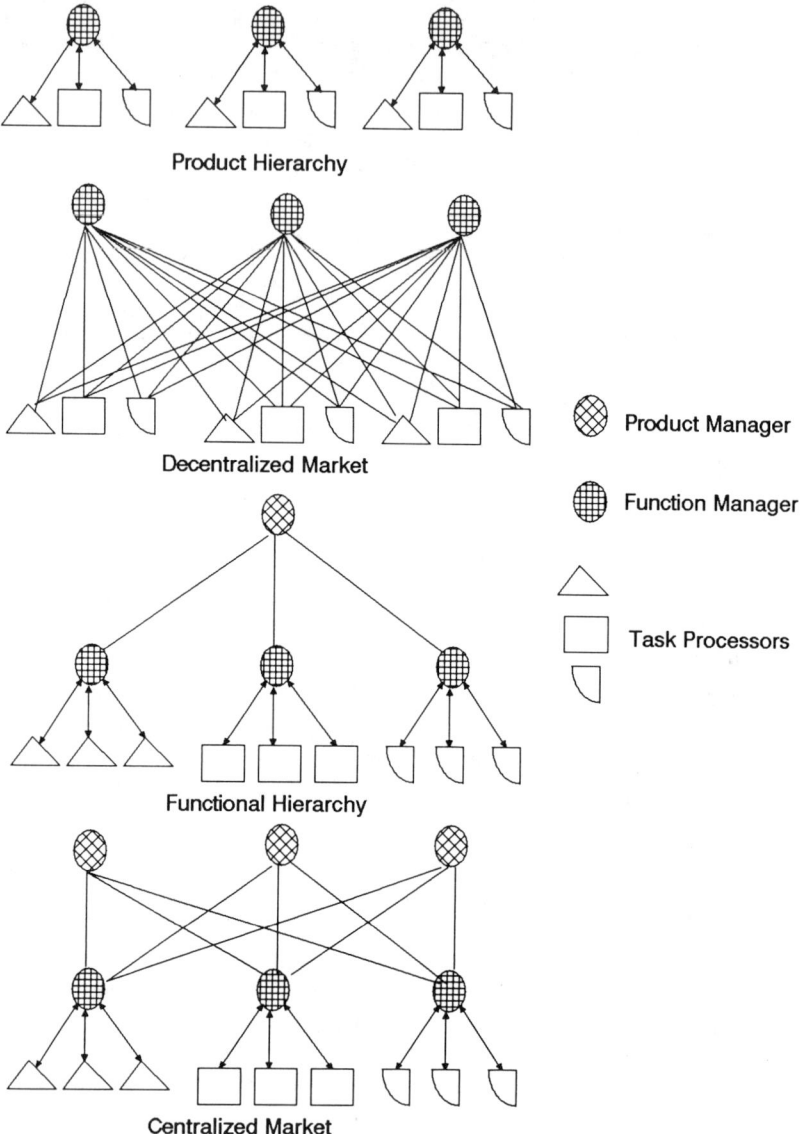

Figure 7.3 Different communication and coordination stuctures (after Malone and Smith [24]).

16. *Comprehensive Work Team Support.* This refers to integrated and comprehensive support, such as perhaps might be achieved through use of the comprehensive DSS design philosophy described in Chapter 5.
17. *Nonhuman Participants in Team Meetings.* This essentially refers to the use of unfacilitated DSS and expert systems that automate some aspects of the process of decision making.

According to Johansen [1], the order in which these are described above also represents the order of increasing difficulty of implementation and successful use. These scenarios of support for decision making are also characterized in terms of support for

Face-to-face meetings (approaches 1, 2, 4, 8)
Support for electronic meetings (approaches 3, 9, 10–12, 17)
Support between meetings (approaches 5–7, 13–16)

Kraemer and King [2] identify six technological foundations on which a GDSS may be based:

1. *Electronic Boardroom*. This GDSS type is comprised primarily of a computer-controlled audiovisual facility. The computer is often only an indirect aid to decision making, as it is primarily associated with acquisition, storage, representation, and presentation of preprogrammed material. Slide-, map-, chart-, and now hypertext- and hypermedia-based presentations are possible.
2. *Teleconferencing Facility*. This type of GDSS is constructed principally to facilitate group and organizational meetings between people at two or more distinct physical locations. Video teleconferencing facilities, with provision of interactive multiway transmission of video and audio, and electronic mail facilities fit into these categories. The Picturephone is a public teleconferencing facility managed by AT&T.
3. *Information Center*. This GDSS type is just that portion of an organization's information technology resources that is dedicated to support of such activities as report preparation and collective inquiry for decision purposes.
4. *Group Network Facility*. This type of GDSS represents an evolution of the teleconferencing facility and is commonly known as *computer conferencing* [29, 30]. Generally, the conferencing is real time and interactive. Each participant is typically seated at a microcomputer workstation, equipped with a mouse keyboard, and telephone communications to enable discourse with other participants. There may be a number of shared applications, such as word-processing files, graphics, and applications software packages. A facilitator or chauffeur usually has process management responsibilities. This differs from the teleconferencing facility primarily in terms of the facilitation efforts and the possibility of direct support for decision modeling.
5. *Decision Conference Facility*. This type of GDSS uses software and processes to provide formal and explicit support for decision making.
6. *Collaboration Laboratory*. This facility will *not* formally use decision models and quantitative analysis techniques. Rather, it concentrates on personal discussions and reports. These are facilitated by taking advantage of text-oriented data representations and graphical conceptions. Although there are others, the Colab facility at XEROX PARC [23] is doubtlessly the best-known collaborative work facility at this time.

There are a number of example implementations of each facility type. Many of these are described in Ref. 2 and references to that article. Rather than provide a description of the present facilities, which are rapidly evolving, we will concentrate instead on descriptions of a taxonometric nature.

A GDSS may and doubtlessly will influence the *process* of group decision making, perhaps strongly. A GDSS has the potential for changing the *information-processing characteristics* of individuals in the group. This is one reason why organizational structure and authority concerns are important ingredients in GDSS designs.

In one study of the use of a GDSS to facilitate group consensus [31], it was found that:

- GDSS use tended to reduce face-to-face interpersonal communication in the decision-making group.
- GDSS use posed an intellectual challenge to the group and made accomplishment of the purpose of their decision-making activity more difficult than for groups without the GDSS.
- The groups using the GDSS became more process-oriented and less specific issue oriented than the groups not using the GDSS.

A total sample size of 82 groups was used for this experiment. The groups were randomly assigned to one of three experimental conditions: a GDSS, a manual paper and pencil support system, and no support whatever. The GDSS used is what will soon be called a level-I GDSS. It provided a menu of facilities for idea generation, rating, ranking, and voting. One of the interesting conclusions of this study was that the GDSS-supported groups, each group consisting of three or four people, performed as well as the paper-and-pencil supported groups and better than the unsupported groups. A related study [32] of the influence of a level-I GDSS on five specific categories of verbal behavior was undertaken. (The categories considered were (1) *initiation behavior*, dealing with the setting of initiating agendas; (2) *goal-oriented behavior*, concerning group goals and jurisdiction; (3) *integrative behavior*, summarizing and integrating the contributions of other group members; (4) *implementation behavior*, concerning actions to accomplished the assigned task; and (5) *process behavior*, dealing with the routines and procedures of the group.) The major finding was that decision-making groups need more training or facilitation in the adoption of a GDSS to their decision-making activities. This is essentially conclusion 2 from the earlier study. It suggests the design of GDSS and group decision processes that involve appropriate training of the group, or the presence of a facilitator to assist in the process. This also supports the notion that we should consider not only GDSS in isolation, but the GDSS as part of a group decision process.

Support may be accomplished at any, or all, of the three levels for group decision support identified by DeSanctis and Gallupe [33] in their definitive study. A GDSS provides a *mechanism for group interaction*. A GDSS may impose any of various *structured processes* on individuals in the group, such as, for instance, a particular voting scheme. A GDSS may impose any of several *management control processes* on the individuals on the group, such as that of imposing or removing the effects of a dominant personality. The design of the GDSS and the way in which it is used are the primary determinants of these.

DeSanctis and Gallupe have developed a taxonomy of GDSS based on the levels of support just discussed. From this perspective, a level I-GDSS would simply be a medium for enhanced information interchange that might lead ultimately to a decision. Electronic mail, large video screen displays that can be viewed by a group, or a *decision room* that contains these features could represent a level-1 GDSS. A level-I GDSS provides only a mechanism for group interaction. What we show in Figures 1.8 or 7.3 could actually be regarded as a level-I GDSS. It might contain such facilities as a group scratchpad, support for meeting agenda development, idea generation, and voting software.

A level-II GDSS would provide various decision structuring and other analytic tools that could act to reduce information imperfection. A decision room that contained software that could be used for problem solution would represent a level-II GDSS. Thus, spreadsheets would primarily represent a level-II DSS. To become a level-II GDSS, there would also have to be some means of enabling group communication. Figure 7.4 represents a level-II GDSS. It is simply a communications medium that has been augmented with some tools for problem structuring and solution, with no prescribed management control of the use of these tools.

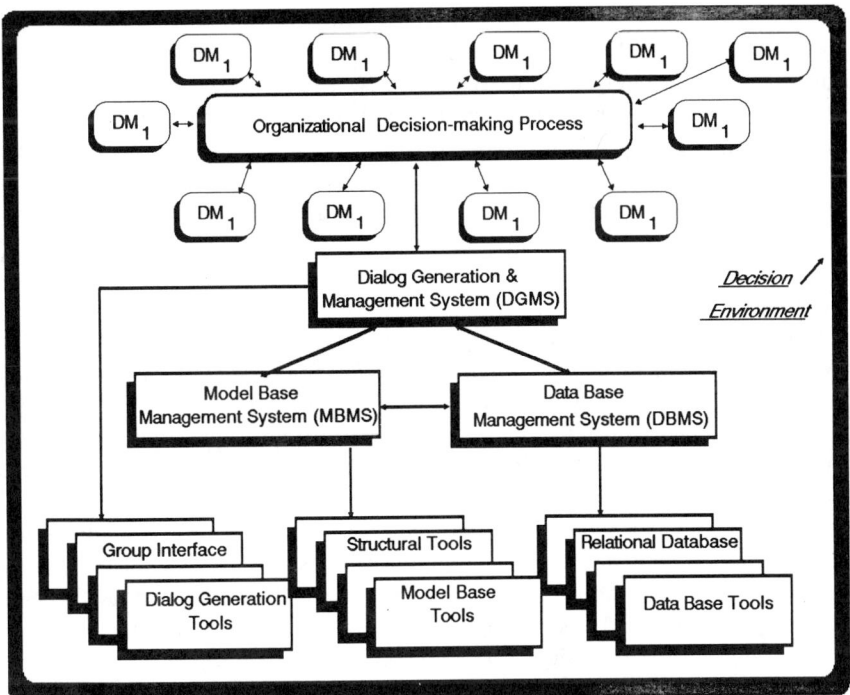

Figure 7.4 LevelI-II (no facilitator) and level-III (with facilitator) GDSS.

A level-III GDSS also includes the notion of management control of the decision process. Accordingly, there is a notion of *facilitation* of the process, either through the direct intervention of a human in the process, or through some rule-based specifications of the management control process that is inherent in level-III GDSS. Clearly, there is no sharp transition line between one level and the next and it may not always be easy to identify at what level a GDSS is operating. The DSS generator, such as discussed in our preceding section, would generally appear to produce a form of level-III DSS. In fact, most of the DSS that we have been discussing in this book are either level-II or level-III DSS or GDSS. The GDSS of Figure 7.4, for example, becomes a level-III GDSS if supported by a facilitator.

In our discussions, we have mentioned the need for a GDSS model-base management system (MBMS). There are a great variety of MBMS tools. Some of the least understood are group tools that aid in the issue formulation effort. Since these may represent an integral part of a GDSS effort, it is of value to describe GDSS tissue formation, as one component of a MBMS, here.

Identifying or formulation of an issue or problem is the first step in any problem-solving process. A problem statement should always be identified prior to the application of solution methods. Frequently, there is considerable merit in identifying the problem in terms of a number of interdependent elements that can be characterized as problem definition elements (needs, constraints, alterables), value system design elements (objectives or objectives measures), or system synthesis elements (activities or controls and activity measures). Too often a notion of a problem is attacked with a large outpouring of energy only to end up back at the starting point, because an immature issue formulation effort has led to solution of the wrong problem. After providing some encouragement for these efforts, we discuss one representative issue formulation method that may be used to aid a decision group in beginning to formulate the problem or issue chosen for study.

One of the difficulties in coping with a complex situation is that often there is no individual with sufficient knowledge concerning the situation to develop a set of elements that describes it. Usually, a most difficult problem area concerns the unsatisfactory nature of available information, since data are commonly incomplete, imprecise, or otherwise faulty.

It has often been assumed that *"two heads are better than one."* Corollary to this would be the statement that *"N heads are better than N−1 heads."* Committees, juries, boards of advisors, boards of directors, citizens' groups, and the like are representative of the many mechanisms for pooling minds to generate ideas that hopefully represent either expert knowledge or collective opinion, each with a high probability of being correct.

There are both advantages and disadvantages to reliance on group opinion. Many times a group will interact to compensate for the bias of individual members of the group, and knowledge of one member of the group may well compensate for ignorance or speculation on the part of other members. It is unfortunately true, however, that "a camel is a horse designed by a committee." Further, opinion can be highly influenced by the individual who talks the most and the loudest. This influence of one or more dominant individuals can be most upsetting to a group, as there is little necessary correlation between loudness or frequency of speech and knowledge. Moreover, unless the group activity is well organized, a bull session may well result in which much more discussion deals with matters of individual and group interest than with the problem at hand. This type of difficulty could well be called *"noise."* In addition, there is often strong pressure for group conformity and avoidance of unpopular and/or minority viewpoints.

As an illustration of one approach that might possibly be utilized as part of an issue formulation effort and supported in a GDSS, let us consider the *nominal group technique* (NGT). This is a structured group approach for the purpose of element or idea generation, as we noted in Chapter 3. In addition to idea generation, NGT is designed to provide for initial screening of ideas. The screening phase consists of a discussion and clarification portion of the meeting, followed by an optional prioritization of ideas.

NGT emphasizes independent or silent idea generation in a group environment. A *"trigger question"* which concisely and clearly describes the issue is posed to the group, generally by a facilitator, in order to elicit responses in the form of ideas. The process is designed to overcome some of the problems encountered with interacting groups, such as unbalanced participation among group members or reduced creativity in element generation due to interference from other group members.

The process usually begins with approximately six to ten participants, selected on the basis of their background with regard to the issue and their motivation, sitting around a table in plain view of one another. Each participant has writing instruments and paper. The trigger question is posed by the group leader, or facilitator. The group leader is a person selected on the basis of familiarity with NGT and general leadership ability. After hearing the trigger question, the group members record a list of ideas on their papers. (An appropriate trigger question might be, for instance, *"What are appropriate objectives for regional mobility that we might support over the next year?"*) This is the first phase of the NGT effort.

At the end of a specified time, 5 to 15 minutes, this phase terminates and the *"screening"* of generated-ideas phase of the NGT process begins. Initially, a structured sharing of ideas takes place in order to clarify, and possibly combine, ideas. This structured sharing of ideas is conducted in round-robin fashion, with each member presenting a single idea from their private list. Ideas are recorded on a flip chart or board by a scribe. This effort continues until all ideas are recorded, after which each is discussed and clarified. It is possible to record ideas for greater clarity, or to combine similar ideas. In essence, this discussion step is the first group interface with each individual's private list of ideas.

Evaluation and criticism of ideas are not appropriate during the discussion, or subsequent voting, portions of this exercise. Rank ordering the ideas is itself a limited evaluation of ideas with relation to each other. However, the primary purpose of NGT is to generate a list of ideas for evaluation and not primarily to decide among alternative courses of action. The prioritized list, therefore, indicates the order in which the group feels the ideas ought to be addressed. The list is generally not an indicator of the worth of ideas or element in resolving the issue under consideration unless the process is specifically guided in that direction by the leader. Usually, this is not a suitable use of NGT.

A most important step in the NGT is the formulation of the trigger question. Unless carefully conceived, problems of interpretation of the question may defeat the intended purpose of the effort. After the trigger question is posed, ideas will be silently generated, and then discussed. Discussion and even preliminary evaluation of these ideas should be postponed until the entire list is compiled. Any discussion or evaluation before that stage can lead to intimidation or fear that an idea would be unpopular, and to minimization of hitchhiking new ideas onto previously stated ones. As a consequence, there would be fewer ideas generated than if discussion and evaluation are postponed.

The final step of NGT is one of clarification, amplification, and prioritization of generated (and hitchhiked) ideas. This phase can easily enter into an infinite circular loop where discussion of minor points or wording can erode available time. NGT follows a regulated systemic approach until priority and weights are applied. Members may be inclined to retain "pet" ideas and exclude unpopular ones from further consideration even though further analysis might otherwise prove their worth. Owing to the subjectivity of this final stage, it may be appropriate to terminate the nominal group process after generation of ideas.

There are many advantages and disadvantages to group techniques. An optimal group technique would result from a maximization of the advantages and a minimization of the disadvantages of several approaches. This is quantitatively infeasible, but we must nonetheless accept the fact of trade-offs or compromise to reach a feasible approach for collective inquiry.

The dynamics of a group will ideally produce more ideas, lessen or eliminate biases (in both questions and answers), and provide open and agreeable interaction processes. Some of the advantages of a group are

Potentially greater sum total of knowledge and information
Greater number of alternative approaches to the problem
Participation in decision making increases acceptance of the final choice
Better understanding and comprehension of the decision

Conversely, some disadvantages to a group effort may be

Social pressure
Individual domination
Desire to *win* the decision
Excessive amiability and esprit de corps

Each of these may result in the replacement of critical independent thought by irrational and dehumanizing actions against outgroups or groupthink.

Consequently, efforts to evaluate the product of group effort are important. Success of a group process is evaluated by comparing the results with the original desires or purposes that led to conduction of the process. The success of the collective inquiry effort can be evaluated using the following criteria:

- *Creative*—Was a sufficient number of creative ideas for the issue obtained?
- *Effective*—Were suggestions and conclusions feasible, and understanding of the issue increased?
- *Efficient*—Were the objectives accomplished within the optimal time span?
- *Organized*—Did every member do their job? Together, did the "whole" team complete the task?
- *Cooperative*—Did members work together constructively toward a group goal or did the meeting become an arena for individual competition?
- *Participative*—Did every member contribute their knowledge and/or perspective?
- *All-encompassing*—Did the group overlook relevant items?

After it has been concluded that these criteria were satisfactorily met, the appropriate fundamental components of issue formulation (as before, formulation, analysis, and interpretation) also need to be examined to determine if they were well executed. Figure 7.5 illustrates a methodological framework for group meetings and its role in the GDSS process. Success of the issue formulation portion of a GDSS process may be discussed in terms of this framework. The components may be evaluated as follows:

1. *Formulation.* Was a descriptive account of the problem obtained? Does it seem to be relatively unbiased? Does it reflect input from the whole group? Does it identify sources of problems and needs rather than simply list the symptoms? Are the ideas clearly identified and stated? Are the ideas responsive to the needs of the issue? Has enough information been gathered and disseminated?
2. *Analysis.* Were forecasts of alternatives or assessment of impacts postulated? Have the ideas been clarified and examined for feasibility or linkages?
3. *Interpretation.* Were alternatives carefully considered and ranked? Is it clear which activities aim at which objectives? Have utility, feasibility, and normative values all been considered? Has a plan been designed for action and implementation of chosen alternatives?

Both the extremes of emphasis and de-emphasis on each of the fundamental components would cause ill effects on a group meeting, as indicated in Figure 7.6. Therefore, it is appropriate to assign a "weight" to each component of the meeting and each subcomponent as in Figure 7.6. This figure shows an attribute tree for performance evaluation of an NGT session. It would be possible to use this to

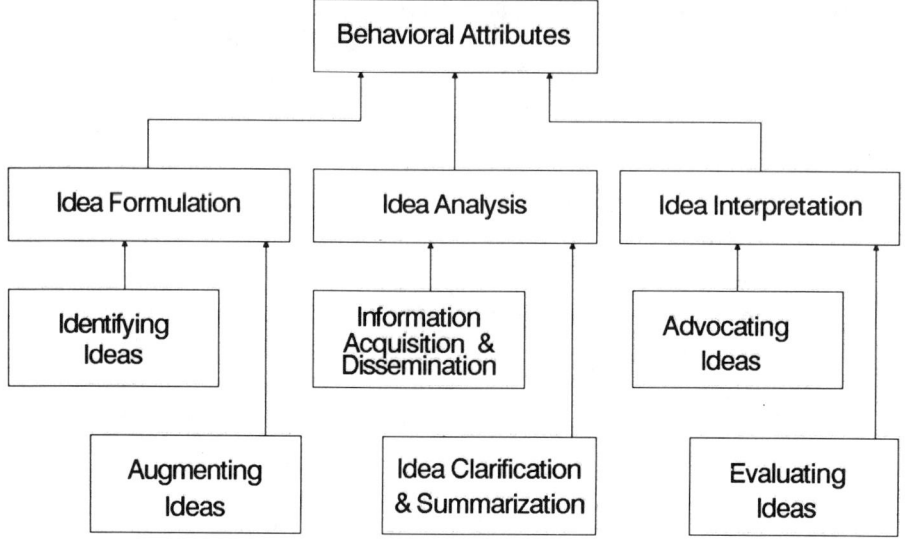

Figure 7.5 Characteristics of group idea (issue) formulation.

evaluate several NGT sessions and, on the basis of this evaluation, select the characteristics of an NGT session that produced the most appropriate results and use it as a paradigm for future sessions. In this way, we are able to design the components of the meeting to obtain as high a score as possible for meeting effectiveness.

This brief diversion into one aspect of MBMS, our presentation of a guide to NGT, illustrates the specific group nature of the concerns for process quality. As noted by George Huber [34, 35] and others, much of the concern in the design of GDSS should relate to the need for trade-offs among

- Human decision-making needs for greater information sharing, and
- The lack of time for, and other resistance to, attending a large number of group meetings.

There is considerable contemporary interest in the subject of GDSS design. Gerardine DeSanctis and Brent Gallupe [33], who initiated the notion of three levels of DSS support just discussed, have provided a recent definitive overview of foundations for the study of GDSS. The taxonomy of GDSS settings that DeSanctis and Gallupe identify include

- *Group proximity*—from face-to-face communication to dispersed communication
- *Group size*—from small groups to large groups

Within this, they identify four recommended approaches:

1. Decision room for small group face-to-face meetings
2. Legislative sessions for large group face-to-face meetings
3. Local area decision networks for small dispersed groups
4. Computer-mediated conferencing for large groups that are dispersed.

They discuss the design of facilities to enable this, as well as techniques whereby the quality of efforts such as generation of ideas and actions, choosing from among alternative courses of action, and negotiating conflicts may be enhanced. On the basis of this, these authors recommend six areas as very promising for additional study: GDSS design methodologies; patterns of information exchange; mediation of the effects of participation; effects of (the presence or absence of) physical proximity, interpersonal attraction, and group cohesion; effects on power and influence; and performance/satisfaction trade-offs. Each of these supports the purpose of computerized aids to planning, problem solving, and decision making identified on page 271:

- Removing a number of common communication barriers.
- Providing techniques for structuring decisions.
- Systematically directing group discussion, and associated problem solving and decision making, in terms of the patterns, timing, and content of the information that influences these actions.

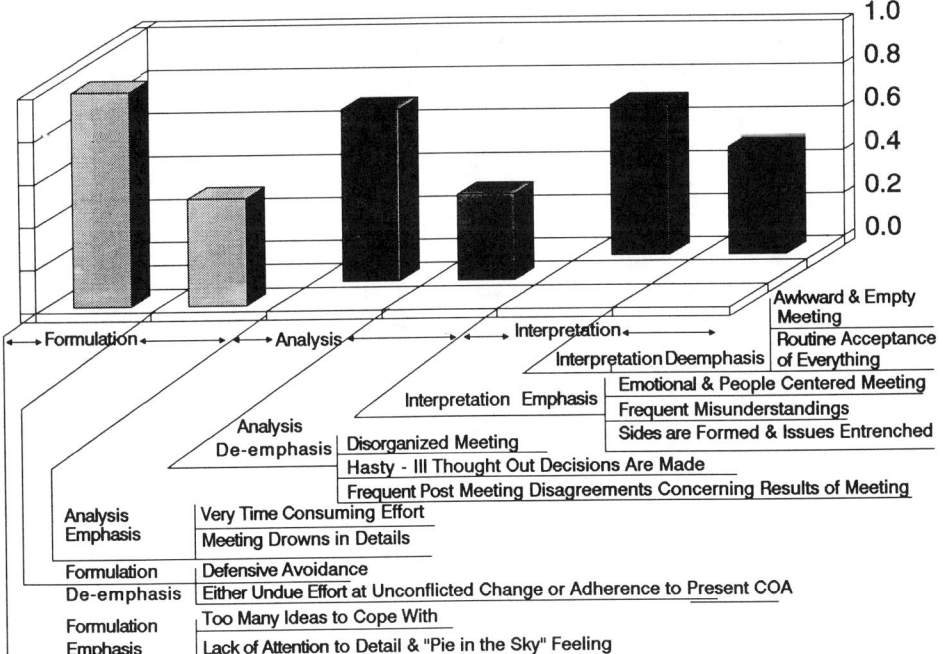

Figure 7.6 Attribute scores for idea formulation (COA-Course of action).

Other relevant efforts and interest areas involving GDSS include the group processes in computer-mediated communications study; the computer support for collaboration and problem solving in meetings study of Mark Stefik et al. [23], the organizational planning study of Linda Appelgate et al [36], and the knowledge management and intelligent information sharing systems study of Thomas Malone et al. [24, 25]. Particularly interesting current issues surround the extent to which cognitive science and engineering studies that involve potential human information-processing flaws can be effectively dealt with, in the sense of design of debiasing aids, for use in operational GDSSs.

Especially interesting complications arise with respect to group decision situations in which the objectives, perhaps owing to different interpretations of and perspectives on information, are in partial conflict. Even this limited discussion makes it obvious that the role of the individual in a decentralized, distributed, group effort may be much different from that traditionally assumed for an individual in a single-person centralized decision situation. In particular, it is essential that individuals in roles such as these be able to combine the tasks of information acquisition, representation, analysis, and interpretation, as well as associated action planning and implementation.

This is not at all an uncomplicated effort, since each individual will have a partially different knowledge base that represents beliefs about others as well as beliefs about the environment and the intentions of others. Further, activities selected for implementation may be brought to full fruition, but not necessarily. Alternatively, they may be eliminated, or modified, owing to the identification of new activities that have higher priority.

All of these influence, to a considerable degree, the roles of the individual in a decentralized, distributed organizational environment with respect to such activities as

Situation assessment

Gathering information or sensing information distribution to others

Potential plan identification or generation

Evaluation of potential plans

Resolution of conflicts with respect to information and activities

Execution of selected plans or action alternatives

Knowledge representation is important, since the form and structure of knowledge exert a strong influence over the way in which knowledge is used. Knowledge will generally be contained in a combination of the DBMS and the MBMS. Knowledge use includes retrieval of information from the knowledge base, and aggregation of this knowledge with human values to enable judgment formation.

If a DSS for a single individual is to be ultimately useful, it must allow for expansion and adaptation in such a manner that the knowledge base is consistent and nonredundant. In a group decision support situation, additional concerns emerge. Data inputs from distributed sources and sharing of data now become requirements. These should be accomplished, from an *efficiency* viewpoint, such that

- Only needed redundancy is obtained
- Only needed consistency is maintained
- Integrated management of the composite knowledge base is possible

Data independence concepts then become an additional desirable requirement that will ensure efficiency, in that modifications to a data base can easily be accomplished. We should like to make the analogous statement concerning information and knowledge. That we cannot easily do this is indicative of additional needs for efforts that better enable us to consider information and knowledge as data. To accomplish this well is a central purpose of a model-base management subsystem in a GDSS.

Security of data, information, and knowledge in terms of authentication, authorization, and various protection mechanisms also becomes vital. The need for local and personal data and knowledge bases is easily established. A top-level manager may, for example, wish to test various hypotheses concerning particularly sensitive resource deployment strategies. The impacts of various strategies will, after implementation, influence other items in the knowledge base. For a variety of reasons, a particular decision maker may not wish these impacts to become part of the shared data or knowledge base immediately. This illustrates the desirability of personal data and knowledge bases in a group decision support situation. In a similar way, loss of portion of the shared data base may require the replacement of the now-missing data with very subjective data, such as that contained in a personal data base. Figure 7.2 has illustrated the role of these various data bases in a more or less generic view of the public and private portions of a GDSS.

Many important elements need be considered relative to these three data bases, and we have identified only some of them here. One interesting concern is that a centralized knowledge base may represent codified group wisdom, doctrine, or standard operating policies. Such centralized knowledge sources have strengths as well as weaknesses. They may well be quite poor in those cases where there is a fundamental change in the contingency task structure that was the basis for their creation. Hence, maladroit results may eventuate from their use in situations where deception, surprise, and use of a new strategy are involved. This may exacerbate a potential crisis management situation. In such circumstances, use of a distributed information system may well yield results that are better than those that could be obtained from a centralized system. Thus, a very realistic question is, *How do we deal with the three possible knowledge bases that may exist for a given decision situation?* These are

- A personal and private knowledge base that the individual may not wish to transmit over the system to others. This is not necessarily sinister in any way. We all have hypotheses that we believe to be "half-baked" and that we desire to explore before telling others about them.
- A personal knowledge base that an individual wishes to transmit openly to everyone on the system.
- A personal knowledge base that an individual wishes to selectively transmit to others, for any of a variety of reasons.

A group can be *centralized* or *distributed*, and therefore decentralized. A centralized group is one where a single group makes all of the decisions, based on all information brought directly to the central location. The group can decide by vote or by other means, including a decision by an individual, who uses inputs for the others in the group, but who has the last say that can override any of the others. A distributed system is one in which the decision makers can be

1. *Territorial*, in which case the decision makers have decision responsibility over a particular geographical or other type of area, and information is cooperatively shared.
2. *Hierarchical*, in that there is a formal reporting treelike structure such that subordinates report to a higher authority, but where they have local decisional responsibility that can be overridden by a higher authority in the hierarchy, and where information is increasingly summarized as it moves up the hierarchy.
3. *Federated*, in which case each decision maker has an equal responsibility for decisions made at a single level, and where all information is shared equally (at least in theory) by all decision makers.

In distributed decision making, there are a set of related decisions that are distributed across a set of organizational decision makers. Not all decisions are made by a single decision maker. The decisions are related in that the consequences of one may affect another and hence must be coordinated in some manner. The decision makers are related by means of their organizational roles, which give them full or partial authority and responsibility for certain areas of the decisional domain. Distributed decisions may be ordered so that higher-ordered decisions take precedence over the lower-ordered decisions. Accordingly, notions of shared decisions and shared information are important. We will examine some resulting issues that are relevant to architectures for distributed GDSS in the next section.

Research by such authors as Jarvenpaar, Rao, and Huber [37] into the effects of technology on group problem solving, generally with semistructured problems, reveals five limitations to the approaches commonly used:

1. Most research used small groups of three or four members only.
2. Past studies generally used students, who were rather naive users of the GDSS technology, as problem solvers.
3. Previous studies were often single-meeting experiments that did not allow learning through repeated use of the GDSS technology.
4. Experimental tasks were often poorly matched with computer-based technology.
5. Many of the prior studies examined "decision rooms" as a whole, and perhaps confounded the effects of different computer-based components such as the personal workstations and the large electronic blackboard.

The design of a GDSS, and the evaluation of use of a GDSS, should seek to avoid these difficulties. If this is not done, it is highly likely that the resulting support system will either not be used or will be ineffective if it is used. In this research, Jarvenpaa, Rao, and Huber [37] examined conventional audiovisual support with computer workstation support and electronic blackboard support. Several attributes of a quality process were examined. These included communication thoroughness, equity and equality of participation, and quality and satisfaction with the process. In terms of performance quality, the conventional audiovisual approach was inferior to both forms of computer support. Satisfaction was rated slightly higher. In terms of communication thoroughness, the conventional method scored higher than either form of computer support. In terms of equity and equality of participation, there was little difference. Both forms of computer support were relatively immature and, hence, the results of the study are somewhat inconclusive. On the other hand, the approach does suggest some design issues for modifications of the support forms.

A single-user DSS must provide single-user–single-model and single-user–multiple-model support, whereas a GDSS *model-base management system* (MBMS) must support multiple-user–single-model and multiple-user–multiple-model support. A *centralized GDSS* induces three basic components:

- A group model-base management subsystem (GMBMS)
- A group data-base management subsystem (GDBMS)
- A group dialog generation and management subsystem (GDGMS)

These are precisely the components needed in a single-user DSS, except for the incorporation of group concerns. In the GDSS, all data are stored in the group data base and models ae stored in the group model base. The GMBMS controls all access to the individually owned and group-owned models in the model base.

A *distributed GDSS* permits each user to have an individual DSS and a GDSS. Each individual DSS consists of models and data for a particular user. The GDSS maintains the group model-base management subsystem (GMBMS) and group database management subsystem (GDBMS), as well as controlling accesses to the GMBMS and GDBMS and coordination of the MBMS of various individual DSS [38]. During system use, the difference between the centralized and distributed GDSS should be transparent to the users. (This might be implemented in the following manner: If user i requests to see the model user j is using, *and if this is not a proscribed transaction*, the GDSS MBMS should copy j's model from j's model base and store it in the GMBMS temporarily for use by user i. User i interacts with the GDSS and does not need to personally take actions involving the technology in order to accomplish the various distributed storage transactions.)

We generally always use models to help define, understand, organize, study, and solve problems. These range from simple mental models to complex mathematical simulation models. An important mission of a GDSS is to assist in the use of formal and informal models by providing appropriate model management. A suitable MBMS for a GDSS can provide the following four advantages [38]:

1. *Reduction of redundancy*, since models can be shared.
2. *Increased consistency*, since more than one decision maker will share the same model.
3. *Increased flexibility*, since models can be upgraded and made available to all members of the group.
4. *Improved control over the decision process*, by controlling the quality of the models adopted.

A MBMS provides for at least the following five basic functions:

1. Construction of new models
2. Storage of existing and new models
3. Access and retrieval of existing models
4. Execution of existing models
5. Maintenance of existing models

MBMS should also provide for model integration and selection. Model integration by using the existing model base as building blocks in the construction of new, or integrated, models is useful when ad hoc models are desired.

7.4 DISTRIBUTED GDSS DESIGN ISSUES

Much recent research in human judgment and choice suggests the need for incorporation of behavioral perspectives in all aspects of system design. This is especially the case for systems, such as decision support systems, that are intended for use by humans to support such fundamentally human characteristics as judgment and choice. In this section, we expand on similar discussions in Section 1.8. We will discuss a framework for GDSS design for distributed decision making that is comprised of three principal integrated and interrelated components:

1. Knowledge acquisition and representation, such as to enable effective and efficient understanding of the decision situation, and to model how people actually use information when solving a problem or making a decision.
2. Information presentation of these representations in a distributed multiagent situation so as to enable evaluation of alternatives from perspectives that are commensurate with experiential familiarity with the task at hand.
3. Organizational structure or architecture, which results in a network of communication channels, in which distributed multiagent decision making takes place.

A purpose for this framework is to guide the design of distributed DSS designs, including resource distribution across nodes in the communication network and associated information presentation and decision support aids, such that it becomes possible to

- Indicate the kinds of impeding interactions between people in distributed decision tasks that result in enhancing support for, or interference with or lack of support to, these distributed decision tasks;
- Understand how one mode of information presentation, for both situation understanding and decision-making purposes, may be better than another in encouraging requests for other information that aids in better understanding of the decision situation;
- Predict the characteristics of a GDSS that provides support for distributed multiagent decision making, so as to make information easy to understand, to relate to other relevant information presentations, and to encourage effective decision making;
- Evaluate distributed GDSS with respect to the extent to which they encourage "effective" decision making; and thereby
- Develop a methodology for the design of distributed GDSS that aid information processing in systems and organizations.

Of the many concerns important for architectures for information systems engineering for distributed decision making, four are particularly critical for the design of GDSS

1. Time sequencing of elements, such as activities and events.
2. Spatial separation between elements in the decision situation, such as cooperating decision makers.
3. Containment of elements within other elements of the decision situation, such as the incremental decisions of a person who must integrate, contain, and coordinate the incremental decisions according to some strategic plan.
4. The inherent uncertainty and imprecision, and other forms of imperfection, that are associated with information inputs and knowledge of the consequences of actions that might be undertaken.

The four concerns just noted, especially that associated with information imperfection in knowledge representation, must be given special attention in developing a design methodology for distributed information systems engineering for GDSS design.

In developing an architecture for a GDSS, careful consideration should be given to the needs imposed by the information and knowledge imperfections that arise in distributed communication environments. These imperfections, such as uncertainty and imprecision, are due to such realities as missing data, erroneous data, incomplete rules for information analysis and interpretation, and erroneous guidelines for information analysis and interpretation. The effects of each of these sources of information imperfection can be potentially corrected by redundancy in the data and information, and redundancy in the guidelines or protocols used for information analysis and interpretation. Associated with this redundancy, however, is complexity. This complexity is due both to the potential number of communication nodes, and to the need for attention to contingencies associated with potential failures in part of the system. Redundancy, if properly exploited, enables improvements in information reliability and usefulness, and related improvements in system survivability and response time.

7.4.1 Individual Information-Processing Realities

A number of human information-processing capabilities and limitations interact with organizational arrangements and task requirements to strongly influence resource allocations in distributed multiple-agent environments. Among individual information-processing characteristics are

1. Humans have extensive wholistic (intuitive affect, reasoning by analogy, etc.) information-processing abilities.

The judgments that follow from wholistic skill-based reasoning may well be sound, but will often be difficult to explain. Consequently, there is the need for decision and knowledge support efforts that will enable construction of knowledge bases and judgment guidelines that follow from skill-based experiential reasoning. This is particularly needed in group situations in which all participants will not have the same level of expertise, but need to understand the rationale behind expert wholistic judgment. Many of our discussions in Chapter 6 relate to these concerns.

Information sharing is one of the many features of a distributed multiagent system. An inherent advantage to knowledge support approaches that allow for the "blending" of formal reasoning, rule-based knowledge, and skill-based expert knowledge is that explanations for judgments are potentially available from each knowledge perspective. This capability significantly enhances the potential contribution of all participants using the distributed multiagent information system for the issue under consideration, by enabling them to use the type of information, and associated information presentation format, most suitable to the perspectives from which they approach the task at hand. To bring these possible advantages to fruition will require considerable additional research in dialog management and associated information presentation principles in distributed multiagent decision support situations.

2. Humans use potentially definable and identifiable judgmental guidelines, perspectives, and rules that are more or less appropriate, depending on their applicability to the task at hand.

The judgmental perspectives that are actually used in a given situation will depend strongly on the format that is used to present various situation assessment and decision-relevant information, and the experiential familiarity of an individual with respect to the task and the environment into which the task is embedded.

That it is possible to identify judgmental perspectives is more a desiderata than a present-day reality. It is essential that we be able accomplish this identification for a variety of knowledge acquisition, representation, and use tasks. It is well known that a diagram is worth many words [39], but we are only beginning to develop a theory of information presentation such that we are able to design information presentation aids for purposes such as situation assessment. Although there is much more to learn, we do know that

- 2.1. When deemed appropriate, especially for unfamiliar and semistructured situations, when *vigilant information processing* is needed, humans will (or at least *should*) attempt to use approaches that stem from the formal reasoning based constructs.
- 2.2. The particular blend of knowledge (skill-based, rule-based, or formal reasoning based in the typology of Rasmussen [40]) used to reach judgments is a function of the contingency task structure. This structure consists of three elements: the internal and external environment in which the task need is embedded; the decision task requirements, including the stress associated with the decision and the "cost" to the decision maker of exercising various judgment strategies; and decision-maker experiential familiarity with the environment and the decision task requirements.

Both formal reasoning and rule-based reasoning approaches contribute to the accumulation of skill-based experiential knowledge through a learning process. The contingency task structure diagnosis leads to determination of the appropriate knowledge perspective. There is learning such that the contingency task structure, for a given individual, changes with experience. Thus, we envision a structure for knowledge acquisition, representation, and use such as that shown in Figure 1.7.

In this figure, we see a symbiotic relationship among three fundamental knowledge perspectives. A meta-level reasoning process results in a decision concerning how to decide how to decide. On the basis of this meta-level decision, a balance of skill-based, rule-based, and formal knowledge based reasoning is used to determine a decision option or problem solution. This will often result in some sort of physical controlling action. Learning occurs, as both a direct and as a feedback process, through observation of what results.

It is certainly now recognized that the mere insertion of a computerized aid for problem solving or decision making will, in no way, guarantee an increase in the effectiveness, efficiency, or explicability of the resulting problem-solving or decision-making task. Just the opposite may well occur. The complexity of tasks may increase, owing to technology infusion, so that there is a reduction in the quality of the resulting information processing and judgments. Clearly then, the amount and extent of technology infusion into judgment and choice efforts affect all of the dimensions of the contingency task structure.

The complexity of a situation and the task requirements, together with the experiential familiarity of an individual with these, will influence how an issue under consideration is decomposed into aspects, elements, or components believed to be tractable by that individual. High complexity will also encourage that this be done in such a manner as to minimize the interaction among the elements so that the human decision maker is able to cope with the resulting disaggregated issue. At least in a formal sense, this complexity will encourage modularization, the hierarchical structuring of issues, and distributed processing of the subcomponents of these issues. On the basis of this hypothesis, it follows that

3. As the amount of information imperfection increases, there will be a much greater need for cooperative interaction among the various human, technological, and organizational elements that comprise the task.

This appears needed owing to the difficulty, especially when the available information about system behavior is of poor quality, of appropriately disaggregating task requirements. This need is particularly acute when expressed for the multiple-agent case, which we will discuss in the next section, since there will exist a large shared distributed data, information, or knowledge base with sophisticated devices to obtain the sensory inputs that enable contributions from a number of individuals who each participate in various aspects of a problem-solving task.

Klein and Calderwood [41] have observed that decision-making issues, in which the fundamental objective is to select a best course of action, are often sublimated into problem-solving issues. In these, the primary goals are situation understanding and immediate selection of a prescribed course of action once a situation is understood. Information imperfections are a primary cause of this lack of understanding and resulting sublimation. The authors describe three types of ambiguities that determine whether a given issue is regarded as a decision-making issue or a problem-solving issue: problem situation ambiguities, appropriate goal ambiguities, and ambiguities in relation to alternative options that will achieve goals. Therefore, these is a need for techniques to enable individual and groups to deal with potentially competing and conflicting hypotheses such that they can resolve discordances due to uncertain, imprecise, or other forms of imperfect information and knowledge. This suggests a relationship between the quality of information available in a given situation and the degree of expertise that a specific person will have about that situation. This does not *in any way* suggest that more information will lead to reduced information equivocality and, hence, better judgment. Just the opposite may well occur! It does suggest the major role of information, and value of information constructs, as major determinants of situation understanding as well as of decision-makming and problem-solving behavior.

This last observation is related to another one that pertains to human allocation of human resources to judgment and decision tasks.

4. The majority of studies of human decision making, especially in organizational settings, shows that people rarely concentrate on one problem at one time but

generally consider, in a simultaneous, often nonsystematic, and parallel manner, a diversity of problem-solving situations [42].

This leads to the observation that

5. Human performance may suffer when the task requirements suggest performance of several subtasks, often in diverse stages of completion, in parallel.

As has been noted many times, humans are limited in their cognitive ability to cope with many bits of stimulus information. The effect of this is often selective perception in which only a portion, often that portion confirming a decision that the decision maker would like to make, of available information is used in the process of judgment and choice. These studies, many of which are summarized in Chapter 6, show that

6. Humans are limited in their unaided ability to process aleatory, or statistical, information.

For example, base rates or prior statistics will not be accorded the weight that they should be allocated, as compared to individuating information. A large number of cognitive information-processing biases that degrade the quality of the resulting judgments have been identified and many of these are discussed in Section 6.5.1. It is also true, as noted by Cohen [43], Baron [44], and Kyburg [45], that

7. Humans often reason quite well based on epistemic and evidential information. Confirmation and denial rules, while potentially very flawed from the strict viewpoint of mathematical logic, frequently yield very acceptable judgments and commonly represent the only types of information available for judgment.

At least two considerations suggest real limits to the behavioral decision theory, or judgment and choice, viewpoint of humans as intellectual cripples who are very prone to the use of seriously flawed information-processing heuristics and the resulting cognitive biases. The first is that, on an individual basis, the continuous adaptive nature of operational judgmental processes acts in such a way as to overcome the discrete statistically based information-processing biases that have been discovered in the laboratory. The second is that there is the *potential* for group-based judgments to be of higher quality than individual judgments.

Especially interesting concerns arise when these notions are considered in a distributed multiagent environment. The concepts of *information sharing* and *shared-concept models* then become especially important. There are many ingredients in this, some of which are the communication nodes and links that exist, the perceptions that the different agents have regarding the internal and external environment, and the situation assessment and decision-making needs of the different agents or actors. A central need in distributed group situations is that of translation of thoughts and ideas into some, more or less, common language so that these can be shared. Questions of dialog generation and management, including information presentation, then become particularly important.

7.4.2 Distributed Multiagent and Organizational Information-Processing Realities

Design of a distributed multiagent decision support system will incur all of the complexities of a nondistributed support system intended to be used by an individual. In addition to distributed decision-making environments being prone to all of the errors of individuals in centralized single-agent situations, there will be added complexities because of the group nature of the support effort. The distributed nature of these systems, generally brought about because of the geographically dispersed sites, imposes at least three additional technological constraints that are generally not incurred in group information processing in a centralized location:

8. Communication channels between sites will often, but not necessarily, be much slower than communication times within a single site.
9. The access time to attach one network to another will be frequently longer than the time required for information transmission, especially in situations such as military conflict where jamming or other intentional message corruption is to be expected.
10. Communication channels and computers will commonly, particularly in military situations, be subject to reliability and survivability concerns such that the knowledge-base system and the support system into which it is incorporated will depend, in effect, on continually changing topologies.

These message delays and associated potential conflicts and discrepancies in information available at various nodes in the communication network, as well as associated concerns relative to file allocation (i.e., location) strategies, result in a critical need for consideration of the architecture of a distributed information system. These technological realities, the finite rate of information flow and the insufficiency and unreliability of information channels, each lead to a situation in which pertinent information is not available in the proper place at a suitable time. The effects of these technological information imperfections must be considered in determining resource allocation strategies, as well as in the development of the resulting information query strategies that are used to obtain information from and for the knowledge base.

Several GDSS design needs are suggested by these observations:

1. The design of decision support system that assist humans in cognitive tasks requires substantial comprehension of the human intellectual activities supporting judgment and choice on both an individual and organizational basis.

This comprises studies of skill-based, rule-based, and formal reasoning based judgment, or the seemingly equivalent larger-dimensioned frameworks concerning judgmental perspectives. Importantly also, it involves the way in which use of these types of knowledge depends on the contingency task structure. Additionally, encompasses a study of ways in which humans process information, especially in distributed environments that are subject to considerable message delays, node failures, and associated uncertainties and imprecision in the resulting data base or knowledge base.

2. Identification of appropriate ways to represent and use knowledge in a multiple- agent support system is a critical issue.

This requires attention to studies that deal not only with the formal reasoning methods common to normative decision analysis, but also to studies of how humans can be aided in reasoning wholistically and affectively, such as reasoning by analogy. Perhaps more significantly, it requires studies of how holistic and wholistic knowledge can each normatively support one another to aid the decision-making processes of individuals and groups in distributed multiagent situations. Further, it requires knowledge of

- How information queries are made, in terms of the number of requests and their distribution across communication nodes.
- The amount of information potentially available across network communication nodes.
- How much of this is used and unused.
- The amount of information ambiguity and imperfection that is present in a given situation.

Research in this area should be, and typically is, concerned with information-processing behaviors in organizational settings. Studies in this category are especially important, since it has been shown that people in an organization will often ignore relevant information in their possession, simultaneously ask for more, and then ignore that new information.

3. Information fusion studies and studies of the diverse interpretations that can result from the same knowledge presentation are critical current issues.

There exists the need to blend descriptive and prescriptive approaches in doing this so that the resulting knowledge support process is behaviorally acceptable.

4. Acquisition and representation of knowledge from multiple perspectives are needed, as well as studies of how to accommodate this within the framework of specific model base and cognitive engine constructs.

This is needed in order to provide the input to the model management, cognitive engine, and associated inference mechanisms that access the knowledge base of a support system. These must be designed in such a way as to consider the special needs that should be associated with a query language structure that may be used to elicit a knowledge base, and the physical locations for various portions of the knowledge base.

5. There are many needs relative to integration of the various knowledge bases, model bases, and cognitive engines such as to enable communication within a distributed multiagent knowledge environment by users of the system.

In a representative distributed multiagent situation, it will typically not be possible, owing to time constraints and other complexities, to evolve a "complete" set of potential action alternatives or plans, and possible ways to implement them. As we have already noted, this will generally lead to use of bounded rationality approaches to decision making, such as the use of a garbage can model of organizational decision making. These realities must be considered in system conceptualization, and the resulting system architecture, such that the resulting designs are ones that people may and will utilize in an efficient and effective way to develop appropriate, and explicable, decisions.

7.5 GDSS EVALUATION NEEDS

A number of overall GDSS evaluation issues need empirical evaluation efforts. In particular, it will be important to evaluate the extent to which the overall concept accommodates and encourages *heterarchical* reasoning—among group and organizational members in the decision situation extant. Trade-off relations that influence functionality and usability can be expected to be quite significant in information systems engineering evaluation efforts. Many interrelationships affect organizational factors and system development and these also must be considered in evaluation.

The GDSS should be *adaptive to user requirements*. It should not force users into a particular mode of thought or force them into using a specific set of decision algorithms or paradigms; nor should it force them into a prescribed protocol or procedure. Above all, the process should yield results that are of value in and of themselves at the moment they are obtained, as contrasted with having to wait until the end of the process to obtain any useful results at all. This is potentially critical, since realistic decision situations are such that there is no known fixed terminal time for the appearance of decision optimality, but a "rolling," often a priori unknown terminal time.

A number of researchers have identified attributes that can be used as metrics for evaluation of GDSS performance, generally in an operational test and evaluation sense. In some recent research, Pinsonneault and Kraemer [46] consider technological support of group decision processes. Figure 7.7 represents an adaptation of their framework to illustrate the three top-level elements: environmental variables, process variables, and decision outcome variables. These are further disaggregated into 11 attributes, as shown in the figure. Each of the three top-level attributes are finally disaggregated into 42 lowest-level attributes. These are illustrated in the attribute tree of Figures 7.8–7.10. Clearly, these can be used to form the basis for an evaluation

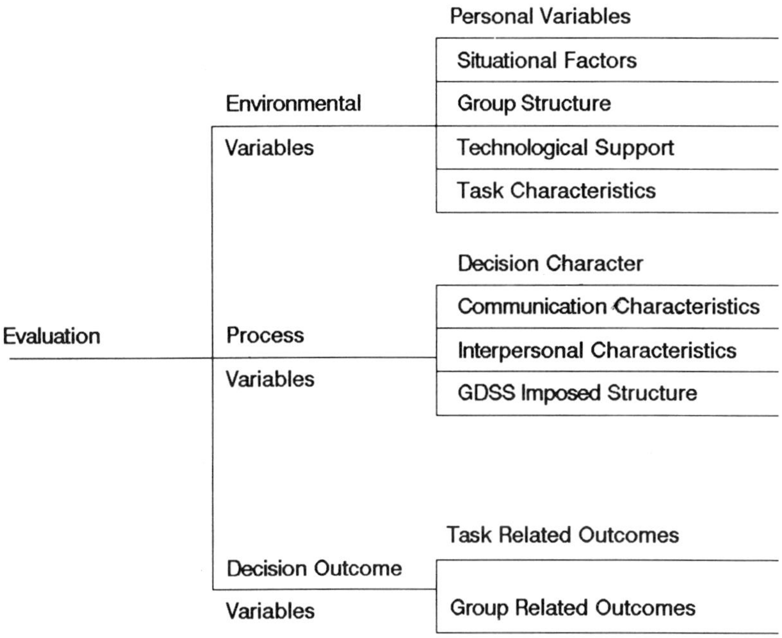

Evaluation
- **Environmental Variables**
  - Personal Variables
  - Situational Factors
  - Group Structure
  - Technological Support
  - Task Characteristics
- **Process Variables**
  - Decision Character
  - Communication Characteristics
  - Interpersonal Characteristics
  - GDSS Imposed Structure
- **Decision Outcome Variables**
  - Task Related Outcomes
  - Group Related Outcomes

Figure 7.7 High-level evaluation metrics from Pinsonneault–Kraemer classification [46].

Environmental Variables
- **Personal Variables**
  - Attitudes
  - Abilities
- **Situational Factors**
  - Individual Motives
  - Experiential Background
  - Reasons for Group Membership
  - Stage in Group Development
  - Existing Social Network
- **Group Structure**
  - Norms of Work Group
  - Power Relationships
  - Status Relationships
  - Group Cohevsiveness
  - Density & Interpersonal Distance
- **Technological Support**
  - Degree
  - Type
  - Unanimity
  - Facilitator Characteristics
- **Task Characteristics**
  - Complexity
  - Nature
  - Degree of Uncertainty

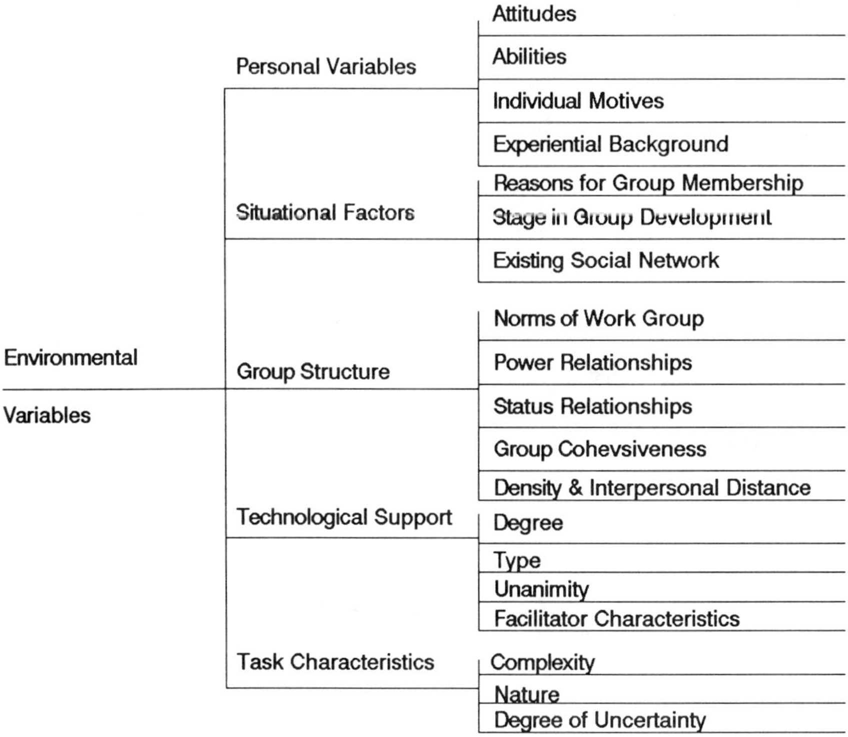

Figure 7.8 Environmental variable metrics from Pinsonneault–Kraemer classification [46].

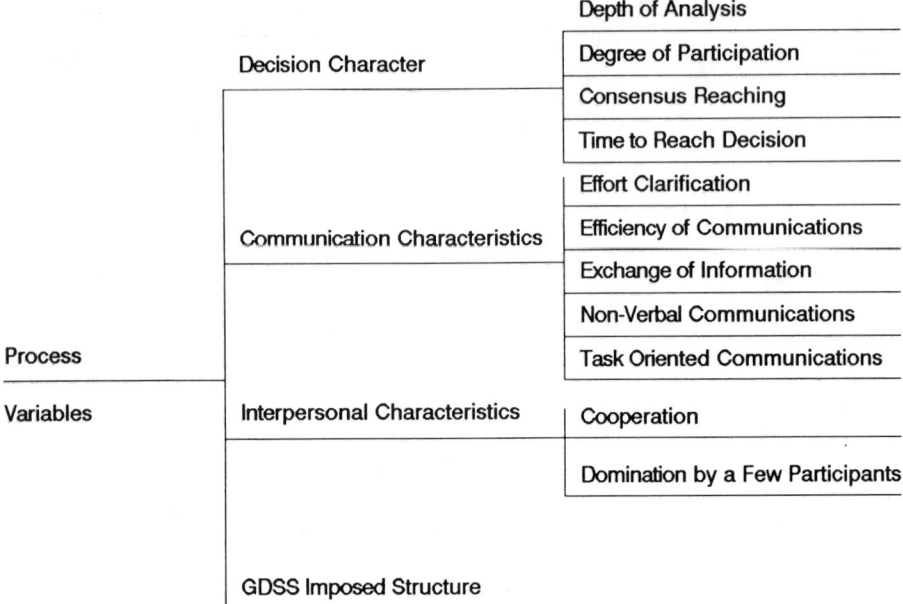

Figure 7.9 Process variable metrics from Pinsonneault–Kraemer classification [46].

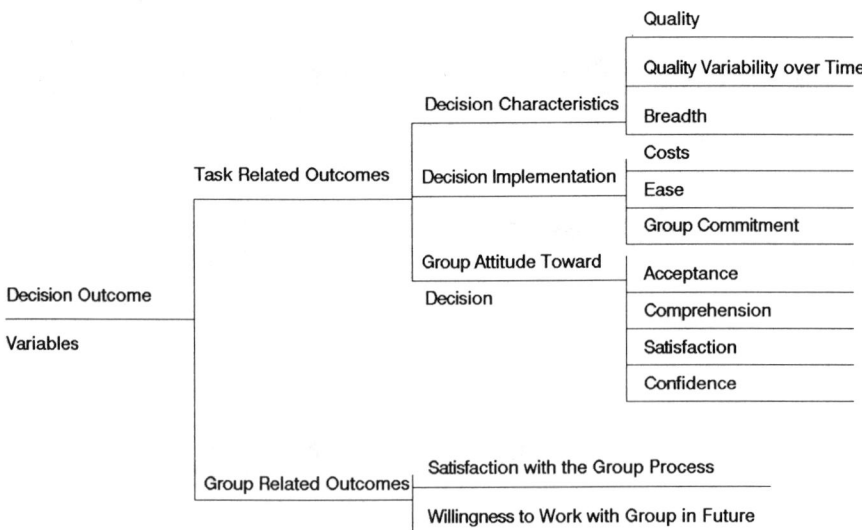

Figure 7.10 Decision outcome variable metrics from Pinsonneault–Kraemer classification [46].

effort. Of course, there are other attributes that can be identified and many have been earlier in this chapter.

Many features of a GDSS should be user-modifiable, or adaptive to the user, to accommodate the abilities and experiences of its users so as to enable them to be more efficient and effective. It must be adaptive from the user in the sense of providing gentle encouragement to the user to modify the initially suggested user approach to the system to facilitate greater user effectiveness and efficiency. It is important also that these approaches be specifically designed to encourage users to avoid poor cognitive heuristics and biases in their expressions of knowledge. Many of these have been identified in the contemporary literature for the single individual information-processing case. Little of this work has been extended to the group decision situation. It should be possible to specifically consider a number of these prototypical situations within an appropriate conceptual information system design framework, and thereby to illustrate the extent to which poor cognitive heuristics and information-processing biases are encouraged or discouraged by the framework chosen. These represent some of the many points that should be addressed when developing evaluation metrics, and when conducting an evaluation of an existing GDSS.

7.6 SUMMARY

We have provided a broad overview of group decision support systems that potentially support group and organizational decision-making functions. Rather than concentrate on one or two specific systems, we have painted a picture of the many requirements that must be satisfied in order to produce an acceptable architecture and design for these systems. Group and organizational issues provide a fertile ground for contemporary DSS research [47, 48].

PROBLEMS

7.1. In this chapter, we provide a characterization or typology of GDSS types according to
   a) Johansen
   b) Kramer and King
   c) DeSanctis and Gallupe
      i. Contrast and compare these typologies.
      ii. Indicate the support that you might expect to be provided by the 17 Johansen groupware types for each of the 15 rationality perspectives described in Chapter 6.
7.2. Develop an attribute tree for GDSS evaluation according to notions of task relevance, representational appropriateness, and equivocality reduction. These were attributes that we specifically identified as useful relative to information value. Contrast and compare these attributes with those presented in Figures

7.7–7.10. Should your new attribute tree be combined with the ones illustrated in these figures? Or will they measure the same thing?

References

[1] Johansen, R., *Groupware: Computer Support for Business Teams*, Free Press, New York, 1988.

[2] Kraemer, K. L., and King, J. L., "Computer Based Systems for Cooperative Work and Group Decision Making," *ACM Computing Surveys*, Vol. 20, No. 2, June 1988, pp. 115–146.

[3] Gray, P., and Olfman, L., "The User Interface in Group Decision Support Systems," *Decision Support Systems*, Vol. 5, No. 2, 1989, pp. 119–137.

[4] Huber, G. P., "Group Decision Support Systems as Aids in the Use of Structured Group Management Techniques," *Proceedings of the 2nd International Conference on Decision Support Systems*, San Francisco, June 1982, pp. 96–108.

[5] Anthony, R. N., *Planning and Control Systems: A Framework for Analysis*, Harvard University Press, Cambridge, 1965.

[6] Simon, H. A., *The New Science of Management Decisions*, Harper and Row, New York, 1960.

[7] Rouse, W. B., "Conceptual Design of a Computational Environment for Analyzing Tradeoffs Between Training and Aiding," *Information and Decision Technologies*, 1991 (to appear).

[8] Keen, P. G. W., and Scott-Morton, M. S., *Decision Support Systems: An Organizational Perspective*, Addison-Wesley, Reading, MA, 1978.

[9] Schum, D. A., *Evidence and Inference for the Intelligence Analyst*, Vols. I and II, University Press of America, Lanham, MD, 1987.

[10] Klein, G. A., "Information Requirements for Recognitional Decision Making," in Sage, A. P. (Ed.), *Concise Encyclopedia of Information Processing in Systems and Organizations*, Pergamon Press, Oxford, UK, 1990, pp. 414–418.

[11] Rasmussen, J., "Models of Mental Strategies in Process Diagnosis," in Rasmussen, J., and Rouse, W. B. (Eds.), *Human Detection and Diagnosis of System Failures*, Plenum, New York, 1980, pp. 241–258.

[12] Welch, D. A., "Group Decision Making Reconsidered," *Journal of Conflict Resolution*, Vol. 33, No. 3, September 1989, pp. 430–445.

[13] Herek, G. M., Janis, I. L., and Hurth, P., "Decision Making During International Crises: Is Quality of Process Related to Outcome," *Journal of Conflict Resolution*, Vol. 31, No. 2, May 1987, pp. 203–226.

[14] March, J. G., "Bounded Rationality, Ambiguity, and the Engineering of Choice," *Bell Journal of Economics*, Vol. 9, March, 1983, pp. 587–608.

[15] March, J., and Wessinger-Baylor, T. (Eds.), *Ambiguity and Command: Organizational Perspectives on Military Decisionmaking*, Pitman, Boston, 1986.

[16] Weick, K. E., *The Social Psychology of Organizing*, Addison-Wesley, Reading, MA, 1979.

[17] Weick, K. E., "Cosmos vs. Chaos: Sense and Nonsense in Electronic Contexts," *Organizational Dynamics*, Vol. 14, Autumn 1985, pp. 50–64.

[18] Starbuck, W. E., "Acting First and Thinking Later," in Pennings, J. (Ed.), *Organizational Strategy and Change*, Jossey-Bass, San Francisco, 1985, pp. 336–372.

[19] Daft, R. L., and Weick, K. E., "Towards a Model of Organizations as Interpretation Systems," *Academy of Management Review*, Vol. 9, 1984, pp. 284–295.

[20] Daft, R. L., and Lengel, R. H., "Organizational Information Requirements, Media Richness, and Structural Design," *Management Science*, Vol. 32, No. 5, May 1986, pp. 554–571.

[21] Sage, A. P. "Information Systems Engineering for Distributed Decision Making," *IEEE Transactions on Systems, Man and Cybernetics*, Vol. 17, No. 6, September 1987, pp. 920–936.

[22] King, J. L., and Star, S. L., "Conceptual Foundations for the Development of Organizational Decision Support Systems," *Proceedings of the Information Systems and Decision Processes Workshop*, Gray, P., and Stohr, T. (Eds.), 1990, (in press).

[23] Stefik, M., Foster, G., Bobrow, D. G., Kahn, K., Lanning, S., and Suchman, L., "Beyond the Chalkboard: Computer Support for Collaboration and Problem Solving in Meetings," *Communications of the ACM*, Vol. 30, No. 1, January 1987, pp. 32–47.

[24] Malone, T. W., and Smith, S. A., "Modeling the Performance of Organizational Structures," *Operations Research*, Vol. 36, No. 3, May–June 1986, pp. 421–436.

[25] Malone, T. W., Grant, K. R., Turbak, F. A., Brobst, S. A., and Cohen, M. D., "Intelligent Information Sharing Systems," *Communications of the ACM*, Vol. 30, No. 5, May 1987, pp. 390–402.

[26] Winograd, T., and Flores, F., *Understanding Computers and Cognition*, Ablex Press, Norwood, NJ, 1986.

[27] Nielson, J., *Hypertext and Hypermedia*, Academic, New York, 1989.

[28] Goodman, G. O., and Abel, M. J., "Communications and Collaboration: Facilitating Cooperative Work Through Communications," *Office Technology and People*, Vol. 3, No. 2, August 1987, pp. 129–146.

[29] Hiltz, S. R., *On-Line Scientific Communities*, Ablex Press, Norwood, NJ, 1982.

[30] Hiltz, S. R., and Turoff, M., "The Evolution of User Behavior in a Computer Conferencing System," *Communications of the ACM*, Vol. 24, No. 11, November 1981, pp. 739–751.

[31] Watson, R. T., DeSanctis, G., and Poole, M. S., "Using a GDSS to Facilitate Group Consensus: Some Intended and Unintended Consequences," *MIS Quarterly*, Vol. 12, No. 2, September 1988, pp. 463–477.

[32] Zigurs, L., Poole, M. S., and DeSanctis, G. L., "A Study of Influence in Computer-Mediated Group Decision Making," *MIS Quarterly*, Vol. 12, No. 3, December 1988, pp. 625–644.

[33] DeSanctis, G., and Gallupe, R. B., "A Foundation for the Study of Group Decision Support Systems," *Management Science*, Vol. 33, No. 5, May 1987, pp. 547–588.

[34] Huber, G. P., "Issues in the Design of Group Decision Support Systems," *MIS Quarterly*, Vol. 8, No. 3, 1984, pp. 195–204.

[35] Huber, G. P., and McDaniel, R. R., "The Decision Making Paradigm of Organizational Design," *Management Science*, Vol. 32, No. 5, May 1986, pp. 572–589.

[36] Applegate, L. M., Chen, T. T., Konsynski, B. R., and Nunamaker, J. F., "Knowledge Management in Organizational Planning," *Journal of Management Information Systems*, Vol. 3, No. 4, Spring 1987, pp. 20–38.

[37] Jarvenpaa, S., Rao, V., and Huber G., "Computer Support for Meetings of Groups on Unstructured Problems: A Field Experiment," *MIS Quarterly*, Vol. 12, No. 3, December 1988, pp. 645–666.

[38] Liang, B. T., "Model Management for Group Decision Support," *MIS Quarterly*, Vol. 12, No. 4, December 1988, pp. 667–680.

[39] Larkin, J. H., and Simon, H. A., "Why a Diagram is (Sometimes) Worth Ten Thousand Words," *Cognitive Science*, Vol. 11, No. 1, 1987, pp. 65–99.

[40] Rasmussen, J., *Information Processing and Human-Machine Interaction: An Approach to Cognitive Engineering*, North-Holland, New York, 1986.

[41] Klein, G. A., and Calderwood, R., *A Preliminary Assessment of Factors Affecting Decision Complexity*, Report No. 96-86.1-F, Klein Associates, Yellow Springs, OH, 1986.

[42] Mintzberg, H., *The Nature of Managerial Work*, Harper & Row, New York, 1973.

[43] Cohen, L. J., "Can Human Irrationality Be Experimentally Demonstrated," *Behavioral and Brain Sciences*, Vol. 4, 1981, pp. 317–331.

[44] Baron, J., *Rationality and Intelligence*, Cambridge University Press, 1985.

[45] Kyburg, H. E., "Rational Belief," *Behavioral and Brain Sciences*, Vol. 6, No. 2, June 1983, pp. 231–274.

[46] Pinsonneault, A., and Kraemer, K. L., "The Impact of Technological Support on Groups: An Assessment of the Empirical Research," *Decision Support Systems*, Vol. 5, No. 2, 1989, pp. 197–216.

[47] Fulk, J., and Steinfield, C. (Eds.), *Organizations and Communication Technology*, Sage Publications, Newbury Park, CA, 1990.

[48] Rasmussen, J., Brehmer, B., and Leplat, J. (Eds.), *Distributed Decision Making: Cognitive Models for Cooperative Work*, Wiley, Chichester, UK, 1991.

Chapter **8**

Operational Implementation, System Integration, and Environments for Decision Support Systems

The environment of an organization includes those factors (physical, technological, social, economic, legal, political, and perhaps others) that are outside of the boundaries of an organization but that still influence the functioning of the organization. It is possible to view the environment as an independent causal variable to which organizations will respond, or as an interdependent variable that organizations may attempt to modify. From the former perspective, the best that an organization can do is to attempt to adapt to the environment, perhaps in an interactive manner. Highly successful adaptation can result in very successful organizational performance. If it is possible for an organization to be proactive such as to predict opportunities for change and to modify its environment accordingly, even greater success is possible.

This chapter is primarily concerned with decision support systems environments, but also with the integration and implementation of DSS and, thus, with DSS design and development environments. While operational implementation and system integration are activities that formally occur near the end of the DSS engineering life cycle, success requires appropriate attention to *concept development, identification of system specifications,* and *overall systems analysis and design—throughout the life cycle*—or operational deployment issues will generally be associated with the greatest of misfortunes.

So, we see that it will be important to understand the environment for DSS design and installation. Our efforts in this chapter will first be devoted to a examining system implementation and integration issues. Then we will turn our attention to DSS environments.

8.1 IMPLEMENTATION AND INTEGRATION

In many cases, a decision support system that is being deployed is *not* a totally new system concept that is being installed in a situation where no other system has previously existed. Frequently, it is a presumably improved version of an existing system and/or must be compatible with existing systems. (For instance, it may be necessary or highly desirable, to utilize an existing corporate data base.) This *new system* will, therefore, evolve from an existing system in a fashion such as shown in Figure 8.1. The new system may be delivered as a result of some contracted effort with an external DSS contractor, or it may be developed *in-house*.

The result of the contracted effort will often be intended to be utilized in future efforts for implementation of some overall system integration concepts as they evolve over time. Both technical and functional integration are usually achieved, each in an evolutionary manner, through systems implementation and integration efforts. The first deliverable relative to achieving this is generally a *DSS implementation and integration plan* that will identify, analyze, and prioritize technical and functional integration issues, and propose solutions to problems extant with the functional deployment of the developed software. To do this efficiently and effectively will require

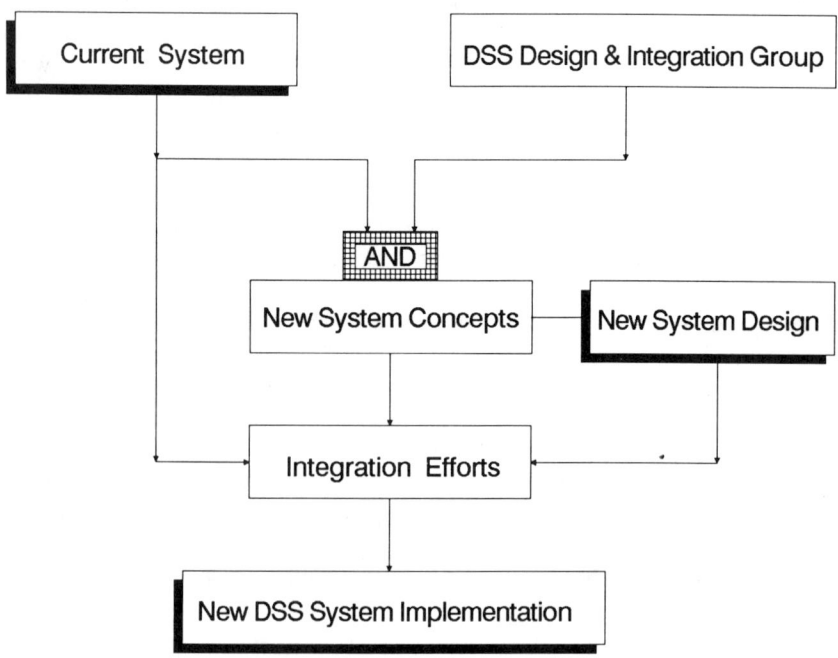

Figure 8.1 Decison support system implementation concerns.

1. Outstanding capabilities in systems management.
2. Thorough understanding of contemporary technology for the development of trustworthy DSS architectures and system integration plans.
3. Technical direction and cost-control abilities.

These DSS engineering capabilities must be present throughout the complete life cycle of development of the DSS. At a number of places in the text, the life cycle of DSS design and development has been discussed. Not generally indicated in these discussions is the distributed nature of the effort, the systems management and technical direction nature of the effort, the multiphase nature of the overall concept, or the iteration and feedback that must be provided back to earlier stages in the DSS design and development process. We emphasize these in our discussions here.

Normally, it will be necessary for a DSS implementation and integration contractor to provide integration concepts and designs. Commonly, the user group will have the contractual ability to approve or disapprove of these concepts as they are developed. In many instances, the DSS contractor will be obliged to assist the user group in the future management and coordination of other contractors, primarily through review of proposed subsystem design specifications. Figure 8.2 describes this systems management notion and indicates the primary role of the integration contractor in the information technology aspects that lead to development of an overall system concept, and the systems management and technical direction role that will often be required as a part of a DSS implementation effort.

Both top-down and bottom-up approaches will generally be needed and used for DSS integration. The top-down approach will be primarily concerned with long-term issues that involve structure and architecture of the overall DSS. The bottom-up approach will be concerned with parallel efforts at making existing parts of the system more efficient and effective such that they can be potentially incorporated into an overall integration concept for the newly implemented DSS. The overall integration design must be such as to take into consideration various existing hardware and software that are not subject to change, and possibly other initiatives that constrain the overall integration concept. This concept must, of course, be consistent with both existing and evolving DSS architectures.

Of central concern in a DSS integration and implementation effort is the system-level *information architecture* of the overall DSS concept. Conceptually, this might appear as shown in Figure 8.3. It should be explicitly noted that the DSS architecture may, especially in the case of a GDSS, be very distributed spatially; what is shown in Figure 8.3 is merely a centralized representation of the system-level architecture.

The intended mission areas for decision support will, naturally, vary from implementation to implementation. The primary systems engineering and technical direction activities of the DSS implementation and integration team involve architectural design of the overall system and integration of specific individual new DSS subsystems into the overall DSS. The first of these activities calls for systems engineering activities on the part of the implementation and integration team. These technical tools and methodologies from DSS engineering involve primarily the top-down

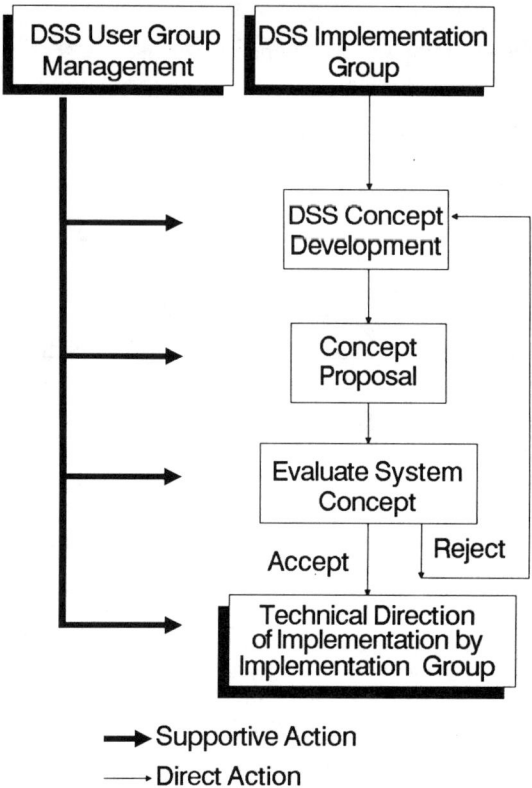

Figure 8.2 Interaction of DSS implementation and user groups.

approaches identified in the initial phase of activity. The second of these activities encompasses systems engineering management and technical direction of other contractors and/or principally bottom-up approaches to the interfacing and interoperability of existing DSS. The phases of effort associated with conceptual deseign and specification of the new components to be added to an existing system are related, as shown in Figure 8.4.

A number of systems technology and systems management issues and challenges are associated with this concept of *DSS implementation and integration engineering*. The technical issues generally involve the conduct, by the implementation and integration team, of impact assessments and the preparation of systems engineering reports on architectural changes and associated integration concerns as they impact the DSS and the organization. The implementation and integration team should also be capable of providing systems management support relative to technical and scheduling decisions. These will usually involve life-cycle costing studies of possible acquisition strategies and configuration management studies as they specifically relate to DSS implementation needs.

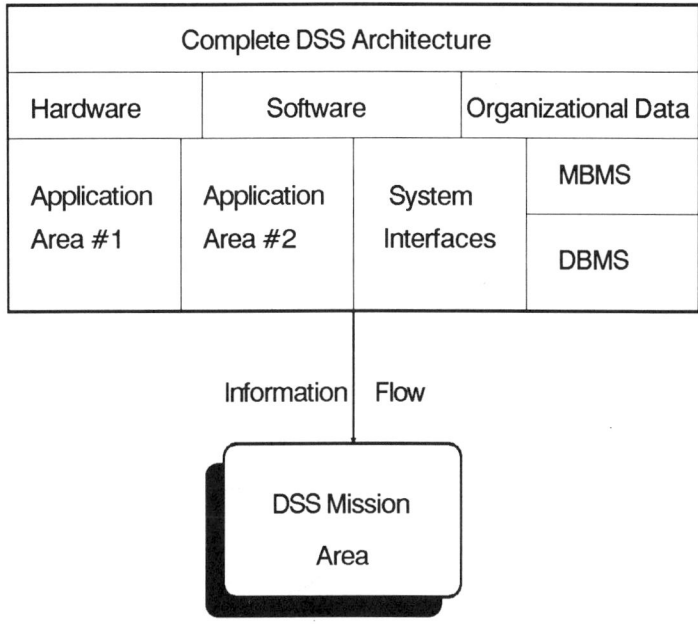

Figure 8.3 Representation of DSS system architectures.

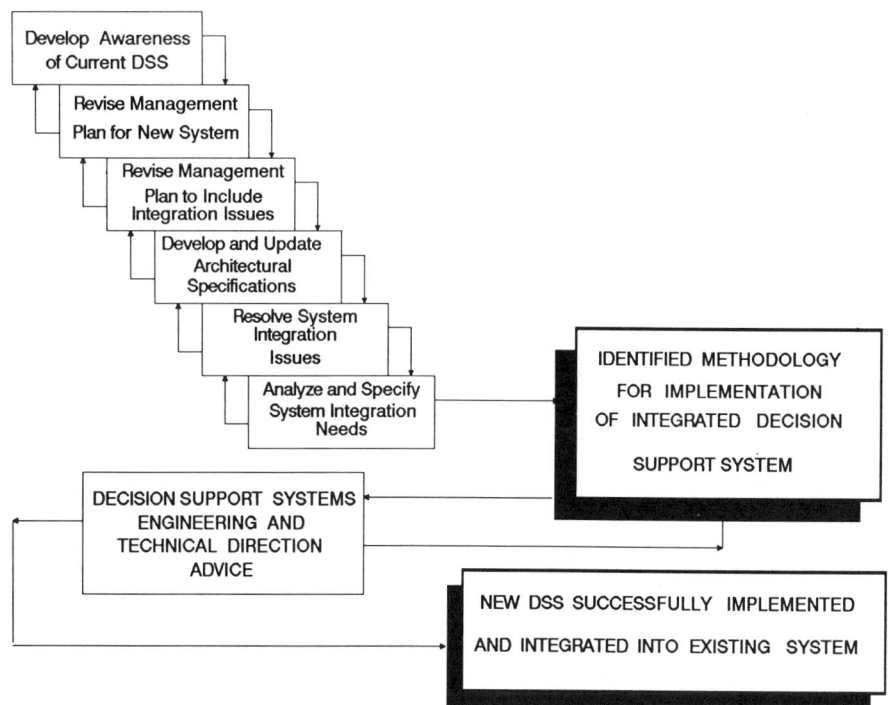

Figure 8.4 Activities in DSS implementation and integration.

When a positive go-ahead to an implementation decision is made, an implementation and integration contractor will typically be tasked to prepare design specifications and a recommendation regarding the method used to accomplish implementation of the DSS. On making a subsequent decision about which implementation method to use, the implementation–integration contractor will generally assist in systems management and technical direction of the DSS implementation effort. Involvement may include performance of an implementation task order, in which case the system user group will independently prepare the task order and determine the acceptance criteria. The implementation and integration contractor would then be responsible for management review and establishment of a management control system to ensure quality-assurance provisions. This will include operational test and evaluation according to contractor-prepared and user-group-approved operational test and evaluation plans. Figures 8.4 and 8.5 illustrate these implementation and integration contractor activities from somewhat different perspectives.

The first effort should generally be to obtain, from a variety of relevant sources, identification of

Where the DSS user group is

Where the DSS user group needs to be

How it should get there relative to system implementation and integration

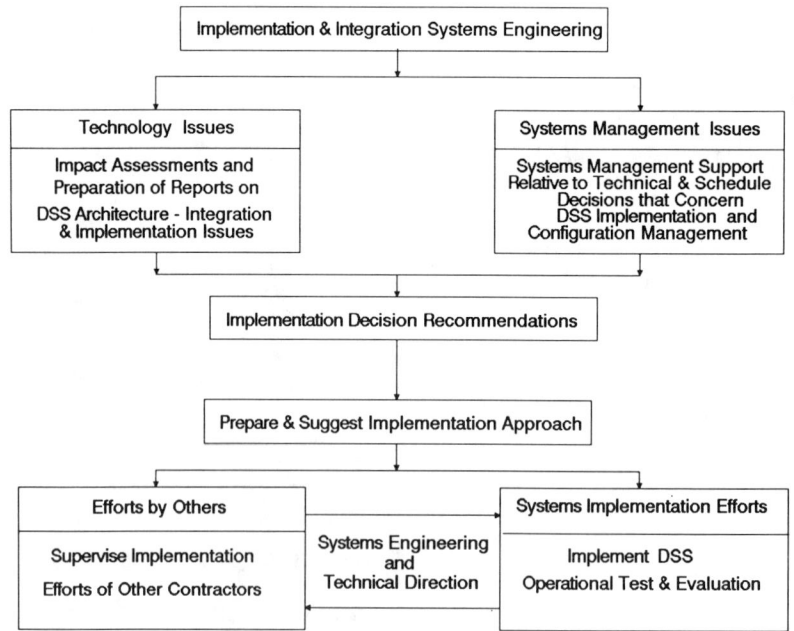

Figure 8.5 Technological and management issues in DSS implementation.

This *situation assessment* effort will result in definition of the problem in terms of the needs, constraints, and alterables specifically relative to the system implementation. Of course, at least a preliminary version of this effort must have been accomplished as an initial part of the requirements specifications effort that led to development of the software system that is now being implemented. Again, this emphasizes the fact the DSS engineering life cycle is really a cornucopialike diagram in which each of the phases within the life cycle have a set of steps associated with them that are not dissimilar to the general activities accomplished within the overall system design phases.

With respect to implementation, there will usually be a baseline configuration, which poses both a reference point and a set of constraints for the existing systgem that is to be modified through augmentation and installation of the new system. Hence, a necessary first task must be to identify potential alternative augmentations, additions, and modifications of this existing system.

These will be subject to analysis and impact assessment activities in which the impacts of these identified alternatives on the effectiveness of the resulting DSS operational implementation will be determined. This step should allow for some refinement of parameters within the assumed architectural structures for the alternative implementations, so that each of the alternatives is optimized for approximately best performance. These alternative systems and processes should be capable of being interfaced and interoperable with some existing systems, integrated with other systems, and compatible with still other DSS. There is a major need for an evaluation and review methodology to verify and validate the software, the hardware, the human interfaces, and the trustworthiness of the resulting system. Accordingly, the many discussions on these topics presented earlier in this text are, indeed, relevant.

Cost and effectiveness indices will be determined for each of the resulting refined alternatives. This will be in the form of a set of planning documents for augmentations of DSS resources that are currently operational. These documents will identify potential integration opportunities within the current technical environment of computer hardware and software, and communications. These impacts will be identified against a background of several alternative future scenarios for conditions that affect the DSS user group or organization.

Also included with each evaluation should be an analysis of risk factors affecting implementation of each alternative. Risk is a very multiattributed concept, and relevant dimensions that affect operational functionality of the system being implemented should be fully explored.

Implementation and integration documents should be prepared. An appropriate system development life cycle will be such that at least a preliminary version of these will have been prepared as part of requirements specifications. Now is the time to revise them! These documents will also include systems management plans for all phases of the DSS implementation life cycle.

8.2 MANAGEMENT OF DSS IMPLEMENTATION AND INTEGRATION

Invariably, the goals of those working on a decision support systems engineering design and development project will include identifying

- New technology approaches that will enhance operational functionality of the new DSS.
- Significant "cost-drivers" that represent a high percentage of total costs of the DSS.
- Methods that will reduce costs while simultaneously retaining benefits.

The task of conceptual design of the system and, most importantly, the methodology for design of this system is basically a top-down effort that requires vigilant attention to DSS engineering management principals. The tasks of implementation of this concept will generally require detailed technical expertise for the many bottom-up tasks that are required. To neglect either is to invite failure in the sense of producing a DSS that will not satisfy the needs of the various users of the system or the organizational goals that the DSS is intended to support. The best way to keep contract costs at a minimum *and achieve a satisfactory implementation of sound concepts* is to select a DSS contractor with the wisdom and experience to manage an effective systems management approach to the various problems that occur throughout the life cycle of DSS design, development, and implementation. There will necessarily be trade-offs between time schedules, standardization of the eventual product, and ultimate functionality and trustworthiness of this product in the operational environment. Consequently, implementation and integration concerns need to be addressed as vital parts of the total DSS effort. To do this effectively will require major efforts associated with environmental management throughout the life cycle. There are actually two environments to be concerned with here. One is the environment of the DSS contractor. The other is that of the DSS user group.

There will be hardware and software issues that will act as cost drivers. Without question, the software cost-drivers will normally be an order of magnitude more critical. In fact, quality software design procedures should enable relatively easy transfer of software from one machine to another as improved hardware evolves. One purpose of quality software design is to make the change of hardware virtually transparent to the DSS user. To accomplish these objectives will require a DSS management team that is well versed in all relevant aspects of systems design and development, including implementation. Systems management activities must be such that a continuous, in-depth knowledge of relevant methodologies for the design, implementation, and management of large software, and hardware, DSS projects is applied. Required also may be the ability to integrate the results of various other hardware and software developers so as to ensure operational functionality of the existing and new DSS subsystems that comprise the overall system.

The concept of operational deployment, or system implementation, is an iterative and evolving one. It is not static over time. Thus, it is that systems that once fit well into a complete DSS at one point in time may not fit it at some future point. This evolving design and development concept is shown in Figure 8.6. The iteration and feedback involved in this is essential and relevant in ensuring continuing functionality of the deployed DSS.

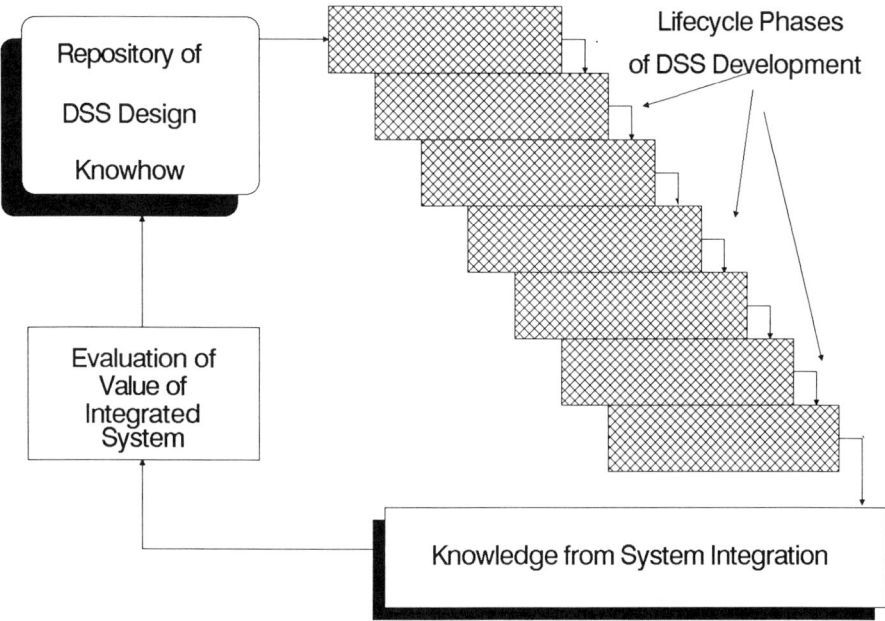

Figure 8.6 Evolving nature of system implementation and integration, and associated learning.

8.3 SYSTEM INTEGRATION NEEDS IN DSS ENGINEERING

A DSS or GDSS implementation effort is a complex human–machine systems design issue. A great percentage of the problems associated with large complex systems are, and will continue to be, associated with the human elements that are related to operating, maintaining, and managing these systems. The tasks of operation, maintenance, and management are each strongly influenced by the requirements specifications and architectures selected for the DSS. Therefore, there is a continuing major need for iteration, interaction, and feedback across and within the various phases of system activity associated with the entire design and development life cycle of DSS.

Several realities emerge from this:

1. It is essential to consider both the design of complex new DSS and the integration of existing and new systems, as well as the operation, maintenance, and management of these systems.
2. A DSS design outlook that enables system designers to anticipate and resolve operational, maintenance, and management problems prior to fielding large-scale complex DSS could do much to support high-quality DSS implementation and integration engineering.

3. Three types of knowledge are vital in design of a DSS:
   a. It is critical to understand the *practice* of DSS design, that is to say, how existing DSS that form a part of an overall system have been designed, how this design affects operational functionality concerns in organizations, and how well existing designs meet existing and projected future requirements, including budget requirements.
   b. To improve on existing systems and to design new DSS, it is mandatory that we understand the *principles* of information technology systems design. We need to understand both top-down and bottom-up perspectives on DSS design, and why a hybrid of these two approaches will generally be needed. We need to be aware of a variety of approaches to DSS design, new information technology products and services, and how these may be integrated into a standardized "design for interoperability" approach that will enhance the integration of existing and new DSS, including associated information management resources within the organization, into enhanced support system concepts and realities.
   c. To accomplish these effectively, we must be aware of future *perspectives* that will enhance prospects for improvements in support systems to meet projected client needs in a timely and trustworthy manner. This will involve future projections of software and hardware technology base, as well as projections of client or user needs for new information technology based DSS.

Although the word does not explicitly appear in this list of three desiderata for technical and systems management in implementation, *standards* is implied in each of the three. In any realistic approach, it must be recognized that more efficient DSS tools (including, of course, the tools that support design and operation of the DBMS, MBMS, and DGMS portions of a DSS) are desirable. Even more important and desirable is the integration of existing and future tools such that they better cooperate in supporting individual and organizational decision-making tasks. We see two basic types of integration in this, tool integration and information integration [1]. We also note the need for top-down integration, where system design precedes subsystem design, and bottom-up integration, where subsystem design precedes system design (this has been called *prefacto design* and *postfacto design*, respectively [1]).

There are other perspectives or aspects from which we can view system integration. In one recent study [2], four aspects are identified:

1. *Integration technology*—which relates to implementations that support transfer of data across different subsystems. These include file-transfer protocols, document protocols, and remote procedure calls. Automatic data transfer, common data-base structures for different applications, and process-to-process communications through well-defined functional interfaces and interaction protocols are examples of how integration technology is accomplished. Some form of integration technology is typically necessary for overall system integration but is never sufficient to ensure it.

2. *Integration architecture*—which relates to intentional subsystem design to ensure easy and secure data and information functionality and sharing across subsystems. This may involve storage of common data in a common data base. It may also include accomplishing distributed data storage through use of an integration architecture that has direct access to data or functional access by activating other systems.

3. *Semantic integration*—which relates to the insurance that either the same concepts mean the same thing in different portions of the system or, alternatively, that there is a known translation mechanism and user interfaces that will successfully resolve semantic inconsistencies (which will invariably exist when the different subsystems of a DSS are procured from different vendors) so as to allow meaningful information sharing and exchange across systems.

4. *User integration*—which relates to the end-user perspective of the DSS that enables a DSS user to concentrate on the task to be accomplished and not the specific details of the computer system at hand. Friendliness of user access and adaptable user interface styles will usually be needed to assure the successful integration of different users in an organization. This will generally require easy access to different applications and systems, uniform user interfaces, consistent data, and consistent use of semantic concepts.

The three approaches to system knowledge we have discussed interact together, and with these four integration aspects, as indicated in Figure 8.7. One major objective of any DSS design and implementation effort should be to provide the systems engineering technology and management capability to reduce implementation risks and enhance trustworthiness of the resulting DSS, and associated decision support process in resolving particular issues. There are some major technical challenges in this. Consider, for instance, a situation that typically exists today. Choice of computer hardware will limit the selection of available data-base management systems. Alternatively, the choice of a particular DBMS will constrain the hardware that may be selected as well as the operating system. A well-designed *integrated* DSS surely needs DBMS independence. This would enable the system to use a variety of validated and verified (and interoperable) DBMS. It would enable application software system expansion to be machine- and operating-system independent. This would foster greater competition among system vendors as well as do much to ensure integrity of the resulting DSS.

What is needed is an approach to systems integration that is able to satisfy present and projected needs in contemporary DSS engineering application environments, that is capable of efficiently and effectively coping with future user needs for hardware and software acquisition, and that will enable the identification, development, and operationalization of an integrated system and related needs. These include need satisfaction regarding DSS implementation in contemporary environments:

1. Accommodating changes in external environment.
2. Accommodating changes in user requirements.
3. Use of product technologies that automate DSS construction.

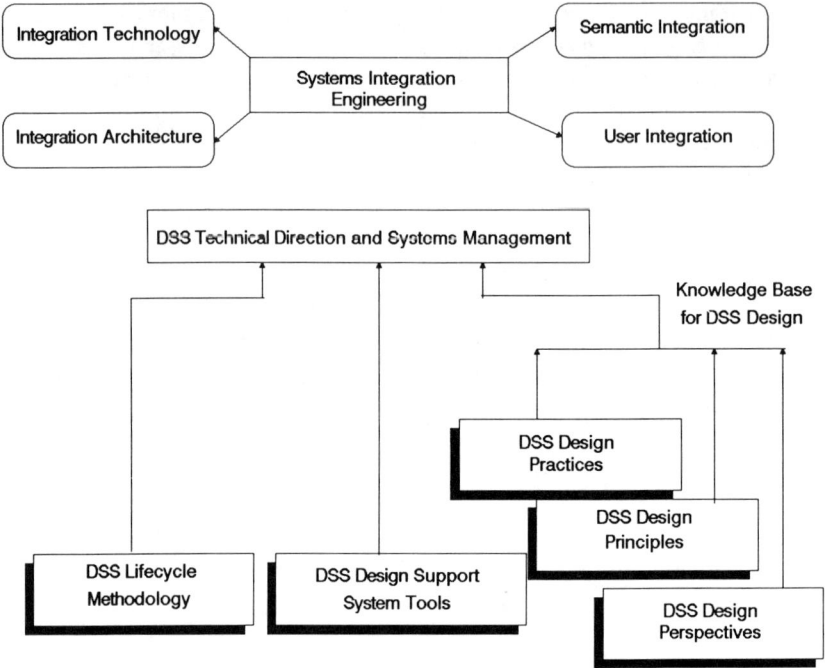

Figure 8.7 Principal knowledge ingredients in DSS integration and engineering.

4. Use of technologies that reduce DSS operating errors.
5. Information management for decision support rather than data-processing procedures.
6. Evolving needs in the computer and software applications environment of the future.

These evolving needs include

7. Providing rapid turnaround for (re)development of applications.
8. Describing the structure of multipurpose systems.
9. Accommodating multiple users in distributed locations.
10. Accommodating effective and efficient software maintenance.
11. Enabling efficient and effective system implementation.

These support specific organizational goals and objectives associated with DSS use [3] in

12. Ensuring that information resource management (IRM) plans, including DSS plans, are in centered on and support strategic plans, goals, and objectives.

13. Providing an overall understanding of strategic direction, context, and functions of the organization.
14. Developing an open information systems architecture that accurately reflects organizational information requirements.
15. Establishing a systemic framework that provides the foundations upon which integrated applications systems development can be based.
16. Planning and implementing an IRM and DSS strategy that is consistent with the supporting of organizational objectives.

Important to each of these is a knowledge of the DSS environment, as it evolves from organizational objectives. Figure 8.8 illustrates one view of some of the many linkages to an operational DSS. Information resource management, including DSS management, is quite dependent on environmental concerns. We now turn our attention to DSS environments.

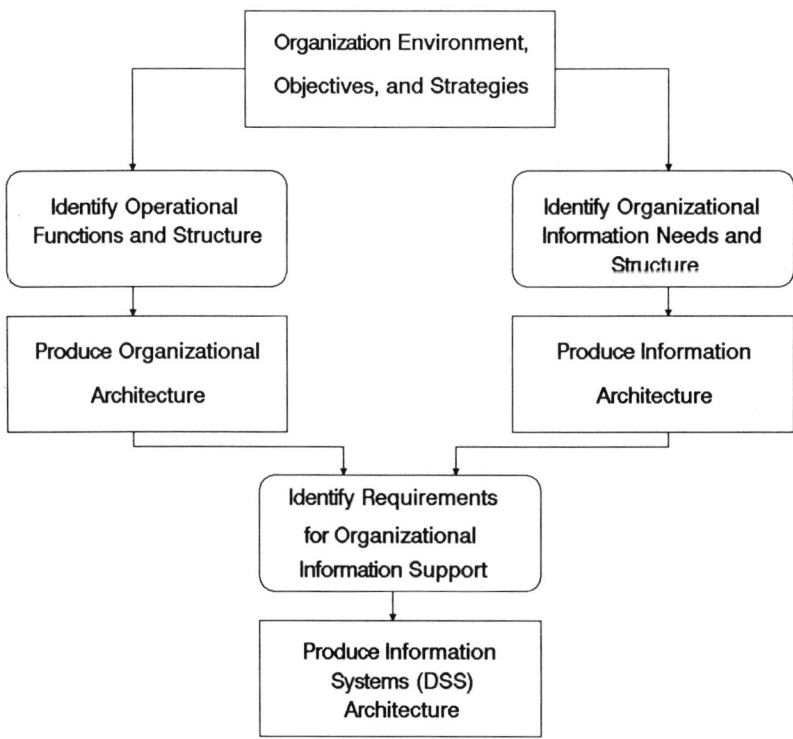

Figure 8.8 Information resource mangement (IRM) components as they evolve from organizational purpose.

8.4 DSS ENGINEERING DESIGN ENVIRONMENTS

In this section, we will discuss *environments* for the design of trustworthy and responsive systems, and decision support systems in particular. We will summarize existing work in this area. To bring about some specificity to the discussions, we will consider a relatively specific application domain. In this connection, we will discuss needs for and requirements to be satisfied by appropriate environments for the design of organizational or group decision support systems.

As we have noted, there are many environments relative to DSS. Here, we need to consider the environment of the designer of a DSS, and the environment of the user of the DSS. The expression *environment for systems design* extends over a wide collection of interpretations. At one end of the spectrum is an interpretation that suggests a set of *computer-aided system design tools* for DSS design, or perhaps just a classic collection of design approaches that have not been subject to computerization at all. At another end of the spectrum are uses of the term that imply an adjuvant that provides *machine intelligence* or *expert system* type support to aid systems design and development of a DSS, potentially through the entire life cycle of system evolution. These two notions are related. The first refers to the environment of the designer and the second to the environment of the client or system user. Still another common use of the term environment, that of *user environment*, relates to the *surroundings* in which the designed system will be used.

Needless to say, it will generally be difficult to understand the environment of the designer or the user sufficiently well such that it becomes possible to model either of them in the knowledge base of a support system. This becomes especially obvious when we realize that systems must not only be designed, but they must be *integrated* with other existing systems, and they must be *maintained* as a user's needs change over time.

For our purposes, we define environment as follows: *A system design and development environment is the set of methods, design methodologies, and systems management processes that, associated with the operational situation extant of the user, is used to produce a trustworthy system.* The methods portion of this definition represents those analytical tools that support the DSS design process.

It is potentially significant to note that this definition indicates that an appropriate DSS design engineering environment is *much more* than an integrated set of methods and tools, regardless of their sophistication, that are useful throughout the technical life cycle of a system. It is important, of course, to surround the system designer with a suitable set of tools, including such automated tools as DSS generators that can be used for rapid prototyping. But this alone will usually not be sufficient for the design of trustworthy systems that satisfy user needs, that are usable, and that will be used by the user.

A successful systems design team must necessarily be aware of appropriate methods, tools, and techniques. They need also to be aware of systems methodologies and design approaches that enable selection of appropriate methods, and appropriate human judgment at the cognitive process level of systems management. Hence, three functional components of systems design engineering are necessary:

- Systems science and operations research methods
- Systems methodology and design
- Systems management

Figure 8.9 shows an expanded conceptual model of the complete systems design engineering process that conceptually incorporates an awareness of the operational situation of the user. Thus, Figure 8.9 represents a conceptualization of an *environment for DSS design engineering*.

The term *methodology* has appeared in our discussions and it is important to discuss it. It is sometimes a misused word, even in systems engineering. It is not simply an overly sophisticated synonym for method. As we use it, a methodology is an open set of procedures for problem solving. Consequently, a methodology involves a set of methods, a set of activities, and a set of relations between the methods and the activities. To use a methodology we must have an appropriate set of methods. Generally, as we have indicated, these are the methods provided by systems and computer science and operations research. They include a variety of qualitative and quantitative approaches from a number of disciplines. Associated with a methodol-

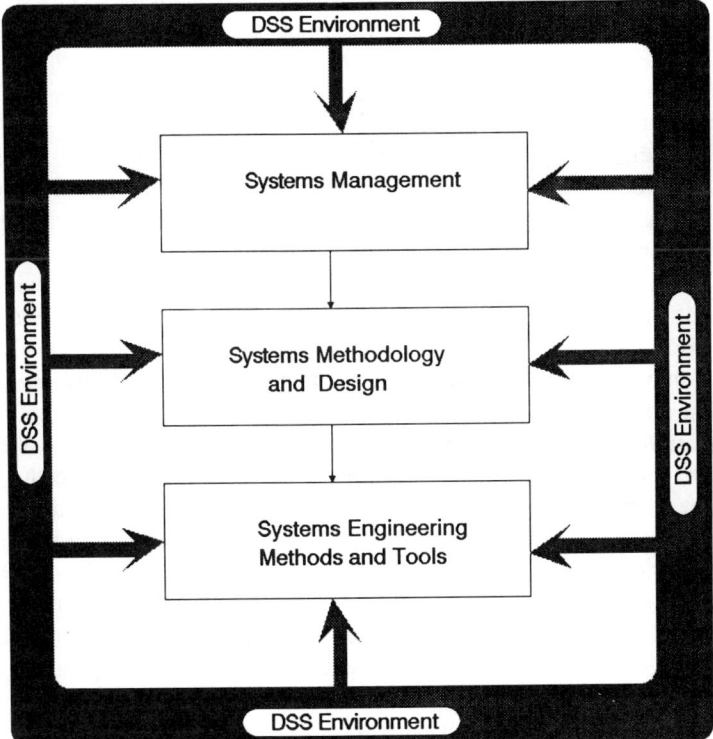

Figure 8.9 Three fundamental levels of DSS design engineering and the environment for DSS design.

ogy is a structured framework into which particular methods are associated for resolution of a specific issue.

DSS engineering efforts will also be concerned with technical direction and management throughout the life cycle that ranges across such phases as requirements specifications, systems design, production, and maintenance. By adopting the management technology of systems design engineering and applying it, we become very concerned with making sure that correct systems are designed, and not just that system designs are correct according to some possibly ill-conceived notions of what the system should do. Suitable tools to enable efficient and effective error prevention and detection in a systems design process will enhance the production of system designs that are correct. To ensure that correct systems are designed requires that considerable emphasis be placed on the front-end of the DSS life cycle, which involves issue or requirements identification, and on the environment for design.

In particular, there needs to be considerable emphasis on the accurate definition of the DSS, what it should do, and how people should interact with it after it is produced. This should occur *before* the system is produced and implemented in an organizational environment. In turn, this requires stress on conformance to system requirements specification, and the development of standards to ensure compatibility and integratability of system products. Such areas as documentation and communication are important in all of this. Therefore, we see the need for the technical direction and management technology efforts that comprise systems engineering. In previous discussions (also see Ref. 4), we have referred to the need for technological systems design and management systems design, and the appropriate use of design practices, principles, and perspectives.

To cope with these just-mentioned needs, a number of methodologies associated with systems design engineering have evolved. Through these, it has been possible to decompose large design issues into smaller component subsystem design issues, design the subsystems, and then *build* the complete system as a collection of these subsystems. Even so, problems remain. Just simply connecting the individual subsystems often does not result in a system that performs acceptably, from either a technological efficiency perspective, or an effectiveness perspective. This has led to the realization that *systems integration engineering* and *systems management* throughout an entire system life cycle will be necessary. Thus, it is that contemporary efforts in *systems engineering* contain a focus on tools and methods, on the system design methodology that enables suitable use of these tools, and on the systems management approaches that enables the embedding of design approaches within organizations and environments, such as to support the application of the principles of the physical and material sciences for the betterment of humankind. The use of appropriate tools, as well as systems methodology and management constructs, facilitates *system design for more efficient and effective human interaction* [5]. Clearly, this is a product of an effective systems design engineering environment. It is what we have attempted to describe in Figure 8.9.

A key issue in this is the design of critical technological systems and critical management systems to implement the technology so that human interaction concerns are dealt with in an effective way in a large variety of plausible contemporary environments in which a system is perceived to be a functionally useful component. Figure 8.10 illustrates this conceptually. The major task of DSS design is to ensure *appropriate* integration across the levels of people, technological systems, organizational systems, and environment such as to assure success in use of the DSS in resolving organizational decision issues. Exactly, this sort of perspective can be taken with respect to use of the DSS itself. Therefore, Figure 8.10 illustrates both the process of DSS design and the process of DSS use. Accordingly, *appropriate* is, here, a very multiattributed term that encompasses such features as risk management, reliability, and modifiability. Differences in the meaning of this term across designer and user groups, as well as the fact that the ultimate application for the DSS design team is the DSS whereas the ultimate application for the DSS user group is some set of specific organizational needs, each suggest that what is pragmatically seen in this figure is quite different across the two groups.

It is meaningful to discuss several types of design environments. One way to do this is to associate an environment with each of the seven phases of the systems life cycle that we discussed in Chapters 1 and 5:

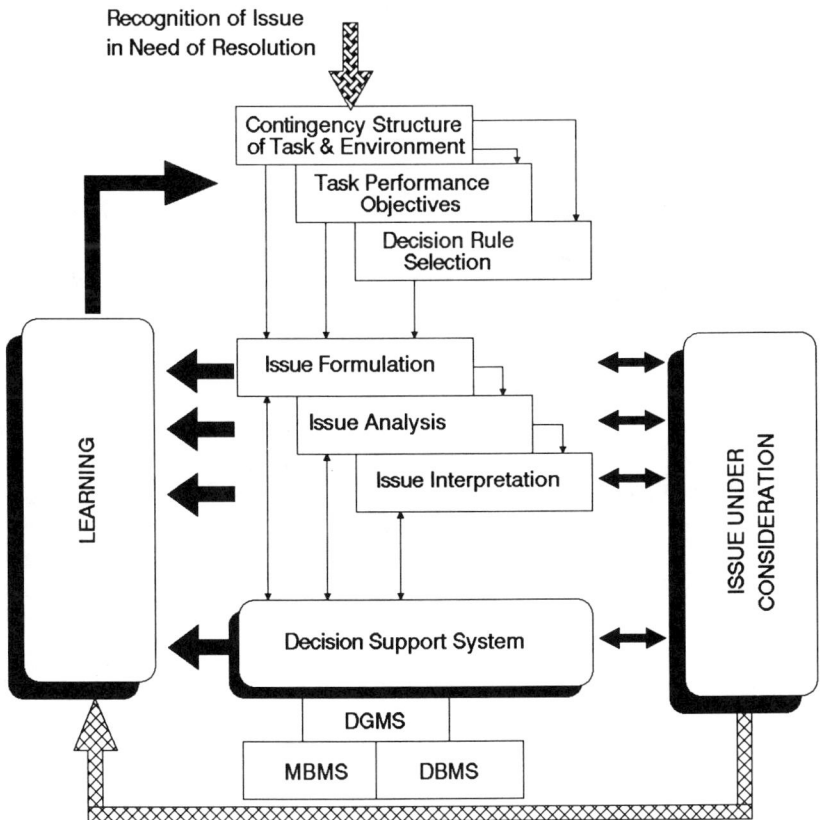

Figure 8.10 The process of decision support.

1. Requirements specifications identification environment
2. Preliminary conceptual design environment
3. Logical design and system architecture specification environment
4. Detailed design and testing environment
5. Operational implementation environment
6. Evaluation and modification environment
7. Operational deployment environment

It will clearly be difficult to provide tools, methodologies, and systems management processes that are invariant across each of these different environments. We would expect to find, therefore, that one specific environment would support the different phases of the system life cycle in differing amounts. At the level of tools, it is quite apparent that very general tools, such as text editors, will support all phases of the system life cycle. However, the support from such a tool may be so general that there is really little automation of the system development process, or achievement of standards of data interoperability.

To achieve truly useful DSS design environments, it seems a certainty that there will have to be specific tools that are primarily useful in only some system life-cycle phases. This suggests, strongly, the need for a systems engineering environment to support *transitioning* from one phase to the other, and to support integration and interoperability across phases and the products of different vendors.

The early phases of the system life cycle are conceptual formulation or *framing* type efforts in which the primary tasks are associated with problem or issue characterization and representation. Then follows a detailed design and analysis, or a *production*, sequence of phases in which a system is actually produced. The final phases in the system life cycle are devoted to interpretation and *evaluation* of the produced system and associated maintenance and modification of the system to make it more effective as time evolves. We can associate an environment with each of these, and we can also speak of a *generic* environment, and of tools associated with this environment. These tools would consist of general-purpose instruments that would be useful across the other more specialized environments. Figure 8.11 illustrates the general relationships among these environments.

We choose this notion of four environmental phases, since they so closely correspond to the general efforts of formulation, analysis, and interpretation that are the fundamental systems engineering steps. The fourth environment, a generic environment, corresponds to tools and support that are ubiquitous across the other three.

The framing environment consists of the tools, the methodologies, and the systems management procedures to accomplish the more conceptual parts of the DSS life cycle. Among the activities involved in these phases are

1. Identifying the need for a system.
2. Determining the general requirements for a system in terms of user needs.
3. Identifying design requirements for the system (conceptual design).

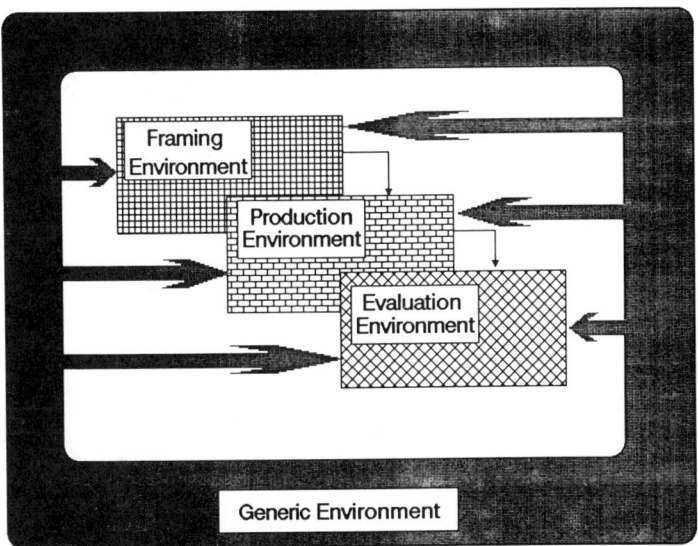

Figure 8.11 DSS support provided in various environments.

4. Determining functional and data requirements for the systems.
5. Identifying resource constraints on system design and development in terms of cost, delivery time, software, and hardware.
6. Performing a cost-effectiveness, or cost-benefit, analysis of the system.
7. Identifying a program and project development and management plan.

Identification or formulation, or *framing*, of an issue or problem is a necessary first step in any problem-solving process. A problem statement should always be identified before the application of solution methods. Often, there is considerable merit in identifying the problem in terms of a number of interdependent elements that can be characterized as one or more of the *issue-framing-elements*. These include

- *Problem definition* elements (needs, constraints, alterables)
- *Value system design* elements (objectives or objectives measures)
- *System synthesis elements* (activities or controls and activity measures)

DSS themselves are particularly useful DSS design support tools for framing environments. There are other tools and methodologies for use in the framing environment that more specifically relate to the translation of identified requirements specification into software technical requirements specifications, as discussed in Chapter 7 of Ref. 6. Figure 8.12 illustrates the production of a DSS in two fundamentally different ways, through the use of tools and through the use of a DSS generator. An expanded conceptual model of the complete DSS design engineering

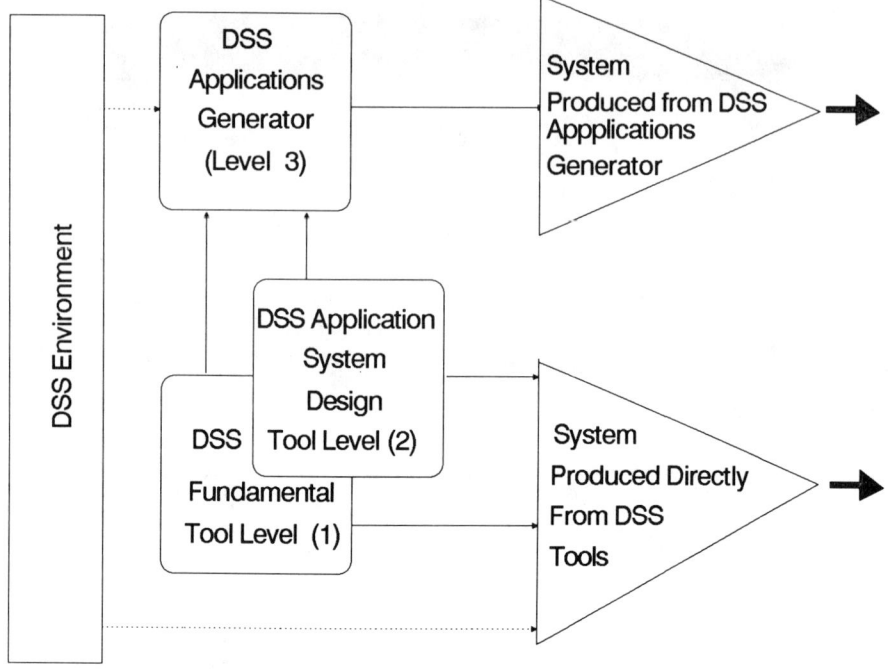

Figure 8.12 Three technology levels for DSS Design.

process conceptually incorporates an awareness of the operational situation of the user relative to the DSS. Hence, a conceptualization of an *environment for DSS design engineering* should include an awareness of both the environment of designers and of users.

Human concerns are especially important in the design of DSS of large scale and scope. These concerns are needed in order that we be able to accomplish the many tasks that will ensure an appropriate DSS:

1. Converting human performance requirements into engineering specifications.
2. Designing to identified human cognitive requirements and needs.
3. Accessing physiological and cognitive work-load potentials to the fullest.
4. Identifying human error potential at very early stages of preliminary system design.
5. Predicting human–system performance capabilities and limitations early enough in the life cycle so that these provide an input to design requirements.
6. Explicitly quantifying human performance factors such as to obtain system designs that are more appropriate for successful human interaction.

The U.S. Army Research Institute's *Hardware Manpower* (HARDMAN) tools [7] are designed to assist in this. These tools enable us to project manpower, personnel, and training requirements at an early phase in the system development life cycle as a function of several potential design strategies that might be adopted. At this early point in the system life cycle, the costs and other resources provided as inputs to a particular design can be analyzed to predict performance and ensure that systems function as intended. While system integration needs occur at later portions of the life cycle, attention to the four primary inputs at an early phase facilitates trade-offs between hardware and manpower when the cost involved is relatively low. It results in technological and management systems (this includes, but would not necessarily be limited to, a DSS) that enable machines to do what machines do well, and humans to do what humans do well.

We can take a methods-based view of *environment*. We can also take a *process* or systems management view. From this latter perspective, we would be concerned primarily with management of the overall systems design process, and with identifying and providing rules and procedures to govern the tasks performed within the environment. In this sense, the process view includes the methods or technological perspective.

The primary objective of the development and use of a DSS design engineering environment is to develop an integrated suite of analysis and design tools, methodologies, and systems management processes that support the efficient and effective design of DSS. The DSS design environment, for automated or prototype DSS design, should have six major functional elements:

1. A system builder or system generator that selects appropriate algorithms and software packages.
2. Data retrieval, entry, and editing capability to allow relevant design data and information to be used by the selected DSS design algorithms.
3. Exercise of the specific DSS design algorithms that are selected to be used for a particular application.
4. Generation of output displays and reports, and presentation of these to the user.
5. A user–system–designer interface to support human–machine communication from both conceptual and linguistic points of view and to assist the system user in efficient and effective use of the resulting *prototype* system such as to enable iterative adjustments toward a *better* system.
6. A knowledge-base life-cycle assistant to determine the implications of design changes throughout the DSS development life cycle.

It may also turn out that decision trees and spreadsheets are effective representations for analytic calculations but not for presentations to the DSS user. Graphic displays, and frame-and-script-type presentations may well be more understandable. For example, the system user may find it much easier to select effective courses of action when domination digraphs of alternative courses of action are presented. A production-rule type representation of implementation plans may well be more easily appreciated than the equivalent presentation in the form of decision-tree-type smart checklists. Thus, it may be appropriate to use these smart checklists and spreadsheets as aids for the analyst, and as convenient data-base representations of decisions and plans, but to use alternative representations for display to the system user.

Methods used to assist the system user in identifying alternative courses of action or alternative designs may play a major role in enhancing the effectiveness of a DSS in an environnment such as the one described here. Often, the initial generation of alternative courses of action is in a very wholistic form and heavily based on experiential familiarity and perceptual feelings relative to the design task at hand. We see that these are closely associated with the *evaluation environment* for systems design and development that we discussed earlier in this chapter.

Generally, neither DSS designers nor DSS users are very knowledgeable about all characteristics of the end system under consideration. This is because they will not have sufficient experiential familiarity with the knowledge domains of the other group to enable full appreciation of the implications of DSS design and development decisions. This is one of the primary purposes of the *DSS design support environment* and why one is quite needed. A purpose of this section is to specify some of the needed features for this environment.

The function and purpose of a design support facility are such that they will facilitate rapid and interactive cycling through the steps and life-cycle phases of DSS design and management activity. The facility will therefore enable and enhance application of the macro-enhancement approaches based on the DSS generator.

8.5 DSS EFFECTS ON THE ENVIRONMENT

It is important to also consider the impacts that DSS, and other forms of contemporary information technology, have on the environment. Huber [8], in an insightful article, identifies 14 propositions that relate to the effect of information technologies on

1. Organizations
    1.1. Subunit structure and processes
    1.2. Organizational structure and processes
    1.3. Organizational memory
2. Organizational situation assessment and decision making

The first three of the propositions deal with the effects on subunit structure and processes:

P1. Use of information and DSS technology leads to a larger number and variety of people participating as information sources in the making of decisions.

P2. Use of information and DSS technology leads to decreases in the number and variety of people comprising the traditional face-to-face decision unit.

P3. Use of information and DSS technology results in less of the organization's time being absorbed by decision-related meetings.

The next six propositions deal with the organization as a whole:

> P4. Use of information and DSS technology in a given organization leads to a more uniform distribution, across organizational levels, of the probability that a specific organizational level will make a particular decision.*
>
> P5. Use of information and DSS technology leads to a greater variation across organizations in the levels at which a particular type of decision is made.
>
> P6. Use of information and DSS technology reduces the number of organizational levels involved in authorizing proposed organizational actions.
>
> P7. Use of information and DSS technology leads to fewer intermediate nodes within organizational information-processing networks.†
>
> P8. Availability of information technology leads to more frequent development and use of computerized data bases as components of organizational memory.
>
> P9. There will be more frequent development and use of in-house expert systems as components of organizational memories.

The following two propositons deal with situation assessment:

> P10. Use of information and DSS technology leads to more rapid and more accurate identification of problems and opportunities.
>
> P11. Use of information and DSS technology leads to organizational situation assessment that is more accurate, comprehensive, timely, and available.

The final three propositions deal with information technology effects on decision making:

> P12. Use of information and DSS technology leads to higher-quality decisions.
>
> P13. Use of information and DSS technology reduces the time required to authorize proposed organizational actions.
>
> P14. Use of information and DSS technology reduces the time required to make decisions.

On the basis of these 14 propositions, Huber identifies five elements or constructs, and obtains a causal structural model as shown in Figure 8.13. This is a fitting concluding picture for this chapter, and this text, as it does indicate the considerable role that modern information and decision support technology can be expected to have in present and future organizational environments.

---

*Two corollaries follow from this proposition. One states that use of information and DSS technology will lead to more decentralization in a highly centralized organization, and to more centralization in a highly decentralized organization.

†As a corollary to this proposition, use of information and DSS technology will result in a reduction of the number of organizational levels involved in processing messages.

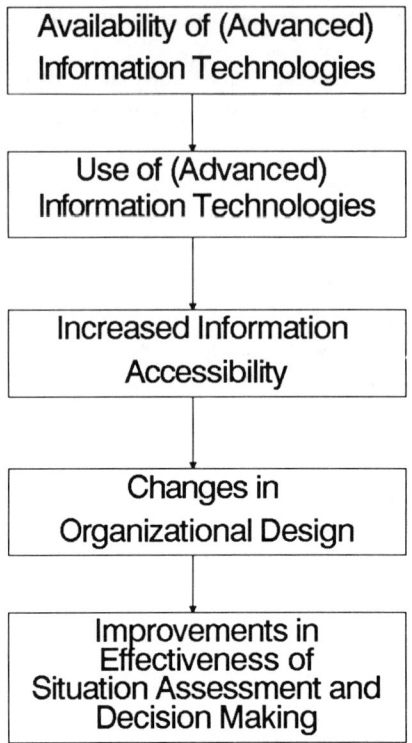

Figure 8.13 Causal structural model of the effects of information technology and DSS on situation assessment and decision making in organization.

8.6 SUMMARY

Quite a bit of territory has been covered in this brief chapter. We began with a discussion of system integration concerns associated with operational implementation of decision support systems. We saw that a critical need is to have a development environment that supports system integration. This led to the topics of DSS engineering environments, and the role and value of DSS in future organizational environments [9].

PROBLEMS

8.1. There are two very popular word-processsing software packages in a large office, and the number of users of each package is approximately the same. Often, there is a need for a report that has been prepared using one format to be used in the other. The office management is concerned with whether to standardize on a single word-processing package or to develop software that will allow data interoperability across packages.

a. Prepare a brief report outlining how an appropriate judgment could be reached concerning which alternative to adopt.

b. Assume that the decision to provide for data exchange between the two formats has been made. Discuss several possibilities for doing this and provide a cost-benefit analysis of each of these alternatives.

8.2. Develop a checklist of activities to be accomplished when operational implementation of a DSS is to be achieved. Discuss the relationships among the activities in your checklist. When in the development life cycle should these activities have been identified?

8.3. Discuss the relationship between DSS *implementation and integration* efforts and *maintenance* efforts.

8.4. Describe the cost influencers for DSS integration. Generally, development changes that change costs at one phase of the DSS life cycle will have offsetting effects at other phases. Prepare a report indicating the trade-off concerns associated with changing the resources allocated to implementation and integration.

8.5. Discuss the statement, *"A DSS development life cycle with lower integration costs is always to be preferred to one with higher integration costs."*

8.6. What trade-offs would you expect among *system integration and implementation* and *system maintenance*? Is it possible that lack of attention to integration will increase maintenance costs?

8.7. Identify how design practices, design principles, and design perspectives may be, or perhaps have been, used to develop a DSS for an application with which you are familiar.

8.8. How do the *framing, production*, and *evaluation* environments differ? What generic support tools would be most appropriate for each environment?

8.9. A DSS could be developed for a large corporation by purchasing hardware and then engaging a software development team to design appropriate software. Alternatively, one could be developed by enforcing a contract requirement that no new software products be developed, except for small utility programs, and that all software satisfy an "in-production in-use" requirement that the software exist in the commercial marketplace a month or so before contract proposals are due. The purpose of this requirement would be to avoid *vaporware*. Contrast and compare the two approaches.

8.10. Is the assumption in the preceding problem that the hardware be purchased before the software is developed, or procured, a good one? Redo the problem using the requirement that hardware and software systems be developed or procured together.

8.11. Examine the 14 propositions identified by Huber. What potentially confirming reasons can you think of for each hypothesis? Can you think of any potentially disconfirming information that might refute one or more of the hypotheses?

References

[1] Power, L. R., "Post-Facto Integration Technology: New Discipline for an Old Practice," *Proceedings of the First International Conference on Systems Integration*, IEEE Computer Society Press, Silver Spring MD, April 1990, pp. 4–13.

[2] Nilsson, E. G., Nordhagen, E. K., and Oftedal, G., "Aspects of Systems Integration," *Proceedings of the First International Conference on Systems Integration*, IEEE Computer Society Press, Silver Spring MD, April 1990, pp. 434–443.

[3] Singh, I. B., and Beyer, R. C., "Information Resource Planning Methodology: A Case Study," *Proceedings of the First International Conference on Systems Integration*, IEEE Computer Society Press, Silver Spring MD, April 1990, pp. 634–642.

[4] Sage, A. P., "Knowledge Transfer: An Innovative Role for Information Systems Engineering Education," *IEEE Transactions on Systems, Man and Cybernetics*, Vol. 17, No. 5, September 1987, pp. 725–728.

[5] Sage, A. P. (Ed.), *System Design for Human Interaction*, IEEE Press, New York, 1987.

[6] Sage, A. P., and Palmer, J. D., *Software Systems Engineering*, Wiley, New York, 1990.

[7] Boorer, H. (Ed.), *People, Machines, and Organizations: A MANPRINT Approach to System Integration*, Van Nostrand Reinhold, New York, 1990.

[8] Huber, G. P., "A Theory of the Effects of Advanced Information Technologies on Organizational Design, Intelligence, and Decision Making," *Academy of Management Review*, Vol. 15, No. 1, January 1990, pp. 47–71.

[9] Strassman, P. A., *The Business Value of Computers*, Information Economics Press, New Canaan, CT, 1990.

Index

Abstraction, 273
Action language, 131, 133
Activities:
    enactment, 230
    retention, 230
    selection, 230
Adaptive user interface, ATI, 149
Adelman, L., 91, 104, 127, 188, 203
Advanced beginner, 219
Advanced data models, 70
Allison, G., 245, 261
Alter, S. L., 1, 36
Altman, R., 72, 80
Ambiguity, 272, 273
Analysis, 10, 11, 88, 170, 287
Analytic model, 245
Anchoring and adjustment, 249
Anderson, J. R., 206, 257
Andriole, S. J., 1, 36
Anthony, R. N., 2, 36, 267, 306
Applegate, L. M., 29, 38, 82, 126, 290, 307
Architectural specifications, 168
Architecture, integration, 319
Arden, B. W., 42, 63, 78
Argyris, C., 231, 233, 260
ARIADNE, 106, 197
Arrow, K., 95
Ashby, W. R., 156, 160
Ashby's law, 156
Aspiration level, 237
Assembly structures, 64
Attention, 208, 209

Attributes, 68
    of hypotheses, 270
    of information, 268
Atzeni, P., 58, 79
Availability, 235, 249
Azjin, I., 226, 259

Barbosa, L. C., 121, 128
Barnard, C. I., 228, 259
Baron, J., 20, 37, 299, 308
Barr, S. H., 189, 203
Base rate, 249
Baserman, M. H., 261, 247
Behavior:
    formal knowledge-based, 214
    goal-oriented, 282
    implementation, 282
    initiation, 282
    integrative, 282
    process, 282
    rule-based, 214
    skill-based, 214
Behaviorally consistent information set, BCIS, 107
Beizer, B., 188, 203
Benbasat, I., 200, 204
Bennett, J. L., 131, 159
Bettman, J. R., 206, 258
Beyer, R. C., 224, 320
Beyth-Marom, R., 252, 262
Blakeslee, T. R., 226, 259
Blanchard, B. S., 92, 127

335

Blanning, R. W., 123, 128
Bobrow, D. G., 26, 29, 37, 273, 281, 290, 307
Boff, K. R., 177, 203
Booch, G., 63, 65, 79
Boorer, H., 328, 334
Boudwin, N. K., 90, 127
Bounded rationality, 237
Bourgeois, L. J., 194, 203
Brainerd, C. J., 212, 258
Brainstorming, 85
Brehmer, B., 91, 104, 127, 227, 259, 305, 308
Broadbent, D. W., 222, 258
Brobst, S. A., 29, 38, 290, 307
Brodie, M. L., 62, 79
Brunswick, E., 156, 227, 259
Bullen, C. V., 174, 202
Bureaucratic politics, 240

Cabinet war room, 264
Calderwood, R., 18, 19, 37
Calendar management, 277
Campbell, D. T., 190, 203
Card, S. K., 144, 146, 152, 160
Carley, K., 244, 261
Carlson, E. D., 7, 9, 13, 36, 50, 79, 82, 126, 133, 138, 159, 172, 178, 197, 202
Cartwright, D., 58, 79
Case-study evaluation, 193
Casual loop diagrams, 86
Categorization, 270
Cats-Baril, W. L., 28, 37, 189, 203
Ceri, S., 72, 80
Chand, D. R., 177, 203
Characteristics, designer, 162
Charette, R. N., 34, 38, 177, 203
Chen, P. P. S., 58, 79
Chen, T. T., 29, 38, 290, 307
Chignell, M., 62, 66, 70, 79
Choice, 227
Churchman, C. W., 245, 261, 264
Clark, C. M., 73, 80
Classification structures, 64
Coad, P., 64, 69, 79
Codd, E. F., 44, 53, 79
Cognition(s):
  higher-order, 206
  lower-order, 207
  cold, 222
  hot, 222
Cognitive illusions, 254
Cognitive model, 245
Cognitive validation phase, 211
Cohen, L. J., 20, 37, 254, 260, 262, 299, 308
Cohen, M. D., 29, 38, 242, 243, 290, 307

Colab, 277, 281
Collaboration laboratory, 281
Collective inquiry, 85, 285, 287
Command language, 134, 141
Command language grammar, CLG, 140, 149
Commitment, 220, 221
Communication structures, 280
Competence, 219
Components:
  environmental, 265
  process, 265
  technological, 265
Computation, 133
Computer-aided software engineering, CASE, 58, 163
Computer-supported conferences, 278, 279
Conceptual design, 168
Conceptual model, 45
Confirmation bias, 249
Conflict analysis, 89
Conflict mode, 223
Conjunction fallacy, 252
Conservatism, 250
Consistency, 147
Contingency task structure, 196
Control mechanisms, 12, 133, 179
Conversational structuring, 279
Cooperative data-base management, 72
Coordination structures, 280
Craik, F. I. M., 226, 259
Critical success factors, 174
Crocker, J., 227, 259
Cross interaction matrix, 86
Cuban missile crisis, 245, 272
Cybernetic model, 245
Cyert, R. M., 229, 241, 259, 260
C^{++}, 66

Daft, R. L., 274, 275, 306, 307
Data abstraction, 62
Data as models, 125
Data-base administrator, DBA, 43, 49
Data-base architecture, 44
Data-base management system, DMBS, 1, 7, 13, 39, 81, 131
Data definition language, DDL, 42, 45, 49
Data dictionary, 47
Data directory, 47
Data entry, 142
Data fusion, 44
Data independence, 39, 42, 69
Data manipulation language, DML, 46, 49
Data model, 13, 44
Data presentation context, 250

INDEX

Data protection, 143
Data query language, DQL, 49
Data redundancy reduction, 39, 69
Data resource control, 39, 69
Data saturation, 250
Data structures, 13, 49
Data transforms, 46
Data transmission, 143
Date, C. J., 14, 36, 44, 53, 79
Davis, A. M., 177, 202
Davis, G. B., 174, 175, 202
Dawes, R. M., 104, 128
Day, M. C., 212, 258
dBase, 50
Debiasing, 253
Decision analysis, 91, 93
Decision conference facility, 281
Decision conflict, 223
Decision flight, 243
Decision making:
  distributed, 292
  proficiency, 217
  under risk, 94
Decision models, 93
Decision paradigm, 220, 221
Decision rooms, 264
Decision situations, 245
Decision support process, 325
Decision support system environments, 309, 330
Decision taxonomy, 267
Decker, K. S., 21, 37
Defensive avoidance, 223
Dekel, S., 252, 262
Delbecq, A. L., 85, 127
Delphi, 85
DeSanctis, G., 21, 28, 37, 282, 288, 305, 307
Design:
  environments for, 322
  factorial, 189
  GDSS, 26, 275
  phases of, 11
  postfacto, 318
  prefacto, 318
Design process, 161
Desire for self-fulfilling prophecies, 250
Detailed design, 168, 184
Device level, 140
Dialectical inquiry system, 246
Dialog, 133
  sequential, 134
Dialog generation, 139
Dialog generation and management system, DGMS, 1, 7, 15, 131
Dialog independence, 148

Dialog management, 133
Diesing, P., 235, 260
Direct manipulation interface, 142
Discrete even simulation, 90
Distributed data-base, 69, 71
Distributed DSS, 300
Distributed GDSS design, 294
Distributed information systems, 21
Distributed system, 292
Dolk, D. R., 125, 129
Dominance digraphs, 108, 110
Dominance structure, 105
Dozono, S., 120, 128, 194, 197, 204
Dreyfus, H. L., 218, 220, 258
Dreyfus, S. E., 218, 220, 258
DSS, distributed, 300
DSS design, technology levels for, 328
DSS effects on environment, 309, 330
DSS implementation, management of, 315
DSS system architecture, 313
Duchon, D., 194, 203
Duncan, K., 153, 157, 160
Dyer, J. S., 125, 129
Dynamic binding, 62

Ease of recall, 250
Ecological interface design, EID, 155
Econometrics, 89
Edwards, W., 101, 104, 127, 128, 254, 262
Effectiveness, DSS, 201
Einhorn, H. J., 247, 252, 261, 262
Electronic boardroom, 264, 281
Elimination by aspects, 92
Empirical, 188
Emshoff, J. R., 246, 261
Ends and means, 241
Engelbart, C. D., 264
Entity–relationship (ER) model, 57
Environment, 31, 33, 162, 326
  enacted, 229
  system design and development, 30, 177, 322
Equivocality, 25, 229, 266, 273, 274
Error, 192
Espoused theories of action, 233
Estes, W. K., 206, 257
Estimation theory, 90
Etzioni, A., 228, 259
Evaluation, 184
Evaluation, DBMS, 72
Evaluation, GDSS, 302
Evaluation of interfaces, 150
Evaluation protocol, 195
Evans, M. W., 34, 38
Event predictions, 270

Evidence, 271
Executive support system, 263
Expectations, 250
Experiments, factorial, 189
Expert data-base model, 61
Expert system, 3, 124
Expertise, 219
Explanation building, 194
Explanations, 270
Explanatory and predictive power, 256
Extensible data models, 70
External dialog software, 148
External model, 45
Eysenck, M. W., 106, 258

Fabrycky, W. J., 92, 127
Face-to-face meetings, 276, 281
Facilitation, 284
Factors, spurious, 191
Fact-value confusion, 250
False alarm, 192
Familiarity, experiential, 162
Feedback, information, 227
Feldman, M. S., 23, 24, 37, 235, 260
File management systems, FMS, 50
File processing systems, FPS, 50
Fishbein, M., 226, 259
Fishburn, P. C., 104, 128
Fiske, S. T., 227, 259
Flavell, J. H., 212, 258
Flavors, 66
Flores, F., 279, 307
Forecasting, 89, 270
Formal reasoning, 2
Forms, 131, 141
Formulation, 10, 11, 170, 287
Foster, G., 26, 29, 37, 273, 281, 290, 307
Frameworks, 167, 196
Framing, 326
Fraser, N. M., 89, 93, 127
Fulk, J., 305, 308
Functional decomposition, 63
Fundamental attribution error, 250

Galing, B., 171, 202
Gallupe, R. B., 21, 28, 37, 282, 288, 305, 307
Gamblers' fallacy, 250
Gaming, 89
Gantt charts, 92
GDSS:
    distributed, 293, 294
    level I, 283
    level II, 283
    level III, 283

GemStone, 62
Generative phase, 211
Generator, decision support, 8, 162
Genetic epistemology, 211
Geoffrion, A., 58, 79, 123, 124, 129
Ginsburg, H., 212, 258
Goals, operators, methods, and selection, GOMS, 146
Goldberg, A., 69, 79
Gould, J. D., 152, 160
Grant, K. R., 29, 38, 290, 307
Gray, P., 264, 306
Greenberg, H. J., 124, 129
Gregory, L., 226, 259
Group, advantages of, 286
Group, disadvantages of, 286
Group authoring, 277
Group consensus, 282
Group decision support system, GDSS, 21, 263, 276
Group memory management, 279
Group network facility, 281
Groupthink, 231, 286
Groupware, 276
Grudin, J., 147, 160
Gustafson, D. H., 85, 127

Ha, Y. W., 252, 262
Habit, 250
Hagafors, R., 227, 259
Hall, A. D., 83, 126
Hall, R. H., 228, 259
Halpin, S. M., 1, 36
Hamlin, G., 160
Hammond, K. R., 91, 104, 127, 160, 227, 259
Harary, F., 58, 79
HARDMAN, 328
Harrison, H. R., 133, 148, 150, 159
Harrison, M., 144, 146, 160
Haye, J., 228, 259
Heninger, K. L., 177, 202
Henrion, M., 256, 262
Herik, G. M., 306
Hershey, E. A., 173, 202
Hersko, R. G., 121, 128
Heuristics, 2
Hierarchical model, 54, 56
Hillier, F. S., 90, 127
Hiltz, S. R., 262, 307
Hindsight, 250
Hipel, K. W., 89, 93, 127
Hix, D., 133, 148, 150, 158, 160
Ho, J. L., 83, 126
Hogarth, R. M., 20, 37, 252, 261, 262

INDEX 339

Holistic evaluation, 2
Holistic reasoning, 2
Hollan, J. D., 136, 137, 159
Howard, R., 87, 127
Huber, G. P., 28, 37, 189, 203, 226, 233, 234, 259, 260, 264, 288, 292, 293, 306, 307, 330, 334
Human information processing, 206, 226
Human information processing biases, 247
Human-computer interface, 148
Hurth, P., 272, 306
Hutchins, E. L., 136, 137, 159
Hwang, S., 124, 129
Hypermedia, 279
Hypertext, 279
Hypervigilance, 223
Hypotheses, 269, 270
Hypothesis testing, 90

Illusion of control, 250
Illusion of correlation, 251
Impact assessment, 88
Implementation, DSS, 184, 310
Imprecise information, 104
Incrementalism, 240
Individual record model, 50, 51
Individuating information, 249
Information:
    attributes of, 4, 268
    value, 173
Information center, 281
Information display, 142
Information hiding, 62
Information presentation, 21
Information processing:
    characteristics, 16
    imperfections, 272
    organizational, 228, 235
Information processing models, 206
Information-processing realities, 296
Information representations, 133
Information requirements determination, 174, 177
Information requirements for design, 171
Information resource management, IRM, 321
Information-retention, 274
Information selection, 274
Information sharing, 299
Information technology, 6
Information value, 24
Inheritance, 62, 63
Input–output analysis, 89
Inquiry system, 245, 246
Integration, semantic, 319
Integrity rules, 49

Interaction, group, 282
Interaction styles, 134
Interface, 133
    direct manipulation, 135
Interface function models, IFMs, 148
Interface purposeful models, IMPSs, 149
Interface structural models, ISMs, 148
Internal dialog software, 148
Internal model, 45
Interpretation, 10, 11, 91, 170, 287
Interpretive structural modeling, 124
Intuitive affect, 16
Issue formulation, 83
Issue-framing-elements, 327

Janis, I. L., 17, 37, 222, 223, 224, 231, 258, 259, 272, 306
Jarvenpaa, S., 292, 293, 307
Jepson, C., 252, 261
Johansen, R., 263, 276, 281, 305, 306
Johnson, G., 150, 160
Joins, 123
Judgment, 227
Judgmental perspectives, 17

Kahn, K., 26, 29, 37, 273, 281, 290, 307
Kahneman, D., 20, 37, 247, 249, 253, 254, 261
Kantorowitz, E., 149, 160
Kaplan, B., 194, 203
Karimi, J., 149, 160
Keen, P. G. W., 4, 36, 200, 204, 233, 234, 260, 268, 306
Keller, L. R., 83, 126, 255, 262
Kendall, K. E., 159
Kenney, R. L., 91, 103, 127
Kent, W., 57, 79
Kerschberg, L., 58, 62, 79
Khoshafian, S., 62, 66, 70, 79
King, J. L., 263, 275, 281, 282, 305, 306, 307
Klayman, J., 252, 262
Klein, G. A., 18, 19, 37, 217, 218, 258, 270, 298, 306, 308
Knowledge acquisition, 21
Knowledge base, 25, 31, 131, 291
Konsynski, B. R., 29, 38, 290, 307
Kraemer, K. L., 263, 281, 282, 302, 303, 304, 305, 306
Krantz, D. H., 252, 261
Kruglanski, A. W., 211, 258
Kumar, K., 199, 204
Kumar, V., 29, 125
Kunda, Z., 252, 261
Kuo, F. Y., 149, 160
Kyburg, H. E., 20, 37, 299, 308

Lagamasino, A., 171, 202
Language, natural, 135
Language extensions, 66
Lanning, S., 26, 29, 37, 273, 281, 290, 307
Larkin, J. H., 17, 37
Larsen, J. B., 125, 129
Law of small numbers, 251
Leal, A., 106, 128
Learning, double-loop, 232
Learning, organizational, 230
Learning, single-loop, 231
Lee, A. S., 194, 203
Lee, E., 150, 160
Lengel, R. H., 274, 307
Leone, R. P., 125, 129
Leplat, J., 153, 157, 160, 305, 308
Level:
  applications, 153
  dialog, 153
  presentation, 153
Lewis, C., 152, 160
Lexical level, 140
Lexicographic ordering, 105
Liang, B. T., 293, 308
Liang, T. P., 121, 128
Lieberman, G. J., 90, 127
Lifecycle, 83, 163
Lifecycle phases, 167, 180, 326
Lindblom, C. E., 240, 260
Linstone, H. A., 245, 261
Location iindependence, 70
Logical data independence, 42
Logical record, 44
Long-term memory, 208
Lorin, H., 72, 80
Lossy joins, 123
Lottery, 95, 99
Luce, R. D., 100, 127, 129
Lund, R. N., 125, 129

McDaniel, R. R., 288, 307
McDonnel, J. C., 189, 203
McGrath, J. E., 85, 127
McKeen, J. D., 174, 202
Macroeconomic models, 89
Maintenance, 187
Maiser, D., 62, 79
Makridakis, S., 252, 261
Malone, T. W., 29, 38, 279, 280, 290, 307
Management control decisions, 2
Management information requirements analysis, 173
Management information system, 5

Mandler, G., 206, 258
Manipulation, direct, 135
Mann, L., 17, 37, 222, 223, 224, 258, 272
Mappings, 45
March, J. G., 23, 24, 37, 227, 229, 235, 241, 242, 244, 259, 260, 261, 272, 273, 306
Markov decision models, 91
Markus, M. L., 194, 203
Martin, J., 14, 36, 73, 80
Mason, R. O., 246, 261
Mastery, 220
Mathematical programming, 90
Mathematical thoeory of relations, 123
Matheson, J. E., 87, 127
Matrix, interaction, 86
Mayer, R. E., 206, 258
MBMS attributes, 121
MBMS functions, 294
Means–ends analysis, 241
Measures, 198
  productivity, 197
Media:
  input, 138
  output, 138
Memory, 207, 208
Memory aids, 12, 179
Mental attributes, 220
Mental functions, 220
Mental tasks, 220
Menu selection, 134, 140
Message handling, 63
Messages, 68
Metersky, M. L., 197, 204
Methodology, 167
Methods, measurement, 196
Microeconomic models, 89
MicroSTEP, 50
Miller, G. A., 208, 258
Mintzberg, H., 6, 20, 36, 228, 237, 259
Miss, 192
Mitroff, I. I., 246, 261
Mixed scanning, 111
Model(s), 82, 88, 134
  garbage can, 242
  time-stress based, 222
Model-base management systems, MBMS, 1, 7, 14, 81, 120, 131
Model-base query languages, 123
Model human information processor, 145
Modeling, 88
  structured, 86
Model mappings, 46
Molich, R., 151, 152, 159
Monitoring, 221

Moran, T. P., 140, 144, 146, 147, 149, 150, 152, 159, 169
Morgan, M. G., 256, 262
Morgenstern, O., 104, 128
Morris, W., 255, 262
Mosier, J. N., 142, 143, 145, 159, 201
Mouse, 134
Mullender, S., 72, 80
Multiple-attribute utility theory, MAUT, 91, 103
Murphy, F. H., 124, 129
Mylopoulos, J., 62, 79

Nadler, D. A., 234, 260
Nadler, G., 167, 202
Natural language, 142
Naumann, J. D., 174, 202
Network model, 57
Network structure, 55
Newell, A., 144, 146, 152, 160
Nielsen, J., 151, 152, 159, 160, 279, 307
Nilsson, E. G., 318, 333
Nisbett, R. E., 252, 261
Nominal group technique, NGT, 85, 285
Nondominated alternatives, 105
Nordhagen, E. K., 318, 333
Norman, D. A., 135, 136, 137, 146, 159, 256, 262
Norman, R. Z., 58, 79
Novel language usage, 66
Novice, 219
Nunamaker, J. F., 290, 307

Object decomposition, 63
Object identity, 62
Objective C, 66
Objectives, DBMS, 81, 82
Objects, 68
Object-oriented data base, OODB, 62
Object-oriented graphical interfaces, 63
Object-oriented style, 66
Oftdal, G., 318, 333
Olfman, L., 264, 306
Olsen, J. P., 242, 261
Operational control decisions, 2
Operational deployment, 169, 186
Operational evaluation, 169
Operational implementation, 309
Operational performance decisions, 2
Operational test and evaluation, 184
Operations, 12, 49, 68, 179
Opper, S., 212, 258
Optimum systems control, 90
Oracle, 50
Order effects, 251

Organization, 266
  definitions, 229
  environment, 309
Organizational decision support systems, ODSS, 263
Organizational information processing, 235
Organizational process model, 241
Outcome-irrelevant learning system, 251
Overconfidence, 251

Padgett, J., 243, 261
Palmer, J. D., 34, 163, 188, 202
Palmer, K. H., 90, 127
Panic, 223
Parsaye, K., 62, 66, 70, 79
Partisan mutual adjustment, 240
Partitioning, 63
Pattern matching, 194
Pattern recognition, 209
Patton, H. A., 90, 127
Payoff matrix, 97
Pearl, J., 106, 128, 254, 262
Pelagatti, G., 72, 80
Perception, 208, 209
Perspective, 220, 221, 235
Phases, lifecycle, 180, 326
Phillips, L., 254, 262
Physical data independence, 42
Physiological information processing, 209
Piaget, Jean, 205, 211
Picturephone, 281
Pinsonneault, A., 302, 303, 304, 308
Pitz, G. F., 197, 198, 204
Placebos, 191
Planning laboratory, 264
Policy capture, 91
Political process model, 241
Polson, P. G., 146, 160
Poole, M. S., 282, 307
Power, L. R., 318, 333
Predictive management information system, 5
Preliminary conceptual design, 168, 182
Presentation language, 131
Presentation support software, 276
Probability, Pascalian, 254
Problem, formulation, 83
Problem, definition, 83
Problem statement language, 173
Process, DSS, 187
Processing, information, 266
Process measures, 198
Proficiency, 219
Proficient decision style, 218
Project and network planning, 92

Project management software, 277
Projection, 63
Prototype, 148, 168

Query language, QL, 49, 135
Question, trigger, 285
Questionnaires, 85
Queuing theory, 90
Quinton, H., 246, 261

Raiffa, H., 91, 100, 127
Rajala, D. W., 106, 128
Rao, V., 292, 293, 307
Rapid prototyping, 168
Rasmussen, J., 17, 37, 153, 154, 155, 156, 157, 160, 214, 215, 216, 258, 271, 297, 305, 306, 308
Rationality:
  bounded, 237, 272
  economic, 236
  garbage can, 242
  legal, 239
  muddling through, 240
  organizational processes, 241
  perspectives, 205
  political, 239, 241
  procedural, 239
  social, 238
  substantive, 239
  technical, 236
Ravden, S., 150, 160
Reason, J., 157, 158, 160
Reasoning:
  analogous, 273
  by analogy, 16
  formal, 17, 274
  meta-level, 17
  rule-based, 17
  skill-based, 17
Reasoning perspectives, 18
Recognition, similar features, 220
Recognitional capacity, 217
Redundancy, 251
Reference, effect, 251
Regression analysis, 90
Regression effects, 251
Relational data base, 44, 53
Relational model, 13, 52
Relevance, 255
Reliability, 190
Repo, A. J., 177, 203
Representational appropriateness, 25, 274
Representations, 12, 178
Representativeness, 251

Requirements:
  applications-level, 174
  organizational-level, 174
Requirements specifications, 162, 168, 180
Retention, 209
Reusability, 63
Riedel, S. L., 197, 198, 204
Roberts, T. L., 150, 160
Robson, D., 79
Rockart, J. F., 174, 202
ROMC, 178
ROMC approach, 13
Ross, B. H., 177, 203
Rouse, W. B., 1, 36, 161, 177, 201, 202, 203, 204, 267, 306
Rowland, A. J., 90, 127
Rule, production, 3
Rule-based reasoning, 3
Ryan, W. J., 177, 203

Saleh, J., 106, 128
Sammes, J. D., 90, 127
Sandberg, G., 53, 79
Sarin, R. K., 128
Satisficing, 237
Schemas, 45–48
Scherer, W. T., 120, 121, 128, 194, 197, 204
Schneider, W., 208, 258
Schneiderman, B., 134, 135, 136, 137, 147, 159
Schon, D. A., 231, 233, 260
Schulman, R. S., 158, 160
Schum, D., 255, 262, 269, 270, 306
Scott-Morton, M. S., 4, 36, 200, 204
Screening-based approaches, 104
Screen-sharing software, 278
Seacord, R. C., 153, 160
Search:
  hypothesis and test, 216
  symptomatic, 215
  topographic, 216
Selective perceptions, 251
Self-interaction matrix, 86
Semantic concerns, 139, 140
Sensation, 208
Sense modalities, 208
Sequence control, 143
Shafer, G., 254, 262
Shannon, C. E., 171, 202
Sharda, R., 189, 203
Shiffrin, R. M., 208, 258
Simon, H. A., 2, 17, 36, 37, 229, 237, 238, 259, 260, 267, 306
Simplicity, 256
Simulation, 88

Simulation models, 89
Singh, I. B., 320, 334
Situation rooms, 264, 265
Skill-based reasoning, 17
Slovic, P., 20, 37, 247, 254, 261
Smith, D. M., 90, 127
Smith, S. A., 279, 280, 290, 307
Smith, S. L., 142, 143, 145, 159, 201
Social interaction, 273
Social judgment theory, 91
Social theory of organizing, 229
Sommerville, I., 177, 202
Spatial layout level, 140
Sprague, R. H., Jr., 7, 9, 13, 36, 50, 79, 82, 126, 133, 159, 172, 178, 197, 202
Spurious cues, 252
Stakeholder, 9
Standard query languages, SQLs, 43, 49
Stanley, J. C., 190, 203
Star, S. L., 275, 307
Starbuck, W. E., 273, 306
Statistical power of a test, 192
Stefik, M., 26, 29, 37, 273, 281, 290, 307
Steinbruner, J. D., 235, 260
Steinfield, C., 305, 308
Steinmann, D. O., 91, 104, 127
Stephanou, H., 22, 37
Stevens, R. T., 186, 203
Stewart, T. R., 91, 104, 127
Stockenberg, J. E., 177, 203
Stohr, E. A., 124, 129
Stone, C. A., 212, 258
Stonebraker, M., 49, 50, 79
Strassman, P. A., 332, 334
Strategic planning decisions, 2
Structural models, 54
Structured issue, 1
Structured modeling, 58, 154
Structuring, 63
Substitution of correlation for causation, 252
Success/failure error, 250
Suchman, L., 26, 29, 37, 273, 281, 290, 307
Sudarsky, O., 149, 160
Support between meetings, 281
Support for electronic meetings, 281
Survey, 85
Sykes, E. A., 120, 128
Synectics, 85
Syntactic concerns, 139
Syntactic level, 140
Systems integration, 44, 165, 309, 317
Systems design:
    functional objectives, 161
    purposeful objectives, 161

Systems design engineering, 163, 166, 167
Systems design methodology, 10
Systems engineering, 9, 10, 12, 83, 165
    life cycle, 170
Systems integration, 44, 165
Systems life cycle, 83
Systems management, 10, 165
Systems methodology, 323

Taggart, W. M., 173, 202
Task, 162
Task level, 140
Task relevance, 25, 274
Taylor, S. E., 227, 259
Technology level for DSS design, 328
Teleconferencing facility, 281
Telephony, computer-based extensions, 276
Tenpenny, P. L., 177, 203
Testability, 256
Text-filtering, 279
Tharp, M. O., 173, 202
Theories in use, 233
Thimbleby, 144, 146, 160
Thinking, future perfect, 273
Thomas, J. J., 153, 160
Thought:
    concrete operational, 212, 213
    formal operational, 212, 213
Tiechroew, D., 173, 202
Tien, J. M., 188, 190, 194, 195, 203
Todd, P., 200, 204
Transaction management, 63
Transitioning, 326
Transparency, 70
Trees, 86
Trend extrapolation, 89
Turbak, F. A., 29, 38, 290, 307
Turbo Pascal Plus, 66
Turoff, M., 281, 307
Tushman, M. L., 234, 260
Tversky, A., 20, 37, 92, 121, 247, 253, 254, 249, 261

Unconflicted change, 223
Unconflicted adherence, 223
Urn model, 98
User guidance, 143
User interface definition language, 153
User interface languages, 49
User interface lifecycle, 146
User interface management system, UIMS, 133, 153
Utility curve, 102
Utility function, 105

Validity:
  conduct conclusion, 190, 191
  construct, 190, 191, 194
  external, 190
  internal, 190, 194
  statistical conclusion, 190, 191
Value of information, 97
Value system design, 83
Van de Ven, A. H., 85, 127
Vicente, K. J., 153, 155, 156, 160
Vigilant information processing, 223-224, 297
Volkema, R. J., 105, 127, 193, 203
von Neumann, J., 104, 128
von Winterfeldt, D., 101, 127, 254, 262
Voting, 92
Vroom, V. H., 233, 234, 260

Wagner, G., 264
Wallace, R. H., 177, 203
Warfield, J. N., 87, 127
Watson, R. T., 282, 307
Weaver, W., 171, 202
Weick, K. E., 229, 230, 259, 273, 306
Weitzenfeld, J., 217, 218, 258
Welch, D. A., 272, 306
Wessinger-Baylon, T., 244, 261, 273, 306

Wheelwright, S. C., 252, 261
White, C. C., 14, 36, 106, 120, 121, 127, 128, 194, 197, 204
White, E. B., 96, 127
Will, H. J., 120, 126
Winograd, T., 297, 307
Wishful thinking, 252
Wong, H., 62, 66, 70, 79
World:
  conversational, 134
  graphical, 134
Wrong problem definition, 193

XEROX PARC, 277, 281

Yadav, B. B., 174, 202
Yadav, S. B., 177, 203
Yeh, R., 62, 79
Yetton, P. W., 233, 234, 260
Yin, R. K., 194, 203
Yourdan, E., 64, 69, 79

Zave, P., 62, 79
Zdonik, S. B., 62, 79
Ziegler, K. Z., Jr., 72, 80
Zigurs, L., 282, 307